D1256336

DEATH AND RITUAL
IN RENAISSANCE
FLORENCE

THE JOHNS HOPKINS UNIVERSITY STUDIES
IN HISTORICAL AND POLITICAL SCIENCE,
110TH SERIES (1992)

1. *Death and Ritual in Renaissance Florence*
   by Sharon T. Strocchia
2. *God in La Mancha: Religious Reform and the People of Cuenca,*
   1500–1650
   by Sara T. Nalle

DEATH AND RITUAL

IN RENAISSANCE

FLORENCE

SHARON T. STROCCHIA

The Johns Hopkins University Press
Baltimore and London

The Johns Hopkins University Press
701 West 40th Street
Baltimore, Maryland 21211-2190
The Johns Hopkins Press Ltd., London

Frontispiece: Anonymous, fifteenth century, *Triumph of Death*. Of particular interest is the funeral procession in the upper left quadrant. Reproduced by permission of Alinari/Art Resource, N.Y.

Library of Congress Cataloging-in-Publication Data

Strocchia, Sharon T., 1951–
    Death and ritual in Renaissance Florence / Sharon T. Strocchia.
        p.   cm. — (The Johns Hopkins University studies in historical and political
    science ; 110th ser., 1)
    Includes bibliographical references and index.
    ISBN 0-8018-4364-2 (alk. paper)
    1. Funeral rites and ceremonies—Italy—Florence—History.   2. Renaissance—
Italy—Florence.   3. Florence (Italy)—Politics and government.   4. Florence
(Italy)—Social life and customs.   I. Title.   II. Series.
GT3252.F56S76   1992
393'.0945'5109024—dc20   92-68

For *Stella* and *Susan*,
and in memory of *Steve*

CONTENTS

Acknowledgments / xi
Introduction / xiii

PART I: THE STRUCTURES OF RITUAL AND SOCIETY / 1
    Chapter 1. The Rules of Order / 5
    Chapter 2. Symbols, Objects, Bodies / 30

PART II: THE MAKING OF A RITUAL FORM / 53
    Chapter 3. The Social World of Late Trecento
    Funerals / 55
        The Triumph of Flamboyance / *56*
        Kinship, Family, Dynasty / *67*
        Patricians and the Gente Nuova / *70*
        Style and the Politics of Chivalry / *75*
        Corporations, Parishes, and Popolani / *82*
    Chapter 4. Civic Ideals and Classicism in the Early
    Quattrocento / 105
        Coluccio Salutati: Chancellor as Poet and Hero / *106*
        From Knights to Statesmen / *120*
        Ritual, Politics, and the Papacy / *134*
        Humanism and the Power of Praise / *143*
    Chapter 5. Spectacle at Mid-Century / 149
        Civic Ritual Comes of Age / *150*
        Social Strategies and the Topography of Tombs / *161*
        Women and the Sexual Politics of Mourning
          Clothes / *170*
    Chapter 6. The Return of an Aristocratic Ethos / 178
        Cosimo de' Medici, "Father of the Country" / *180*
        Patronage, Piety, and Patriliny in Laurentian
          Florence / *188*
        The New Republic, 1494–1512 / *217*
        The New Chivalry, 1512–1527 / *226*

Conclusion / 236
Notes / 239
Index / 303

ACKNOWLEDGMENTS

t comes as the happiest of tasks to thank the people and institutions that contributed to this project, so long in the making. Much of the research for this book was done while I was a Fellow at the Harvard University Center for Italian Renaissance Studies, Florence (Villa I Tatti). I wish to thank for their support the directors and staff of the Villa, and my co-Fellows there, as well as the National Endowment for the Humanities, which funded the project. The staff at the Archivio di Stato, Florence, also deserves warm thanks for helping me find my way through the labyrinths of manuscript work. Over the years the coffee bar adjacent to the archive provided the setting for many memorable discussions about problems of transcription, translation, and cultural meaning, especially with Cristelle Baskins, Tim Carter, Michael Rocke, and John Henderson.

In looking back over the long journey represented by this book, I want to recognize my special debt to my two mentors at the University of California, Berkeley, who started me on the path of Florentine history. Gene Brucker—scholar, teacher, and friend—introduced me to the riches of the archives and offered unflagging enthusiasm and support throughout the project. His love of evidence and a good story steered me clear of many perils while I was writing both the dissertation and the very different book that resulted from it. To my other mentor, Randolph Starn, I owe a sense of what the archives cannot tell us. He taught me how to read between and behind the lines of documents and to appreciate other ways of seeing.

A number of other colleagues generously gave of their time in reading and commenting on parts or all of the manuscript. Stanley Chojnacki, Richard Goldthwaite, Lauro Martines, Ronald Witt, and Jonathan Prude asked important questions, offered incisive criticisms, and encouraged me to say what I meant. James Roark provided enriching conversations and good counsel during the final stages of writing and revision. Woody Hickcox of the Emory University Geology Department generously produced the computer-drawn maps. Many trusted friends–Sonja Ebel, David Kessler, Meredith Shedd, Elaine Lacy, Karen Hegtvedt, Robyn Fivush, and Diane Jones—

also had an unseen hand in bringing this book to completion. The errors in fact and judgment that remain are, of course, my own.

Finally, I want to thank my mother and my sister for their implicit faith in me and my work, even though they are far removed from the halls of academe. Their kinship and caring has informed my scholarship in ways that cannot always be named. It is to them, and to the memory of my father, that I dedicate this book.

INTRODUCTION

his book examines the styles, uses, and meanings of death rites in late medieval and Renaissance Florence, from the Black Death (1348) to the end of the republic (circa 1530). Funerals and requiem masses were formal yet familiar occasions that allowed rich and poor alike to express their sense of honor and identity, their views of obligation and authority, and their commitment to piety and sociability. These brief episodes, lasting only a few hours, nevertheless managed to capture a dense world of power and feeling. What was at stake in these closely patterned, repetitive actions was nothing less than the reconstitution of the social order and one's place in it.

These solemn rites of passage, along with the longer-term activities surrounding mourning and remembrance, offer a valuable way to study continuities and cleavages in social values and patterns of life. By looking at the ways in which late medieval and Renaissance Florentines put together these rites and participated in them, we can discern various forms of social organization, such as household, family, and kinship, as well as catch glimpses of the sentiments attached to neighborhood and friendship. Ritual, however, tells us a great deal not only about the structures of everyday life but also about its dynamics; death rites were not simply static set pieces dedicated solely to the reproduction of a fixed order. Rather, it is more useful to view ritual episodes "as a busy intersection" where a number of social processes and competing claims met head-to-head.[1] This book treats death rites as rather open-ended occasions that Florentines used to revise their social understandings and to mediate the often disparate demands imposed on them by kinship ties, gender roles, civic ideology, spiritual preoccupations, and assertions of self. In this view, death rites appear less as fixed cultural formulas than as social moments fraught with tension and potential conflict.

In examining the history of Florentine death rites, the present work brings together in new ways two subjects that have emerged as important topics of historical research in the last twenty years: the study of death and the study of ritual. The historical experience of death has proven extremely useful to historians as a way to map fundamental changes in attitudes and mentalities, as well as to chart population distribution or social structures. Similarly, the notion of "mere" ritual has given way to a recognition of the essential role ritual played in ordering the collective experiences of early modern Europeans, in creating individual identities, and in establishing some of the most potent and cherished political myths of the age.

Yet each of these new historiographies of death and ritual has developed along a different path, characterized by the use of different sources and methodologies in pursuit of different objectives. Beginning with the groundbreaking studies of Philippe Ariès, the historiography of death in Europe has been dominated by French historians, whose common goal has been to explore collective attitudes, religious sentiments, and changes in mentalities over long periods of time.[2] Although Ariès himself took a rich, eclectic approach to his subject and used a large, diverse body of material, the subsequent history of death has largely taken a quantitative turn, focusing on documents of a more homogeneous sort. Historians such as Vovelle, Chaunu, Lebrun, and Chiffoleau have based their ventures into historical psychology on the systematic, statistical analysis of wills and testaments to examine changes in mentality.[3] Samuel Cohn's fine recent study of death and property in Siena shares similar goals, methods, and sources, despite his contrary contention that mental transformations are often swift rather than slow-moving.[4]

The present study diverges in important ways from this line of approach. First, the focus here is not on determining underlying attitudes but on deciphering the forms of association embodied in ritual actions and behaviors. I have been less concerned with mapping religious sentiments and patterns of thought than with tracking changes in social and political relations through their representation in death rites. Second, although I have counted and measured when possible, the method employed here leans decidedly toward the ethnographic, not the quantitative. I am interested in the ways in which ritual constructed and communicated a variety of social and cultural categories and understandings, ranging from definitions of kinship and gender roles to forms of patronage and political domination. The narrative line here moves back and forth between a number of distinct but, to my mind, complementary tasks. I attempt to decipher social relations between fairly large aggregate groups, examine more intimate exchanges within domestic units, and single out a few detailed portraits of individual lives and deaths that registered both startling departures from, and subtle manipulations of, previous practice. In looking at how death rites revealed and regulated several forms of social relations, I attempt to integrate the methods and concerns of classic social history and some of social history's newer variants.[5]

In pursuit of these objectives, I also attempt to cast my net of evidence as widely as possible, rather than focusing solely on wills. The sources used here include, in addition to testaments, a wide range of narrative accounts, such as chronicles, histories, diaries, and letters; financial records of individuals, families, churches, and corporations; and legal prescriptions and penalties drawn up by guilds and the commune, as well as by bishops, popes, and synods. Figuring into the discussion as well are assorted works of literature and folklore, running the gamut from humanist Latin funeral orations to vernacular satires to popular legends and anecdotes. Visual, architectural, and archaeological sources, including tomb monuments, inscriptions, burial artifacts, chapels, and decorative schemes, also make an appearance. This diversity of evidence affords many additional standpoints beyond those available in a single type of source. Nevertheless, there is a price to be paid for bringing together this rich but disparate mix. Gaps in the evidence, or the predominance of one type of record in particular situations, dictate the pursuit of several common themes throughout the book, rather than the systematic analysis of the same issues over time.

While the present study shares a common subject with the historiography of death, its approach shares greater affinities with recent investigations of ritual and ceremony in early modern Europe. Historians looking at the courts of northern Europe and sixteenth-century Italy have increasingly recognized the importance of spectacles of state to the exercise of power. The valuable studies by Roy Strong, Bonner Mitchell, Lawrence Bryant, Sarah Hanley, Ralph Giesey, and various scholars of Medici ducal festivities document how innovative forms of courtly entertainment merged with older performance traditions to guide pageantry and representations of state in the early modern period.[6] The present work traces its genealogy still more intimately to several studies that take the Italian city rather than the court as a "theater" of power. This book owes an obvious debt to the work of Christiane Klapisch-Zuber, Edward Muir, Richard Trexler, and Ronald Weissman.[7] By illuminating the role of ritual in the relations of everyday life and in the construction of personal and civic identity, they have shown historians how and why we need to take ritual seriously.

The present work attempts to build on these studies of both Italian cities and northern European courts. It uses the rites of death, grief, and remembrance as a lens through which to view the interplay of public power and domestic life. The book seeks to show how ritual occasions themselves displayed and linked changing relationships between women and men, between family and state, and between social groups with often striking differentials of power. One of the major concerns of the book is to connect displays of civic authority central to statebuilding with concomitant changes in family structure, forms of patronage, and neighborhood, parish, and corporate life. In examining this interplay, we also catch glimpses of how ritual defined a distinctly masculine identity for the Florentine state.

Despite the rich historiographical heritage enjoyed by both death and ritual, their joint study nevertheless presents unique problems for the historian, whose chief task is to describe and explain change over time. One of the major stumbling blocks in depicting the history of death rites is that these rites are among the most notoriously stable aspects of all cultures. The rigid conventions surrounding death and burial tend to mask the changes wrought by new historical conditions and processes. To avoid an overly coherent, static picture of death rites, the historian must often look for subtle, nuanced variations in practice, at more overt ruptures with the past, and especially at the context in which rites took place. The challenge here is not merely to tell the difference between minute variations in funerary styles and practices but, as Clifford Geertz says, to make the difference tell.[8]

The organization of this book acknowledges and highlights the historical double nature of death rites—their profound stability and their complex adaptation and transformation—by its formal division into two parts, each with a different purpose. Part 1, "The Structures of Ritual and Society," is an extended essay in historical anthropology which intertwines the methods and concerns of two disciplines. My aim here is to explore and illustrate the contours of a cultural *longue durée* that lasted from the aftermath of the Black Death to the end of the republic, showing how the social and symbolic aspects of death rites fit together in cohesive, intelligible, but imperfect patterns that both constrained change and determined its direction. This account borrows from the techniques of cultural anthropology to analyze the grounds for a persistent collective order and to examine the implicit meanings of ordinary behaviors.

At the same time, however, this account is obviously founded on the particular local knowledge and subjectivity of a historian, who reconstructs past experience from written records rather than from personal observation in the field. It also combines an interest in cultural understandings with more conventional historical concerns, such as politics and social conflict, which animated ritual episodes. In taking this multidisciplinary approach, my goal is a modest one: to contribute to a well-recognized exchange that can expand the range of inquiry for both historians and anthropologists.[9]

Part 1 is composed of two chapters. Chapter 1, "The Rules of Order," examines the social "rules" or grammar governing the highly coded language of death rites.[10] The intention here is to make explicit the patterns of ritual action—their structure, organization, sequence, rhythms, conflicts, and ambiguities—which enabled Florentines to both communicate and control their social experiences. Chapter 2, "Symbols, Objects, Bodies," turns to the symbolic elements that death rites put into play. It looks at the storehouse of symbols and objects from which Florentines made their selections to express honor and represent identity, and links symbols to the social practices that gave them meaning. It also sketches the way in which Florentines viewed and treated that most powerful and "natural" of all symbols, the human body. Together these chapters show how structure and symbol acted as different but complementary channels of communication, whose separate, sometimes conflicting messages nevertheless cohered into a larger statement about persons, groups, and a social and metaphysical order.

Although this description tells us about general features of Florentine social life, it does not tell us about the precise, dynamic context in which social transactions took place, or about the direction, means, and effects of historical change. These concerns are the subject of part 2, "The Making of a Ritual Form," which considers ritual as both a product and a constituent part of changing social and political relations. The purpose of this section is to examine the ways in which death rites partook of larger historical processes, responded to particular events, and represented cultural conflicts as well as consensus. It attempts to deepen our understanding of the complex of conventions explored in part 1 by giving that understanding a chronological dimension and by identifying key breaks in style and practice.

Chapter 3, "The Social World of Late Trecento Funerals," explores the social world of late Trecento Florence, which created a new, flamboyant funerary style. This discussion links rapidly escalating standards of conspicuous consumption with plague mortality, increased social and political mobility, and the civic needs of a commune almost incessantly at war. Chapter 4, "Civic Ideals and Classicism in the Early Quattrocento," traces the more sophisticated, diversified consumption of the early Quattrocento. It looks at the ways in which elitism, statism, and civism affected death rites, and assesses the impact of humanist culture and the theory of magnificence on customary practice. Chapter 5, "Spectacle at Mid-Century," considers how both civic and private rites registered the growing domination of the Medici and the patriciate between Cosimo's ascendance in 1434 and his death in 1464. Chapter 6, the final chapter, examines the polarized, often politicized rites of the late fifteenth and early sixteenth centuries. It considers the effects of patronage, patriliny, and pious concerns on funerary rites during Lorenzo de' Medici's heyday, then tracks the complex cycles of cultural politics following the French invasion of 1494 until the ultimate triumph of Medicean magnificence and the end of the Florentine republic around 1530.

Together these historical developments and their constraints present less a well-ordered portrait of Florentine society than a contested series of exchanges and accommodations in which individuals, families, and the commune put forward their claims to power and prestige while struggling to retain a semblance of community. I have tried when possible to elucidate the ways in which contemporary audiences may have understood the complex, multiple messages embodied in death rites, while recognizing the difficulties in recovering their points of view. Much of this history still remains to be written, as scholars continue to plunder the embarrassment of riches housed in the Florentine archives. Nevertheless, what I hope emerges from this study is a preliminary map of the ways in which late medieval and Renaissance Florentines both faithfully observed and continually reinvented the customs of death.

DEATH AND RITUAL
IN RENAISSANCE
FLORENCE

PART I

THE STRUCTURES OF

RITUAL AND SOCIETY

n November 5, 1445, the Florentine merchant Luca da Panzano made the following entry in his family record book: "I recall how my wife Lucrezia, with whom I had eleven children, died this day, Friday the fifth, at half past two o'clock in the evening." In calm, sure words, Luca registered how the death of his wife and longtime companion had struck him with terrible force. "Her death pained me," wrote Luca, "as if I myself had died, since she had been my companion for twenty years, one month, and ten days." Lucrezia's death had come fifteen days after she gave birth to a stillborn son, who had been baptized at home with the name Giovanni and buried in a local church. As Luca confronted the awful finality of his wife's death, he recalled her life and character using typical Florentine terms of endearment. Lucrezia had been "a good woman, a sweet woman, and seemly," wrote Luca; she had always acted charitably toward others and had borne her fatal illness with "great humility and patience." In light of her many virtues, Luca prayed devoutly that God would "grant her sincere pardon," and further invoked God's mercy to accept Lucrezia into the "seat of His angels."[1]

This poignant memoir offers a rich point of entry into the ways in which Florentines experienced and dealt with one of life's most profound yet commonplace sorrows. Over the course of the next few hours, days, and weeks, Luca da Panzano would participate in an unfolding drama whose basic patterns and characters were known by all Florentines. Death triggered not only intense emotion but also an ordered way of doing things. After the deaths of their wives, husbands, children, relatives, and friends, Luca and his contemporaries engaged in a series of ritual acts that helped them cope with the rage or numbness of grief. Their behaviors, however formulaic, show us how feeling, claims to power and status, and concern for the soul tangled together in an intricate web.

Returning to Lucrezia's story, we find that on the morning after her death Luca quickly notified clergy at the nearby Franciscan church of Santa Croce. Soon afterwards, "at eleven o'clock we made a vigil in the house with priests and friars." Huddled around the body, these clergy intoned the seven penitential psalms in a litany of prayer lasting several hours, probably accompanied by (if not in competition with) the laments of female friends, neighbors, servants, and kin. The prayers of clergy accompanied Lucrezia's soul on its final journey, while serving the less lofty purpose of preventing any popular "pagan" practices from surfacing. This brief interim of the vigil also helped ascertain that death had actually occurred, that Lucrezia's soul would not be an "unquiet" one, threatening to return, and that she would not experience the horror of being buried alive.

With church bells tolling the news, Lucrezia "was buried that day, the sixth of November 1445, in the church of Santa Croce in the tomb of our Messer Luca, to the side of the pier bearing the holy water [font]." Although Luca did not record a detailed description of this portion of the ceremony, we know from other sources that Lucrezia's body would have been suitably washed and anointed, and probably dressed in her best outfit. Placed in full view on a draped bier, her body would have been transported from the house to the burial church of Santa Croce by friars, kin, friends, or neighbors in a slow-moving cortege through the neighborhood. Afterward mourners would return to the house to partake of food and a sense of life. In the meantime, local criers and messengers spread word of Lucrezia's death and invited social familiars to the ceremonies that would follow. Since the next day was Sunday, church law forbade the performance of requiem masses; they were thus postponed one day.

On Monday the eighth, Luca staged a ceremony that captured both his deep personal affection and his social standing in the community. That day, "masses were said in Santa Croce with as much wax and [as many] honors as possible." Dressed as mourners for the occasion were Lucrezia's daughter Gostanza, and another of Lucrezia's kin, Caterina, widow of Filippo di Ghezzo, each wearing the customary garb of mourning mantle and veils. Their garments and their presence made visible the loss of Lucrezia, which Luca perceived as a blow not just to her family but to the whole city. As the last step in the ritual sequence immediately after death, the requiem offered an important opportunity for "the plenty of kinfolk and friends" who attended to honor the dead woman, to mark their special emotional state and status as mourners, and to reconstitute themselves as a community.

However, even though the burial was over, the ritual process was not yet finished. Six months after Lucrezia's death, in May 1446, Luca made an arrangement for additional masses in her honor. It was at once an act of mourning, supplication, and remembrance. Luca agreed to pay his confessor, Fra Attaviano of Santa Croce, a small amount of expensive velvet in return for reciting the Gregorian mass series (one mass daily for thirty days). Standing at a greater temporal distance from the initial rites of funeral and requiem, commemorative practices such as the popular Gregorian series helped to eventually seal off the trauma of grief while keeping alive a keen sense of familiarity and memory. It is to the structures, meanings, and relationships embodied in this unfolding sequence of actions— a rite of passage for both living and dead—that we now turn.

CHAPTER 1

THE RULES OF ORDER

t is because subjects do not, strictly speaking, know what they are doing that what they do has more meaning than they know.

—Pierre Bourdieu

Late medieval and Renaissance Florence was a society that both described and defined itself through ceremony. Florentines placed great weight on the public evaluation of behavior and invested heavily in ritual as a way to maintain social bonds. In hundreds of chronicles, diaries, letters, and other documents, contemporaries recorded both the patterns and the details of assorted rites, along with their evaluations and perceptions of these enactments. These narrative sources offer a way to reconstruct, using participants' own voices, major social values such as honor, obligation, conviviality, and competition, as well as the basic forms of social organization, ranging from the broad collectives of neighborhood and parish to more intimate household groupings. In recording what they did and their impressions of what they saw, Florentines also captured some of the textures and experiences of their daily lives, in which power relationships came face-to-face with feelings and expectations.

The narratives describing death, grief, and remembrance embody not only these fundamental features, however, but also a particular set of tensions. Running throughout these records is a persistent friction between the competing claims of community and solidarity, on the one hand, and the quest for personal honor and family status, on the other. One of the major functions of death rites in any society is to close the circle of community which has been broken by death.[1] Yet while Florentine death rites aimed at reestablishing this sense of order, they also had the conflicting objective of distributing honor to individuals and families. Honor was a principal form of power and authority; according to the savvy humanist Leon Battista Alberti, it was quite simply "the most important thing in anyone's life."[2] Hence in Florence the fundamental human obligation to bury the dead was inextricably bound up with the social imperative to bury them well. The ritual enactments surrounding death and burial were not immune to the competitive, agonistic character of Florentine social relations but rather were structured by it.[3]

This conflicting desire to assert the principles of a harmonious communal order but to lay claim to one's special place in it was a driving force behind both death rites themselves and their representation in narrative. In many instances, chroniclers and diarists told an idealized story about society as they wished it to be, glossing over the frictions of particular occasions and emphasizing instead the "orderliness" of what were probably scattered, disjointed, and sometimes anxious affairs. Even detailed accounts of funerals at times mask the very distinctions that ritual itself aimed to reveal. Other narrators, particularly family diarists, took the contrary tack—greatly embellishing funeral accounts in order to lionize their ancestors, their kin, and themselves for posterity. Because of the differing weight accorded the imperatives of order and honor, we must pick our way through these narrative descriptions and try to read them in connection with other kinds of sources.

This chapter considers how ritual episodes on the one hand put forward the competing claims of individuals, families, and community, and on the other hand mediated between them. The first section looks at how the funeral reproduced and resolved social tensions while at the same time marking conflicting definitions of kinship. The second section examines how the contest between family and community was played out in the use and manipulation of urban spaces. The third and final section turns to the structures, functions, and family dimensions of the requiem. Taken together, the chapter aims to illustrate that death rites, despite their formality, were not static set pieces but, rather, captured the dynamics and problems of everyday life.

I

In late fourteenth- and fifteenth-century Florence, the funeral and the requiem formed the core of public death rites. In narrative accounts these public episodes overshadowed domestic rites such as the vigil, lamentations, and mourning banquets. Despite their shared public character, however, the funeral and the requiem had fundamentally different objectives. The funeral was essentially a political rite: it revealed relationships of power between groups, separated people on the basis of status, and legitimated those distinctions of status by recreating them in the processional order. By contrast, the requiem was a rite of incorporation: its purpose was to strengthen and renew social, communal, and spiritual bonds by gathering into a cohesive community a wide variety of kin, friends, neighbors, trade associates, confraternal brothers, political allies, and occasionally public officials. The requiem liturgy further stressed the common ground of shared religious beliefs among Christians.[4]

In practice, both the funeral and the requiem displayed other, somewhat contradictory, qualities that worked to counter the terrible sameness and sterility of death. Social tensions, threats of vendetta, and the potential violence touched off by grief all brought to mixed funerary gatherings a vitality which could become dangerously explosive in times of war or communal strife. Similarly, social competition, which took forms such as the burning of large numbers of expensive candles and the use of elaborate draperies and richly painted catafalques, enlivened the requiem even while undercutting its integrative function. These paradoxical qualities fitted the funeral and the requiem into a complementary relationship. The funeral sorted out people as they engaged in a common, yet potentially disruptive, activity; the requiem affirmed similarities among individuals while sanctifying distinctions between them.

The funeral achieved its objectives and helped mediate between the competing claims of communal order and private honor primarily by means of its processional structure. Although each burial encompassed different participants and a slightly different style of display, what remained constant in funerals throughout the republican period was their tripartite arrangement. Like most processions studied by anthropologists and historians, Florentine funeral processions were divided into three discernable clusters, with the most important element situated in the middle, marking a symbolic, political, or charismatic center.[5] Marching first in the cortege were the clergy, society's institutional protectors, whose participation marked not only the death of the body but also the passage of the soul. Clerics were followed in this first cluster by a battery of trappings, such as flags, banners, swords, shields, and emblems, that spelled out the public identity of the deceased. Marking the center of the proceedings was the corpse itself, a well-dressed, often heavily ornamented, and always symbolically weighty artifact. Mourners—kin, friends, neighbors, fellow tradesmen, and acquaintances—comprised the final grouping behind the corpse. These three clusters of people and goods made up a formal tableau of hierarchy in action.

As in most Florentine processions, primacy of place in the cortege, when read from first to last, helped map out a hierarchical order of dignitaries. Clergy often jockeyed for the precedence that would assert their institutional status within the city's ecclesiastical hierarchy, giving rise to numerous disputes over protocol that sometimes lasted for generations. In the late fifteenth century, for example, the "longstanding" dispute between the canons of the cathedral and those of San Lorenzo over first place in San Lorenzo parish funerals finally reached a crisis point. In order to avoid a "public scandal" at the 1498 funeral of Giovanni di Pierfrancesco de' Medici, the canons of San Lorenzo agreed to a provisional arrangement negotiated by the Medici in which the San Lorenzo canons marched first, followed by friars from the Observant convents of San Francesco and San Domenico as buffers, with the cathedral canons walking last, nearest the corpse.[6]

This settlement afforded a happy compromise partly because funeral processions invited more than a strictly linear reading. The cortege could be scrutinized not only as a representation of hierarchy from front to back but also as an indication of personal preference and affection when read from the center outwards. Hence participants bound by special ties of patronage or piety enjoyed greater proximity to the ritual "center," the corpse itself. The affluent weaver Guasparre Landini noted these offsetting advantages in recording the clerical participants in his mother Lisabetta's funeral in 1521. Heading Lisabetta's procession were "forty-eight or fifty" pairs of Observant Franciscan friars, followed by forty priests from the Company of the Visitation of Our Lady, to whom Lisabetta "owed a debt." This confraternity also supplied a pall, torches, and 120 candles for the requiem mass. Next in order came eight priests and three clerks from San Jacopo sopr'Arno, where the family had its tomb; then three priests from the outlying parish of San Giorgio, where the Landini owned the house in which Lisabetta died; and finally the priest Ser Antonio di Ser Jacopo da San Casciano, who was probably personally known by the family.[7] The successively closer personal attachment of these groups of clergy to Lisabetta and her family was signaled by its proximity to the body.

The trappings that preceded the corpse were subject to a similar complexity of interpretation. In recording lengthy, often meticulous, lists of trappings and their sequence, observers repeatedly emphasized how this section of the cortege proceeded "with order" or "in an orderly manner." Proudly noting his role in the magnificent funeral arrangements staged by the commune for Guccio da Casale, the lord of Cortona who died in Florence in 1400, Jacopo Salviati carefully noted the sequence of civic honors assembled at the priors' palace. "In front of the bier," wrote Salviati, "there went first the insignia and banner of the Church of Rome that was given by those of Cortona themselves; next came all our flags, one behind the other: first the pennant of the populace, then its crest, then the two square flags, then the pennant and crest of Parte [Guelfa]." After describing the complete assembly, Salviati then noted how "in this arrangement and order" the procession left Santa Croce and proceeded to the Porta San Niccolò, where those trappings headed for Cortona were piled onto mules. Just outside Cortona, all the torches were relit and "all of the aforementioned flags reassembled in their proper order" before making their final entry into the city.[8] This arrangement offered a formal statement about various political authorities' prestige and about their interrelationships.

Yet this linear hierarchical scheme could also be adapted to carve out a special place for personal ties. When Francesco di Tommaso Giovanni recounted the funeral proceedings for the Florentine chancellor Carlo Marsuppini (d. 1453), he indicated how the seven banners carried up to the body in the Piazza della Signoria were all arranged "in their proper order." At the head came the papal flag, followed by the flags of the French king and the duke of Milan, and the Florentine flags from the Parte Guelfa, the Studio, and the Proconsolo. However, the final flag, from Marsuppini's native town of Arezzo, introduced and highlighted a personal connection and in this case functioned as a political gesture as well.[9]

The tension between conceptions of communal order and the imperatives of family and personal honor was probably best reflected, however, in the arrangement of the mourners who followed the corpse. Not surprisingly, kinship, that basic stuff of Florentine social life, claimed its due place immediately behind the body. Lisabetta

Landini's funeral was typical: her husband Matteo occupied the place of honor nearest the corpse of his wife and was closely followed by their three sons. Next came Lisabetta's three sons-in-law and a man described only as a relative.[10] Dressed in the deep mourning of black rather than the lesser mourning signified by brown, these principal mourners informed onlookers that they claimed the greatest grief, sponsored the proceedings, and in turn reaped its reflexive social rewards.

Yet while the participation of kin was fundamental to notions of honor, the larger structures of the social order dictated that only certain family mourners be included. The key determinant here was not degree of kinship but gender. One of the most striking features of Florentine funerals in the late fourteenth and fifteenth centuries is the virtual exclusion of women from the cortege, regardless of their kin attachments. This was a world in which social and ritual activities were frequently segregated by sex, and funerals were no exception. Female kin, along with female friends and neighbors, sat on benches apart from men at the gathering preceding the procession, just as they did in church. Once the procession started, women were admonished by preachers such as San Bernardino, as well as by sporadic communal rulings, to remain in or near the house to continue their laments, and to prepare the mourning banquet that followed the requiem.[11] Messer Guccio de' Nobili described precisely this sexual division of space and labor in recounting the opulent funeral staged for his wife Francesca in 1381: while a crowd of kinsmen, knights, judges, and other eminent citizens paid their respects in the procession, a large group of "many women" remained at the Nobili home in sustained lamentation.[12]

Hence in normal circumstances it was only male relatives, rather than a mixed group of women and men, who formally represented the collective kindred in procession. It appears that widows and other kinswomen walked in the cortege only when the body was not physically present. Jacopo Salviati noted, for example, that Guccio da Casale's widow and other male and female kin marched behind Guccio's bier at the ceremony held ten days after his actual burial.[13] Female kin, friends, and neighbors may have followed behind the procession as a kind of informal addendum; or they may have taken a different route to the burial church for the requiem at which, by contrast, their participation was deemed essential. Nevertheless, as a reflection of social hierarchy and fundamental principles of communal order, the formal absence of women in procession represented in a highly visible, practical way women's marginal public status.

Excluding women from the formal statements made by funerals was typical of other north and central Italian cities as well. Sumptuary laws in Bologna, first passed in 1276 and followed by numerous redactions, strictly prohibited women from leaving the house and going to church before the body was actually buried. The commune of Ascoli Piceno in the eastern Marches passed almost identical provisions in 1377.[14] Similarly, Roman sumptuary statutes enacted in 1471 proscribed women outside the circle of immediate kin from visiting the house of the deceased, and further advised them not to show up at the requiem in a wild or disheveled state.[15] Although it is always difficult to test the level of compliance with sumptuary rulings, these exclusionary practices are confirmed by other types of evidence, ranging from ambassadorial reports sent from ducal Milan in the 1460s, to the separate boat transporting female participants at the funeral of an anonymous "good woman" of Venice in 1421.[16]

This sexual segregation at funerals probably had its inception in the late thirteenth and early fourteenth centuries. An anonymous chronicler writing in Pavia around 1330 noted without further explanation that women recently had been prohibited from their customary practice of walking (each supported by two men) behind the bier in a sequence that varied according to degree of kinship. Once inside the church, however, women still followed the custom of joining clerics in accompanying the body to the gravesite.[17] Davidsohn describes a similar arrangement of women mourners in late Dugento and early Trecento Florence, although these clusters were already placed at the end of the cortege.[18]

We can account for this growing marginalization of women in part by examining the tensions, manifest in mourning customs, between family claims to honor and broader conceptions of communal order. Late medieval and Renaissance Florentines demanded public, visible expressions of grief to convey a sense of loss and to adequately honor the dead. However, it was primarily the responsibility of women to learn, enact, and transmit to others the standard techniques of mourning, which included physical gestures, loud laments, and often dramatic, self-inflicted injuries.[19] The late Trecento novelist Franco Sacchetti, for example, anticipated that a new widow would have the following honorable response to the death of her husband. To signify her loss, Sacchetti wrote, the widow "cuts her hair . . . dresses in black . . . and places her husband in the [public] room on a crude bed on the ground"; over his body she makes "laments and prayers" along with other female kin and neighbors.[20] This behavior was intended not only to demonstrate women's personal loss but to legitimate the collective grief of family and community, as when the corpse of the war captain John Hawkwood "was bewailed by women in the presence of the whole populace of Florence" in March 1394.[21]

However, these outbursts obviously intensified the explosive, emotional quality of funerals, which might result in violence, vendetta, or other breaches of civic order and decorum. To contain these possibilities, Florentines and their Italian neighbors developed a battery of social controls and legal mechanisms designed to limit expressions of honor and grief in the interests of public order. One of the oldest communal strategies was to define the limits of grief through sumptuary legislation. Throughout the republican period, law and custom engaged in a prolonged battle that changed both of their natures and roles but left victory undecided. More effective in transforming mourning customs over the long term were deep shifts in the emotional standards underlying behavior. Humanists from Petrarch on developed new models of grief and mourning, which stressed greater self-control, external discipline, and the internalization of sorrow. Family arrangements also played a practical role in restraining grief; even though the wildly grieving widow who tore her hair represented a cultural ideal, the reality of Florentine marital patterns often meant that a younger widow was transferred rapidly to a new household and marriage bed, thereby eroding opportunities for mourning as well as older loyalties.[22] The continued opposition between family and communal needs which was apparent in mourning practices identified a major fault line in Florentine society, one that neither ruptured fully nor was ever fully resolved.

However, funerals and mourning not only pitted these competing claims against each other but also placed differing conceptions of kinship at the very center of ritual action. Rather than emphasizing a shared understanding and experience of kinship, death rites dramatically distinguished between the family ties enjoyed by women and those enjoyed by men. Both the spatial arrangement of mourners in the cortege and the specific kinship ties mourners represented hinged on the sex of the dead person. Simply put, the processional order at men's funerals claimed patriliny as the dominant form of kinship organization, whereas women's funerals encompassed both patriliny and a older set of bilateral arrangements. Put another way, men's funerals focused on the agnate lineage, while those of women recognized shifting household structures and a wider collective kindred. We can say, then, that funerals in late medieval and Renaissance Florence not only played off communal and familial conceptions and needs against each other; these episodes also brought to the fore a central problem in the long-term evolution of Florentine, Italian, and European family systems, in which patriliny only gradually supplanted an older, bilateral way of reckoning kinship.[23]

These differing representations of kinship deserve a closer look. When the Florentine elite buried their kinsmen, the cortege emphasized the patriline and the patrilineage over two other prominent faces of Florentine kinship, namely the ties of *parentado* and of the conjugal unit itself. The place of honor directly behind the bier was occupied either by household members or by more laterally extended relations, but these mourners were all agnates, not cognatic relations. Pagolo Petriboni, who chronicled a number of important burials in the early fifteenth century, noted the Giovanni Bicci de' Medici's sons Cosimo and Lorenzo, plus an unspecified group of "twenty-eight men and boys of the Medici," followed immediately behind Giovanni's corpse at his funeral in 1429. The same year Petriboni recorded that seventeen men of Matteo Castellani's *casa*, including his son, his brother, and his nephews, mourned him in procession. Two diarists of a later generation singled out the place of honor allotted to Lorenzo de' Medici, duke of Urbino, who walked first among sixty other Medici kin at his uncle's funeral in 1516.[24]

As an image of both social ties and social distance, the cortege for patrician men showed a perceptible gap between blood kin and kin acquired through marriage. Cognatic relations enjoyed no special status in the procession but instead clustered among the friends and neighbors at a greater physical and social distance from the bier. While the extended family networks created through marriage were indeed represented, their role was clearly subordinated to the greater claims of agnates and male offspring. Patrician men's funerals closely restricted recognition of bilateral kinship by formally excluding widows from the cortege, by downplaying cognatic relationships, and by becoming showy occasions for the mutual sharing of honors between fathers and sons. Thus, in a large social and historical sense, funerals for men of established family asserted not only the dead man's reputation but also the primacy of a relatively new type of kinship organization.[25]

In sharp contrast to this emphasis on lineage, the funerals of patrician women reflected a set of more flexible and varied family arrangements. These funerals stressed the household in which the woman had lived at the time of death, whatever its configuration, as the most significant family unit. In family diaries, one often reads accounts of a son or sons honorably burying a "good" mother who had remained in the household after her husband's death; thus Bartolomeo and Francesco Sassetti buried their "good and honorable mother" Betta after a fatal illness in 1430.[26] Less often, one finds brothers burying their widowed sisters who had exercised the right of *tornata* to return to their natal kin. Responsibilities for burial arrangements might also devolve upon a woman's nephews, her uncles, or even her in-laws. The coppersmith Piero Masi noted in his family record book that his father Bernardo had buried his widowed, impoverished and chronically ill sister Mea, who had resided in the household for fifteen years before her death in 1512. Bernardo took charge not only of his sister's funeral but also of those of his wife, mother, and mother-in-law.[27]

Besides highlighting the household, women's funerals also honored the extended social networks and new domestic contexts women created through marriage. That women both generated *parentado* and were, to some extent, defined by it found ample recognition in women's funeral corteges, in which cognates played a much more prominent role than they did at men's funerals. As evidence for the organization of kinship in late medieval and Renaissance Florence, the funeral processions of adult, married women and widows document the simultaneous existence and importance of both the patrilineal and bilateral kindreds that David Herlihy argues characterized early modern European families.[28] These women's funerals also stressed a greater sense of family continuity than did those of their kinsmen, since they included the dead woman's sons-in-law, whose presence acknowledged the marriage alliances and possible offspring of her daughters.

The kin organization of women's funerals was plagued by yet another thorny problem of representing the relationship between conjugal and natal bonds.[29] The ties binding a daughter to her lineage could be legal as well as affective, since marriage did not automatically dissolve a father's power over his daughter (*patria potestas*). Rather, for a woman to attain a separate legal *persona* the enabling act of emancipation was required.[30] Marriage rites also paradoxically sustained these natal ties, at least temporarily, since a young bride returned to her father's house for a brief period after receiving the nuptial ring.[31] Moreover, fathers could reclaim their widowed daughters in order to make new marriage alliances, as when Luca da Panzano, his son, and his nephew rapidly retrieved Luca's daughter Gostanza, along with her dowry of 1,050 florins.[32] Given these conflicting allegiances, it is not surprising that narrative accounts are ambiguous about the place of natal kin in the cortege. In recording the burial ceremonies for his mother Lisabetta, (d. 1521), for example, Guasparre Landini never specified whether her natal kin, the Antinori, formed part of the "lovely crowd of good citizens" following her husband, sons, and sons-in-law, or even whether the Antinori took part in the funeral at all.[33]

Funerals thus offered an arena in which the claims of competing family systems were hammered out over time. The separation of women in the cortege, the stress on patriliny at men's funerals, and the ambiguous place of natal kin in women's processions all point to the gradual evolution of Florentine and European family systems, away from a mixed way of reckoning kinship toward one that was increasingly patrilineal in orientation. During this long period of overlap and structural transformation in the late fourteenth and fifteenth centuries, the particular definition, experience, and expression of kinship depended in fundamental ways on the social fact of gender.

Although kin formed the most important group of mourners in the cortege, other associates who peopled the Florentine social world paid their respects as well. Following family mourners in procession came fellow tradesmen, guild members, and officials, who by their participation fulfilled one of the social obligations typical of corporate societies. Each guild established by statute the number and rank of attendants required to attend a colleague's funeral, generally varying according to his corporate status, and set policies for work stoppages to honor the dead. For example, the 1441 statutes of the Merchant's Court (Sei dei Mercanzia) stipulated that when a chancellor of the court died, all members of both the major and the minor guilds, as well as the magistrates themselves, should assemble at the Mercanzia office, go to the funeral as a group, and return to the office together before disbanding.[34] Corporate officeholders were aptly recognized by special funerary honors. When the goldsmith Matteo di Lorenzo, who had served as consul of the silk guild twenty-two times, died in 1420, "the guild honored him greatly in that the entire guild with the consuls came to the body, bringing with them eight large wax candles."[35] However, as the highest political body and ultimate source of sovereignty, the Florentine priors rarely participated in funerals and restricted their homage solely to requiem services when appropriate.

Although colleagues aimed to enhance a sense of community and solidarity, tensions nevertheless surfaced around the composition and purpose of this group as well. The transformation of guild structures and corporatism over time encouraged both the multiplication and the venality of funeral honors. The increased number of services brought under guild control between 1370 and 1420, coupled with a gradual population recovery in the second half of the Quattrocento, helped swell the ranks of corporate mourners.[36] However, this multiplication of honors and homage had the paradoxical effect of weakening corporate bonds, which were based to some extent on personal affiliation. The extent to which corporatism had deteriorated by the middle of the fifteenth century can be seen by the introduction of venal honors. For a small price, corporations such as the Merchants' Court allowed their emblems to be used by nonaffiliated persons; magistrates of the Merchants' Court, for example, consented to walk in the cortege along with other guild captains but departed before the requiem was performed.[37]

Following the trade associates came the final crowd of mourners—friends, neighbors, and acquaintances—who had been alerted to the solemn news of death and burial by criers, messengers, and bell ringing. Such formal homage was the very stuff of which Florentine social relations were made. Manno Petrucci recalled that his brother Giovanni's funeral in 1443 "was well-attended by many good citizens because Giovanni was well-liked . . . Many peasants arrived as well because [Giovanni] was well-known in the countryside; he had held several offices there, in which many served him."[38] In his testament dated 1463, Manno Temperani specifically told his heirs to invite assorted relatives and neighbors to his obsequies. Even in the absence of such instructions, however, Florentines knew the appropriate social script. Upon Cambio Petrucci's death in the countryside in August 1430, his heirs "called together as many citizens, countryfolk, priests, and friars as were in that place, along with five or six friends, and we honored him as much as it was possible to do."[39] For women, this final group of mourners, like the "sixty or seventy *uomini da bene*" attending Lisabetta Landini's funeral in 1521,[40] probably had more contact and familiarity with the dead women's kinsmen than they had with the women personally.

Yet the right to walk in the cortege was not one to be presumed lightly. Although notions of decorum dictated that participants and deceased had to have shared at least some degree of close personal affiliation, the understandings of different groups about social boundaries did not always mesh perfectly. Hence Lorenzo Strozzi registered his surprise and disdain when, in addition to "the customary crowd of citizens and clergy, with relatives and domestic servants dressed in black" walking in his father Filippo's cortege in 1491, "there also participated—an unusual sight in our city—all the foremen and youths of his projects with architects, woodworkers, smithies, wallers, stonecutters, and all the rest of the more common crowd who worked on his palace from its beginning." Strozzi went on to say that the sight of these well-behaved workers dressed in mourning moved onlookers to tears; apparently, however, they had not been invited by Lorenzo Strozzi himself.[41]

Although funerals throughout Italy in this period were characterized by a similar tripartite structure, the particular ranking of mourners in the final cluster nevertheless reflected the specific social and political arrangements characteristic of each locality. Republican Florence produced one complex configuration of mourners; Sforza funerals in ducal Milan generated another. For example, when Francesco Sforza's mother, Lucia Terziani da Marsciano, died in 1461, the Neapolitan ambassador Antonio Cicinello headed the cortege; at Francesco's own funeral five years later, it was the French ambassadors who assumed pride of place.[42] By ranking foreign ambassadors over immediate family members, these funerals emphasized external political alliances even over dynastic considerations, which dominated French royal funerals of the period.[43] The funeral of Galeazzo Maria's uncle, Bosio, in 1476, took yet a different tack, interspersing Sforza and Visconti family mourners with foreign envoys. As duke of Milan, Galeazzo himself walked first, followed by the Ferrarese ambassador. Next came Galeazzo's young son Ermes, then the Mantuan ambassador, Zaccaria da Pisa; behind them were Francesco's legitimated natural son and Galeazzo's half-brother, Tristano, followed by Galeazzo's two bastards by Lucrezia Landriani, Alessandro and Carlo, and finally, other assorted kin "according to their grade."[44]

Given the political exigencies of court life, courtiers and ambassadors at Milan not surprisingly jockeyed for the status and privileges that funeral protocol could provide. We can glimpse the studied intrigue of court life from a letter written to Barbara Gonzaga, marchioness of Mantua, by the Mantuan ambassador Vincenzo Scalone, dated January 22, 1461. Scalone shrewdly described how various creatures of the court had maneuvered for a favored place at the funeral of Francesco Sforza's mother, Lucia, held the previous day.[45] This was a funeral of enormous proportions, drawing an estimated six thousand participants. One measure of its scale is the sheer length of the cortege: most participants had already arrived at the cathedral before the lesser citizens at the end had even left the court. Scalone noted that the proceedings had gotten under way when Lucia's relatives had gathered in a private chamber, with court magistrates, medical doctors, and other "worthy" citizens assembling in another room. Once the city's parish clergy had filtered into the audience hall of the Palazzo Arengo, where Francesco Sforza held court, various court-appointed officials had been honored with the tasks of handling and transporting Lucia's black velvet, fur-trimmed bier.

As he recalled these proceedings for Barbara Gonzaga's benefit, Scalone was no dispassionate observer. Rather, he was extremely piqued that Ugolotto de Facino, the ambassador from Modena, had preceded him in the cortege. As Scalone explained, he felt entitled to fourth place instead of fifth because of the ties of *parentado* that existed between the Gonzaga and Sforza houses; at the time, Francesco's son and heir Galeazzo Maria was still betrothed to Dorotea Gonzaga, an arrangement that would be annulled two years later.[46] Scalone's sense of propriety was probably offended yet again in the final phase of the ritual, when, as he reported, the mourners briefly returned to the original ducal chamber to ritually cleanse their hands in precisely the same order they had observed in the procession.

Despite the different political ideologies separating ducal Milan and republican Florence, these cities nevertheless expressed a similar ideology of gender in their death rites. Milanese funerals were just as paradoxical and contrary about women's public status and ritual participation as were Florentine rites. Although Francesco Sforza honored his mother with a spectacular court funeral that outshone any ceremony staged for a woman in the Florentine civic world, women of the Milanese ducal court nevertheless were excluded from formal funerary participation and were segregated instead in domestic rites. The ambassador Scalone was explicit that the funeral procession had not involved any women whatsoever. Instead, the duchess Bianca Maria Visconti, unspecified female kin, and a great number of women from the duchy had performed ritual lamentations over the body before assuming appropriate mourning garments. Scalone was equally clear that women had also been excluded from the final hand-washing ceremony, stating that he did not know if the women had performed a similar rite "on their side."[47] Politics and gender intersected in complex ways to give each Italian city a distinct, yet recognizable, set of rules, allowances, and contradictions.

II

The tensions and competing claims that marked the funeral procession also figured into the ritual use of the city's social and symbolic landscape. Unlike the more centralized urban topography of Renaissance Venice, Florence had many centers of social power located in its diverse, socially heterogeneous neighborhoods, which formed the basis of both family and political culture.[48] The sixteen wards (*gonfaloni*), broken down still further into loosely defined clusters of neighborhoods, were the basic units for various administrative functions such as tax assessments, political scrutinies to determine potential officeholders, militia organization, grain distribution, and census gathering. Neighborhoods were also important crossroads for the dense social networks that characterized Florentine life. Among their neighbors Florentines found patrons, clients, friends, godparents, witnesses, charitable donors, business partners, and companions in local festivities.[49]

Contributing to these lively neighborhood scenes, funerals also allowed more affluent households and lineages to throw symbolic weight behind their claims to prestige and control of local resources such as streets, squares, alleys, and intersections. Households' continual use of and association with local spaces established a sense of informal ownership which was identified and referenced in chronicles, tax reports, and popular parlance by a thicket of family names. The old urban core still reads like a historical directory jamming together such family-identified spaces from past times as the Piazza de' Rossi, the Via de' Vecchietti, the Borgo degli Albizzi, and so on. Funerals provided households with legitimate occasions to actively privatize surrounding spaces, and they seized these opportunities with gusto, occupying the spaces with crowds of kin for several hours at a time, cramming them with rented benches to accommodate onlookers and participants, and sacralizing them in the family name through the presence of priests, friars, and religious objects.

This often intense competition between families for recognized control or dominance over neighborhood spaces only entrenched the local, particularist loyalties that constrained the development of civism, so ardently promoted by civic humanists such as Leonardo Bruni. Once again the government used legal strategies to delimit family claims and to expand the commune's purview over spaces and the activities that gave them meaning. Various redactions of sumptuary rulings in the late fourteenth and early fifteenth centuries permitted the display of the corpse only inside or in front of the deceased's own house.[50]

It was the processional route of the funeral cortege, however, that fully mobilized the vocabulary of urban space to serve family interests. Moving through a variety of local, civic, and sacred spaces, processions both created and linked a series of references to the familial use, patronage, or dominance of particular locales. The most basic stage on which funerals played was the neighborhood, with the cortege winding its way from the dwelling of the deceased to the appointed burial church. As patricians cast their marital, political, and patronage networks more broadly in the late fifteenth and early sixteenth centuries, however, their funeral processions reinforced newly expanded citywide claims by traveling both within and outside their immediate neighborhood enclaves.

The most overt instance of a family's use and manipulation of urban spaces, both local and beyond, is the grand funeral ceremony honoring Giuliano de' Medici in March 1516. This ambitious funeral program used Medici imagery to further the family's dynastic ends; as in all that the Medici did, their behavior stood somewhat apart from that of other families. Although the route made reference to particular aspects of Medici history, it nevertheless reflected the workings of a more general social process. The day after Giuliano's death on March 17 at the Badia of Fiesole, an institution much favored by his great-grandfather Cosimo, his body was brought back to Florence for public viewing in the chapter house of San Marco, which also enjoyed a long if troubled association with the Medici. Crowds of Florentines flocked there to see the body; Bartolomeo Masi remarked that he did not believe that "there was anyone in Florence who did not go to see him."[51] Thus, even before the funeral began, the location and display of Giuliano's body called attention to various sites of Medici patronage.

The Medici first marked out the Via Larga, the site of the family palace, as their private territory before laying claim to other urban and religious centers such as San Lorenzo, the Palazzo Vecchio, and the Mercato Nuovo. On the morning of the funeral (March 19), "the Via Larga was completely filled with benches, here and there, on two levels, down its whole length, so that many churches in Florence were empty of their benches. As for the persons who came to this ceremony, if they had been standing still, the lawn of Ognissanti would not have been large enough to seat them all, even if it were filled with benches."[52] That morning Giuliano's body had been transferred from the small church of San Giovannino in the Via Larga to an enormous catafalque erected in the middle of the street across from the Medici palace.

Situated on safe familial ground, Giuliano's funeral proceeded to assert a connection between local Medici aims and the power of the papacy and the grandeur of Rome by making numerous references through costume, style, and symbolism to Giuliano's kinship with the pope, as well as to his Roman citizenship, bestowed in an elaborate ceremony in 1513.[53] Dressed in gold brocade with full armor, sword, and spurs, the corpse also sported a cap that mimicked the papal tiara of his brother Pope Leo X. In the middle of the hat was a gilded *marzocco*, the heraldic lion of Florence, an emblem that made a double reference to the city and to one of Leo's personal insignia.[54]

The catafalque also evoked the power of place: it was surmounted by gold brocade curtains bordered with black velvet in what a chronicler called a Roman fashion.[55]

Moving out from this spot into the city, the procession duplicated the route taken by the triumphal entry of Leo X into Florence three months before (November 30, 1515). This stunning entry was striking both for its visual apparatus and for the fact that it had little other than a dynastic rationale.[56] Leo's entry had taken seven hours to complete, with the pope making numerous stops to hear *canzoni* at each of the triumphal arches erected for the occasion. Giuliano's funeral lasted a mere five hours, but the only stationary part occurred in front of the Medici palace. The sheer physical size of the cortege, which outstripped even Leo's impressive entry, can be gauged from its logistical problems: participating clergy had completed the entire route and entered and exited from San Lorenzo without pause before the body had even moved from its place in the Via Larga.[57] The trappings spelled out virtually the entire range of Florentine official honors and further reinforced Giuliano's Roman and papal connections by symbolically referring to Giuliano's position as Captain of the Church.

Despite the fact that only a few blocks separated the Medici palace from the burial church of San Lorenzo, the processional route chosen was not a direct one. From the Medici palace the procession moved past the cathedral and the Badia, past the Pazzi palace and the Palazzo Vecchio, through the Mercato Nuovo, and up the Via Tornabuoni past San Michele Berteldi and Santa Maria Maggiore; it finally turned into Borgo San Lorenzo.[58] The diarist Cambi quickly recognized that this was a direct and explicit imitation of the route taken by Leo's earlier entry: "Note the turning of this world: that three and a half months had passed since the Pope came to Florence in great triumph by the Porta Rossa and Mercato Nuovo, by the Piazza della Signoria, the Fondamenti, and the Canto alla Paglia, carried on a litter with great triumph. And today his blood brother is carried dead by the same route in comparison with him, and the whole city came to view the aforesaid dead Giuliano who came to see the living Pope."[59]

In its progress, Giuliano's procession touched the city's major religious, civic, and commercial spaces, as well as asserting dominance over the residences of several families either allied with or opposed to the Medici. Since the procession began at the Medici palace rather than at Porta San Pier Gattolino, and ended at San Lorenzo instead of Santa Maria Novella, the route was not an exact replica of papal triumphal entries, which followed a curial formula for the procession and route.[60] Despite the discrepancies at beginning and end, however, the core of the routes was virtually identical, including several of the pivotal points such as the Canto de' Carnesecchi, where the final triumphal arch for Leo's entry had been positioned. Like the Medici art of Leo's time, both the entry and the funeral procession played upon the increasingly familiar tune of a Medici renewal that would triumph despite temporary setbacks.[61] Tracing Leo's footsteps, Giuliano's funeral posited its own hopes for Medici success in the person of Giuliano's nephew Lorenzo, giving spatial expression to the theme of dynasty and destiny that later figured so prominently in the Medici principate.

III

Composed of its three segments, the cortege wound its way toward the requiem, which posed different family claims and united participants in a different form of order. The purpose of the procession was to separate people on the basis of status; by contrast, the requiem incorporated a wide range of civic and family participants into a cohesive community. Those family members deliberately excluded from the procession, or relegated to its periphery, found an accepted place in the requiem proceedings, since it was this gathering process that renewed and strengthened social, communal, and spiritual bonds. The requiem emphasized broader political as well as domestic networks. When appropriate, the Florentine priors attended requiem rites, such as those held for the cardinal of Portugal in 1459, even though the priors were conspicuously and necessarily absent from the funeral itself.[62] Thus there was a complementary relationship between the funeral and the requiem, in that the requiem reintegrated those participants separated in the procession.

This social and religious rite of passage projected different models of family structure and sentiment than did the funeral. While the funeral emphasized the status of a reduced number of claimants, the purpose of the requiem (like the purpose of *cognatio* itself) was to enlarge the kindred. By representing both the group's wealth and its numbers, the requiem recognized and reiterated that the biological survival of the kindred was of paramount importance. Hence the requiem fundamentally restructured the family groupings represented in the funeral: it included cognates as well as agnates, women as well as men. Unlike the ancestor focus of the funeral, which stressed a common line of descent for the participants, the requiem traced out kinship from an ego-focus; that is, it represented kinship networks as spun out from the dead person himself or herself.

Contemporaries repeatedly recognized that women, in their multiple roles as mothers, sisters, wives, daughters, and in-laws, formed the foundation of this new family architecture. The chronicler Monaldi observed how, at the requiem for Niccolò Alberti (d. 1377), "all the close marital and blood relatives of the lineage," including "all the women who had entered or left the *casa*," gathered to honor him in Santa Croce.[63] Honoring Messer Vieri de' Medici (d. 1395) at his requiem were "a very great number of women, among whom were his daughters and his wife," although these women remained "on the other side" of the choir, as was customary in church. Altogether, a total of sixty-eight persons "among men and women" dressed in mourning for the event.[64]

Hence it was through mourning clothes publicly seen at the requiem that Florentine women entered into the organized ritual dramas of death. Put in other terms, mourning clothes were a way for women to negotiate a place for themselves in these representations of family and communal hierarchy. Given this sanction, some women from the commercial classes personally assumed the financial burdens of mourning in order to safeguard their own reputations. When the well-connected businessman Barna Ciurianni died in 1380, his mother Pera and his two sisters Margherita and Lena "said they would pay their share" for their mourning garb, thereby reducing the expenses of Barna's son for their clothes to a mere seven florins.[65] Giemma, mother of the silk merchant Ugolino Michi, proposed a similar cooperative venture upon his death in 1414. As one of the executors for Michi's heavily burdened estate, Giemma "asked the others what they wished to do about the funeral expenses, and after much discussion, it was agreed that Monna Giemma obligated herself for the funeral expenses up to the sum of twenty-five florins." The estate's creditors would bear the necessary cost "to honor Monna Lapa [Michi's widow] in garments and veils" in order that "the burial be made decently as is required." After the burial, however, Lapa promised to return a black gown and the fur mantle to the estate, retaining only the cloth mantle for her own use.[66] Those women with some standing but lesser resources could rent or borrow mourning mantles for the occasion. A purveyor of funeral goods in 1427 listed four women—the widows of two notaries, a physician, and a furrier—among his debtors for benches, bier trappings, and clothes procured for their husbands' funerals.[67]

Mourning outfits gave Florentine widows in particular a central place in the requiem which they sorely lacked in the funeral. Like everyday apparel, however, mourning clothes represented consumption from a particular point of view. The elaborate cuts of cloth, sumptuous linings, and multiple veils that characterized some of these outfits offered yet another way for households and women themselves to assert their wealth and status. In 1380 Valorino Ciurianni spent almost fifty-five florins to dress his father's widow, Lisa Frescobaldi, in a splendid outfit that cost more than twice the amount he spent to dress himself, a manservant, and his father's corpse.[68] Martinella Bardi sported a similarly extravagant outfit at the requiem for her husband Antonio da Panzano (d. 1423). Consuming twenty-six braccia of cloth, over twice the usual yardage, Martinella's gown was then topped off with a beautiful fur mantle and hood purchased by her brother-in-law Luca.[69]

Besides giving wealthy widows visual splendor, mourning clothes helped bolster natal ties between women, which were downplayed by the funeral. The requiem offered an arena in which to reincorporate not only marital kin but also women's own sisters and mothers as highly visible mourners. Dressed in mourning for the requiem of Checcha Masi (d. 1459) were her sister, her mother, her three daughters-in-law, and her husband's niece, as well as her husband and her nine sons. Four women wore mourning at Caterina Parenti's requiem in 1481: her daughters Gostanza and Marietta, her sister Alessandra, and her sister-in-law Selvaggia.[70] In addition to providing opportunities for portrayal of family structures and for self-expression, in many cases the requiem probably demonstrated a deep sense of affection and sociability between women which marriage alliances helped to create.

Yet the requiem and the mourning clothes did not serve to reinforce uniformly all natal ties or other vulnerable areas of Florentine kinship organization. Brothers rarely wore mourning in their sisters' honor, for example. This was in distinct contrast to the way in which sisters honored siblings of both sexes, and to the recognition brothers gave each other. Moreover, mourning clothes measured the limitations of *cognatio* between men of different generations and lineages. When burying his father Parente in 1452, for example, Marco Parenti subsidized clothing for himself, his wife, his mother, and his sister Alessandra, but not for Alessandra's husband Benedetto Quaratesi; indeed, there is no suggestion in Marco's description of the event that Quaratesi ever appeared in mourning. This practice held fast for later generations as well. Among the requiem mourners for Piero Parenti in 1519 were Maddalena Nerli and Maria Rucellai, the wives of Piero's two married sons Marco and Giovanni; both of these women and their husbands wore mourning. Yet although his daughters Caterina and Marietta also donned mourning clothes, their husbands Niccolò degli Agli and Lorenzo Dazzi did not.[71] In this contrary way, the requiem and mourning clothes partially reinforced the patrilineal interests asserted in the funeral.

While the requiem contributed more to a sense of family cohesion and community than did the funeral, it too was undercut by status distinctions that were manifested in liturgy and discourse. Before the middle of the sixteenth century, local versions of requiem masses were determined largely by custom rather than by a fixed, prescribed liturgy. Not until Pius V selected a single requiem formulary for the 1570 Missal was there a standard liturgical text. Nor was a requiem mass actually mandated as an essential part of the burial rite until the creation of the codified Rituale Romanum in 1614.[72] The addition of particular antiphons to the liturgy, such as the antiphon "In Paradisum" popular in Florentine usage during the clerical procession to the tomb, also varied according to locale, as did the use of certain psalms and other prayers for the dead.

Given this flexibility, the particular mode in which the liturgy was performed could help to sacralize social distinctions. The dead were not joined as a community of equals through a common rite of passage; instead they were highly differentiated by the number and status of liturgical celebrants, and by the presence or absence of special honors such as high requiem masses that were sung rather than recited; the addition of an Office of the Dead to the end of the mass; and the addition of organ music that further solemnized and embellished the proceedings. Few Florentines could lay claims similar to those of Lorenzo de' Medici and his heirs: Lorenzo's full requiem services in 1440 involved the bishop of Valvi as chief celebrant, assisted by nine cardinals.[73]

Highlighting these social distinctions was the funeral sermon, which was originally reserved for the rich, the powerful, and the well-born. Although not technically part of the liturgy, sermons following the requiem mass were already customary in Florence by the late Dugento. The Dominican Fra Remigio Girolami delivered a number of funeral sermons praising such Florentine notables as Vieri di Messer Consiglio de' Cerchi (d. 1313), and various members of other magnate clans such as the Adimari and the della Tosa.[74] In the late Trecento, Franco Sacchetti threw often vicious barbs against the lowly social origins or shoddy behaviors of those increasingly eulogized in funeral sermons. With characteristic humor, Sacchetti burlesqued the sermon for the rich peasant and "hearty sinner" Giovanni (*Novelle*, 22), lashing out at greedy preachers who blithely changed sinners into saints for greater material gain.

As is evident in other forms of ritual paradox and contradiction, some of the distinctions voiced in sermons explicitly connected the requiem with the familial themes of the funeral. Funeral sermons used the power of *volgare* preaching to better articulate the tale of family wealth, ambitions, and kinship structures told symbolically in the procession. Despite the fact that comparatively few texts of these sermons survive, diarists sometimes recorded their jist with an eye to family honor. It is worth looking more closely at the biases and claims present in one such account, that made by Tribaldo de' Rossi about the 1494 funeral and sermon for his kinswoman Piera di Antonio de' Rossi, who died in the powerful role of abbess of Santa Felicità.[75]

Tribaldo's account of the funeral proceedings placed Madonna Piera in a deeply lineal context rather than in a religious one, despite the fact that the Benedictine convent of Santa Felicità had received numerous Rossi girls as nuns for centuries. For Tribaldo, the funeral and the sermon, as well as his personal narrative, shared the common purpose of celebrating the larger family traditions into which Piera had been born, and he was thus tightfisted in praising the religious community she had headed since 1480.[76] He began his account by elucidating Piera's ties of kinship to important Rossi men: she was sister to Antonio, the former vicar of Valdelsa, and aunt to Gabrielo, who had invited Tribaldo to the obsequies. Yet Tribaldo established these connections without ever mentioning Piera by her proper name. His lineal biases were also apparent in the way he named the five kinsmen representing the Rossi house at the proceedings, while omitting any reference to female kin except his wife Nannina. Given the importance of nuns and nunneries to female sociability and patronage, this was a particularly glaring omission.[77] Nor did Tribaldo mention the funeral honors paid by fifty priests and four canons, by the archbishop's vicar Messer Filippo Alamanni, and by the archdeacon Messer Rinieri, which figure so prominently in the convent's account of the ceremony.[78]

For Tribaldo, both the ritual process and its narration were inseparably bound up with asserting the place of his lineage in neighborhood and civic affairs. As he recounted in detail, the abbess's funeral cortege paraded family claims to neighborhood space in the Oltrarno, where the Rossi had their various strongholds. Starting from the convent of Santa Felicità, whose square directly adjoined the Piazza de' Rossi and the family palace, Rossi kinsmen carried the bier to the Ponte Vecchio, down Borgo San Jacopo and into Via Maggio, past the Pitti and Biliotti palaces. They then marched on to the Rossi palace itself before returning to the convent. That the office of abbess in this old, affluent house was a matter of considerable local importance can be glimpsed from Tribaldo's awareness that the new occupant was Benedetta Machiavelli, sister to his fellow Oltrarno resident Niccolò.[79]

These family themes found their most explicit expression in the "bela predicha" preached by an unnamed Dominican friar from Santa Maria Novella. Although he did not report the exact text of the sermon, Tribaldo noted how the friar "greatly exalted the Rossi family," praising in particular their special devotion to the Dominican advocate Saint Peter Martyr. Tribaldo dwelled on the recognition the preacher gave to the long history of "our ancient forebears" who defended the saint's cult against those of "bad faith." The preacher also made explicit reference to the column that had been placed by Rossi kinsmen in the saint's honor in the square fronting the church. Finally, in the presence of Rossi kin and their neighbors Tanai de' Nerli and Piero Guicciardini, the Dominican praised the abbess's governing abilities, which had both contributed to and been produced by this rich family heritage. This verbal enactment was the crowning touch to the familial assertions Tribaldo had emphasized throughout his narrative.

In view of these complex representations and conflicting aims, requiem rites thus did far more than simply pose a conception of communal and family order contrary to the ones asserted by the funeral. Clearly the requiem marked a compelling moment of social harmony essential to the contined well-being of the social organism. Nevertheless, the requiem, like the funeral, was both framed by the structures of everyday life and subject to its tensions. Paradoxically, the contradictions embodied within the funeral and the requiem not only defined a set of conceptual opposites but also drew these ritual occasions together into a greater, complementary whole. It was as much the disorder and dynamism of the ritual process as its entrenched structures that helped Florentines write and rewrite the rules of order for their society.

CHAPTER 2

SYMBOLS, OBJECTS, BODIES

W e "see" groups through their symbols.
—Abner Cohen

Death rites took on their shape and meaning not only through patterned action but also by means of particular symbols and objects. The structure of death rites and the symbols these rites put into play were related channels of communication that delivered, each in its own way, complex messages about order and honor, family and community, women and men. In utilizing symbols to construct these messages, Florentines had at their disposal a vast semiotic system from which to pick and choose. The symbolic choices they made to represent themselves, to express power, and to convey emotion in death and burial rites formed an integral part of a broader cultural patterning.

Yet symbols, however venerable or weighty, do not carry inherent or uniform meanings. Rather, objects become symbols only by virtue of the full set of relationships they maintain with their environment. Symbols derive their multiple and often shifting meanings from the everyday situations in which they are used and from the everyday people who use them. Rather than signaling a single meaning, a symbol must be read as part of the overlapping and pluralistic cultural systems that were contained within the larger framework of Florentine society.

This is no less true for that most densely packed symbol of all: the human body. The body was both the mirror and the maker of its historical and natural environment. Historians have increasingly come to recognize that perceptions and regulation of the body were as much historically conditioned and contextually based as were notions of household and kinship. In late medieval and early modern Europe, the physical body not only indexed key social values and practices but also was used as a central metaphor to describe social and political relations. The "head," "members," and various organs of the human body offered a tremendous resource by which to understand and convey the organization of authority in the body politic, or by which to purge or reconstitute metaphorically the body social in rites, festivals, and religious riots.[1]

Taking the lead from Abner Cohen's remark, this chapter attempts to "see" the Florentine social world through the symbols and objects that were used and exchanged in the rites of death. The first half of the chapter examines patterns of symbolic choices, looking at the elements Florentines considered most appropriate for ritual use; the ranking of these elements; and their relationship to particular social structures and practices. The second half of the chapter focuses on the dead body that, as both symbol and artifact, was the centerpiece of death rites. It considers the range of meanings Florentines invested in clothing the corpse, and looks at representations of the body in effigies and other types of images. The chapter ends with a brief analysis of the physical treatment and valuation of the corpse as the detritus of a human life. Although this chapter does not seek to develop a single line of argumentation, it nevertheless aims to reinforce the notion presented in the previous chapter that rather than being isolated, self-contained activities, death rites were closely bound up with other social processes.

I

In late fourteenth- and fifteenth-century Florence, there was no inventory of symbols specific to funerals, and only a few functional mortuary objects were made for the dead (e.g., palls, bier heads, and catafalques). The powerful images and emblems conventionally associated with *memento mori*, or those that figure large in visual representations of the Triumph of Death—skulls and skeletons, reapers and scythes—were not actually used in funerals or requiems of the period. These images became popular in funerals only around the middle of the sixteenth century, by which time both politics and religious taste had changed profoundly.[2] In other words, the iconography of funeral rites in late medieval and Renaissance Florence differed from what later became the standard iconography of death and the macabre.

Instead, the symbols Florentines used to create "appropriate images of honor of and for themselves" in funerals were identical to the items used in other public ceremonies.[3] This symbolic repertoire included flags, banners, standards, pennants, caparisoned horses, shields, swords, escutcheons, books, corporate emblems, and family or personal devices. The symbolic objects conveying public funerary homage to John Hawkwood and Vieri de' Medici in the 1390s, for example, bore remarkable similarity to the ceremonial gifts bestowed on Francesco Giovanni in 1444 when he relinquished the captaincy of Cortona. Given to Giovanni were the arms of the commune, along with "a great taffeta banner with Saint Mark, embellished with gold where necessary," a shield of worked and gilded silver, and a lance.[4] From a practical standpoint, communal accountants made little distinction between the purchase of mortuary items and the outlay for other civic ceremonies. On one occasion in 1397, the treasurer of the fund for civic ceremonies (Camera dell'Arme) paid out just over one hundred florins "to honor Benino di Ghucio at his funeral, and for a pennant and shield given to the podestà Messer Pantaleone, . . . and for three pennants and the expenses incurred for the funeral of Davanzato and Zanobi di Simone Fei."[5]

This shared symbolic system helped Florentines to contend with the facts of death by both embracing and distancing their dead. On the one hand, the living continued to share and enjoy common bonds of recognition with the dead, thereby sustaining the mutual connections and collapsing the distance between the two groups. On the other hand, Florentines distanced themselves from death's disruptive power by using the ordinary emblems of everyday life rather than devising special signs for their funeral processions. This manipulation of symbols not only created a set of orderly relations between the living and the dead but also helped Florentines blunt the emotional force of death.

Political considerations also played a role in the selection of symbols. The symbolic power of a funerary object was determined less by its material value than by the recognized messages of public authority and legitimacy it communicated, primarily by means of the corporate insignia and family coats of arms emblazoned on objects. The importance of these markings to both funerary practices and Florentine social relations more generally can hardly be overstated. Much of the competition for place and honor in Florentine society was organized around arms, emblems, and insignia, which proclaimed not only family identity and corporate affiliation but political allegiance as well.[6] Family coats of arms were used to stake and defend claims to tombs, chapels, and secular spaces and buildings, while judicial punishments often called for defacing an offender's arms in addition to humiliating him in defamatory images (*pitture infamanti*). It was common practice during political upheavals such as the Ciompi revolt (1378), the Pazzi conspiracy (1478), and the ousting of the Medici (1494) to despoil an opponent's family emblems, pictorial symbols, tombs, and collective memorabilia.[7] Moreover, corporate and family emblems not only decorated gifts, ranging from chalices and spoons to wedding chests and armor, but were considered gifts in their own right.[8]

Hence, in marking funeral goods with these common signs, Florentines evoked a rich cluster of socially recognized meanings and symbolic associations that went well beyond the objects' material value. So thoroughly were emblems linked with power and identity that the depiction of emblems often substituted for absent mourners paying tribute to the dead. Pope Eugenius IV sent the banner of the Church along with his own personal flag to the burial of Lorenzo de' Medici in 1440, although the pope himself did not attend.[9] Conversely, to deny these implicit meanings in the interests of piety stood out as a true gesture of humility. The great builder Giovanni Rucellai made a powerful statement when, in his will of 1465, he rejected both an unseemly display of wax and "those flags or banners, either domestic or public, decorated with either domestic or public signs."[10]

Given the significance of emblems, it is not surprising that their integrity and their use in death rites were fiercely defended by corporations and individuals. Jacopo Salviati, one of the two commissioners responsible for Guccio da Casale's funeral in 1400, noted that, among the embroidered escutcheons and small hangings gracing Guccio's bier, "no other arms were placed there than those of our commune, in order not to give others, especially outside of Florence, any [honor] which was not our own."[11] Salviati also recorded how the captains of the Parte Guelfa refused to pay for the enormous pennant bearing the Parte's arms because Guccio had been a Ghibelline. The commune was forced to purchase the pennant with communal funds instead, since the Guelf emblem was such an integral part of communal identity that it could not be omitted, even under these tricky circumstances.

The spatial positioning of emblems on funeral flags and banners also offered a way to signify varying degrees of alliance and affection binding donor and recipient. The officials of the Florentine Studio opted to honor their esteemed colleague the humanist Alamanno Rinuccini (d. 1499) with a whole string of flags that showed the Studio's sign (a red cherub) in close proximity to Rinuccini's family arms.[12] However, this joint depiction could just as easily signal dominance rather than an alliance between equals. To honor their Florentine deputy, Antonio da Panzano, shortly after his death in office in 1423, the neighboring city of Pescia sent to his funeral a huge, beautiful flag whose imagery must have resonated strongly with the Florentine vision of territorial domination so evident in the early Quattrocento. Sitting squarely in the middle of the flag was an outsize depiction of the Panzano arms, flanked by the smaller emblems of all the vicarate's castles and towns.[13]

Given their symbolic force, emblems clearly enhanced the value of funerary goods that formed part of a larger economy of social exchange.[14] Funeral trappings actually figured into two forms of transaction. One was a temporary exchange, in which objects such as wax torches, banners, and bier cloths were loaned by corporate groups to the heirs of the deceased, thereby solemnizing their alliance and binding them through a ritual transaction. Confraternities such as Orsanmichele kept in their inventory of goods a regular stockpile of bier cloths, cushions, and large professional candles mounted on staves, which were temporarily loaned for the obsequies and returned later.[15]

The other type of transaction, in which heirs made outright gifts of trappings to the burial church, was more permanent. In medieval Europe, the presentation of funeral goods (*funeralia*) was originally intended as a free offering, but by the thirteenth century funeral goods may have been considered as restitution to the parish for unpaid tithes or dues. However, there was no fixed sum or percentage that the deceased legally or even customarily owed the parish upon burial. Rather, the wealth of *funeralia* reflected the status of the dead and the generosity of their heirs. Regardless of value, the donation of funeral goods locates a set of everyday patronage activities that penetrated far more deeply into the social fabric than did artistic commissions. Even Florentines of meager means customarily turned over a burial pall and a few candles as gift and compensation. These donations formed part of the complex, reciprocal commerce between churches and patrons, in which goods and revenues were exchanged for prestige and spiritual protection.

While churches generally sold, recycled, or used donated goods, most institutions retained the funeral banners (*drappelloni*) bought for the elite, which were placed around the tomb of the deceased after the ceremonies. Emblazoned with family and corporate emblems, these funerary gifts identified the church's patrons on an ongoing basis. In the sixteenth century and probably well before, hangings taken from family tombs in Santa Maria Novella were used to drape the *ponte* (a kind of rood screen) there for the feasts of Christmas, Epiphany, and other principal feast days.[16] Hung so as to face the main doors of the church, these draperies quickly summed up the church's history of patronage for entering visitors.

Because of these social practices, funeral banners continued to have powerful resonances long after the burial was over. For Duke Cosimo I, the republican associations evoked by various emblems lived on as uneasy reminders of an earlier corporate period, and the renovation of Santa Croce offered him an opportunity to remove family property from several venerable tombsites. Using the rationale of architectural clarity, Cosimo stripped the flags of the Popolo, the Parte Guelfa, and the Ricasoli family from the tomb of the war captain Albertaccio Ricasoli, which had been in place for almost two centuries since his death in 1360. Cosimo took similar action against the tomb of another famous republican citizen, Bartolomeo Valori, removing three flags with various insignia, as well as the three shields and suit of armor posted around the tomb.[17] The parameters of what a family could rightfully do with its dead were clearly different in the principate than they had been in the republic.

Like funeral activities, symbolic trappings helped individuals and families to stake out spatial claims, this time to the sacred geography of a church rather than to neighborhood and city. Families asserted ownership over a church's social and sacred resources not only by placing their emblems on tombs and chapels lining church interiors but also by affixing these emblems to walls, pillars, capitals, doorways, niches, tabernacles, holy water fonts, altars and altar cloths, and other liturgical furniture. With a single church accommodating a large variety of patrons, it must have become problematic to define the points at which different territories converged and to protect the integrity of individual territories, as the following case suggests. In his 1417 testament, the wool dealer Agostino di Francesco di Ser Giovanni included an elaborate set of provisions regarding his private chapel and tomb in Santo Spirito.[18] One of his major concerns was to preserve the sight lines into the chapel from as many vantage points as possible. To this end, he forbade the friars of Santo Spirito to allow the placement of any flag, shield, or other sign next to his chapel or near its entrance. Agostino worried that such emblems might impede the view of his chapel and, perhaps more importantly, create unnecessary confusion about its ownership. In this case Agostino's sense of property and the privatization of a public space extended well beyond the localized display of arms to a more general claim on the church itself. Not only should the living be able to see his chapel, viewed as a social statement; they should also be able to visually visit his dead without the impediments and implications of other family arms.

Florentines used funerary goods to create networks of spiritual as well as secular patronage by depicting sacred images along with family arms on funeral banners. Sacred images, such as figures of the Virgin and of saints, were not only objects of devotion but also active forces for assistance in practical and spiritual affairs.[19] Although generally of negligible artistic merit, these painted images nevertheless offered significant sources of perpetual protection for both living and dead. Unfortunately there are too few descriptions of these banners to undertake a systematic study of spiritual clientage, as A. N. Galpern has done for sixteenth-century Champagne using the evidence of stained-glass windows.[20]

Numerous examples suggest, however, that one of the primary patrons invoked at death was the name saint of the deceased. In 1497, for example, Marco Parenti's heirs commissioned twenty-two flags bearing the emblem of the silk guild, the Parenti arms, and the image of Saint Mark. These flags continued to call on Marco's name saint long after the burial, since "these flags were donated to Santa Maria del Fiore, and hung where [Marco's] body was buried in our customary tomb near the campanile." The heirs of Marco's son Piero created an even wider network of spiritual relations upon his death in 1519. In addition to the usual guild emblems, Piero's flags displayed, along with the Parenti arms, the figures of his name saint Peter, Saint Francis, and the Virgin.[21] The patrician widow Nanna Gianfigliazzi tended to both the spiritual interests of her husband Bartolomeo (d. 1493) and her own reputation when she commissioned funeral flags richly painted with San Bartolomeo's image.[22] The relative affordability of these trappings made the spiritual networks they created far more accessible than those invoked in the monumental art of altarpieces and fresco cycles.

Perhaps the most critical social function of symbolic funerary goods was to identify the social place of the deceased. The clarity and speed of this identification hinged on a close correspondence between symbol and social role. Judges, doctors, and other learned men, such as the Augustinian friar Luigi Marsili, were often represented by books, either carried aloft in the cortege or shown clasped to the dead man's chest on tomb slabs. Similarly, knights were represented by military accoutrements, such as the "belt decorated with gilded silver, [the] small sword with ferrules, also of gilded silver," and the "golden spurs" embellishing the corpse of Vieri de' Medici (d. 1395).[23] Merchants were identified by parading their distinctive short, fur-lined mantles. Hence the Trecento novelist Sacchetti was merely following a mental habit derived from social practice when he tried to match imaginary funeral trappings for Christ with his status as "King above all Kings." Sacchetti concluded that among the many tributes paid to Christ "should [be] four banners" representing the homage of Art, Nature, Morals, and Literature.[24] This matching process had parallels in other activities. For instance, both artists and viewers created and read an iconography of saints by means of their attributes—Catherine of Alexandria's torturous wheel, Lucy's plucked-out eyes, Sebastian's arrows—while the criminal justice system relied on a similar process of identification when punishing some offenders in symbolic, often humiliating, garb.[25]

Venetians followed similar conventions, placing legal codices and digests on the catafalques of judges, books of Hippocrates and Galen on those of physicians. As Venice developed into one of the major Italian printing centers in the late fifteenth and early sixteenth centuries, however, books probably began to assume a more prominent place, at least in some funerals. The renowned publisher Aldus Manutius was surrounded on his bier by books, presumably from his own press, while the physician Tommaso Rangone specified in his testament that his funeral cortege should display certain of the books he had written, opened to predetermined pages.[26]

Accurate identification hinged not only on a set of recognizable associations, however, but also on the restricted use of particular items. Sumptuary law helped establish a cultural system of identification based on exclusion, in which various funerary symbols were assigned legitimately to particular subgroups comprising the elite, such as knights, judges, physicians, and merchants. Those in other occupational roles were not legally allowed any special signs of status, although evidence abounds that these sumptuary proscriptions were often flagrantly ignored.

In assigning symbols by law, Florentines established and marked divisions between genders as well as between status groups and occupations. Signs of professional status and established public authority were always conspicuously absent at women's funerals, regardless of rank. Even wives of such high-ranking professionals as physicians and judges were honored simply by the participation of their husbands' colleagues, rather than by the use of formal emblems. Hence the only official corporate signs available to women in funeral rites (aside from family arms) were the insignia and emblems of religious confraternities. Inspired, produced, and dominated by masculine values and ideals, images of public honor in republican Florence were highly gendered forms of communication and representation.[27]

Women of the Florentine elite nevertheless enjoyed a public persona through their families rather than through formal political participation. Squeezed out of official public affairs, women looked to material wealth, mainly in the form of sumptuous clothing, to establish their honor and identity. In the eyes of moralists from Sacchetti to Savonarola, Florentine women had a particularly vain and frivolous appetite for clothing, which was matched only by their capacity for "feminine" artifice.[28] For privileged, affluent women, it was clothing rather than corporate insignia that carried symbolic weight at death. Beautiful bier coverings, elaborate burial outfits, headdresses, jewelry, and large numbers of candles—goods in which men's status was also reflected—helped underwrite women's personal status and family identity.[29] Some of these items may have been marked with that "public badge of membership," the family coat of arms, which was often woven into or used as an embellishment on articles made for special or even daily wear.[30]

Like the clothes of women mourners, rich burial apparel represented consumption from a particular point of view. The useful splendor of clothing and jewels made affluent women the bearers of their households' reputations, and in a broader sense reflected honor on the city as a whole.[31] Since fathers and husbands often bought and were penalized for the cloaks, mantles, sleeves, overdresses, rings, earrings, necklaces, and head ornaments that became women's emblems, men's status was intrinsically implicated in the *luxuria* that women wore. Yet this steep investment in elaborate burial garb only served to isolate women in a context of goods, far removed from the customary trappings of authority. Through fine clothing, the corpses of privileged women located a confluence of honor and property similar to the one these women had represented in life, when they had guarded the transmission of both patrimony and progeny by means of their proper sexual conduct. Not surprisingly, however, some affluent women seized on the particular authority clothing offered them, using clothing to negotiate a place for themselves within a tightly constricted social world.

II

The subject of clothing takes us into the complex relationship between the human body and the social order. Objects used, worn, or otherwise associated with the body functioned as powerful communicative devices because the body itself was such a powerful symbol, which joined together a whole program of values and meanings.[32] As an extension of the body, clothing made reference to these various and sundry meanings, thereby helping to identify persons on the basis of class, age, gender, occupation, native origins, and so forth. In late medieval and Renaissance Italy, to strip someone of clothing was to strip away his or her acknowledged identity, as attested by the naked, patient Griselda, or by visual representations of naked sinners in hell who were distinguished only by their hats.[33]

Since the dead were frequently transported on biers in full public view (despite laws to the contrary), Florentines could easily evaluate burial garb using their habitual, well-developed sensitivity to clothing. The corpse was enclosed in a coffin only in exceptional circumstances, such as when an individual had died away from the city.[34] The treasurer of San Pier Maggiore noted, for example, that the convent had a coffin ("una chassa da morti") left over "when the dead body of Piero di Vanni arrived from the countryside." The convent later reused this coffin as a temporary holding site for the plague victim Pippo degli Albizzi "because he wanted to have a tomb made in the church." Venetian funerals showed a similarly limited use of coffins, with the corpse openly displayed in procession.[35]

The types of fabric and clothing styles worn by the dead generally reflected the ability to pay, with the elite favoring such colorful luxury fabrics as scarlet silk, purple velvet, and gold brocade. Both traditional color symbolism and the costliness of the dyes and materials made these fabrics the most prestigious, and the most sought after by wealthy Florentines and Venetians alike.[36] Francesco Rinuccini (d. 1381), a wealthy knight who paid the highest forced-loan (*prestanza*) assessment in the city in 1364, was dressed for his burial in "the greatest honor" of vermilion velvet. Niccolò degli Alberti (d. 1377) wore blood-red samite, a type of heavy silk similar to velvet, and a fabric shot through with gold; in the same year, Palla di Francesco Strozzi's body was outfitted in reddish scarlet.[37] Such splendid clothing made the corpse a visual as well as a ritual center of attention, with the dead person's garments adding a spark of brilliance to the crowd of somberly clad mourners. It is a safe guess that less affluent Florentines also wore their best outfits to the grave.

In describing funeral ceremonies, astute observers focused on specific articles of clothing which signified particularly important values for contemporaries. One of the most scrupulously observed objects was the type of headgear worn by the dead. Ranging from the sober to the whimsical, the ubiquitous hats and headgear in which Florentines delighted packed a complex set of associations into a single concentrated object. The power of hats to mark rank and status has already been noted in regard to visual representations of naked sinners in hell, stripped of all but their headgear. The painter Piero della Francesca may have seen firsthand the striking, unmistakable "white hat coming to a point in front" worn by the Eastern emperor, John VIII Paleologus, which Piero later incorporated into his Arezzo frescoes.[38] Specific types of hats, such as the distinctive beret of the Studio's rectors, worn by Carlo Marsuppini's corpse,[39] were sure signs of corporate membership.

As extensions of the body and particularly of the head, hats were jammed with overlapping meanings, connoting authority, rationality, and even charismatic spiritual power. Even amateur political theorists made much of the fact that the head governed the body; hats in turn helped to focus that power, wielded in both social and political terms. The peculiar beret worn by the Venetian doge, as well as the caps of Venetian councillors, figured with the emblem of Saint Mark, signified these individuals' unmistakable authority as "heads" of state. Hats helped to locate and make reference to the specific source from which power originated. The satin cap worn by Giuliano de' Medici at his funeral in 1516, for example, explicitly mimicked the papal tiara gracing the head of his brother Leo X. For religious figures, hats concentrated the essence of both their institutional authority and their charismatic holiness. Of the various articles of clothing from Saint Antoninus's wardrobe preserved as relics, his bishop's hat (*biretta*) worked the most healing miracles.[40] Moreover, hats and headgear also reiterated the sexual differences indicated by other funerary symbols. The bejewelled garlands, crowns, tiaras, ornaments, hairpins, and perhaps even false hair women wore again placed them in a context of goods and property relations, as distinct from the logic of authority that governed men's apparel.

Since Florentines fully expected that the dress of the dead, including hats, would be a sure sign of status, the rejection of that dress in favor of monastic garb was a very powerful statement, especially for rich knights, bankers, and merchants, in whose case the contrast was greatest. Garments made of humble "monk's cloth" were devoid of that rich, often startling play of color and texture that gave Florentine clothing of the period its distinctive character. Thus an individual's rejecting normal attire and opting instead for a religious habit made known in a concrete way the depth of his or her piety. Francesco di Tommaso Giovanni recorded how his eighty-year-old aunt, Simona, assumed "of her own free will . . . the habit of a holy nun, that is, of the order of Saint Augustine; and thus she went to her tomb dressed in the habit of that order on Saturday, March 6 [1434]."[41] Since one had to explicitly choose such a habit, either in one's testament or on the deathbed, burial in religious garb was one of the most significant forms of self-definition available to Florentines.

Rather than reflecting an indiscriminate sense of piety, however, this choice of monastic garb often supported the local, particularist loyalties marked by the funeral route and burial site. The most popular mendicant and eremetic orders—Franciscans, Dominicans, Augustinians, Carmelites, and Vallombrosans—each professed a distinctive type of spirituality and religious organization. Choosing among these options was eased or complicated by the force of neighborhood attachments, such as those apparent in the burial choices made by that venerable statesman Rinaldo Gianfigliazzi (d. 1425). Gianfigliazzi expressed his deep loyalty to his local church of Santa Trinità, site of the ancient family tombs, by choosing to be buried in the monastic dress of a Vallombrosan monk and by designating monks as pallbearers.[42] Yet it should be noted that Gianfigliazzi's piety nevertheless carried only limited obligations: self-representation as a monk or tertiary on the funeral bier made few practical demands on one's behavior in daily life.

Archeological evidence shows that Florentines customarily buried their dead in the same garments worn in the funeral. Excavations below the Florentine cathedral from 1965 to 1974 revealed spurs, brooches, and gold belt-buckles in several late thirteenth-century tombs, while coin finds in graves assisted in dating earlier levels of the church.[43] Religious persons—priests, bishops, monks, and nuns—went to their graves wearing their distinctive religious habits or sacerdotal signs, such as the surplice and amice in which a priest of San Pier Maggiore, Ser Tommaso, was buried in 1382. The tomb transfer of Benozzo Federighi, bishop of Fiesole (d. 1450), corroborates this practice of burial in characteristic costume. During the transfer of Federighi's tomb and remains to a new site in San Pancrazio (1753), excavators found "a small, decayed chestnut box, about one and one-third braccia long, and about a half braccia wide and deep." They found it worthy of note that "in it were the bones of Bishop Benozzo in disarray, without the slightest sign either of his pectoral cross or his miter, or of any other inscription or record." In addition to Federighi's bones, the box contained only some fragments of rose-colored silk, probably from his stole.[44]

Literary sources confirm the practice of burying prestigious figures in precious garments, complete with jewels and insignia. Boccaccio tells a story (Decameron, 2.5) of how a Neapolitan archbishop, Filippo Minutolo, was buried in rich ecclesiastical vestments, along with his bishop's staff, miter, and gloves, and a ruby ring worth more than five hundred florins. Nor surprisingly, in the story Minutolo's tomb became the target of not one but two sets of grave robbers.

The custom of interring the dead in expensive clothing and with official insignia was not unique to Florence. When the French royal tombs were opened during the Revolution in 1793, for example, royal insignia such as a crown and scepter, and often a hand of justice and ring, were found in every king's grave until the time of Charles VIII (d. 1498). From then on, the royal insignia were attached to the king's effigy instead of to his body. However, before 1400 English knights may have been buried only with their insignia because of the extraordinary cost of armor.[45]

There is little doubt that this widespread burial custom invited threats to social, political, and moral order, especially in the form of grave robbery. Both local and canonical rulings condemned the practice of burial in fine clothes and tried to prohibit or at least curb it. As early as 1306, Bishop Biliotti of Fiesole scolded his flock that this habit constituted a tremendous waste of resources that could be put to better social use. In his synodal constitutions, the bishop advised laypersons to seek burial in a cloth of goat hair or some other utterly simple vestment "because if it is done otherwise, one sins against God and brings about the destruction of property, property which could be sold and given to the poor in the name of the defunct." Biliotti enacted the above provision "since funeral pomp is expressly prohibited by law, and since we have heard that recently and in the past some deceased have been exhumed and their bodies robbed of the precious vestments in which they were laid to rest."[46] The commune also recognized the problems of burial in splendid clothing. Every major redaction of sumptuary laws from 1293 to 1473 included a virtually identical provision mandating burial in a simple linen shirt, although these rubrics never specified the grounds for censure.

Rather than abandon this practice, however, Florentines only exacerbated the threat of grave robbery by burying valuables with the deceased. Although we can only speculate about the extent of the problem, incidents of grave robbery were certainly not unknown after Biliotti's time. The gravediggers Lorenzo di Vanni and Lotto Tendi, for example, were severely punished by the commune in June 1345 for digging up the body of Spinello di Dino, who had been buried in the cemetery of Sant'Ambrogio by the two men and another gravedigger, Bartolo Borsi. Together the three men "exhumed the body and stripped it of all the wool and linen cloth that Spinello had on," leaving him nude. They also extracted 150 florins that had been buried with Spinello.[47] A century and a half later, on March 28, 1483, the civic militia (Otto di Guardia) recorded "the scandal committed last night in opening and breaking the tombs that are around the church of Santa Maria Novella, and in other dishonesty," but gave no further details.[48] Stories of tomb pilfering—such as the legend of Ginevra degli Almieri, in which her tomb is opened by thieves intent on stealing the jewels from her body—also abound in contemporary literature.[49] Despite the fact that burial in rich clothes with money or jewels was an economic investment that would never bear fruit, despite stern legal prohibitions, and despite the moral affront of grave robbery, Florentines persisted in dressing their dead well.

The deep reluctance to alter such behavior indicates just how significant the dress of the corpse must have seemed to contemporaries. Clearly clothing was a way to mark status and to order social relations in this world. But clothing also had important implications for the afterlife as well, which added additional layers of meaning to costume. What the dead wore to the grave not only located them among the living, but also projected their social identity into the next world. As a central strategy for the afterlife, burial in fine clothing, complete with money, insignia, and occupational tools, enabled Florentines and other Europeans to bring their earthly status and privileges into that other "modality of human existence," when they joined the community of the dead.[50]

Visual artists may have played on these expectations when they used clothing as a way to distinguish inhabitants of the next world. We can briefly explore this link between artistic and social practice in the depiction of the Last Judgment painted by Fra Angelico circa 1431 (Figure 2.1). In this panel, Fra Angelico depicted heaven as a walled city that strongly resembles a contemporary Tuscan townscape, perhaps even Florence itself.[51] The dead have just been raised from their tombs and now await their assignment to heaven or hell. Before entering the city of Paradise through a turreted gate, the ranks of the blessed stand in various postures of prayer and joy, while on the opposite side, the damned turn away in anxious agitation. Prior to their consignment to the glories of heaven or the pains of hell, both the blessed and the damned are differentiated by their clothing.

FIGURE 2.1. Fra Angelico, *The Last Judgment*, Florence, Museo S. Marco. (Reproduced by permission of Alinari/Art Resource, N.Y.)

Fra Angelico is careful to include a mix of clergy and laity, men and women, rich and poor, in each group. Once the damned enter the hellish torture pits, however, they are stripped of their clothing and of their distinctive rank and identity. Hell is chaotic, disorderly, full of inversions. The social organization that clothing established and reinforced is here totally ruptured, replaced by a crush of stripped-down bodies now grouped only by the hierarchy of punishments to which they are subject. The blessed, by contrast, retain their distinguishing garments, now imbued with a shimmering radiance. The decorum that defines this group is founded on a right order that clothing sustains rather than conceals. In the city of Paradise, the social distinctions of clothing are not erased but are transcended.

Despite this persistent concern with representing a social persona through clothing, Florentines did not exhibit a similar interest in representing the body by means of funeral effigies. Obviously there was no functional need for an effigy because Florentines ordinarily buried their dead within a day after death. When demands of state required that a civic funeral be postponed longer pending appropriate arrangements, the corpse could be preserved for about three days by disembowelling it and embalming it with salt and spices. Yet by comparison with northern Europeans, Florentines showed little interest in preserving permanent images of the whole body in funeral effigies or the figural sculpture of tomb monuments, or on incised tomb slabs.[52]

Instead, Florentines focused their attention on preserving like-nesses of the head and face for commemorative and social purposes. In the "undying faces" of death masks and portrait busts, the physical appearance of kin and ancestors was recorded for future generations.[53] Prominent Florentines such as Lorenzo de' Medici, Luca Pitti (b. 1395), and Niccolò di Giovanni Capponi (b. 1416) had their features recorded for posterity in wax death masks, which were often set later in terra-cotta.[54] Although Vasari incorrectly attributed the invention of death masks to Verrocchio, the practice of making death masks for future use indeed became increasingly fashionable in the second half of the Quattrocento as the authority of antique art and authors took hold.[55]

Commemorative images took two basic forms that had different purposes, clienteles, and audiences. The first type was ancestral images designed for domestic consumption. Ranging from expensive, durable material such as marble to more ephemeral stuff, these images were used by a social elite to promote family traditions. In particular, images of kinsmen served a patrilineal definition of the family, functioning as visual counterparts of or supplements to the written histories found in family diaries. Ornamenting the Medici palace in 1494, for example, was a fine collection of family masks strategically placed on doorways—eight heads over the entrance to the loggia, and six over the garden entry—where a glance upwards quickly indexed the more illustrious chapters of the family's history for visitors and kinsmen alike.[56]

The second type of artifact cut much more broadly across the social spectrum. These were low-cost images made of wax, terra-cotta, and papier-mâché, to be placed in churches for both commemorative and votive purposes. Designed to supplicate the divine, elicit prayers from the living, and perpetuate a physical likeness for posterity, these images had enormous popular appeal. Knights and merchants like Sacchetti's Pero Foraboschi (*Novelle*, 185) commissioned post-mortem likenesses of this type; the vicar of Santissima Annunziata, Antonio da Bologna, contracted for a life-size wax image "al naturale" from the waxworker Archangelo di Giovanni in June 1481; the young, unnamed daughter of Jacopo di Geri Risaliti was depicted in a painted papier-mâché funerary bust, dated 1363, which can still be seen in its Trecento marble niche in the church of San Simone.[57]

Although relatively few of these ephemeral images have survived, their popularity can be gauged from written records. As early as January 1401, the Signoria forbade any further additions to the votive collection at Orsanmichele, except for statesmen and communal leaders, because of the clutter already present. The church of Santissima Annunziata, which housed the vast majority of the city's votive and commemorative images, including those of the Medici, added two large shelves to the tribune walls in 1447 to accommodate the growing number of figures. By 1630, when a formal inventory of votive images was made, the Annunziata housed 600 life-size figures, 22,000 images made of papier-mâché, and 3,600 votive paintings, many based on death masks.[58]

Despite the popularity of death masks, commemorative busts, and votive figures, however, Florentine image making stopped short of funeral effigies for ritual use. Even when effigies might have been functionally appropriate as substitutes for absent bodies, there is little evidence documenting their production or use. When Messer Alessandro dell'Antella died in Hungary in 1379 while serving as communal ambassador, for example, his funeral was held shortly afterwards in San Romolo at state expense. Although the ceremonies featured a draped bier, torches, a caparisoned horse, and numerous family mourners, the detailed description makes no mention of a funeral effigy; records of financial transactions for the manufacture of a wax dummy are also lacking. Similarly, when Simoncino de' Bardi died and was buried in the countryside in September 1372, his funeral was celebrated in Florence "with all the honor and caparisoned horses as if his body were there." At the lavish services held for Guccio da Casale in 1400, the bier was carried by two horses "as if his body were inside," despite the fact that Guccio had been buried at Cortona more than ten days before.[59]

In fact, Florentine political values worked directly counter to the creation of effigies as symbolic representations of the body. The purpose of funeral effigies, such as those commonly used in French and English royal funeral ceremonies, was to ensure an effective transfer of power without interruption of sovereignty. The effigy symbolically perpetuated the fiction that the body natural was still alive, and that it continued to locate the undying power of the body corporate. The king's "two bodies" came together in the effigy, around which an elaborate court ceremonial developed.[60]

Given the corporate political structure and republican traditions of Florence, funerals in the Arno city symbolically confirmed that power was never located in a single person. Florentine civic funerals shied away both from the use of effigies and from a prolonged public viewing that might focus undue attention on the deceased. The bodies of such outstanding public figures as John Hawkwood (d. 1394), Coluccio Salutati (d. 1406), and Carlo Marsuppini (d. 1453) were publicly displayed for only a few hours. Even the corpse of Giuliano de' Medici (d. 1516), the recipient of the greatest and most dynastically oriented private funeral in republican Florence, lay in state for only one day.[61]

Florentines made a great exception to this brief public viewing for bishops and holy persons. The body of Cosimo Pazzi, the archbishop of Florence who died on April 9, 1513, was publicly displayed in the main hall of the bishop's palace for three days, during which crowds came to kiss his hands and feet. The most renowned Florentine bishop of the fifteenth century, Saint Antoninus (d. 1459), lay in state in San Marco for eight days after his death. Despite the detailed descriptions of Antoninus's funeral and requiem, which included Pope Pius II as a mourner and the patriarch of Venice as celebrant, we cannot be sure whether the faithful paid homage to his embalmed, eviscerated body, or to an effigy.[62]

At times Florentines purposely prolonged the period between the death and the burial of holy persons, since this delay might prove critical to the later establishment of popular religious cults. Like other Europeans to their day, Florentines were guided by the expectation that holiness would inscribe itself on the body in some way. A lengthy interim allowed miracles to flourish, as the laity flocked to see and touch the body, to be healed by contact with it, or to witness visions in its presence. A prolonged display also allowed for the demonstrated preservation of the body in the "odor of sanctity," a powerful indication of holiness which was frequently used as essential evidence in sanctification proceedings. Hence the display of holy persons facilitated the creation of new spiritual networks of clients and patrons, while it produced new artifacts of power in the form of relics. Given his reputation for holiness, it is not surprising that the body of San Bernardino of Siena lay in state for twenty-three days in the Aquila cathedral in May 1444. Closer to home, the cult of a local Florentine holy woman, Beata Villana de' Botti, was launched when her body remained uncorrupted for thirty-seven days after her death in 1360.[63] This same invitation to the development of cults meant that the bodies of secular persons were best buried quickly to avoid undue challenges to political power.

Although the neighboring republic of Venice shared similar political concerns with Florence, it nevertheless handled the transfer of sovereignty and its symbolic representation across the boundaries of death in different ways. Here a brief comparison of civic funeral practices in the two cities sharpens our sense of how political distinctiveness cut through cultural similarities. As a patrician oligarchy headed by a doge who embodied civic values, Venice developed a form of funeral ritual that both recognized and limited the doge's primacy. Writing in 1493, the Venetian diarist Marin Sanudo gave a detailed account of how the Serenissima customarily buried its ducal leader.[64] Sanudo reported that the doge's body was dressed in full ceremonial robes, then carried by the canons and chapter of San Marco from the ducal apartment to the main civic audience hall in the company of state councillors. While the bells of San Marco tolled the news, the doge's body was placed on a high catafalque, where it would lie in state for three days.

Once the ducal apartments had been vacated, the councillors reclaimed sovereign power, both physically and symbolically, by moving into the doge's palace. Sanudo carefully noted that their proclamations bore the seal of the eldest councillor rather than the ducal seal, which was smashed along with other ducal insignia.[65] Moreover, their bulletins were signed "Consiliarii Venetiarum, et rectores ducatus; vacante ducatu." The councillors elected twenty-one or more of their number and obliged them to remain in the audience hall for the duration of the obsequies. Dressed in scarlet rather than black robes, these delegated mourners marked the continuation of sovereignty; their outfits were "a sign," as Sanudo remarked, "that although the doge was dead, the Signoria was not dead." In 1485, apparently for the first time, an effigy was substituted for the body of the doge when the plague death of Giovanni Mocenigo necessitated his immediate burial; thereafter, effigies were used only sporadically.[66] Like their Florentine neighbors, Venetians sought to ward off dynastic claims or the development of political cults by avoiding the use of effigies, even though their political rites differed significantly in other ways.

Sanudo's remarks also lead us into the question of how the living handled, treated, and disposed of the dead bodies of people with whom they had once been intimate and familiar. Sanudo and other contemporaries, without reveling in a sense of physical decay, displayed a frankness about death which contrasts sharply both with northern European sensibilities and those of our own day. The northern European world portrayed by the great historian Johann Huizinga delighted in such macabre expressions as *transi* tombs (which displayed an idealized representation of the body over an image of putrefaction) and the *danse macabre* common to painting and literature.[67] By contrast, Italians such as Sanudo often noted in relatively straightforward fashion, for example, the need to disembowel the doge for the public viewing. The doge's body was carried uncovered in procession, "although," Sanudo wrote, "there was a great odor; and if his bowels had not been removed, it would be impossible to keep him above ground for three days because of the stench." The dogaressa was apparently notified on her accession to the post that she would be subject to the same burial honors and the same evisceration procedures as the doge.[68]

For ordinary citizens in both cities, the care of the dead, such as washing, shaving, and anointing the corpses of both men and women, was assumed by gravediggers (*beccamorti*). In Florence this occupational group came under the joint supervision of the doctors' and spicers' guild and the magistracy of the Grain Office (Grascia) only after 1375. The assumption of guild control reportedly stemmed less from hygienic reasons than from a perceived need for wage restraints, due to the "extortion" practiced by gravediggers during plague.[69] After 1376, all those who buried the dead or invited relatives to the funeral fell under guild regulation. In addition to setting wage ceilings for various small tasks such as moving the body, the guild obliged gravediggers to report the name, parish, and quarter of the deceased to the guild notary. However, consistent regulation of burial registers (*libri di morti*) kept under guild auspices took shape only after 1450.[70] When a gravedigger was not available, the corpse was tended by a female relative or friend. Such was the case when Mea, wife of Francesco di Tommaso Giovanni, groomed the bodies of her daughter Nanna and her young grandson (d. 1450) while the family was in the country.[71]

This characterization of Italian candor toward the physical facts of death did not mean that the body was without taboos, that it did not need to be purified and distanced, or that the dead were treated without ambivalence. The very process of preparing the corpse with care was also an act of purification; the interim provided by the vigil ascertained that death had actually occurred and helped assure that the dead would not return.[72] Only when the body was made sufficiently safe was it removed from the house into more public spaces, and the body continued to be dangerous until buried. Sacchetti told a story about the superstitious Lapaccio da Montelupo (*Novelle*, 48), who went to considerable efforts to ward off the bad fortune that might result from touching the dead. The ambivalence Florentines felt toward those who prepared and buried the dead is embodied in the common term for gravedigger, *beccamorto*: that is, one who "pecks" off the dead. Moreover, women's practical role as caretakers of the dead may have exacerbated the misogynistic attitudes stemming from the longstanding ideological association of women and death in Mediterranean culture.[73] There are obviously many more questions about Italian mentalities and behaviors linked with death and burial than can be pursued here.

Whatever the limitations of our current conceptual and empirical framework, it should be apparent nevertheless from this discussion of symbols, objects, and bodies that Florentine death rites conveyed their social messages by means of systems of repeated analogies. Florentines could experience the flash of recognition that accompanies a familiar, well-ordered pattern because elements of both the structure and symbolism of death rites were common to multiple forms of thought and activity. Rather than being unique or isolated episodes, death rites were both recognizable and meaningful because they partook of the functions and significance established in other rites, practices, and situations. In turn, death rites helped fashion other occasions and processes in their own image. In delivering powerful messages about sexual and social differences, about family and personal histories, about the political economy and the economy of the body, death rites realized their many purposes and meanings only within the total field of their social environment.

PART II

THE MAKING OF A RITUAL FORM

ithin the continuum established by the structures and symbols of ritual action, death rites were nevertheless subject to the changes wrought by new historical processes, events, and individual actions. The following chapters examine the ways in which death rites changed as they encountered new conditions and situations. One of our main guides here is style. Style can be defined as the choice, configuration, and emphasis of particular elements in the ritual process: for example, a greater investment in mourning clothes than in wax candles; the use of classical symbols or references in place of, or in connection with, chivalric conventions; and the relative balance between the funeral and the requiem in terms of material consumption and the use of social resources. Rather than being a matter of purely aesthetic concern, style helps mark important disjunctions in social relations, political practice, and cultural ideals, as Florence moved from a corporate society of primarily regional importance to an international urban center dominated by the Medici and the patriciate. Style points us in still other directions: while changes in funerary style signal the beginnings of the modern state, changing styles of mourning help us see the slow making of the modern body.[1]

Not all stylistic changes took place at the same rate, however, or in response to the same historical forces. Funerals and requiems diverged in their historical development, in part because of their fundamentally different logistic characters. While the funeral actively moved through a series of urban spaces, thereby helping to claim them, it offered only limited opportunities for the kinds of static theatrical and rhetorical displays that became an intrinsic part of the requiem. By contrast, the ecclesiastical proceedings of the requiem afforded a greater element of control over self-representations, and over the power of death itself, since the requiem could be strategically postponed briefly to allow more elaborate preparations. Moreover, funerals and requiems also operated under different legal constraints: communal lawmakers closely scrutinized the funeral but had very limited authority over the requiem. Nor did the requiem present an arena in which the tension between ecclesiastical control and "popular" social customs was played out, as did marriage rites, largely because the requiem's basic liturgical format had been fixed for centuries.[2]

Responding to these different logistics and constraints, the complex stylistic history of death rites registers a wide range of changing historical meanings, actors, and consequences. The following chapters proceed chronologically in an attempt to make sense of those changes. Chapter 3 examines the stunning rise in funeral pomp in the second half of the fourteenth century, and links these new consumption patterns to social mobility, the redistribution of wealth, corporate politics, and the psychology of the postplague decades. Chapter 4 analyzes the impact of elitism, statism, and civism on civic and family rites after 1400, and charts the social effects of rising consumption trends to the ascendance of Cosimo de' Medici in 1434. Chapter 5 considers the ways in which spectacle at mid-century maps both consensus and conflict in political values, moral codes, class relations, and the place of women in custom and kinship. The final chapter focuses on complex cycles of change stemming from both the establishment and the rejection of Medici control between 1464 and 1527, a period that saw growing patrician domination and the gradual demise of republican politics.

CHAPTER 3

THE SOCIAL WORLD OF LATE

TRECENTO FUNERALS

n the second half of the fourteenth century, Florence faced a staggering array of challenges and external threats. The Black Death that swept Italy and Europe in 1348–49 was only the first in a recurrent series of plagues to visit the city. Over the next fifty years, the population of Florence declined steadily as plague returned in 1363, 1374, 1383, and 1390, and with particular severity in 1399–1400.[1] Compounding this demographic decline were acute political tensions, economic problems, and heavy debts stemming from recurrent warfare with Pisa, Milan, and other neighboring city-states. Florence's struggle with Pope Gregory XI during the War of the Eight Saints (1375–78) resulted in an interdict that disrupted business and exacerbated civic strife. Political instability was further fueled by violent factionalism between the Albizzi and Ricci parties, by profound tensions dividing powerful and middling citizens, and by the Ciompi revolt (1378) of minor guildsmen and laborers seeking greater representation in the regime.[2]

It was nevertheless in this context of crisis that Florentines developed a new funerary style characterized by conspicuous consumption. This was an age of flamboyance: stunning shows of candles, sumptuous bier cloths, caparisoned horses, and other displays of material wealth became the hallmarks of late Trecento funerals. Interest in the new style reached surprisingly deep into the Florentine social structure, pulling into its orbit not only merchants and bankers but even artisans and laborers, as far as their resources permitted. Plague figured importantly in the genesis and acceptance of flamboyance by redistributing wealth and property and by directing piety and charity in new ways.[3] Yet while plague facilitated these new consumption patterns, it was not the sole cause of ceremonial largesse. Flamboyance should also be linked to the intense competition for political power and social place in these decades, as both established citizens and "new men" used funeral pomp to jockey for greater reputation and for higher places in political and social circles. The desire to represent the commune well to outsiders and foreign powers added still another impetus to rising consumption. Grandiose displays for outstanding civic figures and war heroes such as Pier Farnese (d. 1363) and John Hawkwood (d. 1394) celebrated communal pride and the growing stature of Florence in regional and national arenas.

The second half of the fourteenth century thus witnessed a profound redefinition of what constituted an honorable burial for heroes, officeholders, and private citizens alike. This chapter examines the development, the meanings, and the uses of this new funerary flamboyance. It describes first the basic chronology and forms of consumption, as well as motives for flamboyance and restraints on pomp. It then looks at the implications of pomp for definitions of family and lineage before considering how funeral pomp fit into a broader social and political milieu. The final section of the chapter turns to the collective burial patterns of the laboring classes in order to examine social values, local forms of association, and the role of the parish in burial activities.

The Triumph of Flamboyance

Historians and social scientists have argued recently that human beings commonly respond to times of high mortality by refining their beliefs about death and elaborating their usual ritual behaviors.[4] If this is so, the demographic catastrophe of the Black Death (1348–49) must provide the starting point for any examination of death and ritual in late medieval and Renaissance Florence. As a result of that epidemic, the Florentine population declined from around one hundred thousand to approximately half that number or less, and population recovery was continually hampered by recurrent visits of the disease.[5]

The economic effects of plague included a heightened demand for scarce labor, which caused wages and the average standard of living to rise. The chronicler Marchionne di Coppo Stefani complained that episodes of plague enriched "spicers, doctors, chicken vendors, gravediggers," and others who provided essential services and food-stuffs. He also lamented that the price of goods, including items such as wax and benches which were used in burial ceremonies, showed a similar inflation.[6] As the numbers of dead mounted in the summers of 1348 and 1349, charitable foundations such as the Misericordia profited from a heavy influx of goods and property, although in the long term these institutions were less fortunate. Gifts of money, clothing, and foodstuffs immediately poured into popular mendicant institutions such as Santa Maria del Carmine to subsidize masses for the souls of the dead. These items ranged from an old robe donated by a doublet maker to a short mantle offered by a friar's mother and a measure of wine given by a female tertiary.[7] Over the longer term, altered demographic patterns and a new distribution of resources helped restructure both the Florentine and the European economy in ways that increasingly emphasized the use and production of luxury items, especially fine cloth.[8]

How did the Black Death affect customary burial practices in Florence? The most compelling and conventional answer comes from Boccaccio's preface to the *Decameron*, in which he painted a horrifying picture of social disruption during the initial outbreak of plague. Boccaccio claimed that Florentines were terrified by the disease and altered traditional burial customs "from sheer necessity." Women relatives and neighbors no longer gathered for ritualized laments at the house of the deceased, so that many died "without having a number of women near them"; others died "without a single witness." Kinsmen and neighbors similarly abandoned their customary duties, leaving the honorable work of mourning in procession to low-born, greedy gravediggers. Poor artisans and workers fared the worst, since they were often carried two or three on a bier, taken to the nearest church, and buried without benefit of tears, candles, or mourners. "Things had reached such a pass," said Boccaccio in retrospect, "that people cared no more for dead men than we care for dead goats."[9]

Historians have begun recently to temper this disturbing depiction somewhat, mainly by looking at various legal and administrative responses to the onslaught of plague. In April 1348 the Florentine commune took measures to curb the spread of the epidemic by controlling entrance into the city from affected areas. The commune also tried to protect the transfer of goods, especially to women and minors, against unjust claims. Moreover, the city's charitable associations, such as the Misericordia, and assorted hospitals were active in caring for the sick and the dead.[10] There is also a scattering of domestic evidence that suggests the tenacity of some customary practices, even during the height of the epidemic. In his family record book, for example, the wealthy merchant Pepo degli Albizzi recorded how ten members of his household died of plague between June 4 and July 31, 1348. The last of these victims was Pepo's father Antonio, who died at Pisa. Two days after Antonio's death, Pepo brought his body back to Florence and buried him in the family tombs at San Pier Maggiore.[11] Although plague severely undercut immediate family funeral celebrations for rich and poor alike, established Florentines continued to practice secondary burial, whereby they retrieved their dead kin from abroad at a later date and transferred them to their rightful family tombs in Florence. Secondary burial provided an important resource for Florentines with deep roots in the city, for it ensured family honor and continuity, which undoubtedly helped these families manage the devastating experience of plague.

Not surprisingly, the first encounter with the epidemic in 1348–49 also triggered an anxiety about the afterlife which can be seen in patterns of mass commissions. To assure a speedy passage through purgatory, Florentines of all social levels arranged various mass programs for themselves and their kin. Among the most popular forms of propitiation was the Gregorian mass series, which consisted of one mass daily for thirty days after death. Other Florentines, however, turned to a more dramatic multiplication of masses as a way to assuage anxiety and provide for their own salvation. Throughout the fall and winter of 1348–49, churches such as the Carmine performed hundreds, if not thousands, of masses as instructed by testators and heirs.[12] The Carmine friar Fra Nicola complied with a kinswoman's desire for 100 masses to benefit her soul; Margherita, the wife of Niccolò Acciaiuoli, paid for 128 masses for one of her kinsmen; and the church performed 200 masses for the collective benefit of a certain Piero, his wife, and two other female kin.

Once the onslaught of plague had subsided, however, Florentines turned their attention to commemorative masses that served the more distinct purpose of remembrance. In 1349, the first anniversary of the initial outbreak of plague, the Carmine alone performed 213 commemorative masses. In the vast majority of cases (177), the masses had been commissioned by decedents for their own personal commemoration, and another 32 masses had been commissioned to commemorate kin. Almost all the masses (209) were paid or prepaid in cash, rather than by encumbering real property. Despite the rush of enthusiasm first for propitiatory masses and then for an anniversary celebration, however, these were short-term trends that were not sustained at a similarly high level during the ensuing decades. The number of commemorative offices performed at the Carmine fell to 36 in 1353; a decade later, that figure stood at 39, and in 1370 it fell still further, to 30.

After the epidemic had passed, Florentines quickly returned to their former burial customs as they sought to reclaim the stability inherent in an ordered way of doing things. Yet within five years after the first appearance of plague, funeral practices moved irrevocably toward conspicuous consumption. The event that first ushered in the age of flamboyance for Florence was linked not directly to plague, however, but rather to politics. Plague surely changed the context for the reception of a new funerary style, but it was not immediately responsible. The signal event that introduced what Matteo Villani called a "new and unusual custom" of extravagance was the funeral in April 1353 for Lorenzo di Niccolò Acciaiuoli, son of the Neapolitan seneschal, who died in the Regno.[13] Niccolò transported his son's body north for burial in the new tomb complex he had created at the Certosa of Galluzzo, where he himself ultimately was buried.

Acciaiuoli spared no expense in burying his son. The expatriate Acciaiuoli used this occasion not only to mollify his grief over the loss of his promising heir but also to vaunt to his former fellow citizens his success as a man of the court, a high feudal officeholder, and a royal knight. The funeral bore a staggering price tag—5,000 florins—and included seven caparisoned war-horses, a gold-embroidered silk canopy, and a beautifully draped coffin. Other trappings, such as banners, flags, and shields, gave the cortege an air of a triumphal military parade. Enhancing the event was a large crowd of leading Florentine citizens, who accompanied the body on foot to the city limits of Porta San Pier Gattolino (now Porta Romana), then mounted horses for the rest of the trip to the Certosa. Such conspicuous consumption was thoroughly in keeping with Niccolò Acciaiuoli's vigilant sensitivity to matters of honor. The seneschal was always accompanied by a large retinue of pages and grooms, for example, and even after his son's death he continued these lordly practices. Acciaiuoli reportedly spent 150 florins per day on banquets and festivities while residing in Florence in 1360.[14]

Yet this courtly splendor posed two particular problems for Florentine observers such as Matteo Villani. Although Villani was somewhat dazzled by this display, he also worried about what it meant for a bourgeois civic order whose regime was still feeling its way ten years after the expulsion of the "tyrannous" duke of Athens. Equally disturbing were the family claims put forward by means of pomp, which smacked of the dynastic pretenses of magnate families.[15] Each of the velvet-clad grooms riding horses, for example, bore some form of the Acciaiuoli coat of arms in wrought silver. Banners and flags marked exclusively with private, familial signs celebrated the power and patronage of the Acciaiuoli, trumping up in visual splendor what the family lacked in civic homage. A similar sense of dynasty was embodied in the tomb complex Acciaiuoli created at the Certosa, with its rare examples of armored gisant tombs derived from French models.[16]

The Florentine commune resolved some of these tensions by claiming the flamboyant style of Acciaiuoli's funeral for communal rather than family purposes. In June 1363, ten years after Lorenzo Acciaiuoli's burial, the priors staged a grandiose display for the war captain Piero Farnese, who had been instrumental in Florentine victories against Pisa in 1360–62. Like many other Florentines, Farnese fell victim to the second wave of plague in 1363. In recognition of his role in Florentine expansion, the commune honored Farnese with splendid obsequies that quickly became part of communal lore. The poet Antonio Pucci claimed that "there was no lord of such great excellence within the past hundred years who had such honor and reverence in all things at his burial" as did Farnese. This great civic hero was also accorded the privilege of cathedral burial and a communal subsidy for a tomb monument.[17]

Nor was the commune alone in its growing attraction to burial pomp. The redistribution of resources, renewed psychological uncertainties, and political considerations all worked together during the plague of 1363 to give flamboyance a solid social base among private citizens. It was during the second wave of plague that well-born Florentines consistently began to use more expensive or elaborate bier cloths, more candles, and more tangible signs of material wealth in the cortege. The politically active knight Messer Scolaio

Cavalcanti, for example, draped the biers of his plague-dead wife and son with beautiful cloths, whose resale value was four florins each. In the late 1360s, more clergy began to be integrated into a growing panoply of pomp, and their bell ringing added still another dimension of communication.[18] Lesser merchants and tradesmen quickly joined in this zealous consumption as far as their more limited resources allowed. In 1371 a certain Baldovino da Empoli tried to cover his father's corpse with cloth of silver, a privilege to which he was not entitled by either rank or profession.[19]

By the early 1370s, those features that had seemed so unique at Lorenzo Acciaiuoli's funeral—hugh amounts of wax, luxurious bier cloths, caparisoned horses, military devices, scores of elaborately worked banners—became regular hallmarks of the new burial style honoring well-born men from prominent families such as the Alberti, the Altoviti, the Bardi, the Capponi, the Pitti, and the Strozzi. The chronicler Monaldi captured the essence of this new flamboyant style when he reported the "most worthy honor" paid in 1373 to Domenico Bueri, consisting of "five horses covered in iron and silk, eleven retainers clad in mourning, and a great quantity of wax."[20] Affluent women were also drawn into this effusion of pomp, although they were never honored with the more "manly" trappings: covered horses, weaponry, and signs of public office. In October 1379 Francesca, the widow of Bernardo Bertoldi, was found by communal officials to have been transported on her bier "in such a way that she could be seen and touched in violation of the law," no doubt to better expose her sumptuous burial garments. Communal officials scrutinized the 1383 funeral procession of Bartolomea, wife of Sandro Baracci, to certify that the number of candles fell within the legal limits.[21] Hence the chronology of Florentine consumption patterns confirms aspects of Samuel Cohn's argument for Siena that the return of plague in 1363 had more lasting transformative effects than the initial outbreak of the disease.[22]

One way to evaluate shifting standards of consumption more systematically is to track changes in communal sumptuary policy. Beginning with the first set of sumptuary laws in 1293, the commune walked a fine line between preserving the patrimony of its citizens by curbing excess, on the one hand, and recognizing the social validation implied by ceremony, on the other. Although it is not known to what extent sumptuary laws governing ritual, dress, and social behavior were obeyed, these laws nevertheless are important guides to lawmakers' vision of society as they wished it to be.[23] As ceremonial expectations rose in the 1360s and 1370s, communal lawmakers shifted their strategy in order to establish limits on pomp yet allow the commune to profit from this new taste. In 1384 the commune began selling exemptions to current consumption ceilings as part of its major sumptuary revisions.[24] Priced at a standard fee of 10.5 florins, a sumptuary exemption allowed buyers to display greater amounts of wax, to use luxury cloths of silver and gold when these would normally be prohibited, or to otherwise exceed statutory limits. The response to this policy was extremely enthusiastic. Between 1384 and 1392, the commune sold at least 233 sumptuary exemptions for funerals; in the peak year, 1390, it sold 71.[25]

Yet the triumph of flamboyance was not achieved without contending with powerful forces for restraint. Plague brought with it not only a redistribution of wealth and new strategies for property transfer but also severe sumptuary restrictions during outbreaks of disease. In order to minimize the sense of disruption bred by watching family, friends, and neighbors succumb in great numbers with frightening speed, the commune prohibited the customary bell ringing for the dead during the plague of 1374, limited processional torches to four in number, and permitted deep mourning only to the widow and children of the deceased. In the still more severe epidemic of 1383, the law-abiding merchant Paolo Sassetti struggled to bury his esteemed kinsman Bernardo "with that honor that the plague times and the laws ordained by the commune" allowed.[26] Moreover, prevailing medical and popular opinion advised that plague dead be buried immediately, without regard for pomp. One popular story set in 1396 told the harrowing tale of the rich, noble-born woman Ginevra degli Almieri, who, having lost consciousness, was mistaken for a plague victim and unwittingly buried alive.[27]

Other forms of crisis prompted laws designed to constrain the triumph of flamboyance. In October 1377, during the city's fight with the papacy, the commune passed stringent wartime rulings that set tight limits on wax consumption, the dress of the corpse, and mourning clothes, in the interests of conserving already strained resources. Moreover, these wartime rulings encroached on domestic rites as they sought to eliminate potentially explosive situations. No citizen was permitted to place a bier in front of the house for the usual viewing, and any corpse set out for the ritual lament by women had to be concealed in a wooden coffin.[28] Even without the special restrictions imposed by the papal interdict, however, the regular liturgical calendar prohibited requiem masses and other ritual practices on Sundays and important religious feasts. As the priest Piovano Arlotto told the mother of a rich young peasant who died on Good Friday, "if in these three holy days, the pope and emperor were to die, one couldn't sound the bells, regardless." The distraught mother had to be content instead with the less conventional music made by bagpipes.[29]

In addition to these legal constraints, there were also deep cultural ambivalences about the value and meaning of pomp. Florentines were subject to a set of competing claims that pitted traditional Christian attitudes about modesty and self-effacement, on the one hand, against contrary social imperatives to assert status, on the other. Even within Florentine social mores, there were serious tensions about the appropriate display of wealth. Cautious merchants such as Giovanni Morelli advised their descendants to be guarded in showing their wealth for fear of exciting their neighbors' envy or increasing their tax assessments. Compounding these hesitations were practical considerations such as taxation and the heavy forced loans needed to sustain the ongoing war efforts of the Florentine commune, although it is not yet clear what segment of the population bore the greatest brunt of forced loans.[30]

The fact that flamboyance triumphed despite these tensions and constraints underlines just how important funeral pomp was for Florentines in the late fourteenth century. Before examining the reasons for this development, it is useful to get a comparative perspective on Florentine behavior. Florentines were not alone in their ceremonial flamboyance and in their taste for luxury goods in these decades. Funeral pomp in the region of Avignon, for example, beginning in the late 1330s showed a striking new excess that was vastly accelerated by plague. The popularity of flamboyant burials in this period had psychological as well as material roots in plague. In analyzing the growth of funeral pomp in the region of Avignon, Jacques Chiffoleau has mapped a new periodization of death for that area. Beginning around 1330, the first signs of the transformation of the funeral cortege appeared in Avignon and Orange, with increased numbers of torches, draperies, clergy, and poor mourners.

While Chiffoleau thus suggests that ceremonial extravagance actually predated the Black Death, the plague acted as the great revealer and accelerator of this trend. Around 1380, what Chiffoleau calls "the flamboyant death" triumphed. Individuals organized their own funerals more minutely in their testaments, and funerals were increasingly marked by theatricality and narcissism. The gap between the poor and the powerful widened, not only because the poor could not stage the same kind of display but also because they appeared as mourners in the service of the rich.[31]

Although disparities in the sources make it difficult to compare funeral trappings in Florence and Avignon directly, it is clear that both cities shared similar trends toward the use of pomp. For the urban elite in both cities, flamboyance may have created a kind of ceremonial buffer against the onslaughts of mortality. The greater use of material resources, reflecting a newfound delight in the ephemeral, offered psychological assurances and protection in an environment destabilized by the uncertainties of plague.

Despite this shared enthusiasm for funeral pomp, Florentines and their neighbors in Avignon nevertheless responded differently to the disruptions of plague. For example, the change in Avignonese testamentary formulas from *corpus* to *cadaver* is rarely paralleled in Florentine documents of the period. Moreover, unlike their French neighbors, the heirs of Florentine merchants, bankers, and knights invested more heavily in the rich dress and presentation of the corpse than in small details of the cortege.[32] Perhaps the most striking difference was that Florentines did not regularly employ contingents of poor mourners to enhance the event's theatricality as did the Avignonese. Florentine funerals were certainly occasions for the distribution of alms; for example, Monaldi commented on the largesse of Niccolò Alberti's heirs at Alberti's funeral in 1377, when "a great amount of money was given for God."[33] Yet the poor who did participate generally performed small functional tasks such as carrying torches. While throngs of poor people weeping over the bier added drama as well as additional prayers, the poor rarely figured as ceremonial prisoners in a triumphal parade as they did in Avignon.

Instead, in Florentine funerals mourners were more distinctly individuated by their social roles and their relationships to the deceased. Figuring importantly in prestigious Florentine burials were the deceased's retainers or personal servants (*famigli*) grouped around the bier. Their presence acknowledged part of the dead man's clientage networks and recreated in physical terms the social arrangements of household patronage. Although these famigli are rarely identified by name, their personal connection with the deceased, or at least with his household, was implied by their intermingling with the relatives of the deceased. Moreover, famigli almost always dressed in black, the color of deep mourning. For instance, the beautifully draped bier of Messer Vieri de' Medici (d. 1395), located in the "Medici corner" of the Mercato Vecchio, was encircled by "eight men dressed in black [who were] his servants." Waiting at the nearby Medici house where the body was still stationed were "sixteen of his relations [consorti] all dressed in black and eight servants surrounding the corpse." At civic funerals, a similar honor guard comprised official functionaries known as *fanti* and *donzelli*.[34]

In other words, it was not strictly "a numeric delirium" of mourners[35] that constituted an honorable burial for an affluent Florentine man in the postplague decades. Domestic servants in formal attendance at funerals were always few in number, usually numbering no more than eight, and they never figured into descriptions of women's funerals, regardless of the women's status. What counted was the inclusion of the dead man's clientage networks stemming from and centering on the household. Since famigli probably shared some personal ties or even intimacy with the deceased, their participation also met spiritual objectives in a quest for additional prayers from familiar persons. It was also the social prestige of other mourners and participants that mattered to Florentine observers, not simply their numbers. Despite a common penchant for flamboyance, Florentine funerals in the late Trecento were more contractual and personalized, less theatrical and exploitative than funerals in Avignon.

In explaining these differences, we can fruitfully compare the urban experiences of the two cities. Since there is no study of Florentine testaments comparable to Chiffoleau's, the argument here hinges not on statistical data but on the interrelation of customary burial practices. According to Chiffoleau, the love of pomp and the multiplication of masses were in part reactions to the "mortuary solitude" of those cut off from their ancestors and former burial sites. Chiffoleaus sees the self-absorbed concentration on one's own obsequies which was manifest in Avignonese testaments as a consequence of urban dislocation intensified by immigration and by the demographic restructuring of the surrounding region. The rich elected and secured burial in churches, which were more privileged sites, while their social inferiors settled for less prestigious cemeteries. Even wealthy Avignonese, however, were severed from the communities of their ancestors.[36]

Florentines practiced a different cluster of mortuary customs which located pomp within a different set of social relationships. If, as Chiffoleau argues, urban dislocation and ceremonial flamboyance were related developments, the common practice of secondary burial among the Florentine elite may have curbed the psychological need for certain kinds of excess. Florentines from established families frequently disinterred the bones of kin who died away from the city, bringing them back to Florence for burial in the family tomb. The merchant Lapo Niccolini, for example, transported his brother Niccolò's body from the Romagna in December 1383, four months after his death. Lapo noted that although Niccolò in his testament had elected burial in a local church, "we brought him here to Florence . . . and we had him buried in the church of the friars minor of Santa Croce, in the tomb and the church of our father Giovanni."[37]

This practice of secondary burial continued in full force throughout the fifteenth century. For example, Palla di Messer Palla Strozzi "had the bones of his brother Giovanni and of certain other of his nephews retrieved from afar" in 1423; similarly, Giovanni Arigucci transferred the bodies of his wife and son from Montughi to his family tomb in Santa Maria Novella a few months after they died of plague in 1450. While the vast majority of secondary burials were intended to reconstitute the patriline, a few Florentine women also used this practice to reconstitute their nuclear families. In 1436 Vaggia, the widow of Piero Magli, instructed her heirs that within two years of her death they should retrieve the bones of her husband and son from the Valdelsa for reburial with her in Santa Felicità, where her daughter Mattea was a nun.[38]

The regular use of secondary burial meant that as plague patterns became more familiar, wealthy Florentines organized and experienced a set of collective mortuary arrangements rather than isolated, individualized ones. In contrast to the elite of Avignon, the upper and middle classes of Florentine society, having privatized and controlled their burial spaces more securely, may have needed less elaborate and less legalized funeral strategies. If well-born Florentines were uneasy about the high mortality brought on by plague, they could take comfort from knowing that they were not likely to suffer a mortuary solitude whether at home or abroad. Comparing funeral scenarios in these two cities suggests that it was the particular quality and impact of the urbanization process, rather than the urban experience itself, that influenced the form and the level of pomp. The triumph of flamboyance in Florentine funerals of the late fourteenth century was a triumph that nevertheless was restricted by the demands of kinship and a sense of urban community.

Kinship, Family, Dynasty

The dynastic pretenses of Lorenzo Acciaiuoli's funeral, as well as the centrality of kinship to secondary burial, raise questions about the familial uses and meanings of Florentine funerals in the late fourteenth century. If pomp was intended to celebrate both individual and family, precisely what kinds of family definitions, networks, and values were affirmed? One way to approach these questions is by systematically reconstructing the social profile of Florentines who purchased sumptuary exemptions between 1384 and 1392.[39] In these nine years, the commune sold at least 233 permits to exceed the legal limitations on pomp. Almost three-quarters of the total number were bought to enhance men's funerals (164 exemptions, or 70.3 percent). Unfortunately, for more than half of this latter group we lack specific information about how the buyer was related to the deceased. Eighty exemptions were purchased by persons designated only as the man's heirs, who might include female agnates acting through their guardians, as well as grandsons, nephews, and other more distant relations. In another twenty-seven instances, no relationship between buyer and deceased is specified at all.

However, the fifty-seven cases in which kinship was identified show a clear social pattern. Dominating this group were immediate blood relations rather than laterally extended kin. At least fifty-one exemptions (31 percent of men's total permits) were bought for a member of the purchaser's nuclear family—a father, son, or brother—with whom the purchaser had, at least at one time, shared the same household. The single largest group of permits, twenty-six in number, were bought by sons to honor their fathers. Seventeen exemptions were obtained by brothers of the deceased individuals, eight by fathers whose sons predeceased them, and five by persons sharing the same surname but whose precise relation was not given. Only one exemption was purchased for a dead nephew.[40]

On the basis of this evidence, it appears that the vast majority of flamboyant funerals in the late Trecento were designed to celebrate the patriline rather than extended or bilateral family arrangements. From the standpoint of economic organization, sumptuary transactions in the late Trecento set forth a family identity that revolved around the household; buyers did not dispense patrimony lightly or frequently in the service of more distant kin. In honoring their fathers with pomp, sons displayed their filial responsibility and reverence; in turn, they could reasonably expect to become "the father of a family followed by many of his kinsmen," who was thus shown to be more eminent "than one who is alone and seems abandoned." Not surprisingly, the fraternal bonds represented were most prominent among established families. Twelve of the seventeen sumptuary exemptions honoring brothers were bought by men with such esteemed surnames as Ridolfi, Rinuccini, Cavalcanti, Capponi, Corbizzi, Orlandini, and Tanaglia.[41]

Nevertheless, the nuclear group honored by sumptuary exemptions did not have a distinct dynastic focus. As Richard Goldthwaite has argued, the Florentine upper classes hindered by partible inheritance and by continual shifts in household arrangements as sons died or brothers moved into separate quarters, lacked a sustained economic and demographic base on which to build dynasties.[42] While showy funerals were occasions for a mutual sharing of honor and prestige between fathers and sons, the dynastic connection commonly embraced at most two generations. Even the dynastic hopes of Niccolò Acciaiuoli, whose father and son predeceased him, were short-lived and limited; Niccolò's other sons were not buried with him in the Certosa.[43]

The exemptions purchased for women's funerals (sixty-nine, or 29.6 percent of the total) showed a similar focus on the household but had different social objectives. Rather than honoring intergenerational ties between fathers and sons, the bulk of women's exemptions honored the spousal relationship. Forty-two permits (60.8 percent of the female group) were bought by husbands for their wives, thus interweaving ties of affection with the reflected honors a husband could clearly claim. Some of these funerals could be quite impressive indeed, if the descriptions of husbands are to be believed; in January 1388, for example, the knight Messer Guccio di Cino Nobili paid twenty-five florins for a permit to honor his wife Francesca in a stunning ceremony that, he boasted, was the best funeral ever staged for a Florentine woman. Since Guccio's brother Bernardo purchased an equivalent exemption for his own wife's funeral a month later, Guccio's showmanship may have been quickly outdone.[44]

Second in number to the permits bought by husbands for wives was a cluster of ten exemptions bought by sons to honor their "good mothers"—that is, widows who had remained with their children after their husbands' death. As all ten buyers bore surnames, most from such venerable families as the Albizzi, the Adimari, the Castellani, and the Pitti, there was an important class dimension to this group of permits which may signal differences in domestic organization as well as in sumptuary strategies between established lineages and social newcomers.

However, the privileges and high honors women might enjoy as wives and mothers did not extend to their other roles. Whatever their social status, unmarried girls and widowed sisters living in their brothers' households were poorly represented among sumptuary exemptions. In contrast to relatively strong fraternal bonds, equivalent ties between brothers and sisters were virtually absent; only one brother purchased an exemption for his sister's funeral.[45] Sumptuary permits thus confirm the social distance between brothers and sisters already noted in discussions of requiem masses, mourning clothes, and patterns of commemorative mass commissions.[46]

Of course, all these rites, however flamboyant, were still subject to the code of honor and the social frictions that pervaded daily life. Because Messer Maffeo Tedaldi "was one of the lights of our lineage in his time," his descendant was eager to record the names of the ten family mourners who honored him in 1377 "as an example to posterity."[47] The diary of Paolo Sassetti tells a different story about honor and kinship. Those family members who did not uphold the Sassetti name and reputation were not feted or mourned at their deaths during the 1383 plague. No kinsmen gathered to pay homage to Pierozzo di Doffo Sassetti, who "brought us shame by his desire to die in someone else's house against our will." Nor was Letta, the daughter of Federigo di Pollaio Sassetti, mourned by her kin because of her illicit liaison with Giovanni Porcellini. However, when Pollaio Sassetti's widow Filippa was mistakenly placed in the wrong branch's tomb in Santa Maria Novella, Paolo let the mistake pass. Despite his irritation, Paolo acknowledged that Filippa "was a good woman and always brought honor to our house."[48] Whatever the particulars of kin organization, funeral pomp was always contingent on the norms established and reinforced by the prevailing code of honor.

Patricians and the *Gente Nuova*

Having surveyed the familial and psychological context of pomp in the late Trecento, we must turn now to the relationship between pomp and its broader social and political milieu. From the 1360s to the end of the century, Florentine social relations were colored by an intense competition between established patricians and "new men," which gave tremendous impetus to the increase in consumption. Unlike Venice, which had a formally defined aristocracy, late Trecento Florence was characterized by varying degrees of social mobility which hinged on the interplay of wealth, office holding, marriage, and social perception. Funerals' ability to influence social perception gave them great strategic importance in helping to identify members of a social elite. Conspicuous consumption was a way to represent and measure high status, and at the same time to exclude social inferiors. The sum of more than one thousand florins spent on Matteo Soldi's funeral in October 1379, or the one hundred florins paid in December 1392 by Nepo della Tosa's heirs for his sumptuary permit alone, were clearly beyond the reach of most Florentines.[49]

Critical to the popularity of a flamboyant style were changes in the structure and distribution of wealth, which can be traced in part to the effects of plague throughout the late Trecento. As wealth became concentrated in the hands of an elite urban minority, purchasing power acquired new social leverage that could compensate for the brevity of one's bloodlines.[50] Because it used wealth as the chief indicator of status, funeral flamboyance thus worked to redefine previous social distinctions focused more narrowly on family prestige. For example, the hefty cost of Matteo Soldi's funeral, cited above, helped mask the fact that Soldi was only a wealthy wine merchant rather than a major guildsman from old patrician stock. A common set of burial expectations linked affluent Florentines such as Nepo della Tosa, who came from one of the city's oldest patrician houses, with social newcomers such as the silk dealer Giovanni di Giano. In their daily life these two men shared a common membership in the confraternity of San Pier Martire, through which they arranged their commemorative programs; at their funerals, they shared a common flamboyance.[51] In this sense, late Trecento funeral pomp not only documents the fluidity of wealth that kept Florentine society in a relatively mobile state; it also marks the importance of ritual as a force for social transformation and for a new, wider social cohesion.

By embracing higher consumption standards, the *gente nuova* of the late fourteenth century played a vital role in the triumph of flamboyance. Judging from the sumptuary exemptions sold between 1384 and 1392, flamboyance appealed not solely to an exclusive, patrician clientele but rather to a more heterogeneous social group. Although the vast majority of exemptions were purchased by major guildsmen, buyers of permits were not characterized simply by antiquity of lineage. Sixty-two exemptions (26.6 percent) were purchased by Florentines lacking surnames, including professionals identified as notaries and physicians; the sons of such professionals; and lesser silk merchants and tradesmen. Six of these sixty-two exemptions were obtained by minor guildsmen: the mercer Marco di Tommaso bought a permit for his wife's funeral in June 1385; Francesco d'Agnolo, identified as a *pezzaio*, was honored by his heirs in April 1388, as was the key maker Rinieri di Jacopo in 1390. Another three minor guildsmen purchased sumptuary permits for persons to whom their relation is unclear. Niccolò Bartolucci, described as a knife maker, obtained a permit to honor Messer Giovanni Gherardini (d. 1385); the shoemaker Simone di Michele bought an exemption for the funeral of Monna Betta di Bertino (d. 1387); and the coppersmith Piero di Pero obtained one for Bernardo di Lipi (d. 1390). In addition, the heirs of a certain "Jacopo, called Bianco," also bought a funeral permit (in 1388), but no information about his occupation was given.[52]

As a political group, these newer men stood on the periphery of the ruling class rather than at the heart of political decision making. Their presence in communal sumptuary records nevertheless testifies to the potential for social mobility that created an influx into the Florentine political classes until the 1390s.[53] Filippo Villani voiced his hostility to this process of mobility and incorporation, expressing his resentment against those men who "with the wealth accumulated from trade and usury, in the course of time became very rich. They were able to conclude any marriage which they desired, and by means of gifts, banquets, and persuasion, both open and hidden, they won such influence that they were chosen for office."[54]

As Villani suggests, the fluidity of private wealth allowed "new men" access both to political power and to the trappings of prestige. As opportunities for officeholding diminished around 1390, parvenues still retained the economic means to claim membership in a shifting urban elite, using funerary flamboyance to display their achievements and aspirations. Through the structures of wealth if not of political power, new families and individuals could make their way to more elevated positions in Florentine society.

Shared conventions and flamboyance were also useful in bridging the factional conflicts that threatened communal politics in the late Trecento. In an atmosphere of bitter partisan warfare, a common ceremonial style actively served the interests of the polity by establishing some grounds for harmony. Participants in the Guelf-Ghibelline conflict that erupted in the late 1360s, and partisans of the Albizzi and Ricci factions in the 1370s, shared at least a common interest in elaborate funerals. In the years 1377–79, before the commune began selling sumptuary exemptions, the Albizzi partisan Andrea di Lippozzo Mangioni enjoyed a level and type of funerary display very similar to that of opposing Ricci followers such as Giovanni Magalotti and Matteo Soldi. Scolaio Cavalcanti, that stalwart of the Parte Guelfa, was honored in August 1380 with a ceremony very similar to that held in 1377 for Giovanni Magalotti, who had a consistent record of opposition to the Parte hierarchy.[55] After the commune began its new sumptuary policy in 1384, sumptuary exemptions were purchased for the funerals of such Albizzi adherents as Simone Peruzzi and Vieri de' Medici, as well as for those of former Ricci party leaders Andrea Salviati, Benedetto di Nerozzo Alberti, and Salvestro de' Medici, thereby glossing over the factional conflict that also divided business ventures.[56]

Despite the cohesive value of flamboyance, it was ultimately the competition between great citizens and new men that entrenched this style and pushed consumption to increasingly higher levels. As new men made greater inroads into the upper classes, the mixed social composition of the elite became increasingly fraught with tensions. Franco Sacchetti, for instance, railed against the "mechanics, artisans, and even bakers, and still lower, wool carders, usurers, and cheating barterers" upon whom knighthood was bestowed, much to the degradation of the title. Outbursts such as Sacchetti's became an explicit motif both in the literature and in the judicial records of the late Trecento.[57]

One response to the disturbances created by social mobility came from a small, select group of established patricians, who raised consumption standards still higher. In this mounting competition, Florentine oligarchs measured current pomp against the reference points established by earlier funeral spectacles, both private and civic. In the late 1370s, funerals for extremely wealthy patrician men such as Palla di Francesco Strozzi and Niccolò Alberti (d. 1377) not only matched but surpassed the number of horses, candles, and banners used in earlier public rites such as the huge civic funeral mounted for the war captain Biordo degli Unbertini (d. 1359).[58] More systematic evidence comes from sumptuary permits. Of the five highest fees paid for a sumptuary permit between 1384 and 1397, three were paid by the old houses of the Altoviti, the della Tosa, and the Peruzzi; the other two were paid by two somewhat newer, but still prominent, patrician families, the Medici and the Soldani.[59]

Contributing to and marking this intense competition was the use of pomp for women's funerals. Despite Messer Guccio di Cino Nobili's boasts about the opulence of his wife's burial (1388), elaborate funerals for women were never as numerous or as costly as those staged for their kinsmen. Wives, mothers, and sisters from the commercial classes might reasonably anticipate having the solid but modest sum of sixty to seventy florins spent on their obsequies.[60] Girls who died before marriage, which generally took place when girls were between sixteen and eighteen years old, were honored with lesser ceremonies than their married adult sisters.

Nevertheless, funerals of affluent adult women were routinely scrutinized for sumptuary violations, and the revised statutes of 1384 explicitly recognized such funerals' potential excesses in terms of wax, palls, and costly burial garb. Both patricians and new men seized the social advantages embodied in flamboyant funerary display, with professionals and tradesmen buying sumptuary exemptions (primarily for wives) in proportion to their overall representation among buyers of sumptuary permits. Thus, only a few weeks after the banker Marco Alberti bought a standard sumptuary exemption for his wife's funeral in May 1385, the haberdasher Marco di Tommaso purchased an equivalent exemption to honor his dead spouse. Within these broad class groupings, fraternal rivalries may have contributed yet another competitive spark: in 1390 the Frescobaldi brothers Lambertuccio and Leonardo each secured a permit for his wife's burial, just as the brothers Stefano and Francesco di Giovanni di Ser Segna, who were newcomers to the elite, did in 1387 and 1392.[61] Moreover, some women specifically placed themselves in this prestige economy through their testaments. A certain Monna Filippa (d. 1390) projected such a lavish funeral for herself that the hospital of Santa Maria Nuova, as her executor, was forced to buy a sumptuary permit to meet these demands.[62]

One of the perhaps unintended consequences of these status assertions was to blur the sharp distinctions between genders. There was always a gender value attached to symbolic representations, with men retaining exclusive claim to signs derived from corporate and political life. Yet the trappings of wealth, such as opulent silks in prestigious colors, jewels, and furs, established some common ground between men and women. Messer Guccio di Cino Nobili's detailed description of the burial outfit of his wife Francesca (d. 1388), for example, compares favorably with the luxurious garments in which his and Francesca's eminent kinsmen were buried. Francesca wore a scarlet silk gown buttoned with large pearls; draped over this brilliant garment was a hugh mantle lined with vair and ermine. This outfit was completed by a scarlet, fur-lined hood and scarlet shoes. The bier itself was draped with vermillion velvet trimmed with fur and covered with a gold cloth. Carried in full view on her bier in flagrant violation of sumptuary law, Francesca "was so beautiful and so well-adorned," said her husband, "that she looked like a queen." Moreover, Nobili claimed that so much wax emblazoned the altar during the requiem that the church seemed on fire. Francesca's honors were made complete by the knights, judges, physicians, and other prominent citizens who paid their respects, and by eleven elegantly clad female mourners, as well as by the many women who stayed at home to issue loud laments.[63] In late fourteenth-century Florence, funerary flamboyance became a powerful strategy that addressed the corporate and familial aspirations of patricians and newcomers, both women and men, as well as their individual psychological and religious needs.

Style and the Politics of Chivalry

The triumph of flamboyance in the second half of the fourteenth century should also be linked to a particular political context of corporatism and warfare. In these decades, Florence engaged in a series of dangerous and extremely costly conflicts: the Pisan War (1362–64), won at a price of 1 million florins; the War of the Eight Saints, fought against the papacy in 1375–78, which incurred a communal debt of 3.5 million florins; and the Visconti conflicts in the 1380s and 1390s, during which mercenary payments averaged 100,000 florins per month.[64] These war efforts spurred constitutional readjustments that led to the victory of a more oligarchic regime after 1382. Warfare also helped precipitate an unprecedented fiscal crisis in the communal regime, while the interdict levied by the papacy brought on a near-crisis in public religiosity in 1377. Taxation and political contraction in turn exacerbated social tensions such as erupted in the Ciompi revolt of 1378.[65]

Spectacular civic funerals in the late Trecento were used frequently as a way to focus patriotism and to define the communal ideals that were under attack. The magnitude and ideology of some of these events made them political factors in their own right. The full cavalcade of war-horses, shields, spurs, and crests honoring the wealthy vintner Matteo Soldi (d. 1379), one of the war commissioners involved in the protracted fight against Gregory XI, represented in emphatically military terms his efforts on the commune's behalf, shortly after the conflict ended. Similarly, the corporate trappings honoring Francesco Rinuccini in 1381 recognized both his personal status as knight and his financial support of ongoing war efforts. Rinuccini had paid the highest *prestanza* assessment in the city in 1364 after the Pisan War, and he had been forced to buy seven farms that were part of ecclesiastical property confiscated during the War of the Eight Saints.[66]

During times of high tension such as the spring and summer of 1377, when the commune prohibited flagellant processions and shut down other forms of public celebration, several grand funerals absorbed the civic and religious functions of these activities in order to further political objectives. The funeral for the war commissioner Giovanni Magalotti, held on July 15, 1377, expressly posited the legitimacy of the Florentine cause in the commune's fight with Gregory XI. The war was exacting a terrible price; it had depressed cloth production and trade, severely strained the communal treasury, interfered with the finances and commerce of Florentine merchants, and resulted in a papal interdict against the city.[67]

Magalotti had been excommunicated for his political role as one of the "Eight Saints" resisting the pope. In staunch defiance of the excommunication decree, communal authorities used Magalotti's funeral to shore up flagging morale for the war effort by portraying him as a civic hero and a defender of republican liberty. Occupying a prominent place in the cortege was a banner sporting Magalotti's arms with the motto "Liberty" above. This emblem had been granted to Magalotti, other members of the war commission, and their progeny at the outbreak of hostilities in 1375. By the same provision, the eight war commissioners were knighted at communal expense, and each was given a shield and a pennant bearing his new device, along with other small gifts.[68] Another parade horse showed Magalotti's arms conjoined with those of the populace.

Magalotti's funeral not only took a defiant posture toward the papacy, however, but also glossed over mounting opposition within the city. Behind the celebration of Florentine values and identity in Magalotti's funeral lay a city at odds over the rationale and the cost of the conflict. The sharp factionalism and discord generated by the war's unsuccessful course and economic burdens were masked by a grand show of communal strength and unity aimed at justifying the ways of the commune to foreigners and Florentines alike. Magalotti's public funeral afforded both the occasion and the vehicle to galvanize a deteriorating communal solidarity.

A similar political orientation underlay the funeral of Niccolò di Jacopo Alberti, held a month later on August 8, 1377. Alberti had a long and distinguished record of communal service beginning with his election as prior in 1355, but it was his impressive handling of the Pisan War as Standard-bearer of Justice in 1363 that firmly established his reputation.[69] To mark their gratitude, the Signoria voted to raise Alberti to the rank of knight, and he was invested with sword and spurs by the war captain Piero Farnese in May 1363.[70]

Alberti later undertook numerous ambassadorial missions for the commune and repeatedly held high communal offices, as well as tending to his banking affairs, which netted personal assets of over 340,000 florins. So great was Alberti's public reputation that his memory was invoked in January 1401 during a council debate in an unsuccessful attempt to prevent the exile of his son Antonio.[71]

Alberti's funeral not only honored his personal wealth and distinguished career but recalled his instrumental leadership in the earlier Pisan conflict. In tribute, the Parte Guelfa added twelve torches to the sixty bought by Alberti's heirs. Each of the eight caparisoned horses bore a different corporate emblem or chivalric symbol representing the various facets of Alberti's identity and civic contributions.[72] However, Alberti was buried not in the Franciscan habit he had stipulated in his testament but in a costume of precious red samite and cloth of gold which reflected both his wealth and the ceremony's formidable cost: 3,000 florins. This was a legitimate occasion for public expressions of religiosity which had been forbidden during the preceding tense months. Adding drama to the occasion were five hundred poor mourners weeping over the bier, who marked Alberti's public stature as well as his renowned charity to such foundations as the Orbatello for poor women, and to Santa Croce.[73]

In this context of challenge and crisis, the use of knightly regalia such as shields, spurs, helmets, and caparisoned war-horses in the burials of knights and civic leaders had distinct political uses that went beyond mere conspicuous consumption. Grand chivalric burials illustrated both the political legitimacy and the moral authority of leading members of the regime. Although communal leaders such as Matteo Soldi, Niccolò Alberti, Giovanni Magalotti, and Francesco Rinuccini were not warriors in actual practice, they were represented at death, in a fictive and metaphorical way, as having led the war efforts for the commune's objectives against its various adversaries. Outfitted in their emblems and regalia, these communal "warriors" contributed to the defense of the republic through their capital and political service rather than by their blood. This military imagery appropriate to a commune repeatedly and rightfully at war made a political point on behalf of the commune's past goals and present leadership. Since the military imagery used in Magalotti's funeral was deployed only for men, it also conveyed gender values that represented the masculine sexual ideology of the polity.

In these events that mingled public and private lives, the trappings of chivalry represented less a slavish dependence on northern European forms than a way of expressing civic power and political authority.[74] What this imagery represented was a kind of "civic chivalry," the prerogatives of which were tightly controlled by the commune in the second half of the fourteenth century. Florentines knighted by outside authorities, for example, had to petition the Signoria for confirmation of their status in order to enjoy sumptuary privileges and other communal entitlements.[75] The power to create and recognize a knight of the commune was thus a mark of political authority that conferred legitimacy on recipients and regime alike. For example, the Ciompi government celebrated its victory over the former guild regime in July 1378 by spontaneously creating sixty-seven knights in one day.[76] After the Ciompi were suppressed, however, the incoming regime would recognize these knights' official status only if they were reinvested by a second ceremony. The post-Ciompi government reclaimed its political prerogatives by "remaking" thirty-one of the Ciompi knights, who swore their allegiance to the new regime in the Piazza della Signoria on October 18, 1378. Following the disintegration of the corporate regime of 1378–82, the older, more established political oligarchy signaled its victory over the newer corporatism by elevating twenty men, nineteen of whom came from the city's oldest and most illustrious families, to the rank of knight.[77] In the late Trecento, knighthood was less a search for foreign honor and identity than a validation of a regime's claims to civic power and of knights' participation in that power.

The process by which knights were created, which had a markedly civic quality rooted in both ritual and rhetoric, further clarifies the nature and function of civic chivalry. The commune first appointed a syndic who was responsible for ceremonial arrangements, and then voted a sum of money to cover expenses, usually in the range of one hundred florins. In the fourteenth century, the investiture ceremony, complete with a short oration and the gift of a garland, took place in the main civic space, the Piazza della Signoria. After 1418, these ceremonies were transferred to the cathedral or the Baptistry. Reporting the investiture ceremonies for the thirty-one knights remade after the Ciompi revolt, Niccolò Baldovinetti noted that the knights and their friends and relatives, numbering around one thousand persons, assembled at Santissima Annunziata and then paraded on horseback to the Piazza della Signoria. Baldovinetti described how the knights sat at the feet of the Signoria, "where some words were spoken by the notary of the Riformagione and the chancellor, to the effect that we would be knights of the populace and of the most Catholic, Christian Parte Guelfa; and so we swore to be knights of the people and of the Parte Guelfa."[78] At the ceremony, the new knights were invested with the distinguishing signs of sword and spurs by communal representatives, and each was given a standard and shield painted with the arms of the populace. Through both word and image, these investiture ceremonies repeatedly emphasized the communal nature of knighthood and the making of warriors in service to the city.

The frequency, common symbolism, and express political value of chivalric funeral rites and other public ceremonies in the closing decades of the Trecento gradually made them a more cohesive set of practices. Although there was no uniform style or single policy governing public ceremonies, a distinct body of civic ritual nevertheless began to take shape in these years. The frequency with which various ceremonies were put to political uses, the more explicit recognition of the large-scale political potential of ceremony by communal magistrates, and the prescription of common stylistic elements in diverse ceremonies all point to the formation of a ritual apparatus invested with new authority as an expression or instrument of political rule.

The key episode that pulled together these disparate strands of style and political purpose was the funeral for the English war captain John Hawkwood, in March 1394. Hawkwood's long record of loyal service to the commune since 1375 earned him what late Trecento chroniclers agreed was the most spectacular funeral in the city's history to date. Even during his lifetime, Hawkwood had enjoyed unusual multiple honors; in April 1391, he was made an honorary citizen and given certain tax privileges, and he renegotiated a generous contract with the commune.[79] As he became increasingly aged and ill, however, Hawkwood determined to return to his native land and made new arrangements in early March 1394, shortly before his death, in which he exchanged his pension and castle rights for a flat sum to make the trip.[80]

Within a week of these negotiations, Hawkwood was dead. The commune immediately began preparations "to pay him the greatest honor possible regardless of expense."[81] Judging from contemporary evidence, the commune succeeded magnificently in its task. Chroniclers agreed that, as a didactic tool celebrating civic pride, Hawkwood's funeral had no equal. The honors paid him surpassed even those accorded his famous predecessor Piero Farnese, the victorious captain of the Pisan War, whose burial in June 1363 had brought him "greater honor and reverence in all things" than any man in the past hundred years.[82] Yet in keeping with the trend toward the increase of pomp, Hawkwood's funeral went beyond even this impressive show. In the judgment of Ser Naddo da Montecatini, "until that day the commune had never paid such honor, either to a citizen or foreigner," and this opinion was seconded by a diarist from the Rinuccini family. Narrative descriptions and poems left little doubt that "everything was conducted as honorably as could possibly be done." Hawkwood's funeral was so grand and so charged with political meaning that it became part of communal lore in the fifteenth century; Benedetto Dei, born in 1417, wrote that he knew the sung poem narrating the event by heart.[83]

The citizens' committee selected by the Signoria arranged the ceremonies for March 20, 1394, three days after Hawkwood's death. Set in the Piazza della Signoria and the Baptistry, Hawkwood's funeral represented a large-scale corporate effort that orchestrated magistrates, guildsmen, soldiers, clergy, and citizens in a high moment of communal solidarity. The commune sent four caparisoned chargers bearing the arms of the commune and the populace, along with one hundred torches. The Parte Guelfa contributed two more horses, with appropriate emblems, helmets, and crests, and twenty torches carried by Parte members. Florentine guilds were represented by another twenty large, beautifully worked candles and by guild captains, members of the Merchants' Court, and the guild rank and file. Hawkwood's own men sent a total of eight draped war-horses and eight grooms, six carrying flags sporting his arms and two bearing richly crested helmets. This cooperative enterprise meant that, although the commune itself spent only about 410 florins, the aggregate ceremony was extremely impressive.[84] Corporate sponsorship also showed both Hawkwood and his patrons in the best possible light, since, in Giovanni Morelli's estimation, Hawkwood's relations were too poor "to honor his corpse as it merited."[85] Moreover, the celebration involved the Florentine populace at large. All shops were closed for the day by communal decree, and crowds reportedly flocked to San Giovanni to lament Hawkwood's passing.

Joining these trappings and participants in the square were "a very large number" of mourners from Hawkwood's retinue, heavily hooded in the mourning garb purchased by the commune. Hawkwood's body and bier were adorned with gold brocades, vermillion velvets, and his sword and command baton. With the city's monastic and secular clergy leading the way, the amassed honors preceeded from the Piazza della Signoria to the Baptistry. Here communal authorities introduced an innovative feature, one that set a precedent for civic funerals of the highest order for the remainder of the republic.[86] Rather than being taken directly to the cathedral for a requiem mass, Hawkwood's body was now transferred to a small platform and a second bier that had been erected over the gold-draped baptismal font. It was in this *umbilicus urbis*, where Florentines began their lives through baptism, that the war captain was lamented publicly by numerous women "in the presence of the entire populace of Florence," symbolizing both loss and the city's cyclic renewal. Neither the Baptistry's interior nor its exterior were architecturally reinterpreted by the addition of temporary apparatuses, as was commonly done during the Medici principate. But the symmetric posing of birth and rebirth that characterized the cultural politics of that later era was now introduced into Florentine civic rites by means of this public lamentation, this time celebrating a communal rather than a dynastic destiny.

After this densely symbolic celebration, the scene shifted to the cathedral, where a candle-studded catafalque awaited in the central choir. Once the corpse had been transferred from Baptistry to cathedral by Florentine knights, "a beautiful and graceful mass" was performed by unspecified celebrants, followed by a sermon relating "the most striking deeds" Hawkwood had accomplished. The ceremonies ended after the body was taken into the sacristy and later buried in the choir. Although generous tomb provisions had been made seven months before Hawkwood's death, the marble tomb designed "as much for the magnificence of the commune as for [Hawkwood's] honor and perpetual fame" was never realized. Over forty years later, a very different fresco project by Paolo Uccello was substituted in its stead.[87]

Despite the sorry fate of Hawkwood's tomb project, his funeral crystallized the major themes of ceremonial politics in the final decades of the Trecento. As a celebration of communal pride, Hawkwood's death rites posed a lesson in loyalty and civic legitimacy against outside threats, as well as quelling those dangers closer to home. This cooperative venture, in which an aggregate of honors resulted in a spectacular sum, strengthened and made visible a corporate ethos. Hawkwood's funeral was a high moment in an emergent civic ritual by which the commune created its heroes and reinvested meaning in significant civic spaces. Central to this event was a procession in which the penchant for excess created an ideal image of communal power, a striking picture both of the triumph of flamboyance and of the commune triumphant. It was also a ceremony in which verbal discourse, whether in square or church, played only a minimal role. Civic ritual of the late Trecento embodied its rhetoric less in the formal discourse of orations than in the discourse of custom, gesture, and action. In contrast to the nascent humanism that would soon transform Florentine culture, Hawkwood's civic tribute was an enactment in which the whole polity participated not as listeners but as actors.

Corporations, Parishes, and *Popolani*

Despite the popularity of funeral flamboyance in the late Trecento, this form of display was still simply beyond the reach of most Florentines, who struggled instead to avoid being buried "like a dog," to use Piovano Arlotto's vivid phrase. Although patricians and *popolani* were separated by great disparities of wealth, these social groups nevertheless shared two common habits: an interest in obtaining the most respectable burial possible, and the assumption of burial costs by the closest kin of the deceased. Church records are littered with examples of artisans and laborers who pieced together scarce resources for wax, palls, and a few clerics to enhance kinsmen's burials. Tax returns make it evident that even members of the *popolo minuto* occasionally took on additional debts in order to bury their kin more respectably. In 1427 a gravedigger and purveyor of funeral goods, Luca di Matteo, reported thirty-seven debtors currently in arrears for funeral trappings. Those defaulting were mainly artisans, including barbers, ironworkers, butchers, servants, painters, chicken vendors, shoemakers, and tailors. Among those who had been in debt to Luca for more than four years were a shearer, two skinners, and a carder, workers at occupations that had only briefly been organized into guilds during the Ciompi revolt of 1378. These artisans, small tradesmen, and laborers had eked out a few lire, or even a few florins, to bury their closest kin, as well as more distant relations who died in their houses.[88]

Although this overarching concern with an honorable burial is evident in a variety of records, it is difficult to reconstruct the funerals of individual artisans, laborers, and poor people in any detail. Narrative sources describing the funerals of the popular classes are virtually nonexistent, thereby making a study of stylistic changes unfeasible. Nevertheless, we can reconstruct several important features of these funeral rites, and the forms of association that underlay them, by turning to the legal and economic records of guilds, confraternities, and parishes. These corporations supplemented both the limited household resources and the family traditions of members of the popular classes who sought respectable burial. Some of the information provided by these records is invariably prescriptive; much of it is fragmentary. Creating aggegate data, as I have done when possible to offset some of these difficulties, often masks the richness of individual biographies of artisans and laborers. Within the limitations of the evidence, however, burial practices and preferences not only help us trace values and associations among the Florentine popular classes but also help us clarify the structure and operation of civic and ecclesiastical authority.

The corporate organization of the Florentine labor force offered guildsmen one important form of recognition in their death rites. The required participation of guild colleagues in funeral processions and other religious observances was designed to encourage a greater sense of community and solidarity among those practicing the same trade. Corporate social obligations meant that artisans and small tradesmen such as strap makers, bakers, carpenters, oil sellers, and locksmiths could anticipate some form of collegial homage at their funerals. The 1321 statutes of the armorers' guild, for example, required all members to assemble at the dead man's house, walk in the procession to the church, then return to the house with the rest of the crowd. The consuls of the bakers' guild designated those who were to attend a colleague's funeral; if asked, a baker was admonished to bring at least one companion and to appear respectably dressed, complete with shoes and mourning band. The statutes governing the large, conglomerate major guild of physicians and spicers also required physicians to attend the funerals of their colleagues' wives, although it seems unlikely that a high-ranking physician would have hastened to attend the burial of a tooth surgeon's wife.[89] In addition, many guilds required shops to close during the funeral. Former guild officials could also look forward to additional corporate candles and flags, even if they had never been propelled into the larger arena of civic office.

The corporate support offered by trade associations nevertheless was quite limited, especially in economic terms. Although collegial homage enhanced public honor, guilds did not provide material subsidies in the form of biers, palls, or payments to clergy; moreover, few guilds arranged masses for dead colleagues. While guild membership added an important social dimension to funerals, it neither relieved kin of the financial burdens of burial nor aided guildsmen in burying the women of their households. Trade associations did little to help Florentines meet the new and extraordinary burdens placed on households and parishes by the massive elaboration of funeral pomp in the late fourteenth century.

Instead it was to religious confraternities that increasing numbers of Florentines turned for burial assistance. In the competitive social environment of the late Trecento, confraternities offered access to resources, privileges, and numbers of mourners normally unavailable to artisans and laborers, as well as to women of varying classes. Ritual brotherhoods contributed to the social face of grief through collegial participation in funerals, provided essential trappings that afforded financial relief to members and their households, and addressed powerful spiritual needs.[90]

In offering this multifaceted burial assistance, confraternities not only enhanced personal honor but also helped smooth over tensions between social groups. By distributing honor vertically through the social structure, confraternities assured a great continuum in the funeral displays of rich citizens and those of middling status. Confraternal aid thus mitigated against sharp disjunctions between patricians and popolani which could exacerbate civic strife; paradoxically, however, this aid only fueled the spiral of consumption. While it would be a mistake to ignore the rich spiritual and social attractions of brotherhoods and to consider them simply as burial societies, the

proliferation of confraternities in the late fourteenth century nevertheless should be understood against a backdrop of escalating funeral
consumption yet demographic decline.[91]

For poor and modest tradesmen, confraternal membership was an
extremely important vehicle to a respectable burial. Ritual brothers
banded together to pay for the burials of their neediest brethren,
while fellow members of flagellant companies, which were the confraternities most actively involved in members' funerals, often carried
the bier of a dead brother in the funeral procession.[92] Even the
poorest members of flagellant companies could anticipate burial in
the spiritually prestigious "vesta disciplinale" in which they had
performed their penitential rites.[93] Many confraternal trappings, such
as the torches, golden bier cloth, and vermillion silk cushion sent to
members' funerals by the charitable company of Orsanmichele, were
luxury items marked with confraternal insignia and thus gave poorer
Florentines access to pomp and an important form of symbolic power.[94]
From an economic standpoint, the loan of mortuary items minimized
expenses that might otherwise throw kinsmen of the deceased into
debt.

Confraternal membership also offered access to additional layers
of pomp that satisfied the flamboyant taste of the late fourteenth
century. Bell ringing formed part of the essential vocabulary of pomp
while also serving useful communicative functions. The laud-singing
confraternity of San Zanobi, which met in the cathedral, broadcast
news of a brother's death in the heart of the city by tolling a special
bell for the duration of twelve Our Fathers and Hail Marys.[95] Tens
of ritual brothers, each bearing a small candle while walking in
procession, augmented the honor and the size of the funeral cortege;
these same brothers later multiplied the salutary prayers offered on
behalf of the dead man's soul. Those members who, like the captain
of San Pier Martire, Cieppo di Domenico Fei (d. 1418), distinguished
themselves from the rank and file as confraternal officers earned
additional processional torches (doppieri) in their cortege.[96]

The commune sanctioned these fraternal contributions and perhaps even encouraged membership by permitting members and af-
filiates to exceed the legal limits on wax. Sumptuary rulings specifically exempted confraternal candles from being counted as part of
the permissible amount. Despite these allowances, however, the rubrics of 1384 suggested that confratelli frequently abused their priv-

ileges in pursuit of still more conspicuous funeral displays. These rulings prohibited private individuals and households from sending additional wax under pretense of confraternal sponsorship, while the 1415 statutes railed against borrowing torches from brotherhoods to which the deceased had not rightfully belonged.[97]

Both laud-singing and flagellant confraternities also offered their members access to more privileged burial sites in the companies' tombs. These confraternal burial sites perpetuated the affiliations across lines of class and occupation that characterized many late fourteenth-century religious fraternities. Moreover, confraternal tombs brought together the fictive kin of both past and future generations in eternal rest. Although neither confraternal nor parish sepulchres were individualized, the antiquity of some confraternal tombs, such as the one belonging to Gesù Pellegrino in Santa Maria Novella, offered a burial status more nearly commensurate with that of the great families of Florence, who had begun to privatize their burial spaces *intra muros ecclesiae* in the late thirteenth and early fourteenth centuries.[98] Not all confraternal burial sites were so explicitly privileged, of course; in 1427 the laud-singing confraternity of San Lorenzo had a exterior cemetery in Piazza San Lorenzo adjacent to its chapel, rather than tombs inside the church.[99] Nevertheless, these corporate tombs ensured that many Florentines with limited family traditions would experience neither a "mortuary solitude" nor the greater anonymity of unmarked parish graves.

In offering burial assistance, ritual brotherhoods also cut across lines of gender by making their funeral services, tomb privileges, and memorial masses available to women as well as to men. The role of women in organized lay piety has yet to be investigated fully. Although women enjoyed a marginal status in some singing and charitable confraternities, participating in various rites, they were excluded from the fast-growing flagellant confraternities springing up across Italy in this period.[100] Some flagellant companies, such as that of San Domenico in Florence, did not allow women to share either in their rites or in the spiritual merits of the group.[101] Hence it was primarily singing confraternities that admitted women to worship, making the spiritual fund and practical services of the organization available. Richard Trexler has noted the pressure exerted by Florentine women to be allowed to share in the ferment of organized piety during the interdict-induced crisis of March 1377, which resulted in the admission of women to the cathedral's Company of San Zanobi and other *laudesi* confraternities. In fourteenth- and early fifteenth-century Bologna, women sometimes even outnumbered men in joining singing confraternities.[102]

In extending their resources and services to women, confraternities cut across class and neighborhood boundaries, just as they did for men. Utilizing the commemorative services of the Company of San Pier Martire in Santa Maria Novella were local clients such as Cionella Soldanieri and the butcher's widow Bene, as well as more distant residents such as the sisters Inghilesca and Tessina di Bartolo Corsi from San Lorenzo, and Cionella Migliorati of Santa Maria Maggiore.[103]

Women could obtain these confraternal privileges in two ways: by direct acts of patronage, and by virtue of their kinship with male members. In return for donations of property, confraternities frequently acted in place of kin as direct funeral brokers for women. For example, the Company of San Pier Martire furnished the wax, palls, benches, and other accoutrements for the vigil and funeral of Piera, widow of Giovenco Arrigucci, in June 1418, and supervised the invitation of clerics from Santa Maria Novella and San Pancrazio to her funeral. The company had negotiated similar arrangements for Inghilesca di Bartolo Corsi in 1377.[104] Communal sumptuary rulings specifically permitted confraternities to send additional wax to the funerals of women as well as those of men.[105] Some confraternities, such as the flagellants of Gesù Pellegrino and the *laudesi* of San Pier Martire, also offered women the honor of confraternal burial sites, although there was a distinct, separate depository for each sex, as was the case with private family tombs.[106] Still greater numbers of mothers, wives, and sisters also shared indirectly in corporate spiritual benefits and prayer networks. The Company of San Niccolò da Bari in the Carmine generously embraced in its corporate prayers the "fathers, mothers, brothers, sisters, children, and every other relative [*congiunto*]" of its members, thereby extending the company's spiritual fund well beyond its actual membership.[107]

It was primarily in rites of remembrance, however, that confraternities showed both the full extent of their brokerage functions and the greatest level of gender balance and inclusion. As I have discussed elsewhere, Florentine women of patrician and *popolano* status established themselves as important patrons of the dead by commissioning commemorative masses, including the more costly perpetual mass cycles.[108] The importance of commemorative patronage as an arena for personal expression can be gauged in part from women's high profile as sponsors, with women commissioning roughly half of all perpetual masses in the late fourteenth century and the fifteenth century. In setting up their memorial programs, women, especially widows, frequently used confraternities as agents and brokers to raise funds through the sale of property, clothing, and household goods. Although women's exclusion from administrative responsibilities led to declining retention rates, these corporations nevertheless offered women a cluster of extrafamilial resources that were simply unavailable elsewhere.[109]

Despite the relative inclusiveness and popularity of confraternities, very few poor artisans and *sottoposti* of the wool and silk industries belonged to religious brotherhoods before the middle of the fifteenth century.[110] It was to the parish rather than to confraternities that these laborers, along with beggars, vagabonds, immigrants, the poor, and other marginal persons, turned for corporate burial assistance in the late Trecento. The parish was a unit of ecclesiastical administration centered on the parish church, as well as a bloc of urban space which helped define a neighborhood.[111] Cohn has argued that in the late fourteenth century, working-class sociability revolved around the parish, with marriage patterns documenting a high rate of parish endogamy among the laboring classes. Neighborhood ties centering on the parish church of San Pancrazio were similarly strong until their probable erosion in the last quarter of the fifteenth century. In neighboring Venice, urban parishes also provided local solidarity for Venetians who lacked an established family tradition and the sense of place offered by property ownership.[112]

Florentine parishes nevertheless showed tremendous variation in size, wealth, and administration. This variation affected their roles both in sociability and in burial practices. Of the sixty-two parishes identified in fifteenth-century notarial records, twelve urban parishes were headed by monastic or conventual churches; nine parishes were controlled by other ecclesiastical foundations, such as the hospital of Santa Maria Nuova; and another cluster of urban parishes centered around the cathedral and the collegiate church of Orsanmichele.[113] Parishes in the old urban core tended to be smaller in both size and population than those on the periphery adjacent to the third circle of walls. In 1427 the tiny parish of San Donato dei Vecchietti claimed only twenty-two households; by contrast, the numerous inhabitants of large, peripheral parishes such as San Lorenzo, Sant'Ambrogio, San Pier Gattolino, and San Frediano could sprawl more comfortably into open spaces. From the fifteenth through the eighteenth century, the parish of San Lorenzo alone comprised a full one-seventh of the city's population.[114]

The profile of lay influence and patronage rights at parish churches is similarly complex, with the rights of families to select parish rectors concentrated in older parishes.[115] Balancing these powerful family claims in local enclaves was the greater popularity and the often greater size of churches belonging to the mendicant orders. For example, in 1427 the small parish of Santa Maria Ughi enjoyed income from only two perpetual mass bequests, honoring the wealthy former parishioner Nofri Strozzi and his factor Antonio, whereas the Umiliati friars who headed Ognissanti performed sixty such mass programs the same year.[116]

To understand the role parishes played in the burials of popolani and the poor, it is useful first to review the administrative burdens and benefits assigned to the parish under ecclesiastical law. Despite variations in size and wealth between the city's parishes, each of them was responsible for burying its own parishioners. A primary objective of the parochial law hammered out by canonists in the twelfth and thirteenth centuries was to ensure proper burial for all worthy Christians, regardless of wealth or status.[117] The first full set of constitutions for the Florentine diocese, published under the direction of Antonio Biliotti in August 1310, admonished parish rectors to confess the dying and bury the dead of their parish without regard for material gain.[118] Although parish clergy sometimes received help in burying the indigent dead from the confraternity of the Misericordia, these services remained essentially parochial responsibilities rather than civic or corporate ones.[119]

Biliotti's rubrics of 1310 outlining parochial responsibilities formed the backbone of later episcopal rulings throughout the later Trecento and the Quattrocento.[120] The relative stability of these prescriptions governing parochial conduct and duties contrasted sharply with the jurisdictional battles fought between Florentine bishops and the commune, especially during the tenure of Bishop Angelo Acciaiuoli in the 1340s and 1350s.[121] In practical terms, the removal in 1296 of the old civic cemetery, located between the Baptistry and the cathedral, to make way for the Duomo's expansion helped to physically decentralize Florentine burial sites along parochial lines at an early date.[122]

This established parochial grid could be altered legally only through the intervention of the Florentine bishop, who alone had the authority to cede the right of sepulchre in his diocese.[123] When new religious foundations such as hospitals, oratories, and chapels came into being, they did not automatically enjoy sepulchral privileges but had to petition the bishop for them. Messer Pagolo Vettori, the proud founder of the hospital of San Giuliano, recorded that among the privileges granted the hospital at its foundation in 1364 were the rights "to have an oratory, to sing masses, to have bells and tombs, . . . to confess, give communion and every other church sacrament, and to bury the sick who died at the hospital, as well as those in service to the hospital."[124] Similarly, the canons of San Lorenzo secured an archiepiscopal license in 1445 for jurisdiction over the new tombs created when the church was remodeled.[125] New monastic institutions also sought the bishop's approval of burial rights in their founding charters. Included among the provisions establishing the Benedictine convent of Sant'Appollonia in April 1339 was the episcopal grant of burial privileges for nuns, abbesses, lay sisters, and convent servants.[126]

Parish churches also enjoyed legal claims to burial rights within their territory. Many of the administrative agreements between ecclesiastical institutions, which allowed parishes to control the status and revenues generated by burials at subordinate establishments, were worked out through the Florentine bishop in the late thirteenth and early fourteenth centuries, when the city's population was still expanding. In 1276, for example, the canons of San Lorenzo agreed to permit burials of the French Knights of Rhodes in the church of San Giovanni Battista, located in the parish of San Lorenzo, in return for half of all burial proceeds. In 1325 the Benedictine convent of San Pier Maggiore exercised its parochial authority by severely restricting burials at the neighboring Cistercian house of the Cestello.[127] New institutions founded in the later Trecento quickly found themselves under similar parochial strictures. In September 1365 the bishop's court ratified a pact between San Pier Maggiore and its new neighbor, the convent of Santa Maria di Monteloro, founded the preceding March. The agreement allowed only the Monteloro nuns and servants to be buried in the new cemetery in order "to sustain and not to disturb the parochial right" of the older institution.[128]

There were sound economic reasons for parishes to guard their burial prerogatives closely, especially in the late fourteenth century, when both standards of funeral pomp and mortality rates were exceptionally high. In the plague year 1374, for instance, burial revenues from donated cloth, wax, and clerical fees (exclusive of commemorative offices) accounted for 22 percent of total income at San Pier Maggiore, which was one of the city's largest and most populous parishes.[129] While the percentage of income fell in nonplague years, burials continued to provide a constant, steady source of parish revenues. In a sampling of years between 1374 and 1413, direct burial proceeds amounted on balance to almost 10 percent of the total annual income of San Pier Maggiore.[130] Commemorative masses, which customarily gravitated toward tomb sites, along with banquets rewarding clerics after memorial masses, pushed revenues from death rites even higher. The importance of fees from funerals and offices was poignantly noted in 1427 by the rector of San Niccolò, who claimed that it was only by virtue of this supplemental income that he could survive.[131]

Even fees resulting indirectly from funerals formed an important source of income for parishes and their competitors alike. In March and April 1369, the friars of Santa Maria del Carmine brought in 10.1 percent of all of the church's recorded income for those months by marching in funeral processions. In July of the same year, higher summer mortality rates, combined with an ebb in the liturgical calendar, elevated these processional receipts to 17.7 percent of the month's income.[132]

The great exceptions to this parish burial scheme were the Baptistry and the cathedral, over which the commune retained considerable control. As work progressed on the new cathedral structure begun in September 1294, the communal government ceded jurisdiction over the fabric of the cathedral, including its tombs, to the Lana guild and the cathedral supervisors (operai) in 1331; the commune had already granted supervision of the Baptistry to the Calimala guild.[133]

Under the watchful eyes of lay supervisors, guild consuls, and the communal government, the cathedral was established as a highly privileged burial site only in the second half of the Trecento. In 1357, the cathedral operai voted to prohibit all burials in the cathedral without their approval, with the exception of those of bishops and archbishops, canons, and cathedral chaplains.[134] In succeeding decades, the operai maintained the privileged and civic nature of cathedral burial by successfully resisting the efforts of families and individuals to lay private claim to burial sites. In 1385 the operai took a decisive step in this direction by deciding to remove all private coats of arms from the cathedral.[135]

Even when approving petitions for cathedral burial, supervisors placed severe restrictions on tomb sites and future burial privileges, as illustrated in the following two cases. The operai granted Messer Vieri de' Medici's petition of June 26, 1392, for cathedral burial "because he and his ancestors of the Medici house had shown such singular devotion to the mother church of Santa Reparata."[136] In fact, Vieri's kinsman Giovanni de' Medici had helped stake the family claim by being buried in the cathedral under less stringent circumstances in 1353.[137] Vieri's burial site could display his arms and insignia, but as a monument the operai permitted only a pavement slab, which could not be placed "on the wall or in a prominent place." The operai similarly restricted the form and privileges of the burial site granted Cardinal Piero Corsini in December 1389. In authorizing the cardinal's kinsmen Filippo and Matteo Corsini to construct a chapel and tomb on his behalf, cathedral officials prohibited a display of family emblems on the altar, on the column against which it abutted, and on the altarcloths used for services. Although the operai allocated the Corsini a wall tomb opposite the altar, they again restricted the use of family insignia and limited future burials to other Corsini cardinals and bishops.[138]

In the plague-ridden decades of the late fourteenth century, problems of health, finances, and social control forged the parish into a key unit for civic as well as ecclesiastical administration. After the early reorganization of the city into sixths, parish boundaries had been cut through by the civil jurisdictions of *gonfaloni*, probably in an attempt to curb ecclesiastical power.[139] In the late Trecento, the commune used parochial organization as the basis for new plague legislation. Legislative attempts to curb abuses by gravediggers, ensure legitimate property transfers, and estimate grain needs increased the importance of the parish's administrative functions.

Although civic officials' greatest concern was to protect persons and property during outbreaks of disease,[140] communal lawmakers relied on parishes to administer a variety of new policies. New guild regulations, which in 1375 brought gravediggers under the supervision of the physicians' and spicers' guild, admonished gravediggers to respect the parish preference of the deceased or his or her kin, rather than throwing bodies into open pits or simply consigning them to the nearest, most convenient church, as was frequently charged.[141] In turn, gravediggers were required to report the name, resident parish, and burial place of the deceased to the Grain Office, which began keeping communal death registers, or Books of the Dead (*libri di morti*) in 1385.[142] Even when entries in the Books of the Dead were shortened between 1412 and 1424, the resident parish of the deceased figured as essential information. The rudimentary mechanisms of plague legislation, which after 1385 required gravediggers to submit written proof of death furnished by the rector of the burial church, formalized the links between civic and ecclesiastical administration. These mechanisms also worked to regularize relations between clerics and individual gravediggers, who ran errands for priests and friars, helped them resell burial goods, and customarily turned back to them part of the earnings from gravedigging.[143]

In the fifteenth century, shifting demographics of plague deaths placed increased burdens and responsibilities on parishes. As affluent Florentines began fleeing the city during plague as early as 1383, thereby enhancing their chances of survival, plague found its victims increasingly among the poor.[144] During the epidemic of June 1450, the abbot of San Pancrazio recorded that his parish had received "about 34 corpses, over half of which were buried for the love of God and almost without candles."[145]

By the early fifteenth century, the commune had a stake in maintaining the stability of parish organization not only as part of its health policies but also as part of an evolving criminal justice system. In 1429 the parish priests of San Simone, which stood adjacent to the communal prison (the Stinche), noted their loose contract with the prison. The priests agreed "to visit the sick and to bury the dead of that place," with the church supplying the wax and other necessary burial items, in return for an annual subsidy of thirteen florins.[146] Local parishes received the bodies of executed criminals of Florentine birth who had private tombs; criminals bereft of this advantage were buried in the common cemetery outside the city gates while the corpses of "foreign" criminals from other cities could be procured by medical faculties for dissection.[147] However, succoring criminals on the eve of execution did not form part of the parochial mission. That task fell instead to the Company of Santa Maria della Croce al Tempio (founded 1343), which also subsidized regular masses on behalf of condemned criminals the first and third Sundays of each month.[148]

In the thirteenth and fourteenth centuries, the most serious challenge to parochial control of burial rights and revenues came from the mendicant orders. The growing popularity of burial at Franciscan and Dominican churches siphoned off important revenues from parishes, threatening their economic viability. Competition for both income and prestige led to disputes over burial goods, such as the fight between the cathedral and Santa Maria Novella in March 1311 over the expensive, scarlet, fur-lined robe worn by the knight Berto Brunelleschi to his tomb. Because his widow Mea bore a "special devotion" to Santa Maria Novella, she donated the robe to the friars. However, her decision was formally challenged on two separate occasions that month by the cathedral canons, who sought possession of the robe.[149]

Bishop Biliotti's constitutions of 1310 recognized the growing gravity of the problem and urged parishioners to accept burial in their local parishes in the hope of countering this trend. Anyone desiring burial outside his or her resident parish was advised to have a written statement of that choice notarized, or to publicly express such a wish in front of two or three respectable men of the parish. Acciaiuoli's constitutions circa 1346 took a stronger stance, directing parish rectors to refuse burial to nonparishioners without such proof.[150] Despite these legal directives, the dominance of large mendicant complexes such as Santa Maria Novella remained a serious, ongoing problem for smaller, nonmonastic parishes. The rector of San Donato dei Vecchietti, a tiny parish in the old city center, complained in his tax declaration of 1427 that his already few parishioners preferred burial at Santa Maria Novella, thereby stripping him of much-needed income.[151]

The fiscal competition between parish clergy and mendicants was partially resolved by an administrative apparatus called the *quarta*. First proclaimed by Boniface VIII in 1300 and revoked by Benedict XI in 1304, the quarta was incorporated into the Florentine synodal constitutions of 1310 and firmly reinstated by papal bull in 1312.[152] The quarta system apportioned revenues between institutions in an attempt to balance the free choice of burial site guaranteed by canon law against the legitimate rights of the parish. The quarta required that when a parishioner elected burial with the mendicants, one-quarter of all burial receipts be turned over to the parish of the deceased. This required apportionment was quickly extended to all burials that occurred outside the parish, whether with the mendicants or not. All goods customarily donated to the burial church (*funeralia*) were subject to apportionment, and a payment equal to one-quarter of their value was generally paid in cash soon after burial. For reasons that are not entirely clear, the Franciscans of Santa Croce and the Dominicans of Santa Maria Novella customarily turned over one-half, rather than one-quarter, of wax receipts.

The significance of these revenues can be gauged from repeated disputes throughout the republican period and into the sixteenth century. Santissima Annunziata failed in its attempt to retain all the burial proceeds from Messer Amerigo da San Severino in March 1456 and consequently was forced to pay the quarta to the cathedral canons.[153] The Vallombrosan convent of San Pancrazio, which fell on hard times in the early sixteenth century, had happier results in its lawsuit against Santa Maria Novella. In January 1520, San Pancrazio filed suit against the Dominicans "on account of the many candles owed us, in that they want to give us a quarter instead of half of the said wax as they are accustomed and used to giving us."[154] In June 1578, San Pier Maggiore, Sant'Ambrogio, and other local parishes won a lengthy legal battle with their powerful Franciscan neighbor Santa Croce, which was ordered by both the archbishop and the papal nuncio to distribute to the parishes half of the large wax candles received from funerals.[155]

Parish records of burial income, including quarta receipts, offer a way to evaluate systematically the extent to which the mendicant orders undermined parish ties and revenues in the late fourteenth and early fifteenth centuries. These receipts map the geographical distribution of burial sites, and with them the relative strength of parish loyalties. This information permits us on the one hand to assess how effectively parishes actually fulfilled one of their primary functions, and on the other to measure an aspect of religious preference. Since a citywide analysis would be a prohibitive task, I have selected for study the large, populous parish of San Pier Maggiore, located in the northeastern part of the city, which dominated one of the six "ecological clusters" defined by Cohn. Like several other important parishes, San Pier Maggiore was headed by a monastic complex, in this case the oldest Benedictine nunnery in the city.

The results of an analysis of 252 burial receipts sampled between 1374 and 1413 at San Pier Maggiore are summarized in Table 3.1.[156] It should be noted that these receipts have been culled from regular church accounts rather than compiled from parish burial registers (which are rare for this early period) or from communal Books of the Dead. These figures should not be interpreted as raw numbers of deaths and burials in the parish of San Pier Maggiore; instead, they reflect receipts generated by *funeralia*, mainly bier cloths. Thus the burials of the most destitute parishioners, who were buried at parish expense, are not included in this sample. This is not to say, however, that only the elite are represented by burial receipts. Many parishioners identified by occupation as members of the *popolo minuto*, such as shoemakers, carpenters, bakers, wool carders, shearers, tavern keepers, wine vendors, tailors, and barbers, are represented. Even the burials of several persons identified as "poor" produced a few soldi in resale items. Despite the fact that burial patterns gleaned from receipts are less comprehensive than those compiled from communal burial registers, these ecclesiastical accounts have the offsetting advantage of offering rich contextual information about the social, economic, and religious activities of parishioners.

The urban landscape mapped by the sample shows a highly localized religious topography dominated by strong parish ties. Florentines' local loyalties, evident in both their social organization and their urban experiences, bore a striking resemblance to the localism of their Venetian contemporaries.[157] Ninety-one percent of San Pier Maggiore's parishioners in the sample (220 of 242, with 10 nonparishioners included in the sample) were buried either in San Pier Maggiore or in one of two churches that headed contiguous parishes: Santa Croce, and Sant'Ambrogio (Figure 3.1). These three parishes, bound by numerous sets of associations and exchanges, comprised a distinct neighborhood zone that is better understood in a topographical sense, rather than in strictly administrative terms.

Located at the center of this urban bloc was the parish of San Pier Maggiore itself. A full three-quarters (76.4 percent) of the parish-

TABLE 3.1:

Distribution of Burial Sites, San Pier Maggiore, 1374–1413

Year	No. of Receipts	No. of Parishioners Buried in Home Parish	No. of Parishioners Buried Elsewhere	No. of Nonparishioners Buried in Parish
1374	31	17	12	2
1380	23	17	5	1
1384	17	12	4	1
1388	51	36	11	4
1393	22	16	5	1
1400	44	34	10	0
1412	32	23	8	1
1413	32	30	2	0
Total	252	185	57	10
Percentage of total		73.4	22.6	4.0
Percentage of parishioners		76.4	23.5	

Source: San Pier Maggiore. vol. 68, fols. 19v–22r; San Pier Maggiore. vol. 69, fols. 25r–29v; San Pier Maggiore. vol. 70, fols. 7v–11r, 25v–32v, 53v–58v; San Pier Maggiore. vol. 52, fols. 2r–6v; San Pier Maggiore. vol. 72, fols. 5v–10v, 13r–17v. Figures for 1400 are available only for the period August through December.

ioners in the group sampled, many of whom came from the laboring classes, elected burial in their home parish. Like other parishes in this period, San Pier Maggiore had a heterogeneous social composition that included a range of rich and poor with substantial gradations and discrepancies in livelihood, status, and family traditions. While the truly poor had little choice other than parish burial, even the meager economic resources of minor guildsmen and *sottoposti* gave them a somewhat wider set of burial options. Moreover, parish burial, or even being "put away on the parish," did not carry the social stigma or pronounced sense of dependence that was associated with it in the early nineteenth century.[158] In the late Trecento, social distinctions in tomb sites were mapped out more by privatization and proximity to sacred spaces and objects within churches than by an urban class geography.

These parish account books contain abundant evidence of familiarity and exchange between parishioners and their local clergy dur-

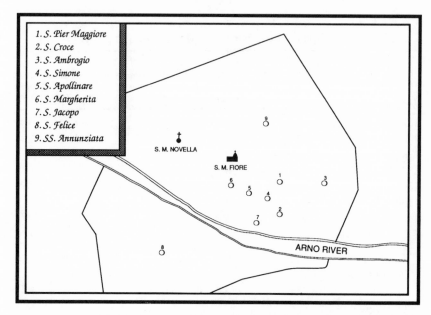

1. S. Pier Maggiore
2. S. Croce
3. S. Ambrogio
4. S. Simone
5. S. Apollinare
6. S. Margherita
7. S. Jacopo
8. S. Felice
9. SS. Annunziata

S. M. NOVELLA

S. M. FIORE

ARNO RIVER

FIGURE 3.1. Distribution of burial sites of parishioners of San Pier Maggiore, 1374–1413. (Data from San Pier Maggiore. vol. 68, fols. 19v–22r; San Pier Maggiore. vol. 69, fols. 25r–29v; San Pier Maggiore. vol. 70, fols. 7v–11r, 25v–32v, 53v–58v; San Pier Maggiore. vol. 52, fols. 2r–6v; San Pier Maggiore. vol. 72, fols. 5v–10v, 13r–17v. Figures for 1400 are available only for the period August through December.)

ing their lifetimes. While the laboring classes have been portrayed as unsympathetic to their parish churches in the late Trecento,[159] these records show successful artisans, minor guildsmen, and women (who were outside the ranks of organized wage labor) actively using their parish church as a local patronage venue. When the soap maker Lionardo offered one florin to San Pier Maggiore to bury his young son during the plague summer of 1400, the abbess of the convent, Antonia Bardi, refused to retain her customary portion because "the said Lionardo restores the convent every day in many ways."[160] On the basis of what must have been a familiar working relationship, the chaplain of San Pier Maggiore, Ser Taddeo, willingly lent the church's gravedigger "Il Grasso" two florins of his own money in

July 1374. Death and burial further intertwined the finances of small neighborhood merchants and the nunnery. The convent ran up a large bill with the local druggists Francesco and Marco after the illness and death of abbess Lucia Falconieri and several other nuns in 1411; in return, the new abbess canceled part of the rent due from the druggist's shop owned by the convent.[161] These local business relationships sometimes directly profited parishioners of modest means, such as the spinner's wife Bartolomea di Feo (d. 1412), who entrusted her funeral arrangements to the parish priests in return for half her household goods. For about eight florins, the parish syndic bought wax and borrowed a bier, bier cloths, and six rows of benches from a local druggist, "all at a discount." He also hired twenty pair of friars from an unspecified church "to do honor to the body" and furnished wine as payment for the gravediggers "so they might enjoy themselves."[162]

Wealthier parishioners joined their artisan neighbors in their common preference for parish burial. A large number (78) of the 185 parishioners choosing parish burial were identified by family names or professional titles, and many were from prominent neighborhood families with long histories of local patronage, such as the Albizzi, the Pazzi, the della Rena, and the da Filicaia. Women and men demonstrated similar parochial attachments, both among those with surnames and among the *minori*. These overarching allegiances to the parish presented implicit opportunities for charity and patronage within the local community. It was the funerary largesse of those wealthy parishioners who heaped wax and expensive cloths on their dead kin that helped underwrite the burials of poor parishioners. Their flamboyant consumption patterns stocked parish coffers, which in turn subsidized burials made "for the love of God," with the parish church acting as a clearinghouse for the circulation of commodities from rich to poor.

Even the small group of ten nonparishioners electing burial in San Pier Maggiore rather than in their own parishes corroborate this localized picture of association and exchange. Four of the ten came from neighboring Sant'Ambrogio; and five came from other nearby parishes (see Figure 3.1), including a carpenter's wife from San Simone; the wife of a Maestro Guerriere from Sant'Appollinare; an unnamed woman from Santa Margherita; Agnolo Bindazzi from San

Jacopo; and Orlando Gherardi from Santa Croce. Only one person in the sample, a certain Lapaccio called "Inpastina," from San Felice in Piazza, came from outside this restricted urban zone.[163]

Those parishioners electing burial away from San Pier Maggiore tell a similar story of local orientation, but one that intersected with more complex patterns of piety. Of the 23 percent who elected burial outside the parish, over half (thirty-three of fifty-seven, or 57.8 percent) chose San Pier Maggiore's prominent Franciscan neighbor, Santa Croce. The Franciscan ideal of poverty and humility worked its power over many Florentines, such as the statesman Bartolomeo Valori, who in 1427 abandoned his ancient family tombs in the Badia in favor of burial with the Franciscans.[164]

Yet it appears from these data that it was not only Santa Croce's spiritual and social prestige that drew parishioners away from the parish but also its proximity. Churches associated with other popular religious orders located at a greater distance were patronized very sparingly. Only one person each elected burial with the Dominicans of Santa Maria Novella, the Carmelites of Santa Maria del Carmine, the Augustinians of Santo Spirito, and the Umiliati of Ognissanti, while no parishioner in the sample chose the Vallombrosans of Santa Trinità or San Pancrazio. The church running a distant second to Santa Croce (five persons) was the Servite church of Santissima Annunziata, which, although not contiguous to San Pier Maggiore, was located in the same zone. It was quite rare for the traffic in ritual and social exchange generated by burials to cross the city or the Arno river.

Those who chose burial at Santa Croce also showed important differences in status and gender from the main group, although the number of persons involved here is too small to form general conclusions. Males greatly outnumbered females (twenty-three of thirty-three), rather than being evenly balanced as in the main group. Moreover, most of these men and boys (sixteen of twenty-three) had either family names or professional titles, indicating their higher social status and the commensurately greater value of their funeral goods. Patrilineal and patriarchal family arrangements also meant that the establishment of new tombs by male heads of household could draw successive burials of their kin away from the parish. Since several patrons of the Franciscans came from families long associated with San Pier Maggiore, such as the Donati and the Salviati, and even the Albizzi, the deflection of their future patronage from the parish must have been especially troubling. The women choosing mendicant burial were drawn from a relatively similar elite group: six of the ten women had family names, including several from households of such traditional parish patrons as the da Filicaia, the Salviati and the della Rena. These findings show that a major strand of the competition between the mendicants and other parishes in the late fourteenth and early fifteenth centuries was a competition for neighborhood resources, local patronage, and dominance in a particular urban sector.[165]

The particularist, local loyalties sketched above are reinforced by another type of funeral evidence drawn from the opposite side of the city. The geographical dispersion of friars from Santa Maria del Carmine who participated in funeral processions portrays similar neighborhood networks and localized ecclesiastical patronage. Inviting additional clergy to march in procession added the kind of luster and prestige characteristic of this rampant conspicuous consumption. It was also a relatively inexpensive form of pomp that could be easily multiplied, since the customary payment to each friar was only two soldi.[166] The popularity of this practice can be judged from the fact that, in eleven years sampled between 1350 and 1380, the friars participated in no fewer than 1,138 funeral processions originating elsewhere. Since the Carmine's population hovered between twenty-two and thirty-four friars in the 1380s and 1390s, funerals obviously claimed a prominent spot on the friars' busy extramural calendar.[167]

The results of a sample of the Carmine friars' funeral participation, taken at roughly four-year intervals between 1350 and 1380, are presented in Table 3.2.[168] The friars attended the greatest number of funerals originating at Santo Spirito, in which parish the Carmine was situated, with San Frediano, a neighboring church, running a close second. As indicated in Figure 3.2, these three churches—the Carmine, Santo Spirito, and San Frediano—shared a bond of close physical proximity, with the Carmine situated about midway between the other two churches, whose parishes formed contiguous units. Seven of the ten parishes visited most frequently shared the Carmine's location in the quarter of Santo Spirito, while an eighth church, Santa Trinità, lay just across the river and was easily accessible (Figure 3.2).

Other aspects of the sample buttress this sense of localism. Of the

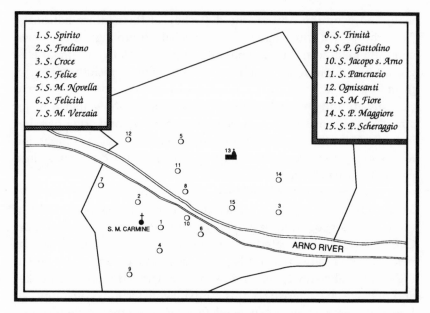

FIGURE 3.2. Processional activity of Carmine friars, 1350–1380 (top fifteen churches). (Data from Conv. Sopp. 113. vol. 81.)

1,138 excursions in the total sample, only five were made to San Lorenzo, one of the most populous parishes; five to Santissima Annunziata; and none to San Marco, all located across the city on the other side of the river. In the plague year 1374, which had the highest single-year participation in the sample, the neighborhood circle around the Carmine contracted still further. The four most frequented parishes—Santa Felicità, San Frediano, San Felice in Piazza, and Santo Spirito—formed a neat arc framing the Carmine. When death rates rose, Florentines in the Oltrarno did not stray far from their neighborhood district in seeking clerical support, but turned instead to clergy who were nearby and familiar. The two great outsiders in this neighborhood scheme were the Franciscan and Dominican churches of Santa Croce and Santa Maria Novella. Persons buried at these two churches may have frequently been of higher status and thus more able to afford additional clergy; at the very least, the Carmelites were not caught in the great rivalries that colored relations between Franciscans and Dominicans, and thus offered a safe complement to the cortege of a patron of either order.

T A B L E 3.2: Participation in Funeral Processions by Friars of the Carmine, 1350–1380 (Top Fifteen Churches)

Church	Quarter[a]	1350	1354	1358	1362	1366	1369	1370	1372	1374	1378	1380	Total
Santo Spirito	SS	2	3	14	16	6	17	13	12	23	11	1	118
San Frediano	SS	6	7	9	12	5	14	4	7	28	6	14	112
Santa Croce	SC	4	6	14	9	4	11	13	9	15	9	12	106
San Felice in Piazza	SS	7	3	4	9	5	4	7	13	24	7	15	98
Santa Maria Novella	SMN	3	9	11	16	4	5	10	4	13	6	10	91
Santa Felicità	SS	1	4	6	6	6	7	4	6	29	6	3	78
Santa Maria Verzaia	SS	1	2	3	7	3	8	5	8	18	9	5	69
Santa Trinità	SMN	3	3	7	2	0	7	4	9	9	7	13	64
San Pier Gattolino	SS	2	3	2	2	2	5	3	2	20	2	7	50
San Jacopo sopr'Arno	SS	0	1	5	4	0	0	2	1	16	2	3	34
San Pancrazio	SMN	1	0	3	1	2	3	2	7	6	2	4	31
Ognissanti	SMN	0	1	0	3	1	3	2	1	8	2	3	24
Santa Maria del Fiore	SG	2	3	2	4	2	2	2	2	1	0	3	23
San Pier Maggiore	SG	0	1	2	1	0	2	2	4	2	1	5	20
San Pier Scheraggio	SC	0	1	0	2	1	0	3	5	1	2	0	15
Subtotal		32	47	82	94	41	88	76	90	213	72	98	933
Total for all churches		37	56	101	118	46	98	92	112	237	92	149	1,138

Source: Conv. Sopp. 113. vol. 81.
[a]SS, Santo Spirito; SC, Santa Croce; SMN, Santa Maria Novella; SG, San Giovanni.

The urban map sketched by tomb sites and processional activity resembles a city of "fitted villages," to borrow a term from modern urban planning, in which neighborhood clusters interlocked to form a larger whole. These neighborhood enclaves set the limited spatial parameters that defined the final ritual experience of most Florentines in the late Trecento and the early Quattrocento. Just as marriage patterns of popolani show a pronounced parish endogamy in the late fourteenth century, so too do burial patterns reveal the parish and its extended neighborhood as the primary geographical arena for association, burial patronage, and ritual exchange. Despite enormous differences in wealth and political power, patricians and popolani in the late Trecento shared a similar parochialism as they pursued their respective paths to an honorable burial.

CHAPTER 4

CIVIC IDEALS AND CLASSICISM

IN THE EARLY QUATTROCENTO

n the first half of the fifteenth century, Florence experienced a number of profound changes in politics, society, and culture which in turn made an impressive mark on death rites. One of the most fundamental changes in the Florentine social and political landscape between 1382 and 1434 was the shift from corporate to elitist regimes and relationships.[1] The early Quattrocento saw the emergence of a more narrowly defined oligarchy and the beginning of Medici domination after Cosimo's return from exile in 1434. These were sweeping changes in "politics," which must be understood not only in the narrow sense of a specific regime and its particular exercise of authority, but also in the broader sense of multiple relations of power and control seen in daily life.

These same decades also witnessed the advent of the humanist revolution in culture, which transformed art, learning, and civic ideology. As early as 1400, civic humanists such as Salutati and later Bruni and Marsuppini used classical models, examples, and rhetoric to articulate civic pride, offer new justifications for civic policies, and promote the place of Florence in an expanding political arena. The newfound enthusiasm for antiquity in the first half of the Quattrocento, guided by the "theory of magnificence," helped transform the urban face of Florence through various buildings, monuments, and decorations done in the new "Renaissance" style. By mid-century, Florence enjoyed a burgeoning international reputation for cultural creativity and leadership.

Funerals, mourning, and rites of remembrance expressed and enhanced many of these important changes. Humanism played a major role in the transformation of customary practice by establishing new funerary conventions, such as Latin funeral orations, that challenged an older chivalric model as the dominant way to express power and authority. Humanists also advocated new models of conduct in mourning which stressed decorum and personal control in contrast to more visible displays of grief. Changes in civic politics were communicated in funerals for statesmen and leaders of the regime, which not only promoted civic ideals but also emphasized the increasingly paternalistic and patriarchal nature of state and society after 1400.

The first three decades of the Quattrocento saw a diversification in style and practice which meant that Florentines no longer enjoyed a standard set of death rites as their common cultural property. Instead, death rites introduced new distinctions and oppositions between social groups and between genders. The net result of these changes in ritual was to affirm and deepen the cleavages dividing oligarchs and lesser citizens, women and men, the lettered and the unlettered. The first third of the fifteenth century represented a critical passage from a relatively mobile society to a more elitist, stratified one, a passage that was enacted and dramatized in death rites.

This chapter examines the complex ways in which funerary conventions and practices were bound up with the changing social, political, and sexual order of early fifteenth-century Florence. It attempts to interweave developments in civic ritual with changes in the funerary styles and practices of merchants, bankers, officeholders, intellectuals, and their kinswomen, since public and familial rites not only sprang from the same context but informed each other. Although the focus here falls on the powerful and well-born, the consequences and transformative effects of these changes in politics and ritual radiated out into the social body at large.

Coluccio Salutati: Chancellor as Poet and Hero

The striking changes in death rites described above were by no means predictable from a demographic standpoint. The century began with the outbreak of a major plague epidemic in 1400, which killed at least twelve thousand people out of an urban population of about sixty thousand.[2] The effects of the city's fifth plague since the Black Death were felt among public officials and private citizens alike. Between April and the end of June, the commune paid out over one thousand florins to subsidize funeral trappings for civic officials who succumbed to plague.[3] Despite the plague's ferocity, the communal government sponsored no new public health measures to deal with the epidemic, but simply retained those sumptuary regulations set in 1383 which limited public gatherings.[4] Unfortunately this episode was only the first in a series of recurrent plagues that kept population levels low throughout the first half of the fifteenth century. Plague visited the city again in 1411, 1417, 1424, and 1430, causing ongoing demographic problems that spurred the communal government to encourage reproduction through a variety of administrative policies.[5]

Given the high mortality, it is not surprising that civic and private funerals departed little from established convention during this episode. One of the more notable plague victims of 1400 was the war captain Messer Brogliole (dubbed "the most valiant man of arms in all Italy" by an anonymous chronicler), whose loyalty to the commune earned him an expensive state funeral after his death at Empoli on July 15. Brogliole's body was brought back to Florence for burial in the cathedral at the city's expense. The costly tribute, which featured standard trappings, numerous retainers, and large quantities of wax, was designed not only to honor the man but also "to give an example to others to serve the Florentines."[6] However didactic its intent, Brogliole's funeral stood firmly in the chivalric funeral tradition, as did the magnificent ceremonies for Guccio da Casale, the *signore* of Cortona, who died in Florence during the last days of plague in October 1400.[7]

Wealthy citizens, who had already begun to flee the city for uninfected rural areas during outbreaks of the disease, also relied on earlier patterns and practices. Despite having fled to the countryside, the merchant Valorino Ciurianni lost two teenaged daughters, a twenty-year-old manservant, and an emancipated female slave in August 1400. Although their funerals understandably were hasty affairs, the burial sites for these household members nevertheless mapped out important social distinctions. Ciurianni buried his daughters in the local church in a privileged site near the altar, while his servant Ciufetto and his slave Maria, of whom he wrote fondly, were buried outside the church.[8] In keeping with tradition, affluent Florentines continued to retrieve kin who had died outside the city for burial in family enclaves. In April 1401 the Alessandri celebrated the return of three relatives brought back for burial in San Pier Maggiore. Several fellow parishioners followed a similar course the same month:

kinsmen of Inghilese Inghilesi retrieved his body along with that of his son Antonio, while Messer Forese Salviati arranged to have his daughter-in-law's body returned from Bologna.[9]

Although plague surely colored Florentine social structures and conditions over the long term, it is not an episode of plague but rather a single political event that we must consider the direct source of some of the new conventions that transformed Florentine funerary practice. This landmark event was the funeral of Coluccio Salutati, who held the position of Florentine chancellor from April 19, 1375, until his death on May 4, 1406. During his three decades in office, Salutati firmly established the prestige of the chancellorship. He helped guide the commune through the city's fight with the papacy in 1375–78, and through the turmoil of the Ciompi revolt in 1378. Under his chancellorship Florence emerged from a protracted series of wars with the Milanese tyrant Giangaleazzo Visconti, dating from the 1390s to 1402, wars that, according to Hans Baron, signaled a decisive turning point in Florentine civic ideology and republican identity.[10] Together with his friend and fellow notary in the chancery Ser Viviano Viviani, Salutati set high ethical and intellectual standards for professional conduct which contrasted sharply with the reputation for greed by which his predecessor, Ser Niccolò Monachi, had been known.[11]

Salutati also fostered the fledging humanist movement, which was to enjoy such great success in later years. As Ronald Witt has recently shown, Salutati's philosophical and political thought was characterized by conflict over the relative value of ancient wisdom and Christian truth, of imperial authority and republican ideals. Yet he was among the first to give a theoretical statement of the Florentine republican tradition implicit in the works of chroniclers and poets who preceded him.[12] Taken together, Salutati's personal and political contributions rightfully earned him a revered place in civic government and communal memory.

When Salutati died on May 4, 1406, his obsequies provided an occasion to bring his personal achievements into focus, as well as to define large communal ideals. Having recently emerged from the costly Visconti wars that had burdened the city for more than a decade, the commune had good reason to celebrate. Yet Salutati's personal and professional career posed certain problems to those who wanted to devise a fitting public tribute. He had been an exemplar of a new breed of civil servant—a professional administrator, notary, and statesman, rather than a soldier or war captain like the heroic Hawkwood. Moreover, his political biography did not conform to those Florentine patterns of officeholding which usually resulted in high corporate homage at death. Even as a public servant, Salutati—unlike his friend, colleague, and successor as chancellor, Benedetto Fortini—had never ascended the *cursus honorum*.[13] Rather, Salutati had been associated exclusively with the chancellorship throughout his long governmental service.

The problem lay not only with Salutati's personal career, however, but also with the nature of the chancellor's office itself. Through his public letters Salutati had given ideological voice to the decisions of communal magistrates, who frequently sought his advice in matters of foreign policy. However, unlike the priorate he served, his office carried no formal decision-making power.[14] Although Salutati's importance as chancellor was unmistakable, even to his enemies, there were few precedents in the ritual repertoire as to how that office should be represented and honored. Salutati's immediate predecessor, Ser Niccolò Monachi, had replaced his own father after the latter's death in 1348, and Salutati in turn had replaced Monachi as chancellor while Monachi was still living.[15] If Salutati's funeral provided an opportunity to represent communal ideals in transition, the precise symbolic form by which to express those ideals had yet to be determined. The commune was thus in the difficult but enviable position of inventing a tradition for the occasion.

The solemn funeral services that successfully overcame these difficulties marked a key moment in the development of Florentine funeral rites and civic ritual.[16] Salutati's funeral added an important new strand to the richly textured fabric of Florentine ceremonial life, which included processions, jousts, festivals, public executions, and military parades. This event came to serve as a standard reference point for the burials of Florentine chancellors throughout the fifteenth century. Staged on May 5, 1406, the day after his death, Salutati's rites inflated the public image of the office of chancellor and inducted Salutati into the pantheon of Florentine civic heroes. The ceremony's heroic and patriotic overtones were reinforced by Salutati's being granted the privilege of a cathedral burial, despite the fact that the chancellor had already prepared a tomb for himself in San Romolo, his neighborhood church.[17]

Given its importance in the development of Florentine civic ritual, Salutati's funeral is worth considering in some detail. This event was not yet a full-blown classicizing ceremony, as the funeral of Salutati's successor Bruni would be, nor did it signal the demise of the chivalric forms so magnificently portrayed in Hawkwood's funeral twelve years earlier. Rather, Salutati's funeral represented a crossroads in both style and ritual practice, blending symbolic conventions and religious elements with marks of an emergent civic humanism. In this sense, his funeral proceedings followed the uneven contours of his own intellectual biography and the changing historical landscape of the world around him. Unfortunately we do not know the identity of the individuals or public committee responsible for the ceremonial program, as we do for Carlo Marsuppini's rites in 1453.[18] Salutati's illness earlier in the year may have prompted those in government circles to consider the eventuality of his death. That the event was staged only a day after Salutati's death, whereas three days had been required to prepare Hawkwood's ceremonies, suggests some fore-thought.

Salutati's funeral aimed at a delicate balance of public and private interests that would represent both self and state. The city's cor-poratism and republican framework precluded the kind of state fu-nerary spectacles devised for rulers such as the Venetian doge, which focused extraordinary attention on a single functionary. Hence the honors paid to the chancellor reflected in somewhat divided fashion on commune and kin. The ceremonies, for instance, were set in the Piazza de' Peruzzi, in front of Salutati's house, as was customary with private citizens, rather than in the urban nerve center, the Piazza della Signoria, where Hawkwood's funeral had been held. The re-ligious facet of the rite was also temporally split off from the civic celebration. In the morning, the Dominican friar Giovanni Dominici preached a sermon in the Piazza de' Peruzzi praising Salutati's "great accomplishments," including his authorship of ten books.[19] Stylist-ically, the ceremonies depended to some extent on older conventions of pomp and magnificence, although the 250 florins spent for Sal-utati's funeral was appreciably less than the 410 florins subsidizing Hawkwood's spectacle or the 600 florins allocated by the commune to knight Jacopo Salviati in October 1404.[20] The procession following later that afternoon also included such characteristic symbols of cor-porate homage as the standard of the Popolo; the banners of the wool guild, the guild of judges and notaries, and Salutati's native commune of Buggiano; and splendid candles purchased at communal expense.[21] But chroniclers tellingly omitted mention of a draped horse in the cortege and fur-trimmed velvets paid for by the commune.[22]

Salutati's distinctive contribution to politics and urban affairs was captured and framed by two innovations that ultimately revolutionized Florentine burial practices: his coronation as poet laureate, and a Latin funeral oration. These features were unprecedented in Florentine funeral rites prior to Salutati's burial. Unlike the material splendor that celebrated Hawkwood's triumphs, these new gestures celebrated Salutati's deeds of the pen as chancellor and statesman, and recognized his powerful feats of letters, acknowledged even by the rival Visconti. In other words, these innovations valorized a new type of civic *gestae*: namely, the political contribution Salutati had made through language. It was by means of these twin innovations that Salutati's funeral helped give ceremonial birth to the "myth of Florence" as a republic of letters. With the introduction of coronation and oration came the beginnings of a civic funerary theater emphasizing dramatic performance over processional pomp and activity.

In front of an assembled crowd of important magistrates, knights, physicians, and the populace, Salutati "was crowned with laurel as a poet by the hand of Ser Viviano di Neri Viviani," his close friend and colleague.[23] Such a posthumous honor no doubt would have pleased Salutati, who defended poetry as the pinnacle of wisdom and a genre possessed of high ethical value. The chancellor's personal reputation as both Latin and vernacular poet had been established as early as 1382.[24] The commune reportedly had petitioned the emperor several years before Salutati's death for the right to bestow the poet's crown, which was an imperial prerogative.[25] That the laureation stood out as the key tribute to Salutati, and the defining act of the funeral, is documented by the numerous references made to the laureation in assorted epitaphs and epigrams honoring Salutati and in various contemporary accounts, and by the communal decree "that from this moment on Messer Coluccio was to be called 'poet.' "[26] Moreover, Salutati's corpse was dressed "like a poet" rather than in chivalric or other garb. The coronation figured regularly into later praise of Salutati, such as Manetti's life of this humanist pioneer written circa 1439. It was also commemorated by a bronze medal cast about 1460 picturing a crowned Salutati on one side, with the motto "Ex decreto publico" surrounding a laurel wreath on the reverse. Cast in a context of greater humanist sophistication, this commemorative medallion was a lasting reminder that "words were fleeting, but coins remained" ("verba volant, nomismata manent"), an important precept governing imperial ceremonies in late antiquity.[27]

On one level, the posthumous crowning of Salutati as poet marks the introduction of classicism which opened new possibilities for cultural creativity in Florentine ritual as well as in learning. This distinctive gesture elevated Salutati to the status of the ancient Roman poets, whose tradition of Capitoline contests for a leafed crown was known but imperfectly understood by Trecento writers.[28] There had been several revivals of this antique practice in the fourteenth century. Alberto Mussato had received a laurel crown at Padua in 1315 in what was part of an academic ceremony; Dante had refused an offer of coronation from Bologna during his lifetime since, as he related in *Paradiso* (25.1–9), he longed for coronation in his native city of Florence instead. According to the late Trecento poet Antonio Pucci, Dante finally received the poet's crown posthumously at his funeral in September 1321.[29] In the succeeding generation, the more classically knowledgeable Petrarch fulfilled his fervent wish for the laurel prize in Rome on April 8, 1341, while a coronation figured into the ceremony dubbing Cola di Rienzo tribune on August 15, 1347.[30] Unlike Salutati's coronation, however, the tributes paid to Mussato, Petrarch, and Rienzo were neither bestowed posthumously nor associated with funeral rites.

The classicism of Salutati's poetic coronation not only honored the man reverently referred to as "father" by Poggio Bracciolini and Pier Paolo Vergerio but promoted and valorized the interests of the whole humanist enterprise as well.[31] Hence its enthusiastic reception within the fledgling humanist community should not be surprising. Bruni had earlier acknowledged Salutati's right to such esteem in his *Dialogues for Pier Paolo Vergerio* (1401), in which the fictionalized Niccolò Niccoli praised Salutati's unique ability to overcome the limitations of his somewhat barbarous times.[32] Aware of the antique origins and symbolism of the laureation, Salutati's disciples abroad were eager for details of the event. "I hear that he was given a splendid funeral," Poggio wrote to Niccoli from Rome on May 15, "and I want you to tell me all about the ceremony [*apparatus*] and its magnificence."[33]

Although humanism would soon flourish throughout the Italian peninsula, the success of men such as Bruni, Niccoli, and Roberto de' Rossi was by no means a foregone conclusion at the time of Salutati's death. For humanists who repeatedly referred to the laureation in their epigrams, epitaphs, and letters, the prize of laurel set apart their new interests and values from contemporary culture; at the same time, the laureation offered a way to instruct a civic audience largely unfamiliar with humanist learning in the power of classical forms.

For all its newness, however, Salutati's laureation signaled neither a classical purism nor a break with the immediate Florentine past. Like other symbols, the laurel crown was a multivalent image combining divergent, often paradoxical meanings. Salutati's funeral program was developed by a regime of mixed interests and constituencies still on the brink of a classicizing breakthrough, and the funeral's unifying theme and justification was overwhelmingly civic.[34] Contemporary descriptions emphasize the civic pride and sense of unity permeating the event, which must have contrasted rather sharply with, and helped to gloss over, the fragmented loyalties and divisive practices of daily life.

It is in this context of civic pride and nascent humanism that the coronation should be read. While the laurel crown clearly revived the glory of ancient Rome, it was also as deeply entwined with the history and the budding myth of Florence. The coronation not only presented Salutati as the equal of the ancients but also claimed him as another "crown" of Florentine letters, in company with the famous Trecento triumvirate of Dante, Petrarch, and Boccaccio. The laurel crown bound Salutati to a distinctively Florentine literary heritage, which he himself had promoted by writing epigrams honoring the five "Florentine" poets for the Palazzo Vecchio, and by supervising the erection of marble monuments in the cathedral to such native sons as Dante and Boccaccio.[35]

But Salutati's coronation went beyond simply making allusions to this common badge of honor: it was Salutati, rather than Dante or Petrarch, who actually brought the crown home to Florence. In a life characterized by wanderings, Petrarch had claimed his laurel wreath amid the Roman ruins, while this honor fell to Dante only in exile from his native land. Through Salutati, Florence succeeded in capturing a ceremonial prize that had thus far eluded the city. With the poet's crown finally in hand, Florence could rightfully claim its place as a republic of letters in both history and contemporary affairs.

The coronation also drew upon other strands of contemporary culture to achieve and communicate a sense of civic unity and pride. Given Giannozzo Manetti's lengthy explanation of the laureation's classical meaning when crowning Leonardo Bruni in 1444, it seems unlikely that the mixed audience of merchants and popolani present at Salutati's funeral was fully aware of the ceremony's antique origins.[36] The laureation's resonance with the ceremony of knighthood was particularly strong, which may have enhanced the event's reportedly positive reception among the unlettered. For example, the investiture rites for communal knights included a crowning with laurel and a brief oration, in addition to the vestment with sword and spurs. Florentines had been reminded of the form taken by such knightly spectacles as recently as eighteen months before Salutati's death, when Jacopo Salviati had been knighted in a lavish ceremony in October 1404 for his valor against foreign rebels.[37] Given Salutati's defense of republican liberties, the suggestion that the chancellor was being knighted posthumously, while resting on his bier, might have seemed quite appropriate. In any case, the gesture would not have been totally foreign to Florentine experience, since the 1322 statutes of the Captain of the People specifically prohibited such a funerary practice, which probably continued into the later Trecento despite its prohibition.[38] The coronation also shared common ground with numerous other festivals of greater public familiarity, such as jousts and processional entries, at which Florentines customarily sported garlands of olive and other leaves.

In view of these complex inferences, it is probably more useful to view Salutati's coronation as an appropriation and expansion of traditional concepts and symbols, similar to the ideological expansion of Guelfism, rather than as a purely humanist innovation.[39] Salutati's laureation, and the oration that followed, established a significant ceremonial connection with an older communal ideology of chivalry, while transforming it into a new civic and humanist program. Like civic humanism itself, the laureation struck a decidedly patriotic note that harmonized vernacular culture, civic pride, and humanist ideas. In the fusion of a multifaceted symbol with a familiar act, Salutati could be simultaneously portrayed as a poetic equal of the ancients, the newest star in the Florentine literary heavens, and (in his role as communal knight) as a champion of republican liberties. By tapping and combining these various traditions and values in an important moment of historical transition, the coronation transformed Salutati into a complex representation of the commune itself.

Salutati's obsequies were also the first in a series of Florentine public funerals to combine rhetoric with ritual activities. After crowning Salutati, Ser Viviani proceeded to formally eulogize the dead chancellor. In front of a mixed audience nestled in the Piazza de' Peruzzi, Viviani praised his former colleague as "an outstanding man of great learning, wise in practical things, of the best nature, upright and God-fearing."[40] The funeral oration should be distinguished here from the funeral sermon, which was usually a thematic exposition on a scriptural verse, and from several other literary genres associated with mourning, such as the consolatory letter (a private document exchanged between individuals) and literary or poetic expressions of grief (for example, Petrarch's laments for Laura).[41] Funeral orations represent part of the self-conscious return to classical models and sources among Renaissance humanists, who were aware that the Romans had publicly eulogized their dead through *laudationes funebres*. Because we lack the actual text of the oration, it is not clear whether Viviani's speech reflected the growing interest in classical rhetoric or conformed more closely to the rules of scholastic discourse.

Nevertheless, the delivery of the eulogy was itself significant. As humanism developed in Florence, civic ritual would increasingly involve citizens and magistrates as listeners in the kind of funerary theater first introduced at Salutati's rites. But the audience addressed by Viviano's remarks extended well beyond the city walls. While the laurel crown located Salutati in a long line of ancient worthies and native sons, the oration thrust him onto the stage of contemporary Italian politics, on a par with some of the most powerful political figures of his age. Even in these early years of humanism, public funeral oratory was rapidly becoming an idiom by which to express political rule and leadership roles. Pier Paolo Vergerio had first revived the ancient practice of verbal tribute to commemorate the transfer of the corpse of Francesco da Carrara to Padua in 1393, and a public oration had figured into the 1402 obsequies for Salutati's great Milanese adversary Giangaleazzo Visconti.[42] Given the growing prestige and political importance attached to artful speaking, the oration for Salutati helped Florentines to display their political and cultural self-awareness to neighboring Italian city-states.

Salutati's rites also introduced the beginnings of what might be called a new tenor in public funerary proceedings. In their descriptions of the event, contemporaries repeatedly stressed the solemnity and dignity of the affair. The chronicler Corazza, for example, noted that the laureation had been conducted "with the greatest dignity," while the procession had commingled "great pomp and solemnity."[43] These descriptions emphasized a growing sense of public decorum, especially in regard to mourning practices, as the city created a new image of itself to add to its already rich ceremonial tapestry. Chroniclers make no mention of the public lamentations characteristic of late Trecento public funerals, such as the "great lament and cries" marking the demise of Pier Farnese in 1363, or the ritual laments for John Hawkwood, who had been "bewailed by women in the presence of the entire populace of Florence" in 1394.[44] Although it is difficult to assign precise reasons for this silence or shift of focus, there are nevertheless clear indications in these and other accounts that a new sensibility was slowly being forged in the early years of the fifteenth century. This is not to argue that Salutati's funeral prompted a radical or widespread shift in customary behavior. Rather, what the observations of chroniclers indicate is that humanists and their admirers were developing a new "art" of mourning which stood apart from, and contrasted sharply with, traditional Mediterranean mourning practices.

Salutati himself had helped to create this new humanist art of mourning. His behavior as chancellor offered important prescriptive examples of proper funerary comportment, in which the demands of state placed limits on the grief expressed by public officers. When death struck Salutati's house in 1396, taking his "most beloved wife" Piera after a two-week illness, the chancellor gave eloquent testimony to a lifetime of reflection about what constituted appropriate public behavior. At Piera's funeral on March 1, 1396, Salutati maintained a proud show of control, despite his struggle "with the greatest grief," which sorely tested his mental and physical powers. Salutati demonstrated his self-discipline and fortitude even further by leaving the funeral early to attend the induction ceremonies of the new priors, as his duties required.[45] The four letters describing Piera's death and his feelings of deep loss make clear that Salutati was neither unfeeling nor unaware of the example he set as a communal official. Several years before, Salutati had chastised the notary Ser Andrea da Volterra for the latter's protracted mourning of his wife and children. Now Salutati was both pleased and relieved that he was able to sufficiently master his feelings at Piera's death.[46]

The point was not lost either on his colleagues or on later humanists. Francesco Zabarella praised his friend Salutati's composure and firm resolve in an exchange of letters in 1400–1401, shortly after Salutati faced the even harsher blow of his son's death.[47] The chancellor's equanimity when confronted with these profound losses earned him still further praise from Giannozzo Manetti, who eulogized the chancellor thirty years after his death for his remarkable constancy.[48]

As Salutati's behavior suggests, the culture of humanism introduced new models of mourning which contrasted sharply with such customary expressions of grief as wailing, tearing one's hair and cheeks, and rending garments. Petrarch had already begun to censure these unseemly practices, which offended the sense of decorum that went hand in hand with his revival of Ciceronian rhetoric. "Order that wailing women should not be permitted to step outside their homes," Petrarch advised Francesco da Carrara in a 1373 letter. "If some lamentation is necessary to the grieved," he continued, "let them do it at home and do not let them disturb the public thoroughfares."[49] Although Petrarch did not deny the power of grief, or even the need for its release, he sought to privatize its customary expressions and to relocate mourning from a public to a domestic setting.

In the two generations after Petrarch, humanists introduced new modes of exploring and expressing grief which substituted an internal discourse for a public one. Rather than grieving openly using ritualized gestures, Petrarch, Salutati, and later Bruni and Manetti stressed the desirability of maintaining outward decorum at funerals; at the same time, they internalized grief, which would be slowly assuaged by the consolations of philosophy and religion. This new humanist art of mourning thus had a twofold meaning for the history of ritual and emotion. On the one hand, humanists explored new psychological territory through their consolatory writings, which allowed them to justify an emotional response to loss rather than to repress it. In his exchange of letters with Francesco Zabarella after the death of Piero, Salutati's beloved son, Salutati himself argued for the validity of sorrow against harsh Stoic injunctions to maintain one's tranquility at all costs. Upon hearing of his mentor's death, Poggio paid his respects to the dead Salutati "with many tears and with heartfelt grief," as he wrote to his friend Niccoli.[50] Grief was increasingly acknowledged as a legitimate feature of the psychological landscape, and its articulation flourished in the genre of consolatory literature.

Yet for all the salutary effects of tears recognized by Salutati and later humanists, the catharsis of mourning was private, internal, and predominantly intellectual: grief was resolved primarily in the privacy of one's study through reflection and literary exchange. Hence while humanists explored the private reaches of grief as a subjective experience, at the same time they sought to limit its public expressions in gesture, action, and clothing. Emotional outbursts were increasingly viewed as unacceptable, especially for men active in public life. For early Florentine humanists, it was the control of private lives that made a public image, lessons of the body that instructed the body politic. Vespasiano da Bisticci praised Palla Strozzi's reaction to the death of his dearest son Bartolomeo, for example, remarking how Palla resolutely put his grief behind him; for "being a wise man, [Palla] saw that he needs must fight against his natural grief and show that he was indeed the man the Florentines deemed him to be." For Leonardo Bruni, "grief should be reserved for those who, when they die, leave nothing that could console their survivors." Hence its open expression was an inappropriate gesture when the deceased had lived his life well through public activities.[51]

These new limits of grief found their way into official communal policy in the generation after Salutati. The acts of moral stamina first exemplified by Salutati as chancellor became part of the requirements of office in Bruni's chancery reforms of May 1436, which denied signs of public mourning to members of the Signoria, principal communal officials, and their notaries, on pain of a 300-lire fine. For Bruni, the moral authority and dignity of public officers, who simultaneously guided the polity, acted as model citizens, and represented the state, required them to put away outward displays of grief. Abiding by these reforms, Bruni's successor in the chancery, Carlo Marsuppini, petitioned for special permission to don modified mourning garb for one day to mark his father's death in February 1445.[52]

These new models of public behavior introduced deep cleavages between the disciplined actions of learned men, on the one hand, and the customary, "disorderly" behavior of women, on the other. Paradoxically, at the same time humanists denied themselves this traditional emotional outlet, they still anticipated that women, especially their female kin, would honor the dead in the usual ways, although preferably at home rather than in the streets. Hence humanists such as Salutati, Bruni, Manetti, and Marsuppini not only distinguished themselves from women and the untrained masses by their controlled public behavior; they also made the customary work of mourning a gendered task. It was women, not men of power and prestige, who performed laments, self-mutilating gestures, and other physical expressions of grief. Bruni was especially aware of how this controlled demeanor at important public events both groomed future intellectuals and officeholders for the appropriate exercise of political power and offered them new definitions of manhood.

Given that the whole matrix of cultural meanings and political relationships was changing in the early Quattrocento, the evolution of new humanist mourning practices should also be seen in relation to the broader discourse about gender roles and relations. This is a large and important area of inquiry which can only be touched on here. Still, it is useful to note how demographic problems and changing social relations prompted Florentine magistrates in the early fifteenth century to try to establish a right order in gender relations that would more securely identify women's and men's respective places in family and society. Humanist strictures on mourning evolved out of this context and addressed similar concerns about appropriate and normative gender behaviors. Between 1403 and 1432, the commune made repeated and wide-ranging efforts to regulate sexuality and to strengthen the institutions of marriage and the family. The licensing of prostitution in 1403 formed part of an attempt to turn men from the "unmentionable vice," homosexuality, for which the city was famous; and proposals to bar unmarried men from office surfaced repeatedly in council debates. Between 1421 and 1432, the commune further regulated the sexual economy by establishing commissions to supervise the purity of nunneries and to control homosexuality, in addition to founding a communal dowry fund that enabled poor girls to marry.[53] The moral authority of these programs and policies was enhanced by preachers such as San Bernardino, who argued for greater adherence to normative distinctions in dress and behaviors among both sexes.[54] Humanist decorum in mourning formed part of a larger ensemble of admonitions, ideals, and policies that assigned specific behaviors to women and men to better meet communal needs.

From Knights to Statesmen

In the two decades following Salutati's death, funerals staged for men of the Florentine elite contributed to the processes of elitism, statism, and civism that transformed Florentine political and social relations between 1382 and 1434.[55] The gradual and uneven shift from corporate to elitist politics had already begun to concentrate officeholding in fewer, more experienced hands by the late 1390s. Simultaneous with this political contraction was the commune's growing administrative need—stimulated by territorial expansion and bureaucratic consolidation—for competent officials.[56] The net result of these developments was to create a regime monopolized by an elite group of experienced statesmen, politicians, and officehold-ers who guided the state.[57] Voicing an elitist point of view, Rinaldo degli Albizzi eloquently told a meeting of seventy important men gathered in Santo Stefano in August 1426 that his audience not only counseled the commune: they *were* the commune.[58] The first two decades of the fifteenth century also saw an intense political fac-tionalism that pitted aristocrats against artisans, as well as a matur-ation of civic consciousness stimulated by repeated warfare and by the articulation of civic ideology by humanists such as Leonardo Bruni, who served briefly as chancellor in 1411.[59]

The emergence of a political oligarchy was supported in the social world by changing habits of consumption. While the precise state of the Florentine economy in the early Quattrocento remains a matter of considerable debate, what seems clear is that affluent Florentines became more willing and even eager to spend their wealth in new ways, despite the burdens of taxation and economic crisis.[60] Accom-panying the development of the state under oligarchical auspices was a greater investment in a wide variety of outlets for status and display, such as sumptuous clothing, and art patronage. There was a new interest in building family palaces and, in the 1420s, a resurgence of interest in monumental tombs.[61] The demands of dowry, whose long inflationary spiral began to accelerate in the early fifteenth century, consumed ever larger portions of the resources of the elite, while the burdens of dowry on lesser citizens were recognized by the creation of the communal dowry fund (*Monte delle doti*) in 1425.[62]

Some of these new attitudes toward wealth and spending can be discerned in the changing sumptuary strategies of Florentine lawmakers in the early Quattrocento. Legislation dealing with the stubborn matter of women's finery showed an increased willingness to accommodate shifting standards of consumption. Although lawmakers did not abandon their customary crusade against the perceived extravagance of women's dress, they nevertheless took a new, more flexible approach to sumptuary legislation in the 1420s and 1430s, seeking a happy medium between ostentation and moderation. Casting about—via numerous redactions—for the perfectly balanced law, lawmakers in these decades formally accepted the desirability of display to a greater extent than had their forebears.[63]

Legislators also tried to reshape sumptuary laws governing funerals into an instrument of political as well as social policy. While the 1415 statutes left Trecento consumption limits and licensing loopholes intact, they nevertheless included a new measure designed to put some teeth into legislative enforcement. The statutes stipulated for the first time that anyone burdened by an unpaid funeral fine could not be elected to, assume, or exercise any communal office.[64] In making this adjustment, lawmakers recognized an increasingly obvious equation between a political class of officeholders and a social elite.

These concurrent changes dramatically altered funerary conventions between 1410 and 1440. In these decades funeral rites showed a number of interrelated developments: the placement of funeral pomp, still conspicuous, within a larger set of family-centered sumptuary strategies among the uppermost elite; a corresponding lessening of pomp among the middling classes, who were unable to keep pace with rising consumption; a more pronounced emphasis on civic rather than on knightly imagery in honoring the political record of statesmen; the use of mortuary occasions as a locus for the assertion and transfer of political authority; and the introduction of humanist innovations that reinforced many of these other developments. Together these trends describe death rites put to new political and ideological uses, and reflecting the growing social distance between elite and populace.

For the most part, however, these changes were accomplished less by the kind of striking innovations marking Salutati's rites than by subtle shifts of balance. There were still important continuities in the use of conventional trappings such as wax, family devices, silks, mourning clothes, clerics, and on occasion caparisoned horses for those who actually held the title of knight, such as Cristoforo Spini and Rinaldo Gianfigliazzi. Moreover, in the early Quattrocento the charms of chivalry continued to hold sway among upper-class Florentines, both young and old, in jousts, pageants, tournaments, and other quintessentially noble sports unrelated to death rites.[65] The returning plagues of 1411 and 1417 served as external checks on funeral pomp, while individual Florentines continued to heed the message of religious austerity forcefully brought home by San Bernardino's fiery Lenten sermons of 1424 and 1425. Within this customary context, however, early Quattrocento death rites posed an impressive set of alternatives to the use of the chivalric code as a way to invoke wealth, power, and authority.[66]

We can begin this analysis of funerary trends in the early Quattrocento by establishing an economic perspective on burial costs, at least for the small number of families who controlled so much of the city's wealth. Dominating the high end of the cost spectrum were the burials of adult patrician men, whose funeral costs, exclusive of tombs and commemorative programs, generally ranged from 300 to 700 florins during the 1410s and 1420s. Niccolò da Uzzano, a wealthy banker who was one of the most eminent political figures of his day, spent 639 florins to bury his brother Agnolo in 1424; the estate of Gherardo Barbadori, a childless patrician, paid about 223 florins for cloth trappings alone in 1429; Francesco Tornabuoni cited in his 1432 petition for tax relief the sum of 1,056 florins recently spent on the funerals of his kinsmen Niccolò and Simone.[67] In 1429 Cosimo and Lorenzo de' Medici reportedly spent 3,000 florins to bury their father Giovanni, in what was undoubtedly the costliest private funeral of the decade.[68] These sums do not appear to be consistently greater than those spent in the late Trecento, and in some cases may even have reflected a slight downturn in expenditures.[69]

Rather than identifying changes in raw costs, however, it is more useful to place these sums within a linked set of economic decisions and relationships that determined the totality of sumptuary expenditures. Florentine lawmakers themselves underscored how consumption patterns interlocked when they complained in new sumptuary provisions of 1433, prefaced by a biting, misogynist preamble, that the extravagance of women's clothing diverted necessary funds from dowries, thereby damaging an already weakened marriage market.[70] The expansion of other cultural investments among the rich gave their funerals a new place both in mortuary rites and in a general cluster of social strategies. While funerals for wealthy, influential men such as Giovanni de' Medici and Nofri Strozzi retained their importance as compelling spectacles that showed individual and family to best advantage, these events often began to fit into a more permanent and more costly mortuary ensemble. That is, funeral celebrations—which were ephemeral—were not devalued but were placed in a different relationship to more enduring forms of honor and remembrance, which became increasingly necessary complements to the rites themselves. Perhaps as a result of changes in plague demography which favored the rich, households of the elite could turn increased attention to the careful planning and completion of tomb commissions.

Nofri Strozzi (d. 1418) is a good case in point. Grand as his funeral was, with some seven hundred pounds of wax lighting the requiem in Santa Trinità, it was only part of a larger and more expensive monumentalizing scheme that included a new burial chapel, a Renaissance-style tomb from the Ghiberti workshop, and an altarpiece by Lorenzo Monaco.[71] None of this display came cheap; four years after the funeral, Nofri's son Palla, assessed as the richest man in the city in 1427, complained that he was still burdened by his father's funeral expenses, whose magnitude nevertheless paled in comparison to the building costs of the chapel and tomb and his tax levies.[72] Palla's filial tribute was immortalized in Nofri's tomb inscription by intertwining the names of both generations, much as Cosimo and Lorenzo de' Medici were to do several years later in their father's San Lorenzo tomb.

The testament of Agnolo da Uzzano, written in 1422, offers another useful example of how funerals fitted into the new spending habits of the elite, which stressed different dimensions of consumption and commemoration. Working from an estate in which his Monte shares alone were valued at over 10,000 florins, Agnolo allocated 100 florins cash to decorate the main chapel of Santa Lucia dei Magnoli, where his tomb was located, plus another 1,000 florins in Monte shares to endow it. He instructed his heirs to distribute 850 florins in charity to a wide variety of clients, supplement each of his three daughters' dowries with an extra 1,000 florins in Monte shares, and dress his wife and daughters in mourning at his expense. Although Agnolo's funeral in 1424, which cost 639 florins, was no paltry affair, it was only one of several important forms of consumption that made a name for him, his household, and his family.[73] The willingness to spend on tombs and chapels probably increased in the 1430s, when the business and political climate stabilized. In his 1435 testament Messer Giovanni Guicciardini included provisions for a new chapel in Santa Felicità; the Scali family, Palla Strozzi's fellow parishioners in Santa Trinità, embarked on a new decorative project for their family chapel around 1434; while the following year the Ardinghelli increased the endowment for their chapel.[74]

Paralleling these developments was a new stress on the familial dimensions of funerals. Increased numbers of family mourners and their more impressive mourning garb highlighted the place of family in the funerals of established, wealthy men. For his uncle Antonio's burial in 1423, Luca da Panzano bought huge mourning mantles and hoods for himself and his two brothers, each made from 14 braccia of fine cloth, 4 braccia more than was customary. To dress these three men, and two principal women mourners, the Panzano family purchased 104 braccia of high-grade cloth.[75] Early Quattrocento observers such as Pagolo Petriboni were far more interested in the richness of mourning garb than in the way the corpse and bier were outfitted. In describing Giovanni de' Medici's funeral (1429), Petriboni paid scant attention to the dead man's costume and bier trappings, details that had figured prominently in accounts of the burial of Giovanni's kinsman Vieri (1395). What interested Petriboni instead was the show of Medici family strength and wealth conveyed by the participation of Giovanni's sons Cosimo and Lorenzo and twenty-eight other "men and boys of the Medici house."[76] This

Medici-centered spectacle followed the spirit of Bruni's advice in his preface to Aristotle's *Economics*, dedicated to Cosimo in 1420, in which he argued that fathers accumulated wealth to better launch the honor and reputation of their sons.[77]

This consumption focused greater public attention on the patriline, rather than on bilateral kin ties. For Petriboni, the heart of the event was the patriline on parade. Petriboni made no mention of marital relatives or female kin, or of the more incorporative requiem rite that surely pulled these diverse kinship networks together. Leon Battista Alberti's pronouncement that the essence of funeral tributes was found in "the father of a family followed by many of his kinsmen" reveals less a generic concept of honor than one grounded in the observances and prescriptions of early Quattrocento Florence.[78] The willingness of sons to indebt themselves for mourning clothes in preference to other types of pomp indicates both the importance of sumptuous dress and the growing centrality of patrilineal claims in early Quattrocento funerals. In 1426 the sons of the influential states-man Vieri Guadagni saddled themselves with a 300-florin debt for mourning clothes alone, at a time when they could ill afford it.[79]

Men of the professional and middling classes also subscribed to this partilineal family ideal when burying their dead. Caught between the competing claims of honor and insufficient cash flow, the five sons of the notary Ser Luca Franceschi, only one of whom was on a solid economic footing around 1427, banded together to pay the funeral expenses for their father. Each brother indebted himself for an equal part of the 245-florin total cost; the lion's share went for mourning clothes rather than for wax, thereby focusing attention on the brother's filial homage as they went about their daily activities.[80] The sons of another notary, Ser Tommaso Masi, were forced to sell all of their parents' clothing and household goods in order to cover the 140-florin cost of their father's funeral.[81]

Not surprisingly, men and women participated in and benefited from shifting consumption patterns in different ways. As mourners, widows and other women asserted their households' wealth and status by means of rich mourning garb. Their outfits followed a path of steady embellishment consistent with general clothing trends in the Quattrocento, which saw the legally approved length of women's trains grow from one-half braccia in 1415 to triple that figure by 1464.[82] Although the customary dark color of mourning clothes limited creativity, mourning outfits were nevertheless enriched by the value and amount of the material used, the type of lining used, and ornamentation or accessories. The sumptuous mourning gown Martinella Bardi wore for her husband's requiem in 1423 was made of twenty-six braccia of fine cloth, more than double the customary amount, and was further enriched by a fur-lined mantle, a fur hood, and twice the usual number of head veils and kerchiefs. Moreover, her daughter Mea wore similarly rich garb.[83] For some widows, such as Niccolosa Rustichi, the young widow of Niccolò Falconieri who returned to her brother's house in 1417, these lavish new mourning clothes formed the core of an otherwise deteriorating wardrobe, to be used while awaiting a new marriage.[84]

Although wealthy women profited from new spending habits in their role as mourners, they were less fortunate when it came to their own burials. The shift in strategies of consumption which favored greater investment in dress and dowry brought with it a corresponding erosion in women's funeral pomp. Here the evidence of sumptuary exemptions permits a systematic approach. Whereas many husbands, such as Agnolo da Uzzano, bought exemptions to better honor their wives in the late Trecento, there was not a single permit purchased for a woman's funeral in the early Quattrocento.[85] This evidence must be balanced against other, less material tributes paid to women in death, such as the Medici tomb inscription praising both the mother and father of Cosimo and Lorenzo, or assorted consolatory letters, or the tender words uttered in praise of his wife by Giovanni de' Medici on his deathbed.[86] Moreover, some affluent women actively sought simplicity in death, choosing burial in a religious habit, as did Francesco Giovanni's aged aunt Simona (d. 1433). An increase in the number of clergy in attendance probably compensated for a lesser show of wax and of expensive palls in some women's burials, especially during epidemics; Luca da Panzano invited forty-six priests to stand vigil over his mother Mattea in 1440, and he staged an impressive requiem for his beloved wife Lucrezia in 1445.[87] Nevertheless, the absence of women's sumptuary exemptions and the new emphasis on men's mourning garb show the uneven privileging of affluent women, on the one hand, and the overall strengthening of a masculine, patrilineal ethos, on the other.

The uneven channeling of sumptuary resources dramatically widened the gap between the costs of marriage and those of burial. Even in the late Trecento, dowries had overshadowed the amount spent on women's burials. But the dowry inflation already apparent by the 1420s introduced striking new discrepancies between the marriage portions of well-born women and their funeral expenses. Examples from the Ciurianni family illustrate this point, although it must be remembered that trends in individual households were always subject to fluctuations in family fortunes, age at death, and household composition. In 1348 Agnesa di Baldo Balsini married Barna Ciurianni, bringing with her a dowry of 525 florins. When she predeceased her husband in 1362, Barna spent approximately 70 florins on the burial. Barna's son Valorino received a dowry of 550 florins when he married his first wife Tessa; in 1382, when she died in childbirth at age twenty-five, he buried her "with great honor" in their family tomb in Santo Stefano for about 33 florins, and also commissioned an altar cloth in her memory for another 15 florins. But the discrepancy between dowry and burial grew much more apparent in Valorino's second marriage. While Caterina Alberti brought a 1,200-florin dowry in 1385, her burial in 1428 at age sixty-six, also described by Valorino as conducted "with great honor," cost only about 26 florins.[88]

These spending patterns probably intensified the competition for resources within all but the most affluent households, and at least in some cases took a direct toll on the burial pomp of men as well as women. The problems experienced by the heirs of Ugolino Michi were symptomatic of these competing economic relationships, for which the dotal system was partly to blame. Michi had served in a variety of important official capacities, including podestà of Pistoia in 1412, and the demands of officeholding reportedly had caused him to neglect his business. Moreover, Michi's already strained estate had to repay three dowries totaling 2,850 florins after his death in 1414. In view of the circumstances, Michi's mother Giemma, to whom the estate owed one of the dowries, agreed to pay up to 25 florins as her share of the funeral expenses. Although Michi's creditors agreed that his widow Lapa should be outfitted in impressive mourning clothes "so that the burial could be made appropriately, as is necessary," she had to return part of the wardrobe to the estate after the funeral.[89] Unfortunately for Michi, the demands of dowry tempered his funeral pomp by deflecting significant funds away from one form of family ritual to another.

Contributing to the financial strains on middle-class households was a deepening fiscal crisis and weakened business climate that gripped Florence for several years, beginning in 1410, brought on in part by civic unrest and war with Genoa. Following on the heels of this conflict, the decade 1413–23 has been dubbed by Brucker a time of "peace without prosperity." Fiscal problems were exacerbated in the next decade by the disastrous Milanese war, which began in 1423. These problems ultimately precipitated the creation of the Catasto commission four years later.[90] While economic problems were undoubtedly experienced across a broad social spectrum of merchants, bankers, and professionals, the effects of a deteriorating business climate and the extraordinary demands of the Milanese war seem to have hit hardest among the middling and modest classes, which may have declined in both size and wealth in the early Quattrocento.[91]

This economic malaise, coupled with the new sumptuary strategies of the elite, served to widen the gap in funeral pomp between a narrowly restricted elite and the professional and middling classes. Unlike the late Trecento, in which the spiral of consumption pulled in a relatively heterogeneous social group, the early fifteenth century saw lavish funerals restricted to a cluster of the wealthiest households. The total number of sumptuary exemptions sold for funeral display dropped dramatically in the early Quattrocento, despite the fact that the 1415 statutes kept the former licensing procedures virtually intact. Only two exemptions were sold in 1416, in contrast to the record high of seventy-one in 1390.[92] In 1419 the sons of Piero Baroncelli, one of the principal architects of the regime after 1403, paid thirty-five florins for a permit, but it was the only exemption sold that year, as was the permit bought for Agnolo da Uzzano in 1424.[93] With the falling off of display for an aspiring elite, the funerals of a handful of wealthy men stood out with even greater clarity.

The growing distance between the funerals of rich men and those of members of other social groups can be graphically illustrated by wax consumption. The large wax candles and torches used at funerals were often lit for a brief period and then extinguished and donated to the burial church. Fifty to sixty pounds of wax, often including some cheaper parched wax, was the norm purchased for burials of physicians and notaries; ten to twenty pounds sufficed for male artisans. From the burial of Cristofano Spini in 1414, however, Santa

Trinità netted over five hundred pounds of wax, and from the burial of his fellow parishioner Nofri Strozzi, over seven hundred pounds.[94] As Florentine society became increasingly stratified in the early fifteenth century, funerals became pageants that more reliably reflected and affirmed social distinctions.

Accompanying these changes in the distribution of wealth, and in consumption, were new ways of defining the political elite. The oligarchical politics of the early Quattrocento made its clearest mark on the funerals of veteran statesmen who crafted policy at the highest level. The most striking change in the state-sponsored contribution to these funerals was the displacement of fictive knighthood by symbols of public authority and massive official tributes. Knightly imagery still prevailed at the burials of war captains, as evidenced by the 1424 funeral for Lodovico Obizzi, but it no longer seemed to the commune and its officers the appropriate way to represent a new breed of statesman.[95]

Increasingly, the funeral rites of city fathers deemphasized chivalric splendor in favor of official signs of officeholding. This trend began in 1414 with the funeral of Cristofano Spini and became especially apparent in 1425–30, when several key leaders in what had become a faltering regime died. While ritual never replaced concrete political action, the funerals of statesmen nevertheless formed part of a larger effusion of oratory and pageantry that facilitated the circulation of civic ideals and helped boost civic morale during a period of factional strife and political disintegration.[96] The civic nature of these rites was enhanced by communal subsidies to purchase various regalia for select councillors and statesmen, including top officials and those who had served in mid-level positions. Only those who died in office were technically eligible for subsidies, although exceptions could be made.[97] The funerary rubrics of 1415 also introduced a new measure that buttressed the needs of civic policy and ideology. In these statutes the communal government for the first time officially exempted itself from all legal limits when honoring high officeholders, as long as the measures allotting funeral subsidies were properly dispositioned in the councils.[98] What these laws sanctioned was the creation of an "official" civic funerary style that quickly merged with private family interests.

Several key examples here will have to illustrate the larger point. Dominating the homage shown to the eminent civic leader Vieri

Guadagni in 1426, for example, was the tribute paid by his colleagues in civic government: his funeral was attended by members of the Colleges, the Ten of War, the captains of the Merchants' Court, the consuls of the wool guild, "the most honored citizens of the land," and hired communal retainers; and flags and banners representing the Popolo and the Parte Guelfa were present. When Rinaldo Gianfigliazzi, Guadagni's colleague at the very center of policy making, had died the previous year at the age of ninety, he had been treated to a similar litany of public honors. Commemorating a lifetime of government service that had drawn heated accusations of tyrannical ambitions as well as assassination attempts, Gianfigliazzi's funeral employed only a minimum of chivalric trappings, in keeping with his fierce guardianship of civic values, despite the fact that he was dubbed the republic's "most noble and renowned knight."[99]

Even in the great family spectacle staged for Giovanni de' Medici in February 1429, official civic tributes shared the spotlight with shows of family wealth, strength, and solidarity. According to the chronicler Petriboni, this funeral was made still more illustrious by the participation of ambassadors from Venice, Bologna, the Kingdom of Naples, and the Holy Roman Empire, as well as numerous Florentine officials, all of whose presence recognized the kind of esteemed political reputation that even money could not buy.[100] To paraphrase Machiavelli, Giovanni died rich in treasure but still richer in fame. Underscoring this diplomatic tribute was a battery of flags, banners, and pennants purchased at communal expense. An appreciation of the event's twin family and civic focus found its way into enduring Medici lore via the work of Scipione Ammirato, who expressed his admiration for the enormity of the political and civic tribute.[101] Those more distant from the centers of civic power, such as the colleagues of the goldsmith Matteo di Lorenzo (d. 1420), may have tried to match these civic outlays with impressive guild homage, as well as by subsidizing large numbers of clerics to march in the funeral procession.[102]

The civic-minded quality of these funerals, which fit well with the regime's patriotic political style, offered their viewers clear depictions of leadership which in turn helped refine an emerging political ideology. Informing a broad, socially diverse civic community, the dominant symbolism of these events served several decidedly civic purposes: rallying patriotic sentiments, shoring up flagging morale in the war efforts against Milan, and masking tensions and fatigue in the inner regime after 1426.

Among the central civic images highlighted in these rites were the emblems of the Parte Guelfa. Although Guelfism was dead as a political force by the early fifteenth century, its emotionally charged symbols and emblems nevertheless continued to embody much of what was both distinctively Florentine and distinctively praiseworthy about a rapidly receding past.[103] It may be, as one social scientist has argued, that these symbols were used with greater emphasis and frequency precisely because the certainty of the moral order they represented was challenged by events.[104] The proud display of civic and Guelf signs for the city's most eminent leaders visually and symbolically stressed a shared ideological commitment to a Florentine brand of republicanism, as did the political rhetoric of council debates; at the same time, this imagery facilitated the transmission of civic ideals of citizenship to the lettered and the unlettered alike. What contemporaries saw was a series of rites, images, and symbols which repeated a similar story with only minor variations. Viewed as symbolic props for the regime, the funeral rites of key civic leaders contributed in their own way to the new idiom of power and civic self-consciousness emerging after Salutati's death.

These rites also merged civic concerns with the social and political interests of an elite. Funerals for members of the inner regime both demonstrated the changed nature of power relations and helped reconcile the peculiar Florentine political tension between elitism and civism that developed in the 1410s and 1420s. Although changes in the distribution of political power and the growth of civic ideology occurred simultaneously, they were to some extent conflicting processes. While civism extended the concept of citizenship and praised civic service, the actual workings of government were increasingly monopolized by an elite. Hence political rhetoric, of which these funerals formed a part, confronted the challenge of nurturing a republican civic ethos in a social body for whom the ideological expansion of citizenship conflicted with shrinking opportunities for political officeholding. The exalted parade of civic emblems hallowed by usage helped resolve these conflicts by creating an apparatus of honor and authority which, while promoting civic spirit, was still restricted to a select group of public officials. This new convention benefited members of the regime such as Vieri Guadagni and the lawyer Lorenzo Ridolfi, whose wealth did not correlate closely with their political reputations.[105]

Concern with the public perception of political roles figured into other kinds of death records and memorials honoring statesmen. The sequence of rites for the high officeholder Antonio da Panzano (d. 1423), disrupted because of his death outside the city, was redeemed in his nephew's eyes by the official presentation of a magnificent banner from Pescia, displaying the Panzano arms surrounded by the emblems of all the district's castles and towns, to be hung proudly near Antonio's tomb in Santa Croce. Similar civic trophies graced the tomb of the great statesman Bartolomeo Valori (d. 1427) until their removal by Cosimo I de' Medici in the sixteenth century.[106] Although Agnolo Pandolfini (d. 1446) outlived most of his compatriots in the inner regime, he did not abandon the political bent of his cohort's self-dramatization. Ambassador, diplomat, peacemaker, officeholder, and savvy teacher of political precepts in Matteo Palmieri's *Della vita civile*, Pandolfini wanted to be immortalized on his marble tomb—constructed in 1420, at the height of his career—in a civil magistrate's cap and gown, helping to author the public peace.[107]

Several narratives describing the deaths and burials of preeminent leaders offer a different way of looking at the connections between death ritual and political practice in these formative years of Florentine statebuilding. Bound up with various mortuary narratives is a marked concern with political succession and the controlled transfer of power between generations. The familial images invoked in these narratives reveal how changing Florentine conceptions of state and society, which shifted from a corporatist ideal to a family-based notion of benevolent elders ruling the polity, penetrated ritual as well as official politics and formal debates.[108] In these records the son rightfully replaced the father, setting up an actual and metaphorical exchange that was seen as a natural flow of power within families, patronage networks, and the state. Similar echoes are found in the language of fifteenth-century formulas for letters of recommendation.[109]

Luca da Panzano, for example, concluded the account of his uncle Antonio's burial with the story of how the family successfully retained the vicarate of Pescia for Antonio's nephew Tommaso; unfortunately Antonio's son, perhaps a more likely candidate, had predeceased him. A similar coda rounded out Petriboni's account of Gianfigliazzi's funeral, with son replacing father on the war commission four days after the burial.[110] On Giovanni de' Medici's death, the commune of Pistoia granted to "all his family who survive him" the privilege of using the commune's coat of arms as a token of regard for Giovanni's service as podestà, during which time he "had always honored and supported this commune in every way."[111] These transfers of office and emblems were, in one sense, commemorative tributes resembling Florentine naming practices: they both paid homage to the memory of the deceased and possibly were intended to "remake" the father's character and contributions in the person of his son.[112] But equally unmistakable are the ways in which these substitutions kept power and authority within a closed circle.

These political intentions are still more explicit in deathbed scenes centering on the legacies of political wisdom fathers left their sons. In a moving deathbed speech, Giovanni de' Medici reportedly entrusted the wisdom distilled from his long political career to his sons Cosimo and Lorenzo, who were to assume his place at the city's helm. Gino Capponi had crafted a similar political testament on his deathbed several years before.[113] True to the concerns of his political cohort, Agnolo Pandolfini charged Alessandro Alessandri, among others, with upholding both the political and paternal duties entrusted to men of the elite, using the language of family. During Pandolfini's final illness, "in most fitting words [he] committed the city to their care [i.e., to the care of his political colleagues] and exhorted them to bear themselves towards it in such manner as would allow them to hand it over to their sons as worthy as it was when they themselves received it."[114]

The most obvious use of a mortuary rite as a locus for the transfer of authority occurred in the unusual funeral ceremony for Messer Matteo di Michele Castellani, a wealthy knight, diplomat, and officeholder. Castellani's son Francesco was far too young to replace his father as one of the sixteen standard-bearers, the office Castellani held at the time of his death in September 1429. What Castellani's funeral did instead was to couch this succession in symbolic terms by conjoining the funeral rites with investiture ceremonies. After Castellani's body had been placed in front of the main altar in Santa Croce, his eleven-year-old son was led to that charismatic space, divested of his black mourning clothes by officials of the Pupilli, and "remade" in the green outfit of a knight by Lorenzo Ridolfi, Palla Strozzi, and Giovanni Guicciardini, all leading political figures with whom Castellani had maintained close ties. Completing this symbolic transfer of power and identity, the commune and the Parte Guelfa vested the young Francesco as a new, unofficial standard-bearer by granting him their standards at the priors' palace a month later, which he and a large entourage then paraded around the city.[115] In this way, Matteo Castellani—father, knight, and statesman—was "remade" in the figure of his son.

Ritual, Politics, and the Papacy

Politics played a central role in the reformulation of early Quattrocento death rites not only in the funerals of statesmen but also in one of the most imposing public funerals of fifteenth-century Florence: the magnificent rites staged in late December 1419 for Baldassare Coscia, the deposed Pope John XXIII. Coscia enjoyed a special relationship with the city both before and after his death. Although the city hosted papal entourages both prior and subsequent to Coscia's final stay, from June to December 1419, he was the only pope ever to be buried in Florence. For fifteen years Coscia was bound to the city by a complex set of relations forged by friendship, political alliance, banking, and humanism. These ties generated such great affection toward Coscia that, according to his friend Giovanni de' Medici, the former pope's death "touched and grieved every citizen."[116] His special connection with the city was immortalized in the monumental tomb in the Baptistry created by Donatello and Michelozzo, one of only four tombs located in that privileged site, which was commissioned in 1422, under way by late 1424, and probably completed by mid-1428.[117]

Coscia's obsequies merged the course of urban affairs with international and papal politics to create a kind of sacralized political theater previously unknown to the city. Although the funerals for Hawkwood and Salutati had also been forms of a civic political theater, the grandiose religious spectacle staged for Coscia differed in important ways from Hawkwood's rites twenty-five years earlier, which had celebrated the commune triumphant in predominantly military and chivalric language, and from Salutati's obsequies, which had enacted new civic and humanist values. Perhaps the uniqueness of this event should not be surprising. As Peter Burke has recently written, the relationship between symbols and power was exceptionally complex in papal rituals because popes themselves were such ambiguous figures, "on the border of some of the main categories of their culture."[118] Certain structural features in papal funerals were prescribed by both liturgy and custom. Yet these complex events also represented nuances of character and biography, communicated the tenor of particular social relations, and reflected the current political conditions of city or court; in practice, then, their structure showed considerable elasticity and numerous permutations.

The complex interweaving of sacred and secular rulership, personal qualities, and political exigencies is nowhere more apparent than in Coscia's obsequies. His funeral services paid tribute not only to his tenure as pope but also to the persistent friendship he sustained with Florence and with several of its leading citizens. Yet for all its distinctiveness, Coscia's funeral also occupies an important place in the overall development of Florentine funerary ritual: first, as a summary of several major political processes of the late 1410s; second, for the way in which the obsequies meshed an ecclesiastical and religious iconic system with a system of public, official, and lay symbols; and third, for its establishment of a reference point for future Florentine burials of ecclesiastical dignitaries, similar to the way Salutati's rites had invented a tradition for Florentine chancellors. Coscia's obsequies contributed to important ways to what was becoming an increasingly coherent system of Florentine funerary ritual, a growing, maturing, self-conscious network of rites defined by a body of ceremonial cross-references and its own set of commonplaces. Given these recurrent references, Coscia's rites need to be analyzed against a backdrop of contemporary Florentine civic funerary ritual (which itself was influenced by private practice) as well as compared to other papal and ecclesiastical obsequies.

In order to understand the program of the funeral, it is necessary to reiterate some important features of Coscia's biography before turning to the more immediate circumstances of the ceremonies.[119] A Neapolitan by birth, Coscia had been elected pope in 1410 at the Council of Pisa, convened to end the Great Schism, but he was forced by international maneuvers to convene a new church council at Constance in the autumn of 1414. Sensing danger to both his person and his office, Coscia fled from Constance in March 1415, only to be arrested on the council's orders, divested of his office in May, and imprisoned in Germany for almost three years. His deposition triggered a debate in the Florentine councils in July 1415 about whether to intercede with the king of France on his behalf. But even though Florentines considered Coscia the true pope, the Signoria decided that such intervention was too dangerous under the circumstances. Complaining that Coscia had been badly treated, Leonardo Bruni among others was outraged over the purported illegality of the deposition.[120] After protracted negotiations between various international powers, it was the Florentines who ultimately secured Coscia's release from captivity in April 1419 after paying a huge ransom.

What prompted such concern for Coscia's fate was his continually friendly posture toward the commune and several of its leading citizens. Beginning in 1405, when Coscia had helped Florence gain Pisa in his capacity as papal legate at Bologna, he remained a political benefactor to the republic, joining forces with the city, for example, in its struggles against Ladislaus (1408). In addition to his official dealings with the commune, Coscia shared close personal ties and business associations with several Florentines, most notably Giovanni de' Medici, well before his advent as pope. Once elected to the papacy, Coscia designated the head of the Medici bank in Rome as depositary-general of papal finances; it was by means of the personal and financial relationship between Giovanni de' Medici and Coscia that the Medici established themselves as the pope's bankers. Although other respected statesmen such as Niccolò da Uzzano and Bartolomeo Valori interested themselves in Coscia's plight, it was Giovanni de' Medici who played the major role in securing the deposed pope's release.[121]

Intellectual ties as well as political alliances linked Coscia to Florence. During Coscia's brief and unsettled pontificate, the papal court became a budding center of Florentine humanism, with the likes of Poggio Bracciolini, Leonardo Bruni, and Manuel Chrysoloras invigorating the provincial atmosphere of Constance in the papal retinue. The rising star of the humanist movement, Bruni, enjoyed close ties with Coscia in his role as papal secretary and, according to Poggio, made "a great deal of money" through the pope's favors.[122]

Coscia's elaborate obsequies were conditioned not only by these longstanding associations, however, but also by more immediate political circumstances, particularly those stemming from the residence of Martin V in the city. Following his election by the Council of Constance in November 1417, Martin had triumphally entered Florence in February 1419 while trying to amass sufficient strength for a southward journey that would reclaim Rome for the papacy. As the duly elected pope, Martin was greeted with appropriate fanfare by the Florentine government, who sponsored a lavish processional entry and banquet costing fifteen hundred florins. The commune also permitted the operai of the cathedral to spend an additional fifteen hundred florins to construct a fitting apparatus in Santa Maria Novella, which housed the papal entourage.[123] Reciprocating this hospitality with his own gesture of friendship, Martin bestowed a jewelled gold rose on the populace in a great public ceremony in late March, shortly before the extraordinary observances marking Holy Week that year.[124]

These mutual ceremonial exchanges masked fundamental tensions and policy differences between Martin and the Florentine Signoria, who showed recurrent signs of devotion to their old ally.[125] An uneasy peace was forged between the commune, Martin, and Coscia once Coscia, after his arrival in June 1419, made public obeisance to the new pope in Santa Maria Novella. In return for Coscia's submission, Martin made Coscia the "cardinal bishop of Tusculum," a title that Coscia changed to "cardinal of Florence," reportedly out of affection for the Florentines.[126]

Unfortunately, Coscia lived as a cardinal for only a few months. He died the morning of December 22 in the house of Antonio di Santi Chiarucci, located near Santa Maria Maggiore. According to contemporary sources, Coscia himself was aware of the relief his death would afford Martin, whose tiara would undoubtedly rest more secure after Coscia's passing.[127] Making his last testament on his deathbed, Coscia named as executors four prominent Florentine citizens: Vieri Guadagni, Niccolò da Uzzano, Bartolomeo Valori, and his trusted friend Giovanni de' Medici.[128] Unlike many of his clerical peers, who in their wills either stressed or rejected the appurtenances of their rank, Coscia left the logistics of his burial to the discretion of his executors, or to any two of them. That the funeral program was actually devised by this group seems clear from their prominent role in the ceremonial proceedings, their later involvement with Coscia's tomb, and Giovanni de' Medici's correspondence with Coscia's nephews regarding Coscia's estate.[129]

By the terms of his will, Coscia also left to civic and pious causes a rich variety of bequests, amounting to a considerable sum, thereby "demonstrating his love the more clearly and fervently by proofs at his departure from this life," as the Signoria said.[130] Among the greatest of Coscia's bequests to the city was his prized relic, the index finger of John the Baptist, the patron saint of Florence. Out of an estate reportedly valued at 25,000 florins, Coscia had allocated 3,000 florins to underwrite his burial and charitable bequests. In actuality, Coscia's estate was sadly inadequate for much of this largesse, but his generosity was nevertheless similar to that of other late fourteenth-century popes, whose funerals were primarily occasions for the distribution of alms rather than grand public entertainments.[131]

The liturgical code governing Coscia's obsequies was the Ordo Romanus, which prescribed a series of requiems held over the course of nine days (*novena*), customarily preceded by a brief public display of the body. Despite these regulations, however, ceremonial practice was far from uniform, especially among Coscia's predecessors in Avignon, such as Clement VI (d. 1352) and Innocent VI (d. 1362). Coscia's funeral took place in an institutional and political context of exceptional fluidity and upheaval, and he himself occupied an ambiguous position as the deposed head of the Christian community. These unusual circumstances made Coscia's obsequies quite malleable and capable of reflecting a variety of civic and religious concerns. By the mid-fifteenth century, once the legitimacy of the Roman papal succession was reestablished, there was an increasing codification of and a greater adherence to ceremonial formulas for ecclesiastical dignitaries, which undoubtedly helped stabilize the prestige of the Roman papal court.[132]

Coscia's funeral began with a simple procession that immediately distinguished his ceremonies from the great civic parade of Hawkwood's rites. His obsequies were performed entirely in the theatrical interiors of the Baptistry and the cathedral, without utilizing secular civic spaces. On the evening after his death, Coscia's body, outfitted in a white miter, with his cardinal's hat resting at his feet, was carried by the canons of the cathedral from his residence to the Baptistry.[133] Heading the cortege were the three processional crosses of the Baptistry, the cathedral, and the church of Santa Maria Maggiore. The canons placed Coscia's bier on the venerated baptismal font, the same location used in Hawkwood's rites, and the place where relics were displayed on special feast days. After the canons recited the office, they transferred the body to a richly illuminated spot beneath the pulpit. There Coscia's body would lie in state for eight days, until December 30, giving his executors enough time to commandeer the formidable resources needed to begin his obsequies in earnest.[134] There is no mention or record of a ceremonial effigy, although a death mask may have been made to aid in the later construction of a tomb effigy; and it is unclear whether Coscia's body was eviscerated. Contemporary accounts are also unfortunately silent about the bell ringing that surely formed a conspicuous part of the tribute, as it did for Coscia's successor: when Martin V died in 1431, every Florentine church tolled its bells nine times nightly for nine consecutive days.[135]

Although Coscia's nine requiems were obviously similar in nature, they should not be lumped together indiscriminately because of their solemnity, splendor, or common liturgical core. The ceremonies for Coscia manipulated the prescribed fragmentation and repetition of requiem episodes into a comprehensive serial tribute, the whole of which was greater than the sum of its parts. Instead of subsuming Coscia's biography into a single funereal occasion, each of the initial three ceremonies paid homage to a different aspect of Coscia's identity: the first honored Coscia the cardinal and former pope, the second treated Coscia's role as an ally of Florence, and the third celebrated Coscia the private man. It was the overall orchestration of these episodes that provided a sophisticated means of political communication.

The first event, to which various citizens and officials were formally invited, was held in the cathedral on December 30 and was paid for out of Coscia's estate. The centerpiece of funeral decor inside the cathedral was a huge, candle-studded catafalque hung with black draperies decorated with Coscia's coat of arms.[136] Seated around the catafalque, situated in the middle of the choir, were eighty mourners in black, all holding lighted candles, among whom were several of Coscia's kinsmen, including his nephew Tommaso Brancacci, the cardinal of Trecarico, outfitted in deep purple. Also stationed in this privileged area, closest to the catafalque, where they might oversee

the proceedings at the heart of affairs, were Coscia's four executors—
Medici, Guadagni, Uzzano, and Valori—who had organized the
spectacle. Coscia's body, however, was not actually resting on the
catafalque; rather, it had remained in the Baptistry, which, along
with the cathedral, was illumined by so much wax that it struck one
observer as nothing short of a miracle. The symbolic stand-in for
Coscia's corpse on the black-draped bier was that quintessential indicator of status and identity, his cardinal's hat. The clerical contingent present consisted of all the regular clergy of Florence, many of
whom had benefited from Coscia's bequests; numerous archbishops
and bishops; and twenty cardinals wearing their prescribed white
miters, who recited the office for the dead. In the midst of such
supposed clerical harmony, the main liturgical celebrant, Cardinal
Antonio Correr of Bologna, could hardly be considered an old friend
of Coscia's: he was the nephew of Coscia's former rival Gregory
XII.[137]

Despite the visual beauty of the setting, the requiem was far from
being either a static or a purely sacred ceremony. Setting up a dramatic rhythm within this formidable assembly was the insertion,
prior to the mass, of a litany of civic and corporate tribute. Once the
clerical dignitaries had assembled, representatives from each of the
major Florentine corporations approached the catafalque, in an order
replicating the city's official hierarchy, to offer funeral gifts. The
sequence of presentation created a pattern of intelligibility suggesting
both a specific political order and a sense that the whole of legitimate
government participated in a common consensus. First the Signoria
and members of the Colleges walked up to the catafalque, bringing
with them a hundred torches. Then they laid over the bier a golden
pall adorned with the emblems of Coscia, Martin, and the city of
Florence, displayed in safe and harmonious combination. As the
heart of communal government, the members of the Signoria not
only enjoyed primacy of place but were also distinguished by their
unique tribute of a gold rather than a black bier cloth. Having made
their offering, the priors took a place of honor in the choir along
with the ecclesiastical elite.

Following the Signoria in sequential homage were the captains of
the Parte Guelfa, accompanied by numerous knights, judges, and
important citizens, offering eighty torches and a black pall decorated
with the arms of Coscia and the Parte. Next came the magistrates

of the Merchant's Court, then the guild captains; each group donated a black pall decorated with Coscia's arms and their respective corporate emblems, along with a total of ninety-six torches. After giving their gifts, these Florentine officials and esteemed citizens assumed their places alongside other prelates on the fringes of the choir. The spatial arrangements described in accounts of the ceremony suggest the attempt to place civic magistrates and clerical dignitaries on a relatively equal footing: the Signoria with the cardinals in the heart of the choir, other officials grouped with lesser prelates. Enhancing this symbolic parity of civic and ecclesiastical worlds, each arranged hierarchically, was the distribution by the four executors of similar-sized torches to cardinals, priors, Guelph captains, and the six captains of the Merchants' Court; all other participants, both laity and clergy, received similar, smaller tapers. The ceremony concluded with a mass, a sermon preached by the Dominican friar Domenico da Figline, and the Office of the Dead; then Coscia's bier was transported to the Baptistry by the canons of the cathedral.

The second requiem mirrored the ceremonial format and tribute of the previous day, but with more pronounced civic overtones. The replication of the ceremony is itself important, with the doubling again posing a kind of symbolic equivalence between clerical and communal homage. Moreover, the attendance and participation of the Signoria at two successive funeral events was without precedent. Customarily the Signoria, as an officially constituted body, played only a limited role even in state funerals. Complementing this exceptional official involvement and gift-giving was the diminished presence of high prelates attached to Martin's court; only one cardinal—Coscia's nephew Tommaso Brancacci—attended, although many archbishops and bishops did. In addition, celebration of the mass by the bishop of Florence could only have stressed the civic dimension of this ecclesiopolitical ceremony.

Furthermore, whereas the first ceremony had been underwritten by Coscia's estate, this time the communal government footed the bill. Such subsidies were not automatically forthcoming for clerical dignitaries, despite their high rank: when Cardinal Albanese died in Florence in June 1412, for example, his funeral was an entirely ecclesiastical affair relegated to Santa Maria Novella, except for a brief exposure of the corpse in the Piazza San Giovanni.[138] According to the enabling legislation, the communal subsidy of 300 florins was designed to show "how dear and acceptable to all the people of Florence were the love and long-standing goodwill displayed in continual benefits" Coscia had rendered toward the "magnificent and potent Commune of Florence." The Parte Guelfa did its part by chipping in an additional seventy florins.[139]

How did contemporaries perceive and understand such a lavish, unprecedented ceremony, especially its messages about communal policy? Giovanni de' Medici, who was by no means an impartial observer, wrote to Coscia's nephew Michele shortly after the ceremonies that "such great honor has been done him by the Signoria here that no greater could be done to any Lord."[140] For all his bias, however, Medici was not alone in his assessment of how Coscia's symbolic tribute figured into a larger set of policy objectives. Similar statements were voiced in the sermon given at the requiem, which stressed that Coscia's burial at public expense was a sign of the symbiotic relationship and past rapport between the commune and the papacy.[141] This verbal rhetoric had its visual equivalent in the familiar civic images, objects, and emblems that formed the city's common symbolic property. These symbols, destined for collective consumption by the civic community, were valued and recognized as direct expressions of the organs of power.

No doubt Martin V was among those the obsequies were intended to address. While explicit statements of communal antipathy toward Coscia's successor would have been impolitic under the circumstances, it is not unreasonable to suggest that the spectacular scale of the proceedings was used to intentionally pique Martin by staking out an independent communal position. Such at least was the opinion of the sixteenth-century historian Scipione Ammirato, who remarked that had Coscia actually been pope at the time of his death, the Signoria would have paid him less homage. Clearly the ambiguity of Coscia's tomb inscription—"Ioannes quondam Papa XXIII," which could be read as implying that Coscia had still been pope at the time of his death—irritated Martin, who demanded unsuccessfully that the Signoria change it to reflect Coscia's final rank of cardinal.[142]

Rounding out the tribute to Coscia was the third requiem, which honored Coscia the private man. This episode, held in the Baptistry rather than the cathedral, emphasized Coscia's relations of kinship and clientage rather than his official face. The bier was situated on the baptismal font, surrounded by Coscia's kinsmen and members of his household, dressed in black mourning garb and bearing fine tapers. Coscia's executors had arranged for forty-four poor men to be outfitted in white at the estate's expense, according to his instructions. These *poveri*, with their crude candles in hand, completed the circle around the bier as visible testimony to Coscia's charity and patronage. After the mass performed by the bishop of Fiesole, the participants accompanied Coscia's kin back to their house, as was customary in private funerals. The same rite and procedure would be followed for the next six days, until the ceremonies were finally completed. This final shading into the more personal, private relations of kinship and clientage was not uncharacteristic of the funerals of great prelates: the cortege escorting Clement VI to his long-awaited burial site in 1353, for example, comprised five cardinals, all kinsmen of the dead pope.[143] Viewed as a complete series of episodes with multiple audiences, Coscia's obsequies linked parallel clerical, civic, and family orders—with Coscia himself as both the center of each and their common linchpin—in a way unprecedented in rites staged by and for Florentines.

Humanism and the Power of Praise

Changes in the political culture and social climate of Florence in the 1420s also helped spread the new practice of Latin funeral orations. Classicizing orations had already begun to gain popularity in humanist circles in the second decade of the Quattrocento. Panegyrics enjoying wide circulation as models for subsequent imitation were Barzizza's oration for Jacopo da Forli (dated 1414), Andrea Giuliano's for Manuel Chrysoloras (1415), Leonardo Giustiniani's for Carlo Zeno (1418), and Poggio Bracciolini's for Francesco Zambarella, then cardinal of Florence (1418).[144] Over the course of the fifteenth century, Latin funeral orations established common ground between state-sponsored rites and some elite funerals, thus linking civic and family rites by a set of shared conventions.

One of the key texts establishing this practice in Florence was Leonardo Bruni's 1428 funeral oration for Nanni degli Strozzi. Strozzi was a Ferrarese general of Florentine descent who died in June 1427 leading a coalition against the Milanese. Shortly after Strozzi's death, several of his friends in Ferrara asked Bruni to compose a eulogy in his honor, but the demands of Bruni's new position as chancellor, which he assumed in November 1427, prevented him from finishing the work until April of the following year.[145] Hence Bruni wrote the panegyric at a time when Filippo Maria Visconti's foreign policy was rekindling fears of Milanese expansion.

The oration's political content as the fullest expression of Bruni's republicanism has been remarked upon by Hans Baron, who saw it as a milestone in the history of culture and political thought. Borrowing heavily from Pericles' funeral oration, Bruni acted as much as a publicist for the regime as he did as a eulogist for Strozzi.[146] By subtly exploiting the topos of birthplace common to orations, Bruni stressed that the virtue and achievements of Florence's citizens stemmed from its climate of political freedom. Milanese contemporaries saw Bruni's oration as a highly effective piece of political rhetoric damaging to the Milanese cause. "Everyone who has read it," wrote the archbishop of Milan, "knows well how greatly it lowers the estimation of the Prince [Filippo Maria Visconti] and of our *patria*."[147]

However, Bruni's eulogy of Strozzi was not actually recited at the funeral, which was long since past, although he composed it "as if it were to be spoken at the very end of the funeral."[148] It is not clear whether there was a public reading of Bruni's oration among friends, a practice upon which the diffusion and success of humanist orations generally depended. But the oration was undoubtedly one of the most popular to circulate in later years, judging from the large number of surviving manuscript copies and its frequent use as a model by other humanists.[149]

Although scholars have analyzed the text in some detail, the Strozzi oration has yet to be situated in the development of Florentine funerary conventions. With its full-blown pronouncements on republican virtues, Bruni's eloquent praise of both citizen and city marks an important step forward in the way in which Florentines exploited the propagandistic value of death rites. Beginning with Salutati's obsequies, funerals began to emerge as a primary locus in which to expound both a republican political ideology and a humanist program, just as funerals at the Milanese court promoted similar praises of monarchical rule.[150] What distinguished early Quattrocento funerals from their fourteenth-century antecedents was the way in which these later rites created and exploited civic myths, ideals, and values in a more concerted ideological direction.

Moreover, Bruni's oration also played an important role in articulating a new, idealized relationship between oratory and trappings in cult practice. Although we are familiar with the resounding success of humanist rhetoric through historical hindsight, the early Quattrocento was a time in which oratory as a device for social and political communication had not yet found an established place in ritual practice. Expounded in a changing framework of consumption and sumptuary investment, Bruni's oration posited the parity of words and "outward things," which together formed a coordinated meaning. The physical trappings of display, Bruni said, "were devoted to the funeral procession," while oratory was devoted "to the praise of those who had perished." In a "public funeral with a splendid display of words as well as outward things," verbal tribute did not replace funeral trappings but instead complemented, reinforced, and clarified their meaning. "When verbal embellishment has been added to the physical display," he remarked, "the gratitude of the living becomes visible and the virtues of the deceased are disclosed as if illumined in a kind of splendor, and the grief of his kinsmen is delineated in proportion to the glory of his accomplishments."[151] Fusing visual metaphors with verbal claims, Bruni argued for a convergence of rhetoric and ritual into a unified public presentation, one that mobilized mourners' ears as well as their eyes. In putting the classical rhetorical tradition to work, Bruni schooled his contemporaries in a new method of perception which engaged them as both listeners and viewers.

With the advent of funeral oratory, the rites of death became an important, recognized meeting ground for humanist values and the claims of a social and political elite. This new rhetorical idiom that spoke of both power and praise was quickly popularized beyond a small circle of chancellors and war heroes to a larger group of Florentine private citizens associated with the humanist movement, either as patrons or practitioners. Poggio eulogized Niccolò Niccoli in 1437 for his donation of eight hundred manuscripts to the city, which created the core of a "public library" that sustained Niccoli's reputation and public service beyond the grave. On his death in 1440, Lorenzo de' Medici was honored with two orations, one by Poggio and one by Antonio Pacini, the tutor of Cosimo's children. Running throughout Pacini's oration were praises of both Lorenzo and his brother Cosimo, who, like famous Roman statesmen, always acted to defend their country's liberty.[152]

By the middle of the fifteenth century, funeral oratory became yet another stable mark of distinction in a well-regulated repertoire of funeral conventions shared by public figures and privileged private citizens. So widespread had the practice become among Italy's educated and social elites that Leon Battista Alberti satirized this vogue by writing a eulogy for his dead dog.[153] Despite Alberti's barbs about the popularized quality of orations, the Florentines honored by humanist orations always remained a highly select group (e.g., political figures such as Giannozzo Pandolfini, Donato Acciaiuoli, Cosimo de' Medici) even in the second half of the fifteenth century, when the humanist movement was in full swing.

Like many of the new funeral conventions that developed in early Quattrocento Florence, humanist orations publicly strengthened the masculine ethos characteristic of these decades. The familial language of rulership, extolled in political debates, formal treatises such as Bruni's *Laudatio*, and deathbed narratives, informed the citizenry in multiple ways that the governance of state and society was a rightfully masculine affair headed by a collection of powerful fathers.[154] Humanist orations fit into this larger rhetorical framework, both in terms of their content and because women were excluded from the select number of those honored. Here republican Florence compared unfavorably with its courtly neighbors in northern Italy. Anonymous orators eulogized Elisabetta Malatesta in Pesaro (the text of the oration is dated 1405) and Caterina Visconti in Milan (after 1410); the great humanist Guarino da Verona in 1439 lauded Margherita Gonzaga, who had been educated by Vittorino da Feltre; and Antonio Lollio wrote at an unknown date in honor of Laudominia Piccolomini, sister to Pius II. The second half of the fifteenth century witnessed a still greater number of orations written outside Florence for distinguished women.[155] The definition and use of Florentine orations as a gendered genre was fully consistent with the political rhetoric and ideology of a regime that sought to strengthen traditional gender roles, moral precepts, and public authority.

Yet the humanist revolution in culture did not leave women's funerary conventions untouched. In singing the praises of well-placed women, however, Florentine humanists chose a different genre: private consolatory letters, whose rhetoric reinforced rather than challenged the gender ascriptions of oratory and formal tracts such as Bruni's *Economics* (1420). Intended for family audiences rather than civic ones, consolatory letters delicately balanced praise of women's achievements with the recognition that these came only within and through the workings of private family life. As Bruni himself noted, "the excellences of a woman's life are reckoned to be (unless I am mistaken) good family, a good appearance, modesty, fertility, children, riches, and above all virtue and a good name," rather than notoriety in public affairs.[156]

The consolatory letter Bruni wrote to Nicola di Vieri de' Medici after the death of Nicola's seventy-four-year-old mother, Bicie, offers a useful guide to gender in humanist precept and social practice. Written in 1433, Bruni's letter measures in one way the transformations wrought in funerary conventions since the death of Bicie's banker husband Vieri, whose funeral in 1395 had been one of the great triumphs of late Trecento style. Bruni recognized that Bicie's activities in business affairs and household management were both deeply enmeshed with, and predicated upon, her husband's social and economic networks. After praising Bicie's qualities of mind and spirit, Bruni quickly went on to say, "The greatness of her prudence can be estimated from the way she governed a very large household, a large crowd of clients, [and] a vast and diversified business enterprise for more than thirty years after the death of her husband."[157] Bruni lauded both her high moral character and her practical abilities, especially the business acumen similar to that shown by women of the Alberti family during their kinsmen's exile in the second and third decades of the Quattrocento.[158] "So great were her powers of administration," maintained Bruni, "that no one felt the loss of her husband's advice and prudence, and there was no falling-off in the regulation of morals, or the discipline and standards of integrity and honor."[159]

Not all consolatory letters acknowledged patrician women's accomplishments so openly. In the more classicizing consolatory letter written to Cosimo and Lorenzo de' Medici upon the death of their mother, Piccarda Bueri, in April 1433, Carlo Marsuppini primarily considered Piccarda's achievements in terms of her sons' activities, with Marsuppini seizing the chance to idealize Cosimo's likeness to the republican statesmen of ancient Rome.[160]

By the early 1430s, most of the leaders responsible for creating the political style and administrative infrastructure of the previous two decades were dead. The innovative funerary conventions of this loose cohort—their depictions of leadership, power, and prestige which fused civic and family interests; the investment in both verbal and visual display; and the politicization of death rites—created and reflected upon sexual, social, and political differences in new ways. Early Quattrocento funerals left an impressive legacy of examples, precedents, and reference points waiting to be incorporated into a wide range of social and political strategies. The passing of this generation of city fathers, coupled with their sons' relative lack of political savvy, paved the way for the dominance of Cosimo de' Medici, beginning in 1434, which in turn created new political conditions and new ritual forms.

CHAPTER 5

SPECTACLE AT MID-CENTURY

he dominance of Cosimo de' Medici from 1434 to 1464 introduced a new politics of perception in which ceremony grew both more spectacular and more politically sensitive. Cosimo's power hinged on working behind the scenes: manipulating electoral scrutinies; utilizing networks of friends and clients; and demonstrating his magnanimity and largesse through ritual and patronage.[1] In this climate where influence and public perception counted for so much, ceremonies became serious entertainments central to the workings of political and social relations. With Cosimo setting the pace, rites of death and devotion developed into full-blown spectacles of family and state, manipulating urban spaces to create a theater of power. The Medici-influenced Magi festival, for example, reached new heights of pageantry between 1446 and 1470, with streets and squares sacralized to allegorically resemble Jerusalem. Private family celebrations followed a similar pattern of development as did corporate spectacles. The wedding decor celebrating the marriage of Giovanni Rucellai's son Bernardo to Cosimo's granddaughter Nannina in 1466, designed to be "the most beautiful and most elegant apparatus that could ever be used at a wedding," blocked off streets to meet family purposes and broke sumptuary laws in the process.[2]

The growth of spectacle was also spurred by a new emphasis on magnificence and liberal spending, in which Cosimo again took the lead. The example he set in several costly building projects undertaken between 1436 and 1450 was instrumental in stimulating the patrician building boom in both domestic and ecclesiastical architecture in the second half of the Quattrocento.[3] Humanists and merchants alike viewed wealth in increasingly positive terms, relaxing the social and moral restraints on spending in the interests of personal and civic honor. The new family palaces and villas, architectural modifications, chapels, facades, and tombs that changed the face of Renaissance Florence and its environs offered eloquent testimony to the "theory of magnificence," which held that civic good resulted from spending. Buoyed by greater confidence about their wealth, patricians shared the view of the active builder Giovanni Rucellai, who wrote circa 1457 that he lived in the best of cities in the best of times.[4]

Not all Florentines would have agreed with Rucellai. Ceremonial splendor reflected not only new economic attitudes but also a more stratified system of social relations.[5] Florence had paid a high price for the successful creation of a territorial state in the early Quattrocento: warfare, heavy forced loans, exile and bitter factionalism, and continued demographic decline. For the pro-Medicean oligarchs who retained their political stature, wealth, and prestige, however, building programs and grand ceremonies helped mark an authoritative social dominance over the lower orders.

This chapter examines expressions of magnificence during the three decades of Cosimo's ascendance for what these expressions tell us about consensus and conflict regarding political values, moral codes, class relations, and the place of women in custom and kinship. It attempts to show how spectacle, especially grand civic rites, summed up Medicean and patrician ambitions, on the one hand, and glossed over deepening political divisions, on the other. The second section of the chapter turns to the social topography of tomb sites at midcentury, assessing the extent to which patrician families dominated ecclesiastical space, to the detriment of notaries, shopkeepers, and artisans. The final section looks at the values and tensions surrounding women's mourning clothes, which became a matter of serious concern to lawmakers, moralists, and women themselves.

Civic Ritual Comes of Age

The middle decades of the Quattrocento witnessed a dazzling array of spectacular ceremonies which reflected the growing stature of Florence, whose position as the center of a regional state was increasingly recognized locally and throughout the rest of Italy, as well as internationally. The visits of international dignitaries such as Pope Eugenius IV and Emperor Frederick III of Austria provided important occasions for the city to show its wealth and to enhance its political profile through ceremony.[6] In turn, these visits exposed Florentines to various different types of rites and festivities, both secular and ecclesiastical, and gave them organizational experience in managing ceremonies on a grand scale. In the late 1430s and the 1440s the prolonged residence of Eugenius's papal court, with its frequent lavish ceremonies marking religious feasts, diplomatic alliances, and the deaths of curial dignitaries, helped solidify this experience and expertise. The high funeral honors accorded members of the papal court, such as the ton of wax honoring the cardinal of San Marcello in 1439, regularly reminded Florentines of the association between pomp and power. The council that was convened at Florence after 1438 to reunite the Latin and Greek churches occasioned still more grand ecclesiastical ceremonies and the refinement of pomp.[7]

Florence also witnessed a series of great propitiatory processions in the mid-1450s. In September 1453, "innumerable women and men" massed in procession for four days and nights hoping to fend off repeated earthquakes; in October 1455, Florentines staged another four days of procession in supplication for victory over the Turks. By the time the nobly born cardinal of Portugal died in August 1459, prompting a magnificent public ceremony that rivaled Coscia's obsequies a generation earlier, the city had become thoroughly accustomed to a variety of elaborate or massive rites.[8] Such spectacles must have thrown into sharp relief the comparatively modest obsequies for Antoninus, the ascetic Florentine archbishop whose death earlier that year had been deeply mourned by the city's poor.[9]

Utilizing these combined experiences and resources, Florentine civic ritual finally came of age in the mid-Quattrocento. Organizational experience, prescriptive legislation, the theory of magnificence, and imitation all played a role in achieving a ceremonial style that would adequately represent the city at home and abroad. This maturation also resulted from efforts to regularize civic ritual. Throughout the 1440s and 1450s, communal magistracies made piecemeal attempts to clarify procedure and protocol. In 1441 and 1451, the Merchants' Court drew up internal guidelines governing the corporate funeral honors accorded officials and private citizens; in October 1460 the priors enacted legislation regulating the scope of festivities at various Florentine churches, and in 1473 they set limits on ceremonial expenses for foreign visitors according to their rank. The concern with establishing an internal order within ritual itself finally culminated in the creation of a ceremonial code book for the city, the *Libro cerimoniale*, in 1475.[10]

However, there was a dual, parallel process at work in this coming of age. It was not only ritual events themselves that were becoming more regularized and orderly, but also their description by humanists, amateur historians, and diarists. Paralleling the greater structure and better execution of civic rites were a host of written and visual works—humanist histories such as Palmieri's *Annales* (1432), and the new pictorial techniques and theories of artists and art theorists such as Uccello and Alberti—that imposed an intelligible order on what were disparate facts, events, and compositional elements.[11] Even merchant diarists such as Francesco di Tommaso Giovanni showed a similar concern with improving the organization of their narratives and a new way of "thinking with things."[12]

These patterns of development can be usefully illustrated by examining three major civic funerals of the mid-Quattrocento: the rites for Niccolò da Tolentino (d. 1435), Leonardo Bruni (d. 1444), and Carlo Marsuppini (d. 1453). Despite their stylistic differences, these events utilized and merged two sets of cultural resources. On the one hand, Florentines continued to adapt imported, northern European conventions to the needs of a mercantile community and Medicean regime, as demonstrated in Tolentino's rites; on the other, the city looked to important episodes of its own past for guidance and legitimation, as evident in the two chancellors' funerals. All three events indicate that, rather than borrowing wholesale from abroad in search of legitimacy, Florentines constantly transformed foreign conventions and turned as much to their own history as to foreign models for sources of inspiration and value.[13]

The funeral of the war captain Niccolò da Tolentino is a characteristically shrewd indication of the Medicean marriage of pomp and power which continued through the republic into the principate. It was by means of this celebration that the Medici fully proclaimed their triumph six months after their return from exile in September 1434. Although Tolentino was a war commander of somewhat debatable skills, he was known as a Medici man and Cosimo's loyal champion.[14] In fact, it was Cosimo's hold over Tolentino and his military forces that in part prompted Cosimo's rival, Rinaldo degli Albizzi, to call for Cosimo's exile in 1433. Sent by Albizzi to fight the Milanese, Tolentino was captured near Imola and died in captivity in late 1434. Six months later, the new Medicean regime retrieved Tolentino's body and on April 20, 1435, staged a public funeral of staggering proportions.[15] Averardo de' Medici's promise that loyal war captains would earn reputation, money, and "the hearts of the men of this city" was more than adequately fulfilled in the rites. The commune contributed a funeral subsidy of 215 florins and continued to employ Tolentino's sons as *condottieri*.[16]

The honors heaped on Tolentino were numerous, including public rites in the Baptistry, the cathedral, and the main civic square. What fascinated contemporary observers, however, was the sheer scale of the material tribute. The numbers here tell an important part of the story: over twenty-five hundred pounds of wax lighting the cathedral, exclusive of another 450 massive torches donated by Pope Eugenius, the Florentine priors, the Parte Guelfa, and other major magistracies and guilds; forty-five grooms dressed in mourning standing guard over the bier, with an additional thirty-seven men-at-arms stationed near the priors' rostrum; and twenty colorful banners, plus four strings of flags with lappets and other adornments, donated by a host of sponsors such as the papacy, the Venetian republic, the Guelf party, and assorted Florentine corporations. Attending this spectacle were representatives of international powers, both lay and clerical, as well as the city's ruling elite.

Nothing in the Florentine ritual record of the preceding century matched this scenario for sheer material consumption. Even the extravagant funeral for Hawkwood forty years earlier paled in comparison. Yet for all its pomp and glory, Tolentino's spectacular funeral paradoxically marked the breakdown of the integrity of chivalric symbols and style. The trappings of chivalry and of the military profession that had loomed so large in Hawkwood's ceremonies—caparisoned horses, helmets, swords, spurs, and shields, the war baton symbolizing command—figured far less prominently in descriptions of Tolentino's obsequies. Instead, honor, power, and magnificence—now couched explicitly in terms of material wealth—were disconnected from the authority of past chivalric exploits or from a long military heritage. A similar disjuncture was marked when the standard-bearer of justice Messer Giuliano Davanzati was knighted as part of the ceremony consecrating the cathedral the following year.[17]

Shoring up these shaky chivalric foundations was a combination of mercantile wealth and humanist ideology which effectively meshed humanist, civic, and Medici interests, especially those concerns stemming from the disastrous battle of San Romano (June 1, 1432). This battle had precipitated Cosimo's exile and Tolentino's subsequent, fatal Milanese mission. Despite the undisputed Florentine loss and Tolentino's lackluster performance in the campaign, Bruni nevertheless attached ideological significance to the battle of San Romano as the real beginning of the city's resurgence. "On that day," Bruni declaimed in his public oration for the civic feast of Saint John the Baptist in 1433, "it may truly be said that the health of this city began to recover from its long and wretched sufferings, and that it regained vigor and enlightenment, learning and hope." Bruni cast Tolentino as a defender of republican liberty against Ghibelline forces, cloaking him with the ancient virtues of courage, military skill, and foresight. Matteo Palmieri ascribed similar qualities and talents to the Florentine commander in his *Annales*, which were begun afresh in 1432 to describe the background of the campaign.[18]

This public rhetoric, which was decidedly at odds with the actual facts of the battle, also glossed over the personal preferences of Bruni and Palmieri for a citizen militia modeled after that of the Roman Republic. Bruni had expounded these notions in his funeral oration for Strozzi and in his tract on warfare (*De Militia*). By endowing Tolentino with ancient virtues in a fight for republican liberty, Bruni removed him from the contemptible ranks of mercenaries, so despised by several prominent Florentines, including Alamanno Salviati, and ideologically elevated Tolentino to the status of civic hero. In Bruni's hands Tolentino underwent a transformation from mercenary to representative of the highest republican ideals. In this way Bruni as chancellor could avoid contravening public policy while making some ideological accommodation to the use of mercenary troops, a practice that was defended by Stefano Porcari in his running arguments with Bruni and Palmieri from 1428 to 1433.[19]

The illusion of heroism and grandeur created by Tolentino's funeral probably attempted to place a similar ideological mask over these communal failures on the battlefield and the broader unresolved tensions about warfare and military leadership. Perhaps a fruitful combination of florins and humanist propaganda might erase the memory of ineptitude and defeat, and replace it instead with an invented "official", memory claiming Florentine victory and celebrating the virtues of the city. Tolentino's funeral offered not merely an occasion for civic propaganda but also a way to rewrite history. Witnessing Tolentino's exaltation as champion of a victorious republic in this event was the whole of Florentine officialdom, as well as papal dignitaries, numerous foreign ambassadors, and the Florentine ruling elite, who solemnly gathered in the Piazza della Signoria to participate in the funeral rites.

There were high Medici stakes involved here as well. Cosimo had been responsible for retrieving the body of Tolentino, who, like Cosimo, had suffered at the hands of Rinaldo degli Albizzi. Moreover, Cosimo and his cousin Averardo had been instrumental in managing the San Romano campaign. Given the close association between Cosimo and Tolentino, this magnificent celebration of the war captain in the guise of civic hero turned what had been a bumbling defeat into a victory for both Florence and the Medici. With an official, public event of this magnitude sanctioned by humanists, the Medici could legitimately proclaim and vindicate their return to power. (This dovetailing of Medici purposes, Florentine patriotism, and the disintegration of chivalric semiotics had a parallel representation in Paolo Uccello's *The Battle of San Romano*, painted under Medici sponsorship at an uncertain date.)[20] Despite the grandeur of Tolentino's funeral, however, his reputation was not so easily or rapidly secured. It was Hawkwood's equestrian portrait, rather than Tolentino's, that was painted by Uccello in the cathedral in the summer of 1436, in a fresco employing new pictorial techniques to represent republican virtue.[21] Twenty years passed before Tolentino was duly commemorated in a companion fresco painted by Andrea del Castagno.

While Tolentino's funeral represents the adaptation of chivalric conventions to Florentine circumstances, the funeral rites for the humanist chancellors Bruni and Marsuppini show Florentines turning to their own past for inspiration. The key to these impressive events was not innovation but imitation. Imitation played a key role in the maturation of Florentine civic ritual, just as it did in other forms of Renaissance cultural achievement. The Bruni and Marsuppini funerals depended on a play of cross-references to episodes, symbols, and practices rooted both in classical antiquity and in the more recent communal past, including extensive borrowing from Salutati's funeral. The cross-referencing of landmark ceremonies— Bruni to Salutati, then Marsuppini to Bruni—projected a sense of Florentine tradition that grew longer and more venerable with each passing generation. Each new edition of an increasingly standardized event served to legitimate the past by reenacting communal history and summing up civic myths. Moreover, the classicism on which all three chancellors' funerals relied was not simply an aesthetic style but rather a powerful technique of public authority which was recognized on local, regional, and international stages. This authoritative use of past prototypes also figured into the permanent monuments erected to the chancellors in Santa Croce. The Bruni tomb, designed by Bernardo Rossellino on commission from the Signoria, appropriated motifs from Coscia's tomb, constructed a generation earlier; in turn, Marsuppini's tomb, by Desiderio da Settignano, explicitly imitated the Bruni monument.[22]

The funeral staged for Bruni in March 1444 also highlighted the continuing evolution of the chancellor's office. Bruni's many talents as civil servant, officeholder, and citizen fixed the stature of the chancellorship. In turn, Bruni was defined by that office; he was neither a notary like Salutati nor a lawyer like the future chancellors Accolti and Scala. During his tenure from 1427 to 1444, Bruni carried greater political weight than had his predecessor Salutati. This authority stemmed from his intellectual energies and professional integrity, the rise in his own social and economic position, and the high moral tone he brought to the office. As Vespasiano reported, Bruni continually emphasized the chancellor's official dignity, serving as a civic exemplar by conducting his daily affairs "with the greatest gravity."[23]

Bruni's funeral both imitated Salutati's rites and resolved some of the ambiguities that had been present in these latter rites. Celebrated in the Piazza della Signoria, Bruni's funeral was a thoroughly secular, civic event that subordinated his private and family identity to the interests of state. Bruni's native town, Arezzo, contributed forty florins, and two years later resolved to erect a statue in his honor.[24] Not surprisingly, however, Bruni's funeral focused attention on his service to the adopted city whose history he had written and which claimed to be the dominant political power in Tuscany. Communal officials canvassed "certain learned men" about an appropriate tribute, and their advice was that "Leonardo [Bruni] should be granted the laurel on account of his extraordinary talent and learning, and that his life should be celebrated in a funeral oration delivered before the assembly, to the end that he himself should be honored in a fitting oration, and that others should be stimulated to splendor and glory."[25]

As in Salutati's rites, the core of the ceremony was a piece of political theater that artfully showcased humanist rhetoric and civic self-confidence. Bruni's corpse was outfitted in chancellor's robes of deep red silk, with his *History of Florence* resting on his chest. The body lay on an elevated bier constructed for the ceremonies, at the head of which stood a huge platform from which Bruni's friend and fellow humanist Giannozzo Manetti delivered a funeral oration "of great richness and elegance." On hand for the ceremonies were a battery of Florentine officials and numerous foreign ambassadors, including emissaries from Pope Eugenius IV, the emperor, and the commune of Arezzo; "all the learned men in every branch of letters who were in attendance upon the Papal court"; Florentine knights, lawyers, and principal citizens; and a huge throng of the Florentine populace, who jammed into the square as onlookers.[26]

It was Manetti's task to address this very mixed audience, and he seized the occasion to give a full explanation of the genesis of the laurel ceremony. Acting as spokesman before a civic and international audience, Manetti not only ornamented Bruni's already brilliant reputation but also presented him as an exemplar of Florentine virtues and achievements, past and future. In Manetti's estimation, Bruni had surpassed the accomplishments of Livy in history and Cicero in oratory. With Bruni to point the way, there could be no doubt that Latin culture flourished once again on the banks of the Arno.[27]

As Manetti spoke, the ceremony built to its emotional climax. "When [Manetti] reached the part of his speech where he was to make it known that the highest honor was to be bestowed upon Leonardo, that he was to be given the crown of laurel as a reward for his outstanding merits, the Orator himself with his own hands placed the crown upon Leonardo's head, binding his forehead with the Apollonian wreath, while the entire populace of Florence looked on."[28] Although the unlettered could not have understood Manetti's elegant Latin, the ceremony nevertheless could focus their allegiance by deploying recognizable symbols, gestures, and imagery that were anchored in communal history. Clearly there was great popular curiosity and enthusiasm about the funeral proceedings, which bore the earmarks of a public holiday. An anonymous eulogist of Bruni later recalled how Florentine officials had to use clubs to clear a path through the thick crowds of people lining the processional route.[29]

For the learned listeners in his audience, however, Manetti's praise of Bruni provided a virtual manifesto of the Florentine humanist program. Stressing Bruni's great erudition, his rhetorical abilities, and his familiarity with moral philosophy, Manetti extolled the ideal of the public servant who used his wisdom and eloquence to serve the commonwealth and to foster moral living. Central to Manetti's evaluation of Bruni as historian, poet, and orator was the conviction that learning and civic service were compatible commitments.[30] Manetti's eulogy served a dual objective: it praised Bruni's virtues in order to stimulate those same qualities in his listeners, while publicizing the humanist message to officials and principal citizens, and to their sons, who would ultimately replace them in civic affairs. Vespasiano noted that copies of the oration were made available to those who desired them, thereby facilitating the wider circulation and greater impact of these ideals.[31]

In commending Bruni, Manetti also referred to the modes of conduct appropriate to current and future officeholders. The humanist "arts" of government and mourning both required a highly developed sense of decorum taught by precept and practice. Humanist orators from Petrarch to Bruni stressed that the excellence of a teacher's character was an important to education as the liberal disciplines themselves. As chancellor and chief exemplar, Bruni had instructed the city at large by virtue of his personal ethos and deportment, modeling his own character to a great extent on that of his mentor, Salutati, and on the severe and dignified mores of republican Rome.[32] In the eyes of both Bruni and Manetti, officers of the state should refrain from emotional outbursts of grief such as those displayed by Tolentino's men, who followed in the tradition of soldiers' laments.[33] Contemporary descriptions are silent about the form or the extent of the mourning for Bruni, with the exception of the noble tribute contained in the tomb inscription written by Marsuppini. Here the disconsolate Muses, rather than living women or loyal retainers, eternally mourned the loss of Bruni with a grief that was stylized, disembodied, and abstract.[34]

Despite the proposed harmony between learning and public life, Manetti's oration also sounded a new discordant note. In focusing on Bruni's crucial role in the rebirth of Greek letters, Manetti emphasized Bruni's intellectual debt to Manuel Chrysoloras, while paying scant tribute to the legacy of Bruni's other mentor, Salutati. Poggio followed a similar path in his eulogy commemorating the anniversary of Bruni's death.[35] This reappraisal of Salutati's role in the humanist revival probably reflects the enthusiasm for Greek learning and the influx of Byzantine scholars that resulted in the more sophisticated intellectual taste of mid-Quattrocento humanists. A generation after his death, Salutati's somewhat rough Latin style was already obsolete, much as Bruni's own style would become by the middle of the sixteenth century.[36] Although Manetti's eulogy recast Bruni's intellectual bloodlines in keeping with current fashions, the genealogy of the rite itself could nevertheless be more securely traced to Salutati, whom Bruni claimed as "father."

Bruni's state funeral in turn provided the model for Marsuppini's obsequies nine years later. Matteo Palmieri continued the chain of Florentine civic tradition by delivering a Latin oration praising the chancellor's ethos and then crowning him with laurel.[37] Yet despite these familiar tributes, Marsuppini's rites in April 1453 were far more spectacular and better orchestrated than those of his two major predecessors. For the first time the Signoria designated an official committee of five men to handle arrangements: the humanists Messer Giannozzo Manetti (newly knighted by Nicholas V) and Matteo Palmieri, along with the prominent members of the oligarchy Niccolò Soderini, Ugo Martelli, and Piero di Cosimo de' Medici.[38] Marsuppini reaped the rewards of the organizational lessons learned from Bruni's funeral, with which Manetti had been deeply involved, as well as from the entry of Emperor Frederick III of Austria and his retinue in January 1452. To handle the logistics of that important diplomatic entry, the commune had appointed seventeen managers, virtually all prominent members of the Medicean oligarchy, including Piero de' Medici.[39]

With its pronounced theatricality, expert organization, and projection of communal confidence, Marsuppini's funeral represents the full maturation of Florentine civic funerary ritual in the Quattrocento. As a part of political rhetoric with a force all its own, Marsuppini's funeral shows us a society formally organizing and defining itself around classical symbols, civic history, and images of wealth. The city government vaunted its traditions as it sought to stabilize and codify them. As with other forms of Renaissance imitation, the lack of originality at Marsuppini's funeral should not obscure the event's importance.

The funeral's lack of inventiveness was counterbalanced by a sense of magnificence and flawless coordination. Lying on an elevated bier in the Piazza della Signoria surrounded by over three hundred torches, Marsuppini's corpse was outfitted in a luxurious red gown with sable-lined sleeves, topped off with the rector's *biretta* of the Florentine Studio. The square itself had been turned into a civic theater by additions to the priors' rostrum in front of the government palace, and by bleachers flanking the sides. Seated around to watch the event unfold were representatives and officials of major Florentine magistracies, such as the Twelve Good Men and the sixteen standard-bearers of justice. Marsuppini's record as humanist chancellor and close friend of the Medici was honored by flags and banners from an impressive array of international powers and local authorities: the papacy, the king of France, the duke of Milan, Marsuppini's native town of Arezzo, the Florentine Popolo, the Parte Guelfa, the Studio, and the notaries' guild. Their funeral gifts also included palls that were sequentially draped over the bier, as had been done in Coscia's requiem. Once again the focal point of the ceremony was the oration, this time by Palmieri, and the subsequent coronation of the dead chancellor as poet. Following Palmieri's oration, the commune mobilized all of the city's clergy, along with a full repertoire of conventional trappings, in a long, slow-moving cortege that proceeded to Santa Croce for the requiem. Altogether the city spent the generous sum of 1,500 florins on the obsequies, six times as much as it had on Salutati's funeral.[40]

One of the most important messages Marsuppini's funeral conveyed was that magnificence could be successfully synthesized with classical imagery, rather than being at odds with it. No doubt the spectacular entry staged for Frederick III of Austria the previous year loomed as a backdrop to the largesse accorded the chancellor. For that occasion, the commune dispensed 25,000 florins to create an impression of liberality and magnificence recognized on both sides of the Alps as noble.[41] Whatever contradictions existed between the humanist values of moderation and the conventions of wealth were happily resolved, or at least effectively masked, in Marsuppini's funeral. The pinnacle of Florentine civic funeral ritual in the fifteenth century was not only an organizational success but a triumph of accommodation: learning and public service, wealth and classicism could all be reconciled and utilized to enhance the greater civic good.

Social Strategies and the Topography of Tombs

In the middle of the fifteenth century, magnificent funerals became the exclusive province of a narrowly defined elite. A systematic examination of the Libri del Giglio, which began recording sumptuary permits in 1457, reveals only a handful of licenses sold over the next decade. In 1459 the commune sold only two permits, one for the funeral of Nerone Dietisalvi Neroni, father of the future anti-Medicean conspirator, and the other for the humanist and former Florentine chancellor Poggio Bracciolini. The next exemptions were sold in 1463 to the heirs of Giovannozzo di Betto Biliotti and to the heirs of Giovanni di Cosimo de' Medici. Two years later, the heirs of Castello di Piero Quaratesi bought a sumptuary permit for his funeral, as did the heirs of Giovanni di Domenico Bartoli in 1466.[42]

Despite the undoubted opulence of these funerals, however, they were mainly conventional affairs that did little to develop a new symbolic vocabulary or even to assert a patriotic ideology. The elaborate burial ceremonies envisioned by Messer Manno Temperani in his fourth and final will of 1463 are a representative example of what were increasingly conventional spectacles honoring well-born men. Temperani wanted his body openly displayed on his bier to better reveal his knightly costume; all his kinsmen and neighbors in the ward of the Red Lion were to be invited to the proceedings; and his funeral cortege was to include copious wax, flags, banners, lappets, shields, a sword and helmet, his coat of arms, "plus every other ornament and honor befitting such a man." This stylistic conservatism paralleled the political thinking of commentators such as Franco Sacchetti, who in 1458 reaffirmed old civic values and traditional modes of political resolution.[43]

The one major trend that can be singled out within this conventional framework is the way in which patrician funerals began to privatize traditional public tributes. Here again the main line of the Medici were pacesetters. The funeral of Cosimo's brother Lorenzo in 1440 marked a turning point in the appropriation and use of public signs for personal and family purposes. While Lorenzo's grand funeral pomp was fairly predictable given his wealth and standing, it was nevertheless quite new that a private citizen who had never achieved extraordinary stature as a statesman or intellectual was honored with the papal arms and personal flag sent by the Medici's friend Pope Eugenius IV, then resident in Florence; with the participation of nine cardinals from the papal court; with the emblems and personnel of all the major Florentine magistracies; and with a Latin funeral oration delivered publicly by Poggio.[44] Lorenzo's funeral signaled that the tributes previously associated with distinguished public service could be privatized and put to new uses, and this strategy was quickly picked up by other members of the Florentine elite, just as the Medici lead in building programs had been imitated by other patricians. The often gaping divide between personal achievement and public tribute was sanctioned in the 1451 funeral guidelines of the Merchants' Court, which allowed corporate emblems and personnel to be sent to private funerals if purchased at citizens' own expense.[45]

However, in the mid-Quattrocento wealthy men from great families increasingly directed energies and resources to tomb monuments, which made more lasting statements about power and memory. These decades saw the arena of competition and interest within the elite shift from the ephemeral displays of funerals to permanent, innovative tomb monuments done in the new, classicizing, "Renaissance" style. Wealthy Florentine men of this generation virtually ignored Bruni's injunction that it was ridiculous to hoard up money and then spend it on a tomb; instead they proceeded with gusto to build new burial chapels and tombs, or to decorate existing ones in the new artistic style. While Bishop Benozzo Federighi's heirs staged a beautiful but conventional funeral after his death in 1450, for example, they focused most of their attention on commissioning from Luca della Robbia a new tomb, which soon became the subject of intense litigation. Similarly, Orlando de' Medici's funeral was a predictable if magnificent affair featuring almost five hundred pounds of wax, from the resale of which his burial church, Santissima Annunziata, realized about fifty-five florins. Yet his tomb by Bernardo Rossellino, which borrowed ornamental details from the Bruni monument, was far more original, as it was the first tomb of its type with paneling below the sepulchral niche. Giovanni Rucellai's bold tomb project patterned after the Holy Sepulchre of Jerusalem was also decidedly at odds with his modest, highly conventional funeral projections.[46]

The reasons for this shift in cultural investment are varied and complex. Richard Goldthwaite has argued that magnificence and private patronage of art and architecture were twin responses to increasingly positive attitudes toward wealth as the century progressed. Samuel Cohn's argument for neighboring Siena emphasizes that the flow of resources to chapels in this "great age of selfishness" was a way to privatize ecclesiastical space more securely, even below the level of the elite. Historians showing a more political bent, such as Brucker, Martines, and Garin, link new forms of artistic consumption more closely to a changing political context. Beginning with Cosimo de' Medici's return from exile in 1434, political exclusion, on the one hand, and advancement through the Medici patronage system, on the other, signaled the contraction and ultimate retreat of what had formerly been an active political class. Medici partisans, who were often newcomers such as the Ginori and the Bonvanni, announced their good fortune by establishing new chapels and tombs, as well as by spending lavishly on public events such as burials and almsgiving. In 1469, for example, the sons of Niccolò Bonvanni reported having a debt of more than three hundred florins for their father's recent funeral; moreover, they were obliged by their grandfather's will to provide a meal for one hundred of the poor every year on the feast of San Niccolò, at which they said more than two hundred of the poor sometimes showed up.[47]

Yet these same strategies and forms of consumption could be used just as profitably by individuals, families, or households excluded from political participation under the Medici regime, to sustain their flagging reputations. F. W. Kent's sensitive exploration of the enigmatic Giovanni Rucellai, who remained suspect for thirty years after Cosimo's return, shows him engaged in building his family palace, erecting a monumental tomb, and commissioning works of art as a way to define his reputation, compensate for the loss of political stature, and remain in the public eye both in this life and beyond. Given these different interpretations by historians and the multiplicity of meanings attaching to both the production and consumption of art, it may be wise at this point to pursue Kent's suggestion that we look hard at individuals and their activities.[48]

One important yet unexamined aspect of this interest in the building of monumental tombs and of chapels is its impact on the availability of tomb sites for minor patrons and lesser citizens. Clearly, affluent men such as Cantino Cavalcanti, who in 1450 bought a site in Santa Trinità between the older tombs of the Bartolini and the Sercialli, had little difficulty procuring specific sites within their preferred churches.[49] But to what extent were notaries, shopkeepers, small tradesmen, and artisans still able to find eternal rest within church precincts in the middle decades of the Quattrocento? That answer is linked in specific terms with the degree of selectivity exhibited by each individual church. This in turn depended on several factors: the church's prestige, parish status, and monastic affiliation; the extinction of older families, which allowed new populations to assume their tombs or chapels; and the expansion or renovation of church precincts and cemeteries.

In more general terms, however, it is clear that popolani still had fairly ready access to intramural burial through the third quarter of the fifteenth century. The continued vitality of parish associations, coupled with social and occupational mobility among artisans and tradesmen, opened up opportunities for patronage, benefaction, or service which frequently earned ordinary citizens a coveted intramural tomb site. In 1453, for example, San Pancrazio granted its keeper of burial records and church syndic, Giuliano di Particino, a tomb site and even paid a small sum to have his emblem sculpted over the tomb "because he is our benefactor." Ten years later Giuliano opted to build a marble tomb in a better spot, undoubtedly reflecting his continued advance from upper artisan ranks to the lower rungs of the elite.[50] Again in 1453, the surprisingly affluent priest Ser Jacopo di Francesco bargained with the convent of Santissima Annunziata for both a new means of livelihood and a guaranteed tomb site. In return for a donation of 150 florins to beautify the convent, Santissima Annunziata accepted him into the community as a full member in life and in death.[51]

These impressions are buttressed by the more systematic evidence derived from the tomb register (*sepoltuario*) begun in 1463 by Piero Bonichi, prior of San Lorenzo. Bonichi's stated intention was to record "the order and form of the new tombs that Cosimo de' Medici and others have made underneath the church, and to whom these tombs are let, and in what place and part they can be found."[52]

Between the inception of the book in 1463 and the last recorded date, 1511, Bonichi and his successors wrote in the name and often the occupation of the owner of each tomb, as well as the date the tomb was acquired. The ongoing nature of the record makes an analysis of acquisitions over several decades more revealing than a year-by-year study. This compilation offers useful information about the social profile of tomb owners at one of the most important Florentine churches, which headed the city's largest, most populous parish.

At the very top of Bonichi's list were the most prestigious sites of the church's social topography: the tombs situated in private chapels belonging to well-known local families such as the Medici, the Rondinelli, the Aldobrandini, the Martelli, the della Stufa, the Ciai, and the Ginori. Chapels also housed three tombs destined for the operai of the church, as well as four tombs for the priors, canons, and chaplains of San Lorenzo. There nevertheless remained a considerable amount of choice burial space in the floor area. Bonichi noted that there were a total of eighty-nine new private tombs (exclusive of chapels) situated in the lower church, which were arranged in four long rows. Of these sites, only sixty-three tombs had been claimed or occupied by 1494. Forty of these sites, including twelve tombs owned by notarial families, belonged to popolani of widely varying professional and occupational status. Among the tradesmen represented in these and neighboring tombs down the nave were goldsmiths, artists, mercers, millers, oil and grain vendors, vintners, spicers, shoemakers, smithies, doublet makers, thread makers, furriers, brokers, stove makers, scrap dealers, sword makers, workers of damask and wool cloth, and secondhand dealers; canons and clerics were also represented. Not one of the tombs was formally owned by a woman, although undoubtedly women found burial in segregated slots in their kinsmen's tombs. Of the remaining twenty-three tombs in these rows, one belonged to a confraternity and the rest to men either identified as bankers or bearing recognizably prestigious surnames such as Medici, Benci, Orlandini, and Bonvanni.

In addition, there were another sixty-nine tombs in the middle nave, thirteen of which still remained available in 1488. The vast majority of these tombs belonged to middling professionals and male artisans of similarly varying occupational status who, according to the register, often displayed coats of arms on their slabs. Bonichi's register shows that the select burial precincts of San Lorenzo still mingled elite patrons with a solid middle tier of local inhabitants.

At other churches, however, popolani of modest status acquired new private burial sites only in locations with less social and spiritual prestige, such as the new cemetery created under the vaults of San Pancrazio after 1456. Among those purchasing tomb sites in the new cemetery in 1463–64 was Zanobia, wife of the barber-surgeon Maestro Dino, from the parish of San Paolo. The scribe noted that "because they [i.e., her family members] are newcomers to be buried here, we assigned them one of the new tombs we had made." San Pancrazio assigned a similar site to the barrel maker Domenico di Giovanni for his unnamed daughter because his household's previous tomb had been destroyed in the course of renovation.[53] However modest these sites, they nevertheless were clearly superior to the communal tombs awaiting immigrants from other Italian cities, day laborers, and poor plague victims.

Although death rites and funerary monuments reveal a general pattern of growing patrician dominance, it is important to recognize as well the many exceptions to this scheme, and to acknowledge the contingencies that shadowed even the best-laid social plans. Despite the disproportionate resources and opportunities enjoyed by the Florentine political and commercial classes, this was not a closed or predictable system but one in which disease, accidents, exile, and other adversities frequently undermined families' expectations and individuals' control of their own final hours. Several vignettes drawn from the diary of the merchant Francesco di Tommaso Giovanni remind us how contingencies turned what otherwise might have been impressive, even strategic social events into hurried improvisations often charged with a sense of failed ambitions. For example, Francesco noted how one of his co-consuls of the Lana guild, Alessandro Arrighi, was killed by a falling object while inspecting the cathedral in 1451: although Arrighi was rewarded with the full guild burial honors, twenty-two flags and eight processional torches, he left an adolescent daughter in such poverty that the guild itself had to supply her mourning clothes. Affecting Francesco more deeply was the accidental drowning death of his nephew Lorenzo in July 1456, which must have been a painful reminder of the similar fate dealt his own brother twenty-five years earlier. Many peasants, country neighbors, and women gathered together at the accident site for an impromptu ceremony, after which Lorenzo's body was brought back immediately for a rather plain burial in Santo Spirito.[54]

Francesco's moving account of his daughter Nanna's death during the plague-ridden summer of 1450 reveals not only the limitations imposed by unexpected turns of events but also the deep, sustained tensions within Florentine family structures which played into the quest for honor and remembrance. In this rich human drama, Francesco paints a small but highly suggestive picture of the competing claims and affections that divided fathers, daughters, and husbands. Here the larger structural conflict between natal and conjugal ties takes on an intimate face. It is worth quoting this episode in full, since it captures so well both the supportive nature of kinship and its conflicted workings.[55]

"I recall that, as was pleasing to God, my daughter Nanna, wife of Giovanni di Filippo Arrigucci, passed from this life on Tuesday the 14th of July, 1450, between the hours of six and seven at night. Shortly before, at the sixth hour, her son Filippo died; he was the eldest of their three children. Both had the sign of the plague, she on her thigh and he under the arm. They were staying at their place in Montughi next to Santa Maria. Their fevers began on Friday the tenth, and on Sunday the plague signs appeared. On Monday morning the 13th, Giovanni Arrigucci came to us in Pian di Ripoli also bearing a plague mark; beforehand he had shown it to the doctor, Maestro Girolamo, who said he was infected. Since I was ill with catarrh, my wife Mea went with Giovanni to Montughi, where only one of their slaves was on hand; she was the wet nurse of Nanna's son Bernardino, then in swaddling clothes. They found the house in a complete state of disarray. Mea discovered that several laborers had assisted Nanna, who that morning had been greatly weakened from lack of food. I also sent my son Tommaso and my manager Pippo to see to their care. Tommaso sent two women from Florence to the house as well: Monna Simona, the wet nurse of [Francesco's son] Giovanbattista, and Monna Caterina [Mea's sister], who went to the house with her. It seemed that God had sent them in order to assist the two sick and to help Monna [Mea]. That same day, Giovanni took the other two children and the slave away with him to Florence, leaving only Monna [Mea] and the two women behind with the sick."

Despite Mea's best efforts at care, "moving from room to room throughout the night," first one patient died, then the other. Nanna's repeated requests for last rites had gone unanswered, since no one was available to fetch a priest that night. In a later marginal note, Francesco consoled himself with the knowledge that Nanna had confessed at Santo Spirito a month before; he also took solace in knowing that, in the absence of a priest, Nanna had nevertheless confessed herself "so devoutly and with such perfect lucidity" that she died untroubled. After the deaths of Nanna and her son, it fell to Mea to dress and arrange the bodies, and to immediately begin making funeral plans. This was not so very unusual: mothers, wives, sisters, in-laws, and other close female kin often played a central role not only in care of the sick but also in making practical arrangements for the dead. To honor his wife and son, Giovanni Arrigucci sent up four large torches, candles, and a coffin in which both bodies were placed, after which mother and son were given local burial in Montughi. But it does not appear from the record that Giovanni Arrigucci himself left the city to attend the funeral, perhaps because he was ill. The "disconsolate" Mea put the house in order, closed it up, and returned to Florence.

Later that year, Giovanni Arrigucci retrieved the bodies of his wife and son for reburial in his family tombs in Santa Maria Novella, although Francesco was unaware of the precise date this transpired. It was customary, of course, for the elite to practice secondary burial, as well as for wives to be buried in their husbands' tombs in the absence of testamentary instructions to the contrary. Yet an apparent strain between father and son-in-law over the proper care of Nanna's soul and earthly memory crept into this marginal note. As Francesco said, "I don't know if an office was ever said for them, but I arranged a meal in exchange for five masses" at Santo Spirito. Francesco expressed his strong sentiment for his daughter by commissioning another office at the Paradiso monastery and thirty masses at the Carmine for her soul.

A different set of adverse circumstances confronted patrician exiles struggling to maintain their family honor and reputation in their native city. Exiles had few opportunities to aid their cause through great funeral displays and elaborate tombs. Here the well-documented story of Matteo Strozzi offers a good illustration of both the disadvantages posed by exile, and the strategies used to surmount them. Although Matteo Strozzi had maintained a neutral position toward the Medici, Cosimo's wrath toward Matteo's cousin Palla, plus the wealth and social prominence of the Strozzi, led Cosimo to exile Matteo to Pesaro for five years. The respect or fear of the Medicean regime for the size, power, and distinction of the Strozzi family resulted in the extension of the ban for twenty-five years, with additional proscriptions for exiles' sons. The Strozzi remained suspect into the 1450s and 1460s. Marco Parenti, Filippo Strozzi's brother-in-law, was removed from the ballot bags by the *accoppiatori* in 1455 on political grounds, and the political position of Giovanni Rucellai, Palla's son-in-law, remained tenuous.[56]

The tributes paid to Matteo Strozzi upon his death in Naples in 1459 reflected these distorted circumstances. Matteo's older brother and fellow exile Filippo "arranged a beautiful burial ceremony" in that city, as he wrote to his other brother Lorenzo in Bruges. Filippo outfitted himself in a long mourning mantle "in the style of Florence" and advised Lorenzo to perform whatever mourning ceremonies seemed appropriate in foreign lands.[57] In Florence, however, honoring Matteo proved a more difficult task, since only private domestic ceremonies and requiem masses were permitted for exiles. The Stoic-inspired fortitude of Matteo's brother-in-law Marco Parenti also worked in practice to hide public grief over Matteo's loss. Writing to Filippo, Marco reflected that "worthy men do not allow themselves to be overcome by misfortunes, but when these occur, they grow in perfection and are a refuge and consolation to others."[58] His steely control contrasted sharply with the kind of customary behavior exhibited in these same years by a rich peasant mother in the countryside, who issued "shrieks, cries, and sobs" to mourn her son, willfully making herself "dishevelled, scratched, and afflicted."[59]

Under these exceptional circumstances, women kin still resident in Florence assumed an exceptional social role, just as they did in the economic affairs of exile families, or in the episode of Franceso Giovanni's daughter. Once news of Matteo's death spread to family members, it was the women who immediately began to make necessary arrangements, as Francesco Strozzi wrote to Filippo.[60] In his deathbed testament, Matteo had recognized the vital role his mother Alessandra would play, and stipulated that his estate should furnish mourning garb for anyone she designated. Accepting the charge, Alessandra sought consolation for this bitter loss not in Stoicism but in religious teachings, and wrote to Filippo that she had tried to muster a celebration that would reflect honorably on all her sons, living and dead. She outfitted her daughters Caterina and Alessandra in mourning at substantial expense (which Filippo would later repay), while paying for her own mourning garb.[61] With the men of the patriline in exile, mother and sisters carried the social burden of marking Matteo's loss for the benefit of friends, neighbors, clients, and even enemies, thus upholding the honor of the entire family. Depending on one's kinswomen for such a critical task may not have fit neatly with many of the patriarchal precepts of Florentine society; but in practice, the efforts and activities of female kin proved fundamental to the survival of a lineage's substance and reputation.

Women and the Sexual Politics of Mourning Clothes

The importance of women's mourning activities for exiles was reinforced by a growing sensitivity to both the value and the meaning of clothing in mid-Quattrocento Italy. Although clothing had long been an established indicator of status in Italian society, it assumed new functions in the social, political, and moral economy of the mid-Quattrocento. The greater material value of fur-trimmed sleeves, brocaded gowns, and embroidered mantles and hoods, as well as jewelry, berets, belts, and shoes, prompted wealthy Florentines such as Dietisalvi Neroni, Giovanni Venturi, and Antonio Segni to keep careful domestic inventories.[62]

Earlier in the century, lawmakers had tried to stem the tide of rising clothing costs by searching for a happy medium between restraint and ostentation. The sumptuary statutes of 1449 continued the crusade against extravagance in a relative spirit of accommodation. But in July 1459 lawmakers took a different ideological tack that did not merely emphasize the economic damage wrought by women's expensive clothing using the usual misogynist rhetoric: the new law also stressed the moral affront such clothing posed to a republican political order. Florentine women were no longer content to go about dressed "like daughters and wives of merchants and private citizens," read the statute, but instead wished to appear "like daughters and wives of great princes and lords [gran principi e signori]."[63] Ironically, this nostalgia proposed that women's finery might function as a political mechanism to help retain fundamental burgher values while, at the same time, Medicean political practice moved ever farther from its republican base.

Mourning garb offered a special slant on the political and sexual relations defined by clothing. That mourning clothes carried exceptional moral value and political significance is made explicit in remarks by Francesco Guicciardini, commenting on an ambassadorial mission of his forebear Jacopo. Sent to console Galeazzo Maria Sforza of Milan shortly after the duke's mother Bianca Maria died in 1468, Jacopo opted for his customary ambassadorial robes of blue-violet. As Guicciardini remarked, Jacopo made this choice because "he did not think it befitting to have to dress in black for the death of a woman." Since the duke was extremely distraught over his mother's death and gave her a huge court funeral, Jacopo followed his better political instincts and dutifully assumed mourning. The question of full mourning for envoys and their retainers had never even surfaced when the ambassadors Messers Bernardo Giugni and Luigi Guicciardini journeyed to Milan two years earlier for the funeral of Duke Francesco Sforza.[64]

Paralleling the sexual politics expressed above was a still-greater stress on the public representation of patriliny via men's mourning clothes. Earlier in the century, patrician men had highlighted their patrilineal affiliation by donning more splendid mourning mantles for male agnates, or by reaching more widely into patrilineal networks to increase the number of mourners at their kinsmen's funerals. In the mid-Quattrocento, these trends were reinforced and enhanced by the continual lessening of the extent to which men observed mourning for cognatic relations. By mid-century, Florentine men of the elite regularly observed mourning only for their wives and mothers, and for men of the patriline. Men of high standing were quick of course to assume mourning for other male members of their lineage, as did several Sassetti for their kinsman Bernardo in 1444. But there was great reluctance to identify oneself as a mourner across lineages. Marco Parenti donned mourning for his father Parente in 1452, for example, while Parente's son-in-law Benedetto Quaratesi did not. Nor did Luca da Panzano assume mourning for his daughter Gostanza's husband Jacopo Risaliti in 1446, and he snatched his daughter back to the natal fold before she could don the expected dark robes.[65] Francesco Giovanni provides yet another useful example of these evolving kinship relations. When Francesco's sister-in-law Checcha, wife of Messer Giovannozzo Pitti, died in 1443, Francesco proudly noted how her two sisters—his wife Mea, and Caterina, wife of Bernardo Sapiti—and her two sisters-in-law received mourning gowns and veils; yet at the same time he noted no special attire for himself.[66]

Men also readily assumed mourning when their wives predeceased them. Domestic bonds, both conjugal and filial, loomed large in the burial of Checcha (d. 1459) the wife of Antonio Masi, who was formally mourned by her husband and nine sons, seven of whom paid for their own apparel. However, the honors accorded to mothers, sisters, and kinswomen in other phases of their life cycle or living in unusual household configurations were far less predictable. When Marco Parenti's mother Tommasa died four years after the death of his father, he may have taken the unusual step of reusing the same mourning clothes, but he apparently did not purchase a new set for the occasion.[67]

In contrast to the increasingly restricted kinship connections dramatized by men's mourning, the mourning garb worn by women continued to cast a wide, complex kinship net beyond the bounds of patriliny. Like women's commissions of commemorative masses, women's mourning reflected their structural position as the nexus between kin groups, as well as the accidents of their personal experience.[68] Although we know comparatively little about the full networks of women's sociability, it seems clear that kinship in its many forms furnished the primary companions for propertied women. These often tangled relations—mingling blood ties, marriage, friendship, and social support—were reflected in illness and care of the sick as well as in death and mourning. For example, Francesco Giovanni reported that when this wife Mea fell ill in 1452 with erysipelas ("Saint Anthony's fire") and needed constant nursing, she was attended "day and night for many days" by a rotating crew of three or four women. Mea's nurses included Bandecha, widow of Francesco's cousin; Lena Salviati, married to Francesco's brother, and Lisabetta Corbinelli, wife of Mea's own brother; another cousin's wife, Bice Ubertini; the wet nurse Simona; and Antonia dalla Porta, whose relationship in unclear. When Mea recovered, much to her husband's joy, Francesco attempted on his physician's advice to limit "the multitude of women who came to visit her," but his instructions were ignored, "especially by her kinswomen."[69]

These various female kin in turn honored their family ties and personal affections as mourners on multiple occasions. Mourning the fecund Checcha Masi, who had borne thirty-six children, were not only her husband and nine sons (her only surviving offspring) but also her mother (who had become a tertiary), her sister, her three daughters-in-law, and her husband's niece.[70] Some of this complexity may have been shaped by personal animosities as well as by affections. It is difficult to know exactly why, for instance, Lulla, the widow of Giulino del Benino, designated her brother's wife Betta as her chief mourner in 1450 and provided her with a respectable mourning outfit, yet made no claims on or provisions for her brother, who was not asked to handle the funeral arrangements although he was still alive at the time.[71]

The restricted scope of men's mourning, on the one hand, coupled with the sustained complexity of women's mourning, on the other, dovetailed with humanist models of decorum, which radiated out into the larger society in the middle decades of the fifteenth century. These enmeshed developments marked out a more stringent sexual division of labor in the tasks associated with grief and mourning. As a result of both the assertion of patriliny and the spread of humanist culture, mourning in the mid-Quattrocento was increasingly viewed as "women's work."

The new moral, social, and political functions attached to mourning dress, as well as its high cost, made it a focal point in both law and literature for various social and sexual tensions. This was particularly true for the dress of widows, who occupied an ambiguous and potentially dangerous status outside the bounds of guardianship and family identification afforded by marriage. Around 1450 the noted bookseller Vespasiano da Bisticci presented a model widow, Alessandra Bardi, whose very appearance resolved the ambiguities surrounding her status. Vespasiano hailed Alessandra as a paragon of female virtue and widowhood, whose exemplary behavior was still more praiseworthy because of her youth. Unlike many wayward widows of her day, Alessandra rejected such "base vanities" as "garments lined with black fur or cloth, or miniver." Instead, she wore a cloak that "was quite plain, her dress high up to her neck, as becomes a widow, with a veil over her eyes." In addition, her mantle and veil covered her face "in such a way that one could hardly see it." Alessandra had patterned her own behavior on the widow Caterina Alberti Corsini, who, according to Vespasiano, kept her house "like a well-ordered convent," a woman those "clothes were suitable to widowhood," and whose face "was always covered" on her rare excursions from home.[72] In his praise of both Alessandra Bardi and Caterina Corsini, Vespasiano made explicit that the ideal garb for a widow stressed her frugality and modesty as it effectively effaced and desexualized her.

As Vespasiano would have been the first to admit, however, not all Florentine widows adhered to this cultural model. There were great variations in the age, economic status, piety, personalities, and household arrangements of widows, even among the elite, and these variations gave rise to a range of social behaviors. Both Vespasiano and sumptuary statutes complained that a sizeable number of Florentine widows and women mourners deviated from sober, conservative norms in their mourning apparel. Lawmakers in November 1459 denounced the extent to which women's newly "degenerate" mourning garb departed from established custom. Like Vespasiano, Florentine lawmakers cast a nostalgic look backwards as they sought to hold on to the conventions of the past. The 1459 statute bemoaned the fact that, instead of conserving the "good and excellent customs of our ancestors," Florentine women undermined the city's honor and reputation by sporting fashionably long trains on their mourning mantles.[73] Here lawmakers seemed to think that, in following the whims of fashion, Florentine women were willfully transforming their mourning duties from something customary and fixed by men to something more mutable and expressive of their own designs. In other words, the lawmakers claimed that women were subverting tradition rather than honoring it. Given that mourning customs themselves were in a state of transition by the middle of the fifteenth century, seemingly small modifications of clothing were perceived as a double violation: they deformed custom, on the one hand, and challenged women's passive acceptance of a prescribed cultural role, on the other.

The 1459 statute made another, perhaps more serious, charge. Lawmakers claimed that under their dark mantles, women wore dresses with huge slits, or with necklines cut so low that "they exposed half their chest." These new fashions introduced an explicit degree of sexuality into mourning garb, bringing nothing but shame to the dead instead of marking their memory "with emotion and sorrow." Three years earlier, lawmakers had decried the low neck-lines on women's gowns in fairly generic terms. The remedies pro-posed by this new law of 1459, however, were quite specific: trains on mourning mantles were limited to a very modest one-quarter braccia; women mourners could not wear dresses with slits, and they were enjoined to cover their chests completely by fastening their collars above the neck, under pain of a twenty-five-florin fine.[74]

The social consequences of these new mourning fashions were clear to lawmakers, who perceived that the way women arranged, changed, or otherwise managed their mourning appeal threatened both the sanctity of social custom and the prevailing moral order. Only a few months before, lawmakers had stressed that in daily life women should dress in keeping with republican values. In the mid-dle decades of the fifteenth century, women's clothing acquired not only a formidable price tag but also powerful moral and civic func-tions. This emerging concern that clothing should both ensure wom-en's public modesty and buttress a political order signals the begin-ning of an important shift in sumptuary law from an economic rationale to a social one. In the second half of the Quattrocento, sumptuary statutes became increasingly concerned with regulating and con-trolling social behaviors, rather than simply with curbing excess.[75] With the legitimation of wealth and spending, on the one hand, and the entrenchment of a political oligarchy, on the other, sumptuary codes were dedicated as much to social and sexual control as to economic conservation.

Although lawmakers made their opinions and rationales known through various preambles and legal prescriptions, it is more difficult to judge the precise motives of Florentine women in purposefully manipulating mourning garb, either as a means of personal expres-sion or as a way to resist encroachments on what they viewed as their customary domain. However, it is not unreasonable to assume that Florentine women as a group used strategies similar to those of other Italian women, who sensitively used techniques of the body as resources of power, whether in manipulating food to achieve sanctity or in artfully defending their right to freedom of choice in clothes. The Sienese humanist Battista Petrucci, for instance, chose to be exempted from all sumptuary statutes as a reward for her public eloquence in 1452. Similarly, the Bolognese patrician Nicolosa Sanuti argued against the 1453 sumptuary laws of Cardinal Bessarion. Sanuti insisted that women should be free of sumptuary restrictions because they depended on clothing, not politics or warfare, for honor and distinction. Dress was at the very heart of women's worth, argued Sanuti: without distinctions in dress, both the conventions of social class and women's special identity would disappear.[76]

The sense that propertied women in particular used clothing as part of a larger set of social strategies, which allowed for some influence, self-expression, and social recognition, is buttressed by the range and depth of women's religious activities and ecclesiastical patronage in the middle of the fifteenth century. Participation in lay religious organizations, as well as gift giving to local churches, afforded propertied women avenues that might alternately enhance, complement, or compensate for their changing role in ritual. Since this is a large area of inquiry which has not yet been studied, the evidence cited here is intended mainly to suggest both the richness of the context and possibilities for future research. As women continued throughout the late Trecento and the early Quattrocento to take advantage of the brokerage services and spiritual benefits confraternities offered, some religious companies responded by becoming more receptive to women's formal membership and participation. The newly approved statutes of Santa Maria della Neve at Sant'Ambrogio (1445), for example, required the company scribe to keep a separate account book "which is called the Book of Women, and to write in it year by year the names of all the women who are now or who in the future will be in our company, as well as their payments, one by one, that is, woman by woman and man by man." The company also dispensed candles to all members in good standing, including women, at its annual feast, had a tomb site for its female members, and obliged itself to recite the Gregorian mass cycle and other prayers for both women and men.[77]

Moreover, there is evidence that in the mid-Quattrocento groups of women also formed their own religious organizations. In 1460 about eighty women, who were "among the most devout women of Florence and from the best, most respected houses" of the city, founded the consorority of Santa Maria del Popolo at the Carmine.

Headed by its first prioress Lisa, widow of Niccolò Serragli, this consorority centered its cult life on the Virgin, as did many other mixed or male companies.[78] Companies such as these may have been prototypes for the sacramental companies of the early sixteenth century, such as the all-female Company of the Holy Miracle at Sant'Ambrogio, founded in 1534.[79] Affluent women also donated numerous gifts of liturgical vessels, vestments, and other objects to churches, perhaps using the growing resources of dowry. In a gesture rich with homage, Francesco Giovanni's wife Mea Corbinelli personally delivered her household's gifts of two large altar cloths and two maniples to the Badia in 1453. On the other side of the river, the Carmine added several new acquisitions bearing the marks of their donors to its already rich collection of chalices, altar cloths, and altar paintings given earlier by women. Among these new acquisitions were an enameled silver chalice decorated with the Pulci arms and the inscription "Domina Albertesca de Pulciis me fecit fieri," and another chalice given by Lisabetta di Lorenzo Segni, which was decorated with enameled pieces and with a split coat of arms of the Segni and the Canisani.[80]

These various activities and objects partially reinforced, yet were also at odds with, other major developments in death rites between 1434 and 1464, which sought to entrench the dominance of the Florentine commune, the Medici, and male oligarchs. Whatever victory the Medicean fathers enjoyed in these decades was riddled with numerous tensions reflected in the poignant laments for older, better days. The very process of constructing spectacular representations that relayed messages about order and authority brought to the fore profound conflicts and contradictions about republican values, the nature of custom, and women's prescribed roles in culture and kinship. Despite the rhetoric underlying spending, the new magnificence paradoxically bred for some a new conservatism and a nostalgia for the past. Even Marsuppini's funeral, which marked the pinnacle of civic funerary ritual, rested on a precarious balance at best. Although the reiteration of older conventions in funerals served to celebrate the city's centrality and to fortify a Medicean order, not even the power and capaciousness of ritual could successfully hold together these contradictions and tensions for very long.

CHAPTER 6

THE RETURN OF AN

ARISTOCRATIC ETHOS

etween the death of Cosimo de' Medici in 1464 and the end of the republic in 1530, funeral rites both elaborated on previous stylistic trends and reflected complex changes in Florentine politics and society. In the second half of the Quattrocento, funeral trappings departed very little from the conventions established earlier in the century. Magnificence generally remained the guiding principle for men of the elite, with a small handful of sumptuary permits marking out an extremely select group of funerals staged for wealthy or distinguished men.[1] The rapid expansion of humanist culture after the Peace of Lodi (1454) gave classicizing funeral orations an ever more secure place in the Florentine repertoire of honors. Impressive tomb monuments and new decorative programs in family chapels, such as those undertaken in Santa Maria Novella by Filippo Strozzi or the Tornabuoni, set apart the great families of Florence in lasting ways. The entrenchment and elaboration of these earlier practices only served to sharpen the contrast between a narrowly defined elite and less privileged citizens.

Working within this conventional framework, funerals nevertheless reflected many of the conditions and processes that dramatically altered the Florentine social and political landscape in the late Quattrocento. As Florence became increasingly governed by patronage networks centered on the Medici, funerals gradually took on features of rites of deference, rites that were both constituents and byproducts of patronage. Changing class relations also reshaped the social composition of parishes and consequently, patterns of parish burial, as laborers were pushed—in part by patricians' building campaigns— from the old urban core to the periphery. Accompanying these large-scale shifts in social relations were changing relations within families and kinship groups; these changes were reflected in sumptuary law and mourning practices. By granting greater privileges to patrilineal kin, new sumptuary laws passed in the 1470s posited patriliny as the dominant way of reckoning kinship. The late Quattrocento witnessed not only the consolidation of control by the patriciate but also the triumphal assertion of patrilineal and patriarchal family arrangements.

However, the direction of change in funerary style and practices in the second half of the Quattrocento was neither simple nor consistent, even among the elite. The 1480s and 1490s in particular witnessed a perceptible backlash against funerary pomp among a sizeable number of well-placed Florentines. The continued growth of spectacle, on the one hand, and its outright rejection, on the other, testified to increasingly divergent views among the elite about appropriate public displays of status in the face of death and divine judgment. Rather than being uniformly accepted, magnificence came to be hotly contested, especially during the tumultuous years of Savonarola's influence between 1494 and 1498. This rift in cultural style and religious taste was compounded by the serious economic and political problems besetting the city, beginning with the French invasion of 1494 and continuing through the harsh interdict leveled by Julius II in 1511.

To a certain extent, this contest between magnificence and moderation was decided by the restoration of the Medici in 1512. Following that family's return to local power, magnificence enjoyed a tremendous resurgence. The effusion of elaborate Medici-sponsored ceremonies in the 1510s and 1520s set important precedents for Duke Cosimo I, who channeled and transformed republican images and ritual practices to serve the Medici principate. Beginning with the restoration of the Medici, funeral style experienced a "rearistocratization" that evoked the chivalric models of northern Europe, freighted with symbols of monarchy and feudal lordship. These same years also saw the rise of the requiem as a new form of mortuary spectacle. Over the course of the sixteenth century, this process moved rapidly to create one of the most striking art forms of late Renaissance and baroque Italy: namely, the "total art" of requiem theater, which integrated effigies, decorative arts, architectural monuments, new forms of music making and liturgy, orations, and printed memorabilia into a complete ensemble designed to defy death and vanquish the limits of memory.[2]

This chapter examines the complex development of funeral rites and mourning practices in the late fifteenth and early sixteenth centuries. The story of death rites necessarily takes on a more explicit political focus in this chapter for several reasons. First and foremost is the fact that politics was an exceptionally important determinant of culture in this period. Historians have increasingly recognized the need to bring the state back into social history and to view culture as responsive to political events, strategies, and individuals whose actions helped change the wider structure. In keeping with this recognition, this chapter attempts to interweave the history of Florence with the history of its most famous family, the Medici. The history of the Medici did not constitute the full story of death and ritual in Renaissance Florence; but neither can that story be told without them. Moreover, the success of the Medici was predicated upon the creation of an elite party sympathetic to their position. This Medicean oligarchy mobilized key civic and local resources in their own interests, which in turn created a new politics of daily life for Medici allies, enemies, and bystanders alike. Finally, in the closing decades of the Quattrocento, Florence became entangled in the actions and policies of mightier European powers, whose intervention in Italian affairs spelled the end of political autonomy for the peninsula. Politics—whether practiced on an international, civic, or neighborhood scale—was one of the prime movers of Florentine culture and social experience between Cosimo's death and the death of the republic.

Cosimo de' Medici, "Father of the Country"

The funeral rites for Cosimo de' Medici, who died on August 1, 1464, capped a thirty-year effort by the Medici to consolidate power while working within the framework of republican institutions. The contemporary remark that Cosimo "was consulted before marriages were arranged, before buildings were constructed, before any decision of importance was taken" has been corroborated by studies of Medicean control over the electoral ballot bags, the preferment of Medici candidates for positions in universities and the Church, and the unprecedented demolition of existing houses to permit construction of the Medici palace. As one contemporary succinctly stated, "Cosimo was everything in Florence, and without him Florence was nothing."[3]

Part of Cosimo's success among the political classes stemmed from his consistent self-portrayal as nothing more than a private citizen. Machiavelli praised Cosimo for his prudence and for his calculated attempts to remain within the bounds of "civil modesty."[4] Image making for Cosimo had a distinct political content and was as integral to his political efforts as it was to those of his grandson Lorenzo, even though the images of both men remain enigmatic. Cosimo chided Pius II, for example, for writing to him "not as a private man who is satisfied with the mediocre dignity of a citizen, but as though I were a reigning prince," and he reminded the pope of "how limited is the power of a private citizen in a free state under popular government."[5]

Cosimo's desire for a simple burial has long formed part of his historical legend. There is no reason to doubt the sincerity of his spiritual concerns, which were especially pronounced during his final days at Careggi, or even his respect for traditional republican values, which tempered his actions and self-representation throughout his lifetime. Cosimo did not make a testament but instead confided his deathbed wishes to his son Piero in the presence of the humanist secretary to the Medici, Bartolomeo Scala, who resided in Cosimo's household.[6] Florence's leading citizen wanted only the clergy of San Lorenzo, San Marco, and the abbey of Fiesole to participate in the ceremonies, thus continuing his well-known patronage of these institutions. He further stipulated that his interment in San Lorenzo was to be "in terra," rather than in the kind of ornate elevated tomb that had become increasingly popular by the time of his death. Piero dutifully discharged his filial obligations by purchasing for the funeral, held on August 2, "neither more nor less wax than required for a modest burial."[7] A month after the burial, Giovanni Bonsi wrote to his exiled brother-in-law Filippo Strozzi in Naples that Cosimo's funeral had been in keeping with his desire for restraint, and other contemporaries corroborated this assessment. Machiavalli was a lone voice when later he imagined a ceremony conducted with "the utmost pomp and solemnity."[8]

Although Cosimo's funeral was less spectacular than it might have been, it could hardly be called simple. Wax consumption amounted to a quarter ton; the estate bought mourning clothes for forty-five persons at a cost of 582 florins; Cosimo's widow Contessina de' Bardi wore a stupendous outfit cut from thirty braccia of fine cloth, over twice the customary or legally permissible yardage.[9] Whatever the historical myths surrounding the occasion, Cosimo's funeral was certainly not distinguished by its austerity.

It could be argued, in fact, that the most outstanding feature of Cosimo's funeral was neither its extravagance nor its simplicity, but its sheer conventionality. Critical to the occasion's success was the careful channeling of wealth in entirely standard or predictable ways, so that the tribute stayed well within the bounds of established tradition. The various trappings of wax and flags all placed Cosimo's funeral squarely among the most eminent patrician burials of his generation but in no way distinguished it as unique or unseemly. Although Piero has often been portrayed as less politically astute than his father, he nevertheless proved himself to be a sensitive master of ceremonies for this important event, steering clear of any overt political or civic fanfare that might jeopardize the interpretation of the occasion as strictly a family affair. He refused the grand tribute of the French king's flag, for example, as incompatible with his father's wishes, only to be rewarded the following year with the privilege of adding the French lily to the family's coat of arms.[10]

Similarly, in keeping with custom, the acknowledgment of ties of kinship anchored the proceedings. Representing the family were Cosimo's son Piero, grandsons Lorenzo and Giuliano, and nephew Pierfrancesco, as well as Cosimo's natural son Carlo. The mourners also included a number of women drawn into Medici households through marriage: Piero's wife Lucrezia Tornabuoni and her two daughters by Piero, Bianca and Nannina; Ginevra Alessandri, widow of Cosimo's son Giovanni, who had died the previous year; Ginevra Cavalcanti, widow of Cosimo's long-dead brother Lorenzo; and Laudomina Acciaiuoli, married to Cosimo's "rustic" nephew Pierfrancesco.[11]

Behind this conventional face of grief, however, lay a subtle new development. Over half of the forty-five mourners were not kin but represented instead an unprecedented mix of political friends, business associates, clients, household staff, and farmhands. Their inclusion demonstrated Cosimo's largesse as head of a great household, while also indirectly referring to his political role as patron and leading citizen. Among those provided mourning clothes at the estate's expense were the humanist Bartolomeo Scala, a self-described "servant of the Medici house," whose appointment as chancellor in

April 1465 stemmed in part from Medici favor, and Nicodemo di Pontremoli, secretary of Cosimo's ally the duke of Milan. Others supplied with mourning included a group of professionals with whom Cosimo regularly did business, such as notaries and the family doctor; thirteen men who worked as factors and stewards at the Medici estates in Careggi and Cafaggiolo; and five serving-women and four female slaves.[12]

In maneuvering around overt statements of political authority, Cosimo's funeral marked his position more by the display of new forms of social power than by conspicuous consumption. In this regard, his funeral stands at the beginning of one of the major developments in late fifteenth-century funerals: namely, the growing complexity of funerals as social events, with mourners of diverse identities taking a more prominent part in the proceedings. During the final decades of the century, patrician funeral pomp came increasingly to be construed in terms of influence or dominion over people, whose numbers and identities furnished social complements to rich material objects.

Cosimo had created much of his power by establishing networks of clients and friends, and his death offered Piero an important occasion to cultivate new ties or strengthen existing ones. After the funeral, Piero turned to charity and commemoration as the chief means of enlarging the fold of Medici clients, both personal and corporate. Cosimo had reportedly left 2,000 florins to be distributed for assorted acts of charity, such as dowering poor girls and releasing prisoners from the Stinche. Rather than donating money anonymously or through institutions, however, Piero instead personalized his giving, recording the names of individual recipients, who no doubt acquired moral and political debts to the new Medici heir along with the handouts.[13] To what extent these relationships cut vertically into the social structure remains a problem for future research.

It was primarily through commemoration, however, that Piero helped multiply the family's capital as institutional patrons. Piero subsidized a huge number of commemorative offices to benefit his father's soul, totaling perhaps as many as twelve thousand masses, at fifty-three different local ecclesiastical institutions.[14] This was a commemorative program distinguished not simply by its sheer numbers but also by its comprehensive, almost global coverage of the Florentine ecclesiastical map. Here Piero's philanthropic strategies differed from those of his father. Rather than focusing on a few select institutions, Piero instead blanketed the city with Medici largesse. Distributing his favors this broadly served the dual purpose of benefiting his father's soul while keeping the Medici name fresh throughout Florence and its environs. Much of the groundwork in establishing the Medici's relations with various ecclesiastical institutions had already been done by Piero's brother Giovanni, who predeceased Cosimo in 1463, and by Giovanni's wife Ginevra Alessandri, an avid letter-writer and patron in her own right who took a keen interest in the workings of several convents.[15]

The diversity of the locations, types, sizes, and affiliations of recipient foundations made Cosimo's commemorative program the most geographically widespread and institutionally varied program among Florentines to that date. Piero solicited services from all the major religious orders in the city, regardless of size or importance, rather than restricting his favors to Observant houses such as that of the Dominicans of San Marco, for which Cosimo had a great affection. Among the foundations targeted were several with which Cosimo had enjoyed a specific personal or familial association. Nor surprisingly, the most obvious focus of attention was the church of San Lorenzo. Piero subsidized a heavy concentration of masses immediately following Cosimo's death: one office of thirty masses for eight days, succeeded by a daily office for the next month. Coupled with the weekly Monday mass, psalms, and procession that Cosimo had commissioned for his father Giovanni, masses for the Medici must have dominated the priests' daily calendar for some time.[16] This cluster was followed by a series of weekly and monthly offices performed over the course of the ensuing year.

When the great porphyry slab was placed on Cosimo's tomb in 1467, his tomb site became the focus of a unique annual memorial service. The tomb itself was strategically located in front of the high altar rather than in the Old Sacristy near his parents' sepulchre. On the eve of the feast of San Lorenzo, the canons were commissioned to cover the slab with a beautiful pall and surround it with burning candles until daybreak. The combination of the site, the materials, and the ceremonial observances created an extraordinary set of classical, imperial, and sacramental associations that made the tomb singular among contemporary monuments. The tomb stood as the physical embodiment of the special relationship Cosimo enjoyed with the canons and church of San Lorenzo.[17]

The web of Medicean ecclesiastical patronage spun around Cosimo's figure nevertheless extended well beyond the predictable bounds of San Lorenzo, San Marco, and the abbey of Fiesole, "churches [Cosimo] had built."[18] Piero solicited special prayers or masses from the aristocratic Vallombrosan convent of Santa Verdiana, where the abbess in 1463 was a kinswoman, Piera de' Medici, and from the Benedictine convent of the Murate, whose shrewd abbess, Scholastica Rondinelli, had exchanged numerous letters with Giovanni and Piero during the early 1460s. Also patronized were the parish church of San Tommaso, an old neighborhood enclave for several branches of the family, and the Observant Franciscans of San Francesco del Bosco in the Mugello, one of Cosimo's favored communities in the Medici's original country seat.[19] This network of commemorative patronage also extended internationally, to numerous places where the Medici had business offices. In Rome, Venice, Milan, Bruges, Geneva, London, and Avignon, Cosimo's associates, clients, well-wishers, and friends gathered together for homage and common prayer.

Viewed as a coherent program, Piero's remembrance of his father thus combined a dual orientation: it strengthened already deep local ties, including those in the *contado*, while branching out into broader urban and international arenas. The Medici, and the patriciate more generally, were moving out of purely local enclaves, where they still retained their interests, to create larger, more complex ensembles of institutional patronage. As the patriciate increasingly forged networks of marriage alliance and political clientage on a citywide basis in the second half of the Quattrocento, the commemorative process was integrated with, and contributed to, broader patterns of control and family interest.

Soon after Cosimo's death, a flood of consolatory letters poured in from such foreign dignitaries as Pope Pius II, the cardinal of Sant'Angelo, and the king of France; Piero assiduously copied these letters into his record book. Cosimo's grandsons Lorenzo and Giuliano also wrote a Latin letter comforting Piero, who had lost both his father and brother within a nine-month period.[20] These letters, which by now had become an integral part of elite funerary conventions, nevertheless reflected both new intellectual tastes and the changing realities of patronage and political rule in Quattrocento Florence. Fifteenth-century humanists often docilely followed the classical rhetorical norms governing the genre of consolatory letters. Even outstanding humanists such as Marsuppini developed little formal novelty or originality of argument.[21] The formulaic structure and classical erudition of these letters contrasted with the more emotional, familiar tone of vernacular letters of consolation exchanged between friends, acquaintances, or even patrons and clients. In a flowing letter written from Siena, Piera Berti consoled Ginevra Alessandri Medici in 1459 on the death of Ginevra's only son Cosimino in language that was openly emotional yet surprisingly restrained in religious content. Bartolomeo Dei's more meditative reflection on the fragility of fortune and the brevity of life, written on the death of Lorenzo de' Medici's young daughter Luigia in 1488, still retains the power to move the reader five centuries later.[22]

Despite the derivative quality of many humanist consolations, these letters proliferated in the second half of the century as humanists intensified their search for patrons and financial support. As a means to possible preferment, the poet Cinelli, for example, sent a consolatory letter to Cosimo de' Medici on the death of Cosimo's son Giovanni in December 1463, openly hoping to be rewarded for his efforts.[23] Francesco da Castiglione, who owed to Medici efforts his appointment to the Greek chair in the Florentine Studio and his position as canon of San Lorenzo, repaid his patrons through eulogies and consolations. Castiglione consoled Cosimo on his son's death in 1463, as had Cinelli, and he also wrote formal consolations to Lorenzo and Giuliano when their father Piero died in 1469. Upon Cosimo's death, however, Castiglione directed his formal condolence not to the immediate family but rather to Cosimo's fellow ruler Alessandro Gonzaga, thereby offering his letter to a wider public audience for appreciation.[24]

Consolatory letters, conventional trappings, and memorial masses were completely acceptable forms of tribute to a private citizen. Yet as a governing body, the commune confronted the far more delicate matter of how to honor its most prominent citizen while remaining within the framework of republican institutions and traditions. Communal policy had traditionally avoided open alignment of the government with a single person or family, and the problem was compounded by Cosimo's status as a private citizen at the time of his death, which made him technically ineligible for the funeral subsidy often granted to those who had repeatedly held office. The solution to this problem was arrived at only in March 1465, when the committee of ten men appointed by the commune posthumously awarded Cosimo the title *pater patriae*, which became his most famous historical epithet. By 1467 the tomb slab bearing an inscription referring to the title was in place in San Lorenzo, and commemorative medals cast circa 1470 also awarded Cosimo the honor.[25] It is worth stressing, however, that neither the title nor its accompanying oration formed part of the actual funeral proceedings. The long delay in awarding the tribute was attributed in the enabling legislation to the dispersal of the citizenry because of plague. In practical terms, the disjunction between the burial and the awarding of the title ensured that Cosimo's funeral could not be construed as a civic event. Although in the later Quattrocento and the Cinquecento Cosimo was the subject of numerous eulogies that developed a Medici myth, the humanist Donato Acciaiuoli declaimed only a brief, cautious oration on behalf of the citizens' committee when the title was actually awarded.[26]

The humanist ideals underlying the title have been ably explored by Alison Brown.[27] In a revival of Roman practice, Cosimo was cast in the role of republican hero, one who helped achieve a much-desired peace in Italy. Yet the title "father of the country" should also be seen in light of earlier trends in political rhetoric and funeral practices. The honor represented the culmination of paternalistic ideals of state and society that had been developing in Florence since 1400. The language of family was central to Quattrocento conceptions of power and statecraft, permeating council debates, diplomatic correspondence, consolatory letters, and symbolic modes of communication. Those seeking favors from the Medici tugged on fictive bonds of kinship in personal letters, addressing Cosimo, his sons, and his grandson as "father" or "brother." Medici wives such as Ginevra Alessandri and later Lucrezia Tornabuoni, who often facilitated patronage, were addressed as revered "mothers" or "sisters."[28] In what was the fullest, most explicit articulation of these trends to date, the title *pater patriae* redefined the boundaries of kinship to project the citizenry as Cosimo's children and subordinates, who owed respect and filial deference in return for his protection.[29]

In keeping with this political ethos, Piero de' Medici fell heir to his father's reputation and achievements. Donato Acciaiuoli expressly lauded this generational legacy, writing that Piero was "not only the legitimate heir of a very generous patrimony" but also "a most careful imitator of [Cosimo's] admirable virtues, in the very esteemed tasks which public as well as private affairs bring to you."[30] However, Piero's political inheritance was short-lived and riddled with tensions. His lesser skills and poor health, coupled with growing anti-Medicean sentiment and financial crisis, resulted in a failed conspiracy in 1466. His death only a few years later, on December 2, 1469, precipitated a crisis for the regime.[31] A meeting of Medicean *veri amici* the evening of Piero's death demanded the preservation of the Medici "in reputation and greatness," despite the youth of Piero's sons Lorenzo and Giuliano. Lorenzo himself later reported how the city's principal citizens came to his house to ask him to assume the governance of the state previously entrusted to his father and grandfather.[32]

Given this uneasy political situation, and in conscious imitation of Cosimo's funeral, Piero was buried in San Lorenzo on December 3 with little public ceremony. The Milanese envoy Sagramoro reported to the duke of Milan that Piero "had ordered a funeral without pomp, like his father."[33] The duke of Milan and other foreign dignitaries sent letters and embassies of condolence, as they had done for Cosimo. Donato Acciaiuoli's affectionate letter of consolation to Lorenzo mourned the loss of this "common father of the republic" and encouraged Lorenzo to imitate his father's virtues for the greater good of the city.[34] The reins of Medici power now passed to the young and untried Lorenzo.

Patronage, Piety, and Patriliny in Laurentian Florence

Lorenzo's assumption of the Medici political mantle inaugurated what traditionally has been considered the richest period of Florentine ceremony before the advent of the principate. Image making, public shows, and the manipulation of social perceptions were fundamental to Laurentian political culture, particularly after Lorenzo consolidated power following the Pazzi conspiracy of 1478 which left his brother Giuliano dead. Lorenzo brutally revenged himself on the conspirators, rounding up and killing seventy culprits, and then marked his triumph with a striking set of images. While the traitors were hung and then further degraded in *pitture infamanti* painted by Botticelli, Giuliano's person and memory were distinguished first by grandiose funeral ceremonies and later by a kneeling wax votive image in Santissima Annunziata which may have incorporated his death mask. Joining this figure shortly afterward was a life-size wax votive image of Lorenzo himself. Vasari later reported that friends and kin of the Medici set up two additional wax figures of Lorenzo in other churches, one dramatically dressed in the bloodstained garments worn during the assassination attempt.[35] Supporters of the Medici vented their spleen on the failed conspirators' family tombs, desecrating them and despoiling them of their emblems. Subsequently, reverence for Giuliano's memory took a more literary turn in the small booklet of unknown authorship entitled *Lament for Giuliano*. The printing press affiliated with the Dominican convent of San Jacopo di Ripoli published one hundred copies of the work in October 1478, with a second edition following in June 1479.[36]

As Lorenzo stabilized the regime in the 1480s, the city became synonymous abroad with ceremonial splendor. Florentines secured their reputation with festivities ranging from carefully orchestrated ambassadorial entries, jousts, and tournaments, to more exotic fare such as the public showing of a giraffe sent by the sultan of Babylon in 1488 as a gift to Lorenzo, which even cloistered nuns clamored to have brought around to their convents for viewing. Aspects of ceremonial protocol were codified in the *Libro cerimoniale* of 1475, and were then sporadically amended and refined over the next two decades.[37] Largely with Lorenzo's help, "magnificence" became a common cultural currency that successfully bridged courtly preciosity and familiar civic conventions.

The importance of so much public show to both the civic life and the foreign policy of Laurentian Florence has been variously recognized by contemporaries and historians alike. Savonarola remarked that Lorenzo distracted the populace with festivities so "that they may think of themselves and not of him," and Francesco Vettori attributed similar cunning motives to il Magnifico.[38] Modern historians have traced the shift in the center of public ritual and political gravity from the Piazza della Signoria to the Medici palace, with Lorenzo hosting foreign dignitaries at home, dispensing favors on the streets, and gradually withdrawing his support from communal festivities such as the feast of Saint John the Baptist.[39] However, Lorenzo realized his success more by accomodating or manipulating traditions and procedures of civic ritual than by abandoning them outright. Despite Alamanno Rinuccini's declaration that Lorenzo sought to establish a tyranny, his regime was noted for its formal legality.[40] The Signoria continued to vote funeral subsidies to distinguished officeholders for the customary trappings; moreover, Lorenzo luckily escaped confrontation with the civic heritage of chancellors' funerals because of the long tenure of Bartolomeo Scala as chancellor from 1465 to 1497.

Yet civic funerals clearly did not occupy the same place in the civic imagination or historical record of Laurentian Florence as they had earlier in the century. There was no funerary equivalent to the ceremonies for Salutati, Marsuppini, or even Tolentino during Lorenzo's regime. To a certain extent this was the result of stylistic trends. Civic funerals that used traditional trappings no longer stood out quite so clearly among a constellation of more novel ceremonies. More importantly, funerals of private citizens took on various features that had formerly been associated with communal officials, while magnificence and humanist culture blurred the boundaries between civic and private rites. Pomp, public funeral orations, and commemorative medals crossed the lines demarcating citizen and officeholder, so that honors granted on the basis of the decedent's official status became less distinguishable from those commemorating his personal career, family wealth, or philosophical pursuits. As the lines separating public and private power became increasingly unclear under Lorenzo's aegis, and with the dramatic expansion of humanist culture after the Peace of Lodi (1454), funeral pomp became a grab bag of honors that defied sharp typological distinctions. The result of these trends for both Laurentian politics and culture was not two contrasting alternatives—a princely style and a republican one—but rather an interpenetration of conventions which created enormous fluidity and variation in practice.

This blurring of status boundaries and overlap of conventions was particularly noticeable in the funerals of noted humanists. For example, Matteo Palmieri acquired civic stature in part by delivering Marsuppini's funeral oration, although he himself never held the chancellorship; Palmieri in turn was publicly eulogized by Alamanno

Rinuccini in 1475. At the same time, Palmieri was heaped with family honors and buried in his local parish church, San Pier Maggiore, in a new private chapel paid for by his wife and nephew.[41] In Cristoforo Landino's 1478 funeral oration for that "excellent citizen" Donato Acciaiuoli, the growing prestige of philosophical pursuits tipped the balance toward a greater concentration on Acciaiuoli's prodigious intellectual achievements than on the many civic commissions by which he had fulfilled "the duties of the republic."[42] The institutional development of civic or quasipublic academic bodies such as the Florentine Studio or the Platonic Academy (founded 1462) also offered humanists career avenues and public funerary recognition, breaking down the exclusive association of humanism with the chancellorship. When the prominent Studio member Alamanno Rinuccini died in 1499, a commemorative medal was struck "by public consensus," as had first been done for Salutati, while Marsilio Ficino's great accomplishments and Medici friendship earned him cathedral burial in 1494 and a public eulogy by Marcello Adriani, Scala's eventual successor as chancellor.[43]

The diminished place of funerals in the pantheon of civic ceremonies nevertheless should be linked with fundamental changes in civic life. This shift did not necessarily signal withdrawal to a villa culture, or the complete destruction of the commune as a ritual entity. Arthur Field has recently shown that Platonic humanists such as Ficino and Landino, whose ideas were already fashionable in the 1450s, were not idle contemplatives. Rather, they sought instead to reach a wide Florentine audience with their doctrines of love and harmony and their conceptions of friendship, which ultimately created a new ideology for the Medici party. However, more and more well-born Florentines willingly pursued these goals only in the context of detachment and contemplation provided by Ficino and his Platonic Academy.[44] Moreover, between 1471 and 1480 Lorenzo engineered important constitutional changes and redefined informal political processes to revolve increasingly around his own interests and brokerage.[45] Historians are still debating the nature and effect of these changes on Florentine politics and society. Among the questions that remain open or contested are the extent to which patronage networks extended vertically to incorporate ordinary citizens, and whether patronage networks were themselves centered around humbler figures; the ways in which patronage affected the meanings, sentiments, and administration of neighborhood life; and the relative strength and motivations of the Medici party in the Laurentian political equation.

While many of the dynamics of Laurentian society remain to be investigated, one of the trends this new civic context put into play was a more stylized, theatrical ostentation on the part of Florence's greatest citizens. Churches began to acquire more pronounced theatrical qualities resulting from the extensive use of draperies, hangings, and canopies. Dress standards for mourning clothes grew still more sumptuous, as men's mourning mantles inched ever longer and women's mourning was elaborated both at home and across the Italian peninsula. In Milan, Ferrara, and Mantua, the death of the Ferrarese duchess Eleonora of Aragon in October 1493 prompted a flurry of letters, as her daughters Isabella d'Este Gonzaga and Beatrice Sforza sought to discover and outdo each other's mourning finery.[46]

These ephemeral expressions, important in their own right, had more enduring counterparts in the building or decoration of private chapels in the last quarter of the century. A number of late Quattrocento commissions expressly emphasized family claims through the visual propaganda of fresco decorations and coats of arms. Among the most renowned was Ghirlandaio's celebration of Tornabuoni family myths and history in his fresco program for the main chapel of Santa Maria Novella, begun in 1486. Far more common was the plethora of family emblems affixed to buildings and assorted objects. Giovanni Falconi considered the presence of identifying emblems so important that his bequest of two hundred florins to the friars of Santa Maria Novella in 1478 hinged on the stipulation that the friars never, under any condition, remove the Falconi arms from the family chapel.[47]

Falconi was not simply being petulant. At stake in the use of family emblems in chapels and burial sites were legal evidence of ownership and the protection of patriline or lineage. Both the legal and the social importance of family signs are abundantly clear in the 1474 dispute over burial rights between the merchant and amateur historian Marco Parenti, and Rinaldo di Piero, descended from the dyer Ciliago. As the oldest male of the only surviving Parenti line, Marco felt obliged to defend his ancestral tomb site in Santa Croce, even though his immediate forebears and descendants had abandoned this site in favor of a new one in the cathedral. Marco offered three forms of evidence to support his claim to the Santa Croce tomb: the presence of his ancestor Parente's coat of arms depicting three bears; the Latin inscription surrounding the tomb ("Parentis Orselli et suorum"); and a written entry in the church's tomb register. Opposing Marco's claim was Rinaldo, who argued that once the Parenti had abandoned the tomb, it had become customary over the years to bury his own family's dead there. Marco happily reported that the operai decided in his favor, and Rinaldo was ordered to clear out the bones of his kin under pain of a fifty-florin fine.[48] Obviously emblems shared by a more flourishing lineage than Marco's might add to family frictions rather than increase solidarity. A common coat of arms only confused the claims of different branches of the Spini to burial rights in the family chapel in Santa Trinità during an intralineal dispute in 1473.[49]

In the later Quattrocento, coats of arms provided an important social and psychological resource for artisans as well as for households of the elite. Male artisans with modest means used these symbolic representations to formally mark the beginnings of a patrilineal family grouping. Written evidence makes it clear that in the second half of the century numerous artisan households, such as those listed in the burial register of San Lorenzo, concocted personalized emblems, devices, signs, and coats of arms as ways to distinguish their tombs and establish and express their budding family heritages, and thereby claim both a sense of identity and a certain standing in the community. This process formed a visual corollary to the increased use of surnames among artisans in these same decades. Although it is difficult to know exactly what many of these signs looked like, they probably represented the tools of trade, occupational habits, plays on personal names and nicknames, allegiances to particular saints or locales, or simply individual fancies that defy easy explanation. Looming over the tomb of the druggist Agnolo Grifi in San Pancrazio, for example, was "as coat of arms, a pair of deer antlers."[50]

Sometimes these distinguishing signs were added by descendants well after death, when the stone or marble tomb slab was already in place. In June 1489 the monks at Santissima Annunziata granted to the sons of the butcher Giuliano di Salvestro (called "Tanbellone") the right to place "their sign or arms" on their father's unmarked sandstone slab in the church, where Giuliano apparently had been buried for some time. This gesture brought honor to both father and sons, asserted a sense of patrilineal continuity, and confirmed the reciprocity of living and dead in meeting each others' needs. In return for this privilege, Giuliano's sons promised to donate six florins and to pay various debts their father owed the convent. However, a later undated entry noted that the agreement had to be cancelled because the sons were unable to pay off the debt.[51]

Drawing together these trends in stylized magnificence and family claims was the greatest private burial in Laurentian Florence, the one staged for Filippo Strozzi in 1491. A banker who amassed a tremendous fortune in exile, Strozzi became a "symbol of successful repatriation" to his kinsmen and to other Florentines as well. The artisan Piero Masi, a neighbor familiar with many of Strozzi's doings, marveled that "by public repute" Strozzi's fortune amounted to more than 300,000 ducats. A considerable part of this fortune was earmarked for construction projects such as the new family palace begun in 1489, designed to outshine that of the Medici. Strozzi's bold new tomb complex in Santa Maria Novella, decorated by Filippino Lippi at a cost of one thousand florins, ensured the permanence of his reputation following the hardships of exile.[52] Both projects remained incomplete at the time of his death on May 14, 1491, however, and his body was temporarily placed in a sealed casket, walled in his chapel to await final burial.[53] Strozzi's carefully crafted testament, running to over fifty folios, delegated the actual details of his funeral to his second wife, Selvaggia Gianfigliazzi, his son Alfonso, and Filippo Buondelmonti, the husband of his niece Costanza Parenti. He did specify, however, that he wanted his burial "to be ornate and provided with divine offices and honors, and with those honors and expenses regarding offices, masses, and other appropriate things" as seemed fitting.[54]

Filippo Strozzi's son Lorenzo boasted that his father's funeral was the largest, most extravagant private funeral the city had ever seen, and the evidence supports his claim. Preparations took three days to complete, and the ensuing event was recorded and commented on not only by the dead man's kin but by other contemporaries as well. Subsequent ceremonies held in Rome and Naples, where Strozzi had business offices, reportedly brought the total costs to three thousand ducats, although this sum seems somewhat exaggerated.[55] The obsequies orchestrated a full range of funeral honors and motifs. The clergy in attendance comprised four orders of friars, the full clerical compliment of the cathedral and of San Lorenzo, and 150 confraternal brothers of the Company of San Benedetto. Outfitted as mourners were "all of [Filippo's] kinsmen," an unspecified but undoubtedly substantial number, considering that the Strozzi clan had 120 men eligible for office in 1524. Four menservants walking behind the corpse "dressed like sons," with dignified long mantles trailing behind them, reinforced a lineal orientation. The cortege also included assorted guild captains, forty processional torches, and two strings of emblazoned lappets, while the church of Santa Maria Novella was richly draped with black cloth and illuminated by unprecedented amounts of wax.[56]

Yet Filippo Strozzi's funeral represents more than a mere catalog of late Quattrocento pomp and magnificence. It also marked the initial penetration of market relationships into funeral proceedings and the growing involvement of social subordinates in rites of patronage. Lorenzo Strozzi himself remarked that "in addition to the usual multitudes of citizens and clergy, with kinsmen, domestics, and servants dressed in black, there also intervened, in a spectacle unknown to our city, all the masters and youths of his building projects, with architects, carpenters, smithies, bricklayers, stonecutters, and the rest of the more vile crowd engaged since building on the palace had begun."[57] There is no way to know the exact size of this group, but it probably numbered at least fifty. Dressed of their own volition in respectfully dark clothes, these craftsmen comported themselves in the cortege with "such devotion and melancholy" that, according to Lorenzo Strozzi, "it moved to tears all those gathered to witness the funeral pomp."[58]

Expressing his surprise at both the turnout and the unexpected decorum of these workmen, the son's retrospective account, written long after his father's death, smacks of arrogance and of contempt for the laboring classes. Relations between employers and workers in the city have been characterized as tense, with few vertical ties binding rich and poor.[59] Filippo Strozzi nevertheless seems to have maintained somewhat personalized relationships with his construction workers. He oversaw much of his pet project in its initial phases and kept individual accounts for each laborer, a practice that continued after his death and ceased only in 1499.[60] The tribute paid to him suggests, on the one hand, that the labor market was still to some extent structured and regulated by personal arrangements and relationships. The sense of obligation, familiarity, and even intimacy created by these workmen's homage offers testimony to the kind of ambiguous, tangled social relations, blending elements of friendship, loyalty, and reciprocity, that Ronald Weissman argues were pervasive in Renaissance Florence.[61]

Yet on the other hand, this tribute also marks a new sense of deference and dependence emerging in patron-client relations. Filippo Strozzi's funeral was neither a gathering composed simply of kin, neighbors, colleagues, and friends, as funerals a century earlier had been; nor was it a rite that identified the rich and powerful by social exclusion. Rather, it was an occasion that conveyed status in terms of social deference. In this sense, Strozzi's funeral is emblematic of the ways in which the rites of death and remembrance enacted changing class and social relations in the late Quattrocento. As patronage became established as the key social process in Laurentian Florence, it acquired a more deferential face, with the respective positions of patron and client marked out through various gestures and ritualized activities.

Acts of deference figured not only in funeral ceremonies but also in commemorative arrangements. In 1487, for example, the wealthy patron Piero del Tovaglia struck a bargain with the monks of Santissima Annunziata, where he had endowed the chapel of San Gismondo. In addition to the customary obligation of an annual mass on the saint's feast day, del Tovaglia also required the convent to send eight novices bearing white candles to his house (or eventually to that of his descendants or his brother's offspring) on another feast day, in homage to his piety and largesse. If the monk defaulted on this latter obligation, the contract stipulated that they were to spend an additional twenty-five florins on the chapel's decoration.[62]

The changing face of class and clientage created permanent divisions in the ways in which Florentines of differing means defined an "honorable burial." The greater disparity in both material and social resources enjoyed by powerful citizens, middling burghers, minor guildsmen, aspiring artisans, and the *popolo minuto* introduced profound cleavages that could no longer be more than partially assuaged by confraternal assistance. For the Florentine elite, status continued to rest on the established formulas of multiplication and magnificence, which took on a special social twist. At the other end of the social spectrum, it was hardly status that was at stake but the bare necessities of honor and dignity: a decent bier, a few candles, several priests and mourners, and a burial mass. Between these two poles there evolved a highly refined calculus of honor that calibrated wealth and standing by minute degrees. Wax provided a major axis of differentiation: additional or larger candles on the altar, purer grades of wax, and gifts of candles to priests in procession all added luster to the occasion and respect to the memory of the dead. Bell ringing, sung liturgies and antiphons, more priests and masses, and fancier bier cloths each contributed an extra layer of pomp and a key to social distinction. But the kind dynamic competition between middling and affluent Florentines that had sparked consumption in the late fourteenth century was no longer a viable proposition.

These deepening discrepancies were apparent not only in funeral celebrations but also in the way in which burial sites mapped out social divisions. The Laurentian age represented the critical passage to a permanent domination of choice ecclesiastical space by the patriciate. Here several examples drawn from the parish of Santa Trinità give a human face to this process. The burial honors afforded in 1472 to Lucia, described in convent records only as "a poor person" and the unmarried daughter of the shearer Marco di Bartolomeo, consisted of a tiny bit of wax and the dubious distinction of burial in the communal parish tomb. Similar fates awaited two of Lucia's co-parishioners: the widow Caterina, who the convent scribe reported "did not have a tomb for her use," as well as Nastasia, who had been a serving woman of the bookseller Vespasiano da Bisticci and was murdered by her husband in 1482. Not only did these women command insufficient wealth to muster more than a rudimentary burial; they were also outside the particular networks of family, corporation, and clientage that might have earned them greater tomb privileges. The burial site awaiting their co-parishioner the seven-year-old Maria Gaetani offered a striking contrast. Although Maria's youth precluded an elaborate funeral ceremony, her membership in one of the most prominent patron families of Santa Trinità nevertheless destined her for the house's old, prestigious tomb located beneath the choir. More privileged still was Lena Mancini, widow of Gherardo Gianfigliazzi, who donated 400 florins to the Gianfigliazzi chapel, her chosen burial site, to endow a daily mass benefiting her own soul and Gherardo's after her death in 1474.[63]

Obviously there was still some room for parishioners, local residents, and newcomers to negotiate more desirable tomb sites by capitalizing on patronage, obligation, and services promised or already rendered. As abbots and priests at several institutions avidly sought to improve their buildings, they welcomed patrons who took on modest as well as monumental tasks in exchange for intramural burial. In 1482 the abbot of Santa Trinità ceded the tomb formerly belonging to Pace Brunetti, whose line had died out, to a certain Giovanni from the Casentino, who in return promised to repair one of the church windows at his own expense. Similarly, the monks of Santissima Annunziata conceded an available tomb located within the confines of the church to the brothers Bernardo and Niccolò Mini from the tiny parish of Santa Maria Nipotecosa in 1497 as repayment "for the many services done for the convent."[64]

Confraternities also continued to make available their corporate tombs, which offered a valuable option for minor guildsmen such as the flask maker Giovanni di Niccolò, who elected burial with his confraternal brothers of Saint Sebastian in Santissima Annunziata in 1489, as well as for some foreigners.[65] Like their male counterparts, women from the class of artisans and small tradesmen, especially widows, also availed themselves of these valuable extrafamilial burial resources. For example, in 1495 the draper's widow Ginevra turned to the Company of Saint Peter Martyr, to which she donated a house in return for burial in the company tomb and an annual anniversary office for her soul and the souls of her husband and their descendants and relatives. In similar fashion another Ginevra, twice-widowed, whose son was a Dominican friar, in 1499 elected burial in the tomb of the Company of Saint Catherine of Siena housed in Santa Maria Novella, as did Marta, a former serving woman to the Popoleschi family in 1491.[66]

However, women's varied roles in family structures and arrangements added yet another degree of complexity to patterns of burial sites which reflected basic class or corporate options and local ties. By and large, most adult married women and widows found burial in the tombs of their husbands. In the many cases of multiple marriages, however, widows had to choose among their former spouses. For instance, in her will of 1482, another twice-widowed Ginevra, daughter of Giovanni Albizzi, elected burial in the tomb of her second husband, Leone de' Pilli, in Santa Maria Novella, rather than that of her first husband, Jacopo dal Borgo.[67] Church records contain numerous examples of wealthy widows who contributed substantial sums to endow or decorate their husbands' tombs or burial chapels, where in turn they themselves would find eternal rest. In 1481, because of the great mutual affection between herself and her late husband, Angelica, widow of the exchange broker Gaspero di Zanobi da Lamole, made good on her husband's unfulfilled intentions to establish a chapel dedicated to the Magi in Santa Maria Novella. Angelica instructed Giovanni Caroli, prior of Santa Maria Novella, to purchase within six months sufficient goods to render a minimum annual return of three florins to subsidize a perpetual mass in the chapel for Gaspero and his descendants.[68] Similarly, San Pancrazio netted one hundred florins toward the decoration of the Minerbetti chapel in 1489 per the bequest of Bartolomea Alessandri, widow of Giovanni d'Andrea Minerbetti. In another case, Nanna, widow of Bartolomeo Gianfigliazzi, commissioned in 1492 "a string of flags with the Gianfigliazzi arms and with St. Bartholomew painted in very rich and beautiful fashion" for display in the family chapel in Santa Trinità during the memorial masses she sponsored to benefit her husband's soul.[69] These patronage activities focused on husbands ultimately bore additional fruit for the affluent female donors themselves after their own burials at the same sites.

Yet obviously not all women enjoyed these opportunities or exerted this kind of forceful influence through patronage. Women from artisans' households often worked within a more scrambled set of options and affiliations, and certainly had more limited resources. Women's burials described in the intricate family history of the locksmith Piero Masi tell what was probably a more common story.[70] In 1484, Bernardo, Piero's father, arranged the burial of his mother-in-law Agnola, a widow who had lived in Bernardo's household since his marriage in 1477. Since Agnola already had a tomb site in the church of San Tommaso in the city center, she was buried there. Eleven years later, Bernardo lost his wife Caterina, a baker's daughter, who died at age forty and was buried the same day in the family's current parish of San Donato de' Vecchietti. Unfortunately Piero, writing in retrospect, did not note when or where his father had procured a separate tomb site for household members.

The next year, in 1496, Bernardo buried his mother Piera, a woman more than seventy-five years old, who had remained a widow since her husband's death in 1458. In fact, she and her children had continued to live in the house she owned on Via de' Pepi for many years before moving to the Strozzi neighborhood on Via de' Ferravecchi. This Piera, the daughter and widow of carpenters, was also buried in San Donato, "in the same tomb," as Piero noted, "where Monna Caterina, my mother and her daughter-in-law, was buried." Bernardo remarried two months after his first wife's death in 1495, and the couple had a daughter Piera, named after her dead grandmother. But this infant died at nine months of age in 1499, and was buried in the Masi's new parish church of San Michele Visdomini, where the family had recently moved, "in the tomb of the virgins" along with other infant girls and young, unmarried ones.

The last burial of a kinswoman recorded in Masi's diary was that of Bernardo's sister Mea, a sixty-five-year-old widow of a barber, who had resided in the household for fifteen years before her death in 1512. Although Piero did not record her final resting place, he did leave this sobering story as a warning to his descendants and future readers:

"[Mea] lost her dowry because, at her husband's death, not a single asset was found, except for a house of which he was heir by the male line during his lifetime. [Mea] did not have any male heirs, and so the house reverted to the chapter of Santa Maria del Fiore, and no pledge of her dowry was found. My father Bernardo, Mea's brother, had to take her into his house, provide her expenses, and keep her until her death. Most of the time until she died she was ill with syphilis [mal francese], which she had caught from her husband Bartolomeo. So . . . you who find this record, beware when you give dowries. Someone should be appointed custodian, so that you will not find yourselves obliged to take into your house your sisters or daughters with no resources."

If it is difficult to describe with precision the family traditions of male artisans, at least some of whom, like Piero Masi, had patrilineal dreams, it is still more problematic to construct family typologies for women outside the elite on the basis of their burial patterns. Not only were women's burial sites subject to the vagaries of household arrangements that shifted radically according to the women's place in the life cycle; they were also affected by the relocation of the women's resident households to other sectors of the city, which severed ties with local parishes. As the Masi examples illustrate, even women of widely different ages and natal origins who were brought together in a single household during their lifetimes did not always find final rest as a distinct family unit.

As Florentine society became more markedly stratified in the late fifteenth century, one of the few remaining commonalities in the burial practices of rich and middling citizens was the incorporation of large numbers of clergy into funerals and requiems. The proliferation of clergy in death rites was one of the most pronounced trends in the late Quattrocento which reflected the new forms of corporate and confraternal devotion springing up after 1470. Around 1473 a neighbor commented that at the burial of the wealthy Cyprian physician Messer Giorgio, who had married a Bardi woman, virtually every priest and friar in the city had intervened.[71] By the end of the century, the sight of varied brigades of priests and friars marching in funerals had become so common that contemporaries considered the mere four orders of clergy involved in Lorenzo de' Medici's funeral in 1492 a mark of simplicity.[72]

Burials in the Parenti family over three generations tell a similar story of growing ecclesiastical participation. Attending the obsequies of Parente Parenti (d. 1452) were eighteen canons and thirty chaplains from the cathedral, where the family had its principal tomb. The funeral of his widow Tommasa four years later involved roughly the same number and kind of participants. At their son Marco's rites in 1497, the cathedral clergy were joined by the Observant Franciscans of San Salvatore near San Miniato and the conventual friars of Santa Croce. This proliferation became still more apparent in the early decades of the sixteenth century, as populations of clergy started to rise in various foundations. Present at the obsequies for Piero di Marco Parenti (d. 1519) were fourteen priests from San Michele Visdomini, along with ninety-seven priests and chaplains of the cathedral, six clerks from the cathedral school, and the full complement of Franciscans from Santa Croce. By contrast, Piero's vigil, a far less public rite, involved only four friars.[73]

However, it is not only the numbers that are important here. This multiplication both reflected and contributed to the erosion of strictly local interests in favor of a more comprehensive patronage of major ecclesiastical institutions scattered across the urban map. Part of this proliferation thus involved a restructing of ecclesiastical patronage away from the distinct localism of a century earlier, and toward the kind of diffused global coverage seen in Cosimo de' Medici's memorial program. The final quarter of the century probably saw a weakening of neighborhood and parish attachments and the creation of a citywide grid of ecclesiastical patronage by the patriciate.[74] In terms of funerals, however, this development signaled less a complete displacement or surrender of local ties than a broadening out from parochial interests or narrowly defined affiliations. In choosing clerical mourners, Florence's great citizens generally retained their traditional local attachments but now added to their funeral rites a varied conglomerate of clergy from other prominent institutions.

Even the homage paid to religious dignitaries showed similarly expanding networks of exchange. When Vincenzo Conci, Vallombrosan abbot of San Pancrazio, died in May 1491, his procession boasted "a great honor of wax and of ecclesiastical persons" that included members of the Florentine College of Priests and the chapter of San Lorenzo, and the friars and monks of the Carmine, Santa Maria Novella, and Santa Trinità, as well as monks from his home convent. The Vallombrosan abbot of San Salvi officiated at the splendid obsequies, while an Augustinian theologian from the Carmine delivered the sermon.[75]

The long-term effects of these developments for lay-clerical relations and ecclesiastical institutions remain to be investigated. The immediate result for patrician funerals in the 1480s and 1490s, however, was to involve an extremely diverse and eclectic mix of clerical participants in ritual activities of death and remembrance. The Medici church, San Lorenzo, gained a number of new patrons outside the parish who sought to profit from its newfound prestige, but the most consistent winners in this development were the friars, especially the Franciscans. Ironically, the newly established Observant foundations of San Marco (Dominican) and San Salvatore near San Miniato al Monte (Franciscan) were among the most favored in this effusion of pageantry. The austerity and spiritual intensity of these communities attracted the support of well-to-do citizens as well as civic subsidies.[76] The growing presence of Observants in the funerals of wealthy Florentines in the 1480s and 1490s highlighted not only the greater complexity of these events but also a mounting tension between ascetic ideals and ostentation that finally exploded in the Savonarolan period.

The expanded role taken by clergy in funerals generated heated disputes among institutions over processional protocol and precedence. At stake here were less the revenues accruing from burial than the assertion of institutional status. Rivalries between Franciscans and Dominicans persisted, but the key struggle—for recognition as the city's premier institution—arose between the Medici church of San Lorenzo, and the cathedral. The latter competition was no doubt intensified by the relative proximity of the two churches, which also made this a struggle for the geographical heart of the city. In 1484 conflict broke out between the canons of San Lorenzo and those of the cathedral over pride of place in the funeral cortege of Giordano Orsini, who died in the house of his kinsman Lorenzo de' Medici while traveling through Florence. Orsini's death brought with it the chance to put a powerful competing set of Medici connections to the test; in a small, concrete way the episode measures the inroads made by Medici prestige into civic culture. The position of San Lorenzo was enhanced by the fact that Orsini's procession originated in that parish, which allowed the canons to call on their parochial rights. The two institutions temporarily resolved their dispute by alternating their respective hierarchies of clerks, chaplains, and canons, with the prior of San Lorenzo situated in the final pair of clerics between two cathedral dignitaries.[77] Neither side was the clear victor, but the arrangement put the two churches on a newly equal ceremonial footing for funerals originating in the parish.

This harmonious settlement was not to last long. Conflict broke out again in the more strained political climate of September 1498, when the Florentine captain Giovanni di Pierfrancesco de' Medici died. The problem of protocol was compounded by the civic honors granted in recognition of his military service, as well as by the inclusion of the city's Conventual and Observant Dominicans and Franciscans, and an additional one hundred priests. In order to avoid "public scandal," or offense to the Medici, the canons again agreed to provisional arrangements with the cathedral clergy, but the dispute surfaced repeatedly until its final resolution by a papal nuncio in San Lorenzo's favor in 1555.[78]

In the late Quattrocento, contemporaries also perceived an elaboration of the liturgical services associated withh death and remembrance. Sumptuary laws in 1473 complained about the crowds of mourners flocking to requiem and other masses; testaments decried the waste involved in performing great numbers of offices of the dead and annniversary celebrations; churches were visually transformed by more spectacular draperies and apparatuses, as well as made more musically splendid by organ playing for these various liturgical occasions. Both women and men of means commissioned additional masses for themselves and their kin, with affluent women using the economic resources of their dowries. Liturgy was fast gaining a greater visibility in the complex of death rites as the Quattrocento drew to a close.

However, it is difficult to measure with precision the extent to which contemporaries were justified in perceiving a proliferation of masses and liturgical ceremonies. The task of making a comparative census of perpetual mass programs based on the major ecclesiastical tax returns of 1427 and 1478 is hampered by fragmentary evidence and incomplete reporting. Sample returns from thirteen churches and three confraternities, chosen for their diversity of size and affiliation, and the existence of reports for both years, show only small real gains in the number of perpetual mass commissions over fifty years (Table 6.1).[79] The bulk of the gain can be attributed to administrative changes resulting in Santa Maria Novella's more complete tax return rather than to widespread upward trends. More useful information emerges from a detailed analysis of perpetual commissions at the prominent laud-singing confraternity of Saint Peter Martyr, located in Santa Maria Novella. Of the ninety programs in effect in 1427, twenty-four had failed by 1478 because of funding problems; only fifteen new bequests had been instituted during a fifty-year period, giving a net loss of nine programs.[80] The numbers probably increased somewhat in the 1480s and 1490s, but the need to commit shops, farms, or the usufruct of other permanent investments for perpetual endowments placed intrinsic ceilings on the growth of these commissions. On the basis of this often sketchy evidence, it seems unlikely that endowments for perpetual masses were the reason for contemporary critiques.

Yet there almost certainly was an explosion of masses in the last quarter of the fifteenth century, whatever the problems involved in

T A B L E 6.1:

Perpetual Mass Program Census, 1427 and 1478 Catasto

Church or Confraternity	1427	1478
Churches		
Sant'Ambrogio	0	17
Sant'Appollinare	0	0
Santa Brigida	0	0
Santa Cecilia	0	0
Santa Felicità	0	≥5
Santa Maria del Carmine	0	2
Santa Maria Maggiore	3	12
Santa Maria Novella	11[a]	125
Santa Maria Ughi	2	2
Santa Margherita	0	0
San Simone	0	0
Santo Spirito	12	0
Santa Verdiana	0	0
Totals	28	163
Confraternities		
Laudesi of San Frediano	3	2
San Pier Martire (Santa Maria Novella)	90	81
San Zanobi (Santa Maria del Fiore)	6	4
Totals	99	87

Source: Catasto. vols. 184, 185, 194, 989.
[a]Only Monte subsidies reported.

measuring it. This is a large area of inquiry for which only a small body of evidence exists at present. Judging from a wide reading of commemorative bequests, however, the perceived increase in the number of masses resulted from a cluster of related developments. Among the most significant were the simultaneous performance of the already popular Gregorian mass series (one mass daily for thirty days after death) at several religious houses rather than at a single institution. Jacopo di Messer Bongianni Gianfigliazzi, whose father had established a distinguished new tomb site for his line in the main chapel of Santa Trinità, left provisions in his 1497 testament for Gregorian masses to be said at five monasteries beginning the day after his death.[81] When distributing his extensive farm holdings in his will of 1494, Guido Boncianni hoped to avoid litigation between his grandsons after his death by requiring them to mutually sponsor the Gregorian series at both Santa Maria Novella and San Donato a Scapeto; Boncianni also wanted another fifty masses said for his soul at each church within six months of his death, as well as a ten-year-anniversary mass at Santa Maria Novella. In addition to the multiplication of the Gregorian series, the number of masses per anniversary office commonly expanded in the late fifteenth century from twelve or fifteen to thirty, as was stipulated for the annual office benefiting Guasparre di Melchiore dal Borgo, who also stipulated in his 1489 will that he wanted his heirs to be notified at home of the exact day the office would be performed.[82]

Moreover, greater numbers of clergy were drawn into requiems, masses, and anniversary celebrations as well as into funerals. While the wealthy patron Federigo Federighi (d. 1477) instructed his heirs to spend what they chose for his funeral, he was adamant that he wanted at least fifty priests to perform Gregorian masses at San Pancrazio within one month of his death; San Pancrazio was to supplement its own clergy with Observant Franciscan friars from other local houses if necessary. At the same time Federighi left instructions for a cluster of ceremonies that proudly celebrated the ideology of lineage: a daily mass in the family chapel, an annual mass for his father Jacopo and his male antecedents "in the fourth degree," another annual mass for his own soul, and a splendid feast of the Annunciation complete with vespers and organ music. This ambitious program became the basis for a protracted lawsuit—lasting from 1477 to 1532—between San Pancrazio and Federigo's son Filippo; ironically, one of the reasons Filippo defaulted on this lineal celebration was the need to repay the twelve-hundred-florin dowry to his dead brother's wife. More typical of early fifteenth-century anniversary programs was the one commissioned sporadically by Antonio Rustichi for his mother Filippa between 1417 and 1426, which involved ten priests from his local church of San Romeo.[83] That some clergy abused the growing demand for their services is implied in the revised capitular constitutions of the cathedral redacted in 1484. These rubrics admonished canons participating in requiem or anniversary masses to remain in the choir for the better part of the liturgy, instead of rushing off before the end of mass.[84]

Late fifteenth-century mass programs sometimes showed new or additional forms of liturgical embellishment as well. When making her will in May 1496, the wealthy widow Caterina del Vigna instructed each of the eight Dominican friars present to recite the Gregorian series, to be followed by a sung annual mass accompanied by organ music and including the popular antiphon "Libera Me Domine." This solemn office was to be staged at a portable altar set up in front of the crucifix attached to the pilaster nearest her tomb, thus drawing the holy and the dead into an intimate locus.[85]

Also cropping up repeatedly in late Quattrocento church records and testaments are provisions for short-term anniversary masses, commonly to be performed five, ten, or twenty-five years after death. Although more limited in scope than perpetual programs, these commissions nevertheless allowed notaries, minor guildsmen, foreigners, shopkeepers, and small tradesmen to provide for their own spiritual well-being and earthly remembrance. Widows of varying household means also figure prominently among these shorter-term commissions. For instance, Vezzossa, widow of the physician Maestro Ugolino di Piero, in 1480 requested an annual office performed for ten years in Santa Maria Novella; Annalena, both daughter and widow of notaries, opted for a similar program in 1498, while the patrician widow Ginevra Albizzi de' Pilli in 1482 instructed her heirs to make only a five-year commitment to the same church.[86]

The financial advantages of shorter-term mass programs for testators are obvious, since they cost less to establish and freed up property or long-term revenues for use by one's heirs. Whereas Mattea, the widow of Giovanni del Paglio, in her 1489 will left a house in the parish of San Simone to subsidize her anniversary program at San Pancrazio in perpetuity, Mea (d. 1490), the widow of Tommaso Raffacani, had to set aside only one florin for the Gregorian series to be performed once at the same church after her death. Tita Baroncelli Rucellai allocated the same sum, one florin, to be spent yearly on a ten-year mass program at Santa Maria Novella in her 1498 will.[87]

Beyond this economic rationale, however, the popularity and widespread appeal of liturgical celebrations in the late Quattrocento also reflect new directions in piety and underlying religious attitudes. Critical to our understanding here is not simply the interest in numbers but the shift in timing. In the way these multiple masses tended to be concentrated soon after death, they show a more distinct orientation toward suffrage for the soul of the deceased than toward long-term remembrance. The focus of many new commissions was to alleviate the pains of purgatory rather than to perpetuate the earthly memory either of oneself or one's kin. In this shift of emphasis, changing patterns of mass commissions point not only to new patterns of piety, as Cohn has argued for Siena, but also to a heightened sense of spiritual anxiety in the Laurentian age, particularly among the upper echelons of Florentine society.[88] The full-scale plague epidemic of 1479, with its high death toll, once again paraded unsettling reminders of mortality and fragility, and probably brought the elaboration of liturgy to greater public attention.[89]

There are several points to be made here about this ebullient enthusiasm for masses in Florence, as compared to other areas of Italy and Europe. First, although the quest for prayer was a common religious expression across late medieval Europe, in Florence it had a specific sacramental and liturgical focus.[90] What Florentines wanted were masses, not simply the prayers of their fellow citizens. Unlike the inhabitants of sixteenth-century Champagne, who used stained-glass windows, altar cloths, and public pronouncements to actively solicit prayers from onlookers, Florentine men and women placed the mass at the heart of their propitiatory programs. This sacramental emphasis also distinguished Florentines' behavior from some of the strategies developed by their Sienese neighbors, who shifted their focus of attention from good works and sacraments to family and property.[91] In Florence, the prayers of family and friends surely clustered around these liturgical occasions but were not themselves the centerpiece.

This intense concern for one's own soul represented an important cross-current to the "civic Christianity" that had characterized Florentine religious behavior by 1400.[92] This earlier interest in public charity had prompted the foundation of varied institutions (e.g., the charitable confraternitites of the Misericordia and Orsanmichele, the widows' asylum of Orbatello [founded in 1372], the Innocenti orphanage [1419], and the renowned Florentine hospital system) geared toward helping the poor, sick, and abandoned. In the second half of the Quattrocento, however, the direction of public charity shifted away from handouts to the solitary, traditional poor (*miserabili*) toward a more paternalistic policy designed to preserve and strengthen family solidarities among the "deserving poor" (*poveri vergognosi*).[93] Charity, along with political discourse, helped construct the paternal Florentine state. While it is tempting to see masses as part of this redefinition of family and community, it is worth stressing that even in the late Trecento, which featured a broad-based social charity, Florentines did not in any appreciable numbers sponsor masses for those outside their kin groups. Still, Florentine patterns of piety resemble what Cohn has dubbed the "great age of selfishness" in the way in which patrons of masses often deeply entangled their heirs and their heirs' property to celebrate an ideology of family and lineage.[94]

These increased mass commissions had the practical effect of funneling money and property into church coffers, which in turn provided the necessary structures and personnel to support these new patterns of piety, patronage, and mental attitudes.[95] While the evidence is sketchy at present, there was undoubtedly a dynamic relationship between these trends in masses and the growing number of flagellant confraternities, priests, chaplains, canons, and monks in Observant houses, who could staff and administer mass programs and were in turn supported by them. San Pancrazio hired a priest from the country town of Poppi on a contract basis in 1489 to take up some of these new liturgical burdens, for example, and the church regularly brought in outside priests to help officiate at offices for the dead.[96] When several major donors defaulted on mass bequests in the 1480s, San Pancrazio was plunged into hard times that threatened the integrity of some patron-client relations. The church was forced by serious financial need to bring a protracted but unsatisfying suit in the archbishop's court from 1490 to 1497 against Brancazio di Niccolò Rucellai, who had failed to uphold his father's property bequest. San Pancrazio fared more successfully in obtaining the one-hundred-florin donation made by Bartolomea Alessandri Minerbetti to officiate and decorate the Minerbetti chapel, after it threatened to sue her executor, Santa Maria Nuova, in 1489.[97]

If masses signaled a sense of spiritual anxiety in Laurentian Florence, what contributed to that uneasiness were deepening conflicts about values among the elite. These conflicts surfaced over a variety of political and moral issues, ranging from sodomy prosecutions (which diminished during a "golden age" of tolerance in the late 1480s), to a questioning of the social and spiritual utility of funeral pomp.[98] The very ceremonies and tolerant practices that helped establish the reputation of the Laurentian elite at home and abroad also prompted a backlash against magnificence and a call in certain sectors for greater thrift, asceticism, and moral rigor. The 1480s in particular saw a noticeable breakdown of consensus in patrician conceptions of an ideal moral order, with both political and spiritual struggles fought out partly in cultural terms.

Here differing funerary projections crafted by wealthy men in their testaments offer useful illustrations of an obvious polarization in religious sensibility and social values. At one end of the spectrum, some well-off merchants left elaborate instructions detailing the number of friars and candles to be involved, as did Francesco Bonaparte in his testament of 1489. At the other end, an appreciable number of prominent men explicitly rejected or modified in their wills the kind of pomp that otherwise would be considered commensurate with their social standing. Gino Capponi wanted his obsequies done "simply and moderately . . . and without pomp" (testament dated 1480); Angelo Strozzi indicated that his funeral display should remain within legal limits (1480), as did Antonio Albizzi (1476). Girolamo Martini, a Venetian residing in Florence, wanted no pomp and specified in his 1490 will exactly which friars should attend. The notary Alberto Serruchi also prohibited pomp, desiring only the presence of the Franciscans of Santa Croce and the priests of San Pier Maggiore according to his testament of 1475.[99]

Personalized combinations of pomp and austerity gave other funerals and testaments a unique stamp that cannot be easily categorized by type or by political alignments. Filippo Strozzi was apparently buried in the confraternal habit of San Benedetto yet was otherwise surrounded by magnificence; conversely, the great Franciscan patron Tommaso Spinelli chose the most expensive outfit he owned, to be openly flaunted on the bier, yet prohibited flags and excessive wax.[100] The involvement of clergy as mourners presented the thorniest problem and evoked the greatest range of responses. Some Florentines saw brigades of friars as a form of "gloria mundana," while others saw the friars' presence as an indication of fervid piety. However beautiful the facade, the pomp and ceremony characteristic of the period masked conflicting values and divergent cultural meanings, social relations based on dependence, and a growing mood of political and spiritual uncertainty.

Indicative of these shifts and conflicts in values was the change in communal sumptuary policy away from an earlier search for accommodation, toward greater stringency. Comprehensive new sumptuary laws passed in April 1473 clamped down on extravagance in funerals, weddings, baptisms, and banquets in an attempt "to restore the people to good customs."[101] It was hoped that the examples of relative thrift set by Florence's greater citizens would encourage the populace to follow suit. Several of the funerary rubrics repeated traditional provisions; other rubrics, such as the one that limited the number of clergy who could participate in funerals, and regulated their payments, were directed specifically at new abuses. Provisions to exceed sumptuary limits were retained, but the fee levied for the required license jumped from ten florins to either twenty-five or fifty, depending on the purchaser's social rank.

Underlying this legislation was an important moralizing rationale that went beyond traditional economic arguments about the futile dissipation of patrimony. A special point of contention was the spiritual value of multiple masses. Already by 1473 communal lawmakers represented this form of pomp as spiritually useless or even harmful. One of the rubrics claimed that "the practice of making masses with pomp, a great deal of wax, and crowds of people [is] a fruitless expense for the soul of the deceased." The provision authorizing the legislation was still more explicit about the detrimental effects of these ceremonies. It stated that the rising tide of funeral pomp not only served to "burden the heirs with expenses, but more importantly it harmed the souls of the deceased," although the lawmakers did not proceed to articulate their reasons for the latter belief.[102] The resulting rubrics mixed older political and economic motives with new encroachments on ecclesiastical territory, prohibiting large gatherings of either women or men at memorial masses and continuing to regulate wax consumption.

This change in sumptuary policy away from accommodation toward renewed stringency has been explained in various ways. Machiavelli tied the passage of these laws to the excesses associated with the entrance of the Milanese duke Galeazzo Maria Sforza in March 1471, which seems unlikely given the two-year interval, the explicit moralizing bent of the legislation, and the variety of ceremonies to which Florentines were almost constantly exposed. Guicciardini rather snidely claimed in retrospect that the magistrates undertook the revision because they had little else on their agenda to occupy them. More recently, Richard Trexler has attributed this shift in policy to the desire of Lorenzo de' Medici to curb patrician privilege, thereby limiting competition between the Medici and other great families for social and political predominance.[103]

However, the measures regulating funerals do not bear out this last interpretation. In fact, in setting limits on wax, flags, clergy, and mourners, special allowances were consistently made for communal officials, knights, physicians, and jurists in ways that not merely preserved but actually extended their customary sumptuary privileges. Members of these groups were allowed six torches and two banners, for example, others only four torches and one banner; the number of mourners for an ordinary citizen was restricted to fifteen persons other than neighbors and kinsmen, whereas there were no restrictions for the designated elite. Social rank also determined the permissible number of clergy, as well as the dress of the corpse. For the first time the law permitted corpses of the elite to be publicly displayed on the bier, a privilege denied to ordinary citizens. Although knighthood thus retained its formal attraction and legal utility to merchants, these allocations of privilege on the basis of occupation or title were interpreted loosely to include a broader elite of wealth. Despite the new ceilings placed on consumption, the 1473 sumptuary laws only served to enhance and legitimate patrician privileges at the expense of a poorer populace. In this regard, sumptuary policy paralleled changes in class relations and judicial practice which were more explicitly aimed after 1460 at controlling the lower orders.[104]

Besides targeting consumption, the 1473 statutes also instituted new forms of social control directed at customary mourning practices. For the first time, the rubrics limited the permissible number of mourners and prescribed the duration of mourning; they also attached greater mourning privileges to particular kinship bonds, addressed the problem of men's mourning clothes, and introduced distinctions based on age. Although this type of proscription was unprecedented in Florence, similar laws had been passed in Rome in 1471. The Roman rubrics severely restricted the number of mourners and allowed mourning garb to only one son or nephew, one woman (the deceased's widow, sister, or other close kin), and, for members of the upper classes, one valet. Moreover, the Roman statutes showed their conservative social orientation when admonishing women to wear the "traditional" Roman mourning garb of a simple gown and mantle, instead of more fanciful wear. These same rubrics also gave added legal weight to decorum as a model of civic behavior: women were ordered not to appear at the requiem in a disorderly or disheveled state.[105]

In Florence, these novel regulations had the larger effect of helping to selectively redraw the boundaries separating family and community. The 1473 sumptuary statutes intruded into areas that had long been part of an unregulated body of familial and social custom. Bruni's mourning restrictions of 1436–37, for example, had applied only to communal officials, not to the citizenry at large. The new statutes still trod gingerly in claiming new jurisdictional ground for the polity. The limits set on the number of mourners and their kinship connections applied only to those Florentines who had not left specific instructions for mourning clothes in their wills. Nevertheless, all Florentines were subject to the new legal distinctions drawn between black clothing made specifically for mourning (*panni neri imbastiti*), ordinary black clothes (*vestiti di nero*), and lesser degrees of mourning (*panni bruni*). Moreover, the permissible mourning period defined by law applied to all citizens regardless of rank.[106]

These new communal claims were predicated on a complex interplay of social and sexual ideologies that highlighted sexual distinctions and contributed to their inequities. While the statutes determined pomp on the basis of class, they allotted mourning privileges by gender, allowing more extensive mourning to honor men than to honor women, regardless of social status. Men could be "deeply" mourned by a variety of kin, including sons, grandsons, mothers, fathers, daughters, daughters-in-law, and widows. Other patrilineal relations, such as brothers and nephews, might wear a lesser degree of mourning. Moreover, knights and physicians who were related to a cleric as reckoned "through the male line" could legitimately invite him and his colleagues to participate in the funeral. By contrast, the laws stipulated that only one woman other than the children of the deceased might don deep mourning to mark a woman's death. This single mourner was, in order of preference, either the woman's own mother, the wife of her eldest brother, or her eldest sister. "In whatever circumstances," read the rubric, "the result should be that only one female from the woman's side [*dallato della donna*] is outfitted." Measures regulating the duration of mourning similarly permitted longer periods to mark the deaths of husbands, fathers, grandfathers, and brothers than to mark the deaths of female relatives. Marco Parenti was quick to note in his diary his compliance with these rubrics when his wife Caterina died in 1841, although in fact he violated the code.[107]

As new legal norms, these provisions struck hard at women's burial honors, their customary prerogatives as mourners, and the representation of complex kinship ties in ritual activities. Such a stringent reduction in female mourners severely diminished the honors permitted a dead woman, since the vast majority of women's mourners were female kin. The implications of this move for living women and for family systems more generally were equally significant. By cutting off a woman from an extended group of kin, this reduction symbolically isolated the dead woman from identification with a hodgepodge of kin acquired through multiple marriages, household transfers, and the accidents of life. Natal bonds between women suffered a particular blow in the preference of a brother's wife over a woman's own sister as the designated mourner. At the same time that these laws disadvantaged dead women, they also reduced the traditional opportunities living women enjoyed as mourners to dramatize the complexities of their kinship ties. The model of family and kinship posited in this legal code was an explicitly patrilineal one, stripped of bilateral complexities and focused on descent through the male line. Late Quattrocento sumptuary law made inroads into the domain of customary family activities by specifically targeting bilateral and cognatic networks that had been created by women.

As sumptuary law carved out a new set of patrilineal privileges, fashion trends highlighted still further the special status of sons. Black mourning mantles worn by sons and grandsons to honor their male forbears grew longer, more voluminous, and more expensive to tailor; at times, they even outshone the mourning costumes of female kin.[108] Filippo Strozzi's cortege even sported four fictive "sons" wrapped in huge mantles that trailed behind them, whose presence added visual splendor and symbolic weight to an already gaudy occasion. As the Quattrocento drew to a close, both law and clothing projected funerals as masculine family affairs. Given these new legal restrictions and costume trends, and the complete absence of sumptuary permits bought for women's funerals under Lorenzo's aegis, it is evident that public representations at death affirmed a much more pronouncedly paternalistic conception of state and society than they had done a century earlier.

However, it is difficult to build up a corresponding picture of significant changes in the funeral pomp of well-born and middling women in the absence of detailed descriptions. Late Quattrocento merchant diarists such as Marco Parenti and middling artisans such as Piero and Bartolomeo Masi proudly claimed that they had buried their wives, mothers, and grandmothers "honorably," but they left few particulars about the ceremonies.[109] Even the funerals of Medici women such as Ginevra Alessandri and Ginevra Cavalcanti have left little trace in the historical record. Ecclesiastical sources document that humbler folk such as shoemakers, butchers, bakers, and millers frequently hired six or ten pairs of friars for the funerals of their mothers, wives, and daughters, and that these same men sponsored masses to benefit their kinswomen's souls. Yet it is not possible to offer a comprehensive analysis of changes in the formal patterns and characteristics of women's funerals—reflective of both their personal desires and their place in household, family, and community—without a full-scale recovery of women's testaments and of documents detailing their ecclesiastical patronage and political activities, a task that lies beyond the scope of this book.

The magnificent but troubled rule of Lorenzo de' Medici came to an end with his death at Careggi on April 8, 1492. With his passing, the chronicler Benedetto Dei remarked that "the splendor, not only of Tuscany, but of the whole of Italy, has disappeared."[110] Like his grandfather, Lorenzo reportedly forbade any pomp in his honor. His body was carried to Florence the next morning, where it was laid in the meeting place of the Magi confraternity in San Marco for the remainder of the day, bewailed, according to Piero Parenti, by great and humble citizens alike. The funeral took place in San Lorenzo on the tenth with relatively little flourish. The church was "devoid of hangings and canopies," and the only funerary participants were clerics from Santissima Annunziata, San Marco, and San Lorenzo; and Medici kin.[111] To Dei, the lack of pomp seemed irrelevant, "for no matter how pompous the ceremony might have been, it would always have proved too mean for so great a man."[112] Lorenzo first was buried in the stunning porphyry sarcophagus, designed by Verrocchio and situated in the Old Sacristy, that contained the bodies of his father, brother, and uncle. When his body was translated in an elaborate, myth-laden ceremony to Michelangelo's New Sacristy in 1559, his corpse was reported to be desiccated but completely intact, and his white burial outfit and scarlet beret virtually untouched by time.[113]

Lorenzo's death was marked both at home and abroad by a variety of tributes. The King of Naples and his entire court donned mourning in honor "of the benevolence [Lorenzo] had borne towards the King." Poliziano wrote a poem in honor of Lorenzo's death, and two funeral orations were subsequently composed, one in Naples by the bishop of Martorano, the other by Antonio Pacini. However, Lorenzo was never eulogized publicly in Florence, and it was not until the second decade of the sixteenth century that Lorenzo's mythic stature as patron began to be propagated in funeral oratory.[114]

The commune cast about for a suitable tribute, as it had for Lorenzo's grandfather Cosimo. The solution arrived at was a clear imitation of the recognition paid the *pater patriae*, emphasizing the generational continuity of power and again representing the state as a Medici family, albeit with characteristic communal restraint. Three days after Lorenzo's death, the Signoria and the Colleges voted by a majority of nearly eight to one that "whereas the memory of Lorenzo needs no outward adornments . . . it has been determined to transfer to Piero, the eldest son of the deceased, the heir of his father's dignity, and the successor to his fame, the public honor due to his father and his ancestors." The succession of Piero to the Medici political legacy was to be regarded as "a public testimonial of gratitude to the memory of so great a man, in order that virtue may not be unhonored among the Florentines, and that in days to come others may be incited to serve the commonwealth with might and wisdom."[115]

The signs and portents accompanying Lorenzo's death seemed in retrospect to tell of the troubles and evils to come. Over the next two years, death claimed several other leading lights of Laurentian Florence—Pico, Ficino, Ghirlandaio—whose demise marked the end of a cultural era.[116] In the political realm, Piero fell heir not only to Lorenzo's achievements but also to wobbly alliances, anti-Medicean sentiment, and the growing might of foreign monarchs. Elaborate diplomatic games and foreign intrigues involved language that grew seemingly more elusive in meaning.[117] Piero contributed to his own difficulties by mismanaging foreign affairs and by alienating the Florentine patriciate. Although Florence would soon be plunged into crisis, what had been wrought in Lorenzo's lifetime was not so easily squandered: namely, the restructuring of social connections, of urban ecclesiastical patronage, and of legal norms which declared the victory of patrician domination.

The New Republic, 1494–1512

The entry of Charles VIII into Florence in November 1494 marked the beginning of a lengthy political crisis that ultimately resulted in the collapse of the Florentine republic.[118] The French invasion brought in its immediate wake the exile of Piero de' Medici, the loss of Pisa and other Florentine territories, and the revival of popular government. Having rejected the Medici, the "new republic" broadened constitutional representation to an unprecedented degree by the creation of the Great Council, with some three thousand eligible members. However, changing political opinions among the patriciate, turbulent foreign affairs, and the fluctuating influence of Savonarola made the practical exercise of power by the republican regime extremely fragile.[119] After 1496, the city was further disrupted by plague, famine, financial crisis, grain riots, conspiracies, and a string of interdicts that took an enormous toll on Florentine religious and ceremonial life. The times still seemed so stormy a decade later that Francesco Guicciardini advised wise men to avoid festivities if they could; Guicciardini himself reported that he celebrated his wedding in November 1508 with as little pomp as possible.[120] Given the practical difficulties of these years, it is not surprising that there were only a small handful of impressive funerals scattered throughout this period.

This retrenchment also testifies, however, to the advent of a new cultural politics. In this context of crisis and reform, the tensions between competing conceptions of an "honorable burial" which had surfaced in preceding decades, especially among the elite, became more overtly politicized. Magnificence and its rejection now intermingled religion and politics in new ways: each strategy helped declare one's allegiance to particular political styles, factions, and moral values. In other words, death rites in the new republic became an area of explicit ideological activity. One of the ways in which prominent men such as Piero Soderini, Piero di Gino Capponi, and

Alamanno Rinuccini demonstrated their strong republican leanings was by breaking with, or severely modifying, the conventions of magnificence that had become the hallmark of Laurentian Florence. Soderini, Capponi, and Rinuccini all explicitly forbade various types of standard funerary honors in their testaments: Soderini prohibited "all pomp and apparatus"; Capponi denounced displays of "worldly glory"; Rinuccini elected burial in a Franciscan habit.[121] Similarly, a number of affluent women made their moral stance visible through their sober taste in necklines and mourning garb. The rejection of magnificence as a governing concept was, of course, an integral part of Savonarola's program for moral reform and political renewal. Savonarola lashed out against rich Florentines not only for their vanities in this life but also for their pompous vanity in death. The Dominican had nothing but scorn for those "gentlemen and lords of the world" whose beautiful tombs revealed their reluctance "to rot unless in a luxurious place."[122]

By contrast, those ceremonies noted by contemporaries for their opulence or extravagance seem to have all been associated in some way with a pro-Medici faction, especially after the establishment of Piero Soderini as *gonfaloniere* for life in 1502. In the new republic, cultural style not only expressed honor and ambition, but also helped trace out broad political alignments. The diarist Landucci, for example, remarked on the "great pomp" surrounding the 1504 wedding of Lorenzo Strozzi and Lucrezia Rucellai, daughter of one of the staunchest Medici sympathizers, Bernardo Rucellai. In 1508 the city witnessed a requiem of truly enormous proportions staged for Rinaldo Orsini, the former archbishop of Florence, whose kinship and alliance with the Medici helped solidify a Rome-Florence axis. Similarly, Archbishop Cosimo Pazzi, Orsini's successor and a Medici candidate, took office with more than the usual flourish.[123]

Following Piero de' Medici's exile, the desire to dissociate the new republic from previous Medicean magnificence while still preserving communal honor presented practical difficulties for civic ritual. The solution was a series of uneven compromises. Receptions for ambassadors and foreign dignitaries between 1494 and 1512 were quite respectable events, for example, but none approached the grand scale of earlier receptions or the dazzling entry of Leo X in 1515.[124] This more modest form of magnificence was no doubt buttressed by the commune's serious financial woes and the need to demonstrate fiscal probity. Yet this strategy was not simply a money-saving device. Rather, it formed part of a larger, serious campaign by the Signoria to reestablish a republican iconography through images, symbols, and rituals. Almost immediately after Piero's exile, the Signoria attempted to erase some of the most obvious signs of Medici rule, ordering the Medici coat of arms removed from public buildings and replaced with the arms of the populace. The civic magistrates also directed that the tomb inscription of the *pater patriae* be effaced, and confiscated a collection of fourteen commemorative family busts gracing the grounds of the Medici palace.[125] The Signoria was not content with simply removing these vestiges, however. Donatello's statue of the tyrant-slayer Judith was quickly transferred from the Via Larga to the government palace, with a new inscription alerting viewers to the evils of tyranny; in 1504 Michelangelo's *David* joined this earlier work to form a dual proclamation of republican sentiment.[126]

Civic funerals in the first years of the new republic similarly advanced the cause of *governo civile*. In contrast to the novelties of Savonarola's youth processions, however, the communal government took a profoundly conservative approach in honoring statesmen and heroes, one that played on the patriotic conventions of the Florentine past. The civic homage paid in 1496–97 to Piero Capponi, who died while heading a campaign to recapture Pisa, and Gino Ginori, an eminent statesman and supporter of Savonarola, was pointedly traditional in form, involving massive numbers of torches bought at public expense; flags displaying the arms of various civic magistracies such as the Ten on Liberty, the populace, and assorted guilds; and public recognition accorded by civic officials.[127] Viewed in their larger context of political and iconographic reform, these rites provided visual and symbolic analogues to Savonarola's praise of traditional republican forms, expressed in works such as the *Trattato circa el reggimento e governo della città de Firenze*.[128] Even after Savonarola's downfall in May 1498, the regime clung to a similar conservative strategy. The ceremonies honoring the noted humanist and Medici critic Alamanno Rinuccini in May 1499 bore such republican hallmarks as a funeral oration delivered by the Florentine chancellor Marcello Adriani, the commission of a commemorative bronze medal, and extraordinary guild homage accorded by the Studio.[129] Similarly, sumptuary laws in the last years of the republic aimed to strengthen rather than to significantly revise established policies.[130]

Given the way in which images and ceremonies formed part of a larger political agenda, it is not surprising that factional tensions between the Medici's enemies and allies surfaced repeatedly in public funeral rites. The obsequies for Giovanni di Pierfrancesco de' Medici in September 1498, some four months after Savonarola's execution, became a focal point for political tensions as the regime tried to exploit rivalries within the Medici family to celebrate broader republican sentiments. Giovanni and his brother Lorenzo, often referred to as the popolano branch of the family, had both been exiled by Piero in 1492 after a long-simmering family quarrel, only to return after Piero himself was ousted. Giovanni's civic service as commissioner general for the Romagna, on the one hand, and his membership in the city's most famous family, on the other, allowed both sides to claim his funeral as an occasion to gain political advantage. The huge public obsequies held at San Lorenzo fifteen days after his death once again pitted the canons of the cathedral and those of San Lorenzo in a heated dispute over processional protocol, while forcing the body of civic magistrates and resident ambassadors into uneasy accommodation with a phalanx of Medici relations.[131]

The death of Giovanni's brother Lorenzo in 1503 became a still more politically contested occasion. Piero Soderini had been installed as *gonfaloniere* for life the previous year; in January 1503 Piero de' Medici drowned, an event that was greeted with jubilation by the anti-Medicean forces in the city.[132] In Lorenzo's funeral, however, members of the Colleges and other principal civic magistrates, whose presence added a specifically republican tribute, were forced once again into an uneasy mix with more private signs of Medici wealth and power, such as a lavish wax display in San Lorenzo and one of the largest clerical contingents ever assembled for a layman's funeral. For this occasion, ranks of clergy were used less as a mark of piety than as counters in an elaborate political game. The playoff of factions resulted in a spectacular, highly politicized event that was dramatically out of proportion to Lorenzo's personal achievements.[133]

The new popular government confronted not only these crises of representation, however, but more urgent problems of plague and famine which threatened an already tenuous order. In April 1497, soaring food prices sparked riots led by a handful of poor women which drew an estimated three thousand female participants. Their cries for bread ("pane, pane") became dangerously confused with cries of Medici allegiance ("palle, palle").[134] Not surprisingly, subsistence problems hit hardest at the urban poor, whose inadequate diet made them easy targets for disease. From 1493 to 1498, the city experienced recurrent episodes of plague and plague-like diseases, although none as harsh as the full-scale epidemic of 1479. The legislation that established civic plague officers (*ufficiali del morbo*) in March 1496 and the following year created a plague hospital to treat poor plague victims cemented the association of plague and poverty, an association that emphasized social control of the lower orders.[135] However, this legislation still did not make the city responsible for burying the growing numbers of indigent dead. That task continued to fall to the charitable confraternity of the Misericordia, whose major reorganization between 1490 and 1501 better equipped it for this role.[136]

Mortality associated with plague, famine, and poverty also highlighted changes in urban class geography and neighborhood residential patterns. The opening up of the city center to make way for building projects such as palaces and squares, especially in the second half of the Quattrocento, displaced laborers and artisans in this area. By the late fifteenth century, 80 percent of the *popolo minuto* was concentrated in eleven large parishes on the city's periphery.[137] These changes in the social composition of parishes resulting from demographic redistributions and, to a lesser extent, from immigration gave rise to a greater dependence on the parish and a new sense of parochial affiliation, which are reflected in burial patterns. The availability of a comprehensive burial register for the large, outlying parish of Sant'Ambrogio, with a predominantly working-class population, allows us to systematically survey the burial sites of parishioners between 1480 and 1510. The vast majority of entries identify the parishioner by occupation and sometimes place of origin, as well as by name. The results of a sample taken at alternating two- and three-year intervals, totaling eleven hundred burials, are summarized in Table 6.2.[138]

Compared to an earlier sample drawn from the neighboring parish of San Pier Maggiore between 1374 and 1413,[139] this survey shows a greater reliance on parish burial (83.4 percent versus 76.4 percent), with consistently higher percentages after 1500. This concentration exceeded the patterns seen in other sixteenth-century cities such as Paris, where 76 percent of testators studied by Pierre Chaunu named

T A B L E 6.2: Parish Burial Patterns at Sant'Ambrogio, 1480–1510

Year	Total No. of Burials	No. of Parishioners Buried in Parish	Percentage
1480	49	39	79.6
1483	81	64	79.0
1485	71	55	77.5
1487	40	31	77.5
1490	63	47	74.6
1493	92	82	89.1
1495	113	88	77.9
1497	205	179	87.3
1500	54	49	90.7
1503	55	49	89.0
1505	71	65	91.5
1507	149	121	81.2
1510	57	48	84.2
Total	1,100	917	83.4

Source: Conv. Sopp. 79. vol. 458, "Libri di morti, 1478–1511." There are some slight gaps in the evidence: no burials were recorded for January 1505, or for March and August 1510.

their parish church as their preferred burial site.[140] Moreover, exchange into the parish after death slowed to a virtual halt: in the entire sample, only one person residing outside Sant'Ambrogio elected to be buried there. Concentration of burial sites within the urban zone of Sant'Ambrogio, San Pier Maggiore, and Santa Croce saw a corresponding rise, with burials in these three churches accounting for 92 percent of the total. The great Franciscan church of Santa Croce continued as before to draw off the largest number of parishioners, both popolani and members of important families with long-standing parish traditions, such as the Zati and the del Caccia; as in the earlier sample, men comprised more than half this group (thirty-six of sixty-one). However, those electing burial outside this zone mapped out diffuse allegiances to parishes scattered across the city and to rural communities in the contado. Spanning the occupational gamut from tailors, doublet makers, and rag dealers to gardeners, victualers, and cooks, this small subgroup testifies to a displaced laboring class seeking to honor former familial and neighborhood attachments.[141]

The growing importance of the parish and class segregation in the late Renaissance was accentuated and reinforced by the privatization of burial sites. The monopoly of select tomb sites and ecclesiastical space by established lineages, a monopoly that had taken shape over the previous century, found explicit legal backing in the synodal rulings of 1517, which prohibited intramural burial to anyone who could not already claim an ancestral tomb within church confines.[142] These rubrics reinforced the control of privileged burial space by those great families who had already spread their wealth, patronage, marriage networks, and ancestral claims to urban areas beyond their local parishes and neighborhoods. At the same time, these rulings worked in the opposite direction to localize the burial patterns of middling Florentines such as notaries, druggists, and butchers, who most often enjoyed access to prestigious intramural burial only in their local parish. By the 1520s, burial sites traced out a class geography both within ecclesiastical spaces and across the urban landscape.

Parishioners of modest means seeking to escape either the anonymity of burial in an unmarked communal tomb, or the corporate nature of confraternal burial, still had a few options. Their most likely chance for a private tomb site was a subterranean tomb in one of the newly expanded cemeteries built by some local parishes. In September 1519, for instance, the baker Domenico di Jacopo was able to purchase a tomb for his father in the underground cemetery of San Pancrazio, with the understanding that if he failed to wall the site and donate nine lire by the following March, the abbot could bury his father's body in any communal tomb he wished.[143] Alternately, domestic servants or even the displaced members of great families might attach themselves to their patrons in such a way as to procure better burial sites. In 1510 Piero Soderini's wife Argentina Malespina contracted with the convent of the Murate to allow her seven-year-old niece Caterina to act as her personal servant in the room Argentina maintained for her own use at the Murate. The agreement stipulated that Caterina could be admitted later as a nun if she chose, or in any event could be buried in the church when she died. This kind of intervention by Argentina was not unusual; Soderini drew fire from his opponents for allowing her to write letters of recommendation for her friends to various magistrates in and out of the city.[144]

The focus on parish burial should also be linked, however, to new forms of parish religious activity developing in the late fifteenth and early sixteenth centuries. The turbulance of these decades accelerated the collapse of traditional confraternal life drawing on citywide networks. From the Savonarolan period to the Council of Trent, confraternities were frequently suppressed.[145] With the decline of confraternities and broader civic communities, the popular classes turned to local parish and neighborhood organizations for their ritual life. The reinvigoration of local associations was already evident in the Sant'Ambrogio sector in the 1490s. The Company of Santa Maria della Neve at Sant'Ambrogio, founded in 1445, reissued its statutes in October 1493 to permit greater involvement of parishioners, both male and female, in the company's activities.[146] At neighboring San Pier Maggiore, a new confraternity dedicated to the Virgin emerged in August 1493. The company obligated itself to assist with various parish feasts and processions, and the company's officers—a linen weaver, a tailor, and a dyer—reaffirmed these parochial duties in 1516.[147] With the establishment in the 1520s and 1530s of local sacramental confraternities such as Sant'Ambrogio's Company of the Holy Miracle (1533), the cultic life of Florence began to center firmly in the city's parishes. The parish subsequently offered a stable unit of social control for both church and state under the Medici dukes.[148]

These new directions in Florentine social life and in pre-Tridentine piety bound clergy and laity in still more complex ways, and this interdependence was nowhere more evident than in rites of death and remembrance. As Florentines became increasingly divided by wealth, geography, and cultural politics, clergy became the most important—often the only—common element of public mortuary practices. The presence of clergy might be multiplied, politicized, used to mediate factions and ideals, contested, or interpreted in other ways: whatever the case, clergy were essential to this cult management. In turn, by the early sixteenth century both parochial and monastic institutions came to depend heavily on such public recognition of their ritual services and on the economics of death. Lucrative revenues flowed not merely from the customary gifts of funeral trappings, which had formed a significant part of church income in the late Trecento. Clergy now benefited from the whole ensemble

of masses, meals, prayers, processions, tombs, and chapels Florentines had elaborated during the Quattrocento. Proscriptive ecclesiastical legislation gives one indication of how important and attractive
death revenues had become. Cosimo Pazzi's episcopal constitutions
of 1508 sounded a familiar theme, denouncing clerics who flocked
to burials uninvited in search of alms. The synodal constitutions of
1517, however, added a new condemnation of clerics who neglected
duties at their own churches on Sundays and feast days and during
Lent in order to celebrate anniversary or votive masses at other
institutions for pay.[149]

Moreover, Luther's polemical charge that clergy "ate" off the dead
rings true in one tangible sense, at least at large monastic complexes
such as Santa Maria Novella. Commissions for tombs and burial sites
often brought in their train regular, ongoing provisions for special
meals (*pietanze*) commemorating a testator's death day or some other
specified occasion. These meals, ranging from relatively humble fare
to virtual banquets, were offered to friars as partial compensation
for services and in hopes of stimulating additional prayers. By the
early sixteenth century, *pietanze* furnished an impressive part of the
friars' regular subsistence, especially considering the serious food
shortages that plagued the city under siege. In November 1528, a
peak liturgical month, the friars of Santa Maria Novella enjoyed
pietanze on twenty-one of thirty-one days. From December through
the following July, commemorative meals bolstered the convent menu
on more than one out of every three days (36.6 percent).[150]

The complex ways in which clergy and laity needed each other to
maintain cult life and clerical livelihood help to put into context the
powerful leverage exerted by a string of interdicts in the new republic. The most severe of these was the interdict levied by Julius
II in September 1511. Caught in a swirl of international affairs, the
Signoria dove headlong into conflict with the papacy and forced six
major churches to continue celebrating mass. In other churches,
however, the interdict was observed, thereby giving individual Florentines the option of compliance.[151] Under the terms of the interdict
all customary burial rites and practices were suspended. As the diarist Masi reported, clergy were "not able to accept the corpses of laity
in any sacralized place; nor were clergy able to walk in processions
to bury the dead, either with or without a cross, as was church
custom."[152] However terrible the spiritual and social costs, the pro-

hibition of burial in hallowed ground posed further practical problems of civic hygiene. During what must have seemed a long, confusing autumn, as the interdict was lifted then reinstated, the bodies of dead parishioners at Sant'Ambrogio were buried in sand to retard putrefaction, or placed in coffins and chests that served as interim tombs.[153]

Not all Florentines were disturbed by what seemed a desperate turn of events. Former followers of Savonarola, such as Giovanni Cambi, thought the interdict had a beneficial impact on death rites, since rich citizens "were unable to spend money on wax and priests, or on masses or flags, which was very useful for the city." Cambi further speculated that the interdict would have long-lasting salutary effects in keeping with *piagnoni* moral reforms. "When things return to normal," Cambi mused, "this will cause less pomp in candles and bell ringing, and the things of God will be held in greater reverence."[154]

Cambi's hopes were nevertheless short-lived. Leading Florentines such as Filippo Strozzi recognized the profound weaknesses of the popular regime and had already begun to move closer to the Medici. These internal conflicts and the interference of foreign powers paved the way for the reentry of the Medici in September 1512 after an eighteen-year exile. Ensuing changes in the civic constitution and in government personnel assured the domination of the Medici and their aristocratic followers over affairs of state.[155] The Medici restoration also had profound effects on the cultural politics of the city, as the new rulers of Florence declared their victory through a resplendent ethos of magnificence that left no doubt about the relation of ceremony and power.

The New Chivalry, 1512–1527

Within months after the Medici restoration, the cultural politics of the new regime became readily apparent. Giuliano and Lorenzo were welcomed with pageantry, the replacement of Medici armorial symbols throughout the city, and a host of verses. In March 1513, the city celebrated the election of Giovanni de' Medici as pope with a grand clerical procession and much gift giving. Later that year, the new pope Leo X bestowed Roman citizenship on his brother Giuliano and nephew Lorenzo in an elaborate ceremony.[156] Magnificence also celebrated the Medicean political and familial connections of the Florentine archibishop Cosimo Pazzi upon his death in April 1513. Pazzi's mother Bianca was the daughter of the ill-fated Piero de' Medici; his father Guglielmo was a staunch Medicean and a member of the newly empowered permanent Balìa; Pazzi himself had been instrumental in solidifying the connections between Rome and Florence upon which Medici power rested. After Pazzi's body had lain in state for three days, a massive procession around the heart of the city outstripped in pomp and theatricality even the honors paid to Pazzi's predecessor Rinaldo Orsini in 1508. The crowning touch was the donation of a rich banner displaying the Pazzi and papal arms, which was to be hung in the cathedral as a perpetual memorial.[157]

In all these examples, however, Medicean cultural politics rested on far more than the kind of conspicuous consumption and largesse typical of the late Trecento or even the Laurentian period. What was new about this image making was the nature of the resources upon which it rested, as well as the consistent way in which these resources were mobilized, managed, and manipulated. In ceremonies such as the elaborate entry of Leo X in November 1515 and the funeral of Giuliano de' Medici the following year, the Medici emphasized rather than masked the power stemming from the Rome-Florence axis they had carefully nurtured over the preceding century. Unlike earlier state entries, the extravaganza for Leo was not a vehicle for dialogue between political equals; nor was the funeral of Giuliano an expression of mutual obligations between social groups. In these events there was little attempt to disguise the Medici's domination of civic and social processes, of patronage activities and networks, of ecclesiastical space and personnel. Moreover, there was a hint of force about these ceremonies, which openly incorporated the retinues of armed guards of soldiers and courtiers officially commanded by Lorenzo de' Medici after May 1515. Abandoning the covert strategies of Cosimo and il Magnifico, Medici ceremonies after the restoration depended on and made direct reference to the family's multiple power bases in Florentine institutions and international alliances, now newly backed by military might.

Deploying these new resources, Medici festivities in the 1510s and 1520s functioned as both boundary and bridge between the republic and the principate. These years saw what was perhaps the most critical transition in the use of ceremony as an instrument of political rule. Ceremonies did not yet present a full program of political ideas or the elaborate political allegory typical of the principate, yet Medici ceremonies during these decades nevertheless anticipated later court spectacles of state in both their form and their political connotations. Through a powerful combination of chivalry, humanism, and theater, these stage-managed affairs created images of a Medici prince and of a Medici dynasty as the legitimate rulers of Florence.

The building of a Medicean cult through ceremony can be seen in the elaborate funeral arrangements for Giuliano de' Medici, duke of Nemours, who died on March 17, 1516. This funeral, engineered by Giuliano's nephew Lorenzo to bolster his own reputation, was reckoned by one contemporary as the most magnificant funeral ever staged in Florence for a private citizen.[158] It would be a lengthy undertaking indeed to catalog fully the honors paid to Giuliano— the fifteen strings of flags; multiple banners and torches; caparisoned horses; brilliant brocades; tapestries, silks, and detailed armor—or to enumerate the ranks of participating communal officials, guildsmen, and clergy, or the two hundred Medici kin in voluminous mourning cloaks. Michelangelo immortalized several of these accoutrements and aspects of dress in Giuliano's monumental tomb in the New Sacristy of San Lorenzo.[159]

What is most important to note from a stylistic standpoint is the way in which Giuliano's funeral encapsulated the chivalric revival already under way in tournaments and other festivities. This "new chivalry" marked the rearistocratization of Florentine society yet had different, more explicit, political meanings than did the chivalry of the late Trecento. The new chivalry of the early sixteenth century deployed northern traditions and symbols for the deliberate purpose of drawing or transferring the allegiance of courtiers and bystanders to the figure of the "prince."[160] This manipulation of chivalry went beyond the direct references made by Giuliano's burial armor and trappings to his position as titled duke, Captain of the Church, and the pope's brother. Visual combinations and ritual activities suggested in addition that the Medici owned, dominated, or otherwise controlled a variety of powerful republican and chivalric symbols. For example, Giuliano's hat, fashioned like a papal tiara, was emblazoned with the Florentine seal of the *marzocco*; prestigious signs such as papal banners and the command baton were for the first time carried by Medici kin rather than by anonymous grooms; and the cortege laid a forthright claim to the city center as a theatre of Medici power, in direct imitation of Leo X's earlier processional route.[161]

Complementing this new chivalry was a new kind of funerary theater that exploited the dramatic potential of customary action. Although it did not devise new forms of liturgy, music, or commemoration as would the grand requiem spectacles of the Medici principate, Giuliano's funeral nevertheless functioned as a rudimentary form of court theater in the way in which it manipulated space, created dramatic tension, and established roles for players and audience. Following an unprecedented public display of the body at San Marco, Giuliano's corpse was placed on view in front of the Medici palace—the new political center of gravity—for several hours before the ceremonies got under way. Hundreds of officials dressed in brown (significantly, these did not include the Signoria), ambassadors, Medici relations, clients, and well-wishers packed the stepped benches lining the Via Larga. There these spectators awaited the appearance of Lorenzo, Giuliano's widow Filiberta, and other close relatives who issued from the house.[162] With the assembly complete, the audience was now primed for a formal recitation of the Medici's virtues by the Florentine chancellor Marcello Adriani.

Adriani's eulogy added an important political articulation to this unfolding drama. The chancellor did not shy away from calling the Medici *principes*, a term whose republican meaning—"first citizens"—was increasingly giving way to more monarchical interpretations. More importantly, Adriani focused on the topic of family and ancestry to develop a clear rationale for Medici rule. This was a politically charged topic that previously had been avoided in Florentine oratory; now it became the central way to advance the mythic stature of the Medici. Tracing Giuliano's illustrious geneaology, Adriani praised Cosimo *pater patriae*, Lorenzo il Magnifico, and Pope Leo X as civic servants, patrons, peacemakers, and forces for public order. A similar set of themes inspired the funeral oration by Francesco Cattani da Diacceto for Lorenzo de' Medici three years later, composed at the request of Cardinal Giulio de' Medici.[163] Hence by 1520 humanist orators already identified both the prestige and the destiny of the city with the activities and fortunes of the Medici dynasty, an identification that provided one of the driving themes of Medici art under Duke Cosimo I.[164]

After Giuliano's death, his nephew Lorenzo became the last hope for continued dynastic succession in the main line. Lorenzo was far more ambitious, aggressive, and abrasive than his uncle, and his disagreements with Leo did little to win him additional favor with the Florentines. After Lorenzo took charge of the city upon the family's return in 1512, there developed a widespread perception that Lorenzo wanted to establish himself as *signore* of Florence. The naming of Lorenzo as captain of the Florentine armed forces in May 1515 further reinforced this perception, as did his marriage to the French princess Madeleine Tour de l'Auvergne in the summer of 1518.[165]

Both Lorenzo's ambition and the main Medici line came to an end with his premature death on May 4, 1519. To describe the particulars of his extraordinary burial ceremony would be largely to repeat with still greater embellishments the features of Giuliano's funeral. As one contemporary put it, Lorenzo's obsequies in San Lorenzo "vanquished in every way those celebrated for his uncle, which lacked nothing."[166] This was an exercise in the pure glamour of power: for four hours observers were treated to what was perhaps the most spectacular piece of funerary image making in the history of the republic. Prefiguring the requiem theater of the later Cinquecento, Lorenzo's services exploited the physical setting of San Lorenzo for its theatrical possibilities by means of draperies, escutcheons, and lighting. Following the obsequies, Cardinal Giulio received formal condolences from the citizenry at the Medici palace. Lorenzo's death brought great pomp but few tears: many Florentines apparently breathed a sigh of relief or secretly rejoiced at his passing. No amount of pomp and ceremony could disguise the fact, however, that the Medici now confronted a dynastic crisis. The family mantle passed first to Leo, then after his death in 1521 to the cardinal and future pope Giulio, who exercised control in Florence via various minions and allies.[167]

However grand these spectacles, there was perhaps no better indication of an emerging court society centering on the Medici than the funerary tribute paid Lorenzo's wife, Madeleine Tour de l'Auvergne (d. May 1519), and his mother, Alfonsina Orsini Medici (d. February 1520). Their lavish, well-attended public ceremonies in San Lorenzo greatly surpassed the burial honors previously given any woman in republican Florence. One observer remarked that the proceedings for both women more closely resembled the customary tributes for "some great master" than those for women.[168] To some extent, these elaborate requiems reflected the women's personal status and accomplishments, particularly in the case of Alfonsina. As an active patron, Alfonsina had accumulated prodigious influence in the years following her marriage to Piero in 1487, using both her wealth and personal connections. For example, she and her mother, Countess Caterina Orsini, spent considerable sums of money to expand and improve various female religious communities, especially the Dominican convent of Santa Lucia. At that house, Alfonsina and Caterina even built for their personal use "several rooms near the street that goes to San Marco," which in 1516 the nuns swore to keep available to these women, also promising to receive them any time they wished.[169] Alfonsina's purview extended to the broader civic community during the late summer and autumn of 1515, when she governed the city in her son's absence, and her ongoing intervention in political affairs earned her the dislike of many.[170]

But these unprecedented funeral honors had a more instrumental political use in the transition from republic to principate. The reorganization of public life in the early sixteenth century also involved a reconsideration of the way in which gender and state had been mutually constituted since the early Quattrocento. While it is likely that Alfonsina actually wielded greater influence than previous Medici women, this public staging of female power so contrary to custom at least symbolically undermined the way in which representations of authority had been gendered over the preceding century. The unabashed richness of these public events declared that Medici interests and family claims superceded even the entrenched paternalism of republican politics. A similar indication of this displacement had already come with the more prominent role accorded to Giuliano's wife Filiberta in his obsequies. Although we are still a long way from the full court burial spectacle honoring Duchess Eleonora of Toledo in 1562, in terms of both a cult of the ruling family and a formal "liturgy of state," these early sixteenth-century requiems took a decisive step in that direction by redefining one important aspect of the relationship between gender and politics.[171]

While the Medici confronted dynastic problems after Lorenzo's death, other aristocrats used similar cultural strategies to confirm their own social place, building on the political stability and new resources the Medici brought to Florence. If the funeral of Bartolomeo

Ginori in 1519 is any indication, ephemeral trappings as well as costly tombs began to command a high level of artistic merit; Ginori's funeral sported flags painted by the young Pontormo, which were much praised by Vasari.[172] What was particularly striking about the effusiveness of early sixteenth-century funerals, however, was their concentration on a flamboyant piety that functioned as both display and consolation. Ecclesiastical pomp continued on its earlier trajectory to reach a pinnacle of pre-Tridentine grandeur. It was not at all uncommon to involve hundreds of clergy in the public burial rites of well-to-do Florentines such as Piero Parenti (d. 1519), with a corresponding diminution of the number of clergy present at private services such as the vigil.[173] Affluent women such as Lisabetta Antinori Landini shared in this effusion, which in some women's funerals emphasized the special connection between the dead woman and a cult or ecclesiastical institution. Lisabetta's funeral in 1521 drew almost two hundred clerics, considerably more than those attending the burial of her husband Guasparre a decade later.[174] Paradoxically, pomp was fed in some cases by an express desire to escape this spiraling display, or to channel it in other directions. Girolamo Tornabuoni stipulated in his will (1524) that if his sons exceeded the pomp specified in his instructions, they had to match the amount of excess with public almsgiving.[175]

Once again, however, it is not only the numbers but also the manipulation of timing which tell an important story. Beginning around 1490 and accelerating rapidly in the early sixteenth century, requiem and memorial masses began to acquire an independent status, as the performance of these rites was more regularly separated from the standard ritual sequence. Since the middle of the fourteenth century, the normal custom had been to perform the funeral and the requiem together on the day after death. In exceptional cases, the requiem might be postponed for an additional day because of conflicts with the liturgical calendar, or to afford more time to gather kin and embellish the church. These rhythms were increasingly broken by the enormous popular demand for large-scale mass celebrations aimed at suffrage and consolation, on the one hand, and by the desire of great men and their heirs to control the details of spectacular mortuary scenarios, on the other. For instance, Piero Parenti's seven sons buried him the day after he died in May 1519, yet they waited six days before staging a set of sixty-one requiem masses in the cathedral. In the interim, the Parenti kept torches stationed around his tomb, had a set of exquisite taffeta banners made for public donation to the church, and had mourning clothes made for fifteen persons.[176] During these same years, musicians in Italian, French, and Flemish cities and courts began to explore the potential of the requeim mass as a medium for new, polyphonic musical expressions.[177] Under the combined forces of popular religious currents, Tridentine decrees, and ducal politics, the funeral ultimately gave way to the requiem as the central event in the ritual sequence as the century progressed. This displacement was codified in 1614, when the Rituale Romanum declared the requiem to be the principal part of the burial and prescribed its use by liturgical law.

Testaments offer additional evidence for the formation of a new religious taste, whose relationship to the cultural politics outlined above remains to be explored. Besides documenting a continuing increase in the number of offices and clergy, some testaments reveal a heightened sensitivity to specific aspects of the liturgy used at memorial services. The commemorative program designed by Francesco Tornabuoni in his 1525 testament offers a case in point. Tornabuoni left fifteen florins annually to subsidize his memorial services at Santa Maria Novella, roughly three times the amount customary a century earlier. He obliged his heirs to celebrate in perpetuity the annual feast of his name saint with both a special feast-day mass and the Gregorian mass series. In addition, Tornabuoni commissioned the Dominicans to sing a solemn mass on his actual birth and death days, using fifty torches on the altar, after which they were to walk in procession to his tomb, singing the antiphon "Libera Me Domine."[178]

The setaiuolo Giovanni Stecchuti showed a similar attentiveness to particular aspects of liturgy. In 1513 Stecchuti enjoined the friars of Santa Maria Novella to celebrate annually the feast of Saint Anne in his family chapel located under the vaults. He instructed the friars to sing the popular "Libera Me Domine" after mass, following which they were to be rewarded with a meal. Shortly after this bequest was made, Stecchuti's grandson Mariotto confirmed the donation but wanted still greater liturgical specificity. Mariotto preferred that the mass honoring Saint Anne be read rather than sung, but he added to the program low masses on two other feasts and costlier types of candles.[179]

In the 1520s plague introduced a stark set of contrasts between the way in which affluent Florentines controlled their visions of death and remembrance, and the experiences of growing numbers of poor. Epidemics struck the city with such fury in 1523 and 1527 that the urban population declined by 20 percent between 1510 and 1530. The diarist Lapini claimed that the death toll from the 1527 plague alone reached between forty thousand and fifty thousand persons; although this figure is grossly exaggerated, given an estimated urban population of eighty thousand in 1520, it nevertheless conveys a vivid sense of how contemporaries registered the gravity of the situation.[180] Mortality patterns hit hardest at laborers, artisans, and the poor, with initial outbreaks in 1522 concentrated in two major zones: the Oltrarno, near San Frediano and Camaldoli; and on the western periphery toward Porta al Prato. The uneven distribution of plague mortality severely undercut the city's labor force; the number of cloth workshops operative in Florence fell from 270 in 1480 to only 63 by 1537.[181]

The virulence of these episodes, which created obvious problems of hygiene and public order, forced a more complex reorganization of corporate and municipal responsibilities for plague victims. Institutional responses to plague combined a two-pronged strategy: on the one hand, charity toward victims; on the other, their isolation from the rest of the community. The Misericordia extended its traditional succor to poor plague victims, who after 1523 were quarantined in their houses for forty days or transferred to a plague house (*lazzaretto*). Assisting the Misericordia in its task of burying plague dead was the newly founded Company of San Sebastiano (1523), comprising seventy-two men. Their corporate mission was to bury poor plague victims in their local parishes with the rudiments of honor: a bier, a processional cross, torches, and a winding sheet. Henceforth plague victims were to be buried "as one would do for those who had not died of plague," instead of being transported on ladders "like beasts" without benefit of trappings or mourners.[182]

This charitable program worked in concert with a growing emphasis on quarantine as a way to curb the spread of disease. Medical practioners' gradual acceptance of the idea of contagion was supported by practical experience indicating that quarantine helped mitigate the effects of plague. Quarantines both isolated the city from surrounding regions and imposed restrictions inside it. Beginning in

1522 the Signoria ordered varying forms of blockade which barred pilgrims and laborers from entry but still permitted visits from ambassadors and state dignitaries. Despite the limited success of blockades, they became a standard part of government plague policy in the sixteenth and seventeenth centuries.[183]

The effects of internal regulations were somewhat more successful from a public health standpoint, as well as more socially pernicious. In 1523 the commune moved to isolate both plague victims and suspects in *lazzaretti*, and to limit personal contacts and commercial exchanges with those infected. These restrictions resulted in greater unemployment and the further impoverishment of the laboring classes and working poor.[184] Plague measures also became more intrusive: in September 1525 the commune appointed a public medical officer vested with the authority to inspect residences where plague was suspected. The final piece in this comprehensive program fell into place when municipal plague officers were given permanent status after the 1527 plague.[185]

By the time the Medici were ousted once again in 1527 and the last Forentine republic was instituted, plague and its controls stood as a kind of metaphor for the way in which politics and society had changed over the preceding century. The discourse of disease helped constitute a centralizing state endowed with greater powers and authority; it also reflected a cordoning off of rich from poor which was supported by mortality patterns, social behaviors, and an urban class geography. In short, Florence had already been transformed into a stratified society of courtiers prepared to honor a Medici prince as a small price to pay for dominion over the rest of the social body.

This is not to discount the whirl of events that made the precise constitutional outcome of the 1520s uncertain. Nor is it to minimize the resistance of staunch "democrats" and anti-Mediceans who hoped for the return of a broad-based republic upon Giulio's election to the papacy in 1523, or the explosive hatred shown in the ravaging of Medici artifacts during the last republic of 1527–30. Ensuing events proved the fragility of both republican and pro-Medicean regimes and the important role played by foreign powers in finally securing the Medici principate.[186] But the politics of death as they were practiced by 1530 offer important evidence that patterns of control achieved over a century were too deeply entrenched to permit more than nostalgia for a lost republicanism.

CONCLUSION

n 1608 the Englishman Thomas Coryat made the following observation while traveling through Italy: "The burials are so strange both in Venice, and all other Cities, Townes, and parishes of Italy, that they differ not onely from England, but from all other nations whatsoeuer in Christendome. For they carry the Corse [*sic*] to Church with the face, handes, and feete all naked, and wearing the same apparell that the person wore lately before it died, or that which it craued to be buried in: which apparell is interred together with their bodies. Also, I obserued another thing in their burials that sauoreth of intollerable superstition: many a man that hath beene a vitious and licentious liuer is buried in the habits of a Franciscan Frier; the reason forsooth is, because the beleeue there is such vertue in the Friers cowle, that it will procure them remission of the third part of their sinnes: a most fond and impious opinion."[1]

Coryat's remarks emphasize not only his Protestant sensibilities but also the persistence of Italian mortuary customs and ritual forms over many centuries. The first part of this book has tried to elucidate some of those long-term continuities both in social behaviors and in the storehouse of symbols from which Florentines drew throughout the late fourteenth and fifteenth centuries. Flags, banners, coats of arms, books, shields, and clothing in symbolic colors and fabrics all constituted the means of ritual and social exchange throughout the republican period. Even the symbols and forms borrowed from antiquity—the laurel crown, orations and medals, classicizing images—were often hybridized to blend with other conventions of republican iconography. In Florence the funeral remained the centerpiece of ritual action until about 1550, when a new politics of death and remembrance backed by the Medici principate and Tridentine piety took firm hold. Then, in a move away from earlier cultural patterns, the popularity of skeletons and the macabre signaled a new fascination with death, while the "total art" of Cinquecento requiem theater—polyphonic mass settings, printed commemorative books, lifelike effigies, eloquent orations, monumental catafalques—signaled new ways to triumph over it.

Yet this profound continuity still evident in Coryat's remarks should not obscure what were obviously decisive changes in the style, uses, and meanings of death rites as understood by participants themselves. Beginning in the 1360s, funerals embarked on an upward spiral of conspicuous consumption that remained unchecked throughout the republican period. The triumph of flamboyance was fueled by the social competition between established families and "new men," by the redistribution of wealth and political power, and by repeated episodes of plague that paradoxically underscored the bonds of family and community. Confraternities contributed their part to this excess, distributing honor vertically through society. It was nevertheless the parish that assumed the bulk of mortuary responsibilities and commanded the localized loyalties of rich and poor alike.

In the early Quattrocento, flamboyance diversified to include new architectural complexes, grander mourning clothes, and the rhetoric of classicizing funeral orations. By mid-century, spending could be ideologically justified by the "theory of magnificence" emanating from humanist circles. Yet style was also put to new social and political uses after 1400. As Florence became transformed from a corporate society to an elitist one, funerals helped promote a set of paternalistic and patrilineal ideals. These rites posited patriliny as the dominant way of reckoning kinship for the "fathers" who also ran the state. Humanist praise furthered these claims. This eloquent rhetoric was gendered both in terms of its genre and its content; while public orations declaimed the noteworthy, even historic, deeds of powerful men, consolatory letters quietly spoke of women's skills as household managers and moral exemplars. Sharpening gender distinctions still more was the humanist "art" of mourning, which stressed outward decorum and the internalization of grief for learned men and officers of state.

Interwoven with these developments was the birth and maturation of civic funerary ritual. From the chivalric splendor and inchoate republicanism of the late Trecento, the funerals of Coluccio Salutati and other statesmen helped coalesce a formal civic ideology. The growth of civic ritual hinged on a cross-referencing of rites between generations (Salutati, Bruni, Marsuppini), on an accommodation of humanist, chivalric, and mercantile values (Tolentino), and on an explicit didactic intent (Coscia). Many of the conventions first developed in civic rites were later deployed among a wider elite in Laurentian Florence, a dissemination that signaled both the blurred boundaries of public and private power and the erosion of civic culture.

In the second half of the century, the growing magnificence of ceremonies revealed deep cleavages between and among social groups. Pomp both contributed to and marked social and sexual stratifications, fixing an urban class geography by the last quarter of the Quattrocento, and remaking the gender precepts embodied in mourning practices. Sumptuary policy supported these changes. Moving from the late Trecento's strict, ineffectual prohibitions to the early fifteenth century's policy of greater accommodation, sumptuary law targeted behaviors more than consumption after 1470. Plague measures enacted in the 1520s introduced yet other, more pernicious, forms of social control which were retained in the emerging modern state of Duke Cosimo I.

Yet funeral pomp in the late fifteenth and early sixteenth centuries also acted as a lightning rod for conflicts within the elite. The breakdown in cultural consensus beginning in the 1480s became obvious during the crisis of the Savonarolan period and its aftermath in the new republic. As affluent Florentines both embraced and rejected pomp, clergy came to a new prominence, bound to the laity in profound interdependence through the business of death. Death rites in the early sixteenth century also made visible the expanded nature of the resources upon which Medici power rested, incorporating that family's international business stature, ecclesiastical position, diplomatic networks, and force of arms.

Students of Florentine history will find these chronological patterns familiar. Rather than simply recasting the traditional history of the city, however, the history of death rites shows us instead the sheer intricacy of how ritual and society defined each other. These episodes point us toward culture in action: the tangled, dense, and decidedly unstable relations binding family and state, gender and politics, word and image.

NOTES

Abbreviations used in the notes are as follows:

ASF.	Archivio di Stato, Florence
Carte Strozz.	Carte Strozziane
Comp. Relig. Sopp.	Compagnie Religiose Soppresse
Conv. Sopp.	Conventi Religiosi Soppressi
MAP.	Mediceo Avanti il Principato
NA.	Notarile Antecosimiano
Provv. e Massai. Campioni.	Provveditori e Massai del Comune. Campioni d'Entrate e Uscite
BNF.	Biblioteca Nazionale, Florence
BNF. Conv. Sopp.	Biblioteca Nazionale, Florence. Conventi Soppressi

Unless otherwise stated, all manuscript references are to the Archivio di Stato, Florence.

Introduction

1. I borrow this concept from Renato Rosaldo, *Culture and Truth: The Remaking of Social Analysis* (Boston, 1989), esp. pp. 16–21.

2. Philippe Ariès, *Western Attitudes toward Death: From the Middle Ages to the Present*, trans. P. Ranum (Baltimore, 1974); idem, *The Hour of Our Death*, trans. Helen Weaver (New York, 1981).

3. Michel Vovelle, *Piété baroque et dechristianisation en Provence au XVIIIe siècle: Les attitudes devant la mort d'après les clauses des testaments* (Paris, 1973); Pierre Chaunu, *La mort à Paris: 16, 17, et 18e siècles* (Paris, 1978); Francois Lebrun, *Les hommes et la mort en Anjou aux 17e et 18e siècles: Essai de démographie et de psychologie historiques* (Paris, 1971); Jacques Chiffoleau, *La comptabilité de l'au-delà: Les hommes, la mort et la religion dans la région d'Avignon à la fin du Moyen Age, vers 1320–vers 1480* (Rome, 1980).

4. Samuel K. Cohn, Jr., *Death and Property in Siena, 1205–1800: Strategies for the Afterlife* (Baltimore, 1988).

5. I refer here to the two "ideal types" of social history set out in the incisive remarks of Natalie Zemon Davis, "The Shapes of Social History," *Storia della storiografia* 17 (1990): 28–34.

6. Roy Strong, *Art and Power: Renaissance Festivals, 1450–1650* (Berkeley, Calif., 1984); Bonner Mitchell, *The Majesty of the State: Triumphal Progresses of Foreign Sovereigns in Renaissance Italy, 1494–1600* (Florence, 1986); Lawrence M. Bryant, *The King and the City in the Parisian Royal Entry Ceremony: Politics, Ritual, and Art in the Renaissance* (Geneva, 1986); Sarah Hanley, *The Lit de Justice of the Kings of France: Constitutional Ideology in Legend, Ritual, and Discourse* (Princeton, N.J., 1983); Ralph E. Giesey, *Cérémonial et puissance souveraine:*

France, XVe–XVIIe siècles (Paris, 1987). On Medici ducal festivities, see the fine collection of essays edited by Marcello Fagiolo, *La città effimera e l'universo artificiale del giardino: La Firenze dei Medici e l'Italia del '500* (Rome, 1980).

7. Christiane Klapisch-Zuber, *Women, Family, and Ritual in Renaissance Italy*, trans. Lydia G. Cochrane (Chicago, 1985); Edward Muir, *Civic Ritual in Renaissance Venice* (Princeton, N.J., 1981); Richard C. Trexler, *Public Life in Renaissance Florence* (New York, 1980); Ronald F. E. Weissman, *Ritual Brotherhood in Renaissance Florence* (New York, 1982).

8. Clifford Geertz, *Works and Lives: The Anthropologist as Author* (Stanford, Calif., 1988), p. 114.

9. There are obviously tensions between ways of doing anthropology which cannot be discussed here. For some of the current turmoil besetting ethnography, see James Clifford and George E. Marcus, eds., *Writing Culture: The Poetics and Politics of Ethnography* (Berkeley, Calif., 1986). There are also theoretical limits to be confronted in this disciplinary collaboration, as discussed by Jean-Claude Schmitt in his introductory remarks to the special issue on "Gestures," *History and Anthropology* 1 (1984): 1–28.

10. Peter Burke, *The Historical Anthropology of Early Modern Italy* (Cambridge, 1987).

Introduction to Part I:
The Structures of Ritual and Society

1. The following account is taken from Carte Strozz. ser. 2. vol. 9, fol. 122r. Hereafter, "ser." is omitted before the series number in citations of this manuscript collection. All translations are mine unless otherwise noted. The Florentine calendar began each year on March 25. All dates given in the text and notes have been modernized.

Chapter 1: The Rules of Order

Epigraph. Pierre Bourdieu, *Outline of a Theory of Practice*, trans. Richard Nice (Cambridge, 1977), p. 79.

1. The classic formulation of death rites is Arnold Van Gennep, *The Rites of Passage*, trans. Monika B. Vizedom and Gabrielle L. Caffee (London, 1960).

2. Leon Battista Alberti, *The Family in Renaissance Florence*, trans. Renée Neu Watkins (Columbia, S.C., 1969), p. 149. Among the many useful works exploring Mediterranean perceptions of honor are J. K. Campbell, *Honour, Family, and Patronage* (Oxford, 1964); and J. G. Peristiany, ed., *Honour and Shame* (Chicago, 1966). Colette Beaune, "Mourir noblement à la fin du Moyen Age," in *La mort au Moyen Age: Colloque de l'Association des historiens médiévistes français réunis à Strasbourg en juin 1975 au Palais universitaire* (Strasbourg, 1977), pp. 125–43, examines the forms and functions of honorable burials in late medieval France.

3. For the agonistic character of Florentine social relations, see Ronald F. E. Weissman, *Ritual Brotherhood in Renaissance Florence* (New York, 1982).

4. On the functions and historical development of the requiem, see Mario Righetti, *Manuale di storia liturgica*, 3d ed., 4 vols. (Milan, 1969), 3:470; H.-R. Philippeau, "Introduction à l'étude des rites funéraires et de la liturgie des morts," *La Maison-Dieu* 1 (1945): 37–63; J. Jungmann, *Missa Solemnia*, 2 vols. (Turin, 1953); and T. Maertens and L. Heuschen, *Doctrine et pastorale de la liturgie de la mort* (Bruges, 1957). For specific aspects of the requiem liturgy, see "Les funérailles chrétiennes" (special issue), *La Maison-Dieu* 44 (1955).

5. Clifford Geertz, "Centers, Kings, and Charisma: Reflections on the Symbolics of Power," in *Culture and Its Creators*, ed. J. Ben-David and T. N. Clarke (Chicago, 1977), pp. 150–71. See also the civic processions described by Edward Muir, *Civic Ritual in Renaissance Venice* (Princeton, N.J., 1981).

6. Domenico Moreni, *Pompe funebri celebrate nell'imperial e real basilica di San Lorenzo dal secolo XIII a tutto il regno mediceo* (Florence, 1827), pp. 25–27. This lengthy dispute was ultimately resolved to the satisfaction of both institutions only in 1555.

7. Libri di Commercio. vol. 102, fol. 17v. Since Ser Antonio di Ser Jacopo da San Casciano and the parish priest of San Jacopo sopr'Arno, Ser Girolamo, were the only two clerics out of more than 150 to be specified by name, it seems likely that the family knew them both personally. It is not clear from the entry what kind of debt Monna Lisabetta owed the confraternity. My thanks to Judith Brown for bringing this document to my attention.

8. *Cronica fiorentina di Jacopo Salviati*, in *Delizie degli eruditi toscani*, ed. P. Ildefonso di San Luigi, 24 vols. (Florence, 1770–89), 18: 194–95.

9. Carte Strozz. 2. vol. 16 bis, fol. 16v.

10. Libri di Commercio. vol. 102, fol. 17v. Landini named the following mourners: "Matteo d'Andrea di Piero Landini suo marito; Giovanfrancesco di Matteo d'Andrea suo figliuolo; Guasparre di Matteo d'Andrea suo figliuolo; Girolamo di Matteo d'Andrea suo figliuolo; Generi 3: Donato di Francesco di Donato purgatore; Lucha di Sandro tessitore; e Domenicho di Pagolo legnaiuolo; e Chosimo d'Antonio di Cosimo parente."

11. For these practices in late Dugento and early Trecento Florence, see Robert Davidsohn's *Storia di Firenze*, 7 vols. (Florence, 1965), 7: 709–10, which also cites a mishap at a funeral in 1239 in which the temporary structure supporting the women mourners collapsed, killing twenty-six women. San Bernardino's admonitions are noted by David Herlihy and Christiane Klapisch-Zuber, *Les Toscans et leurs families* (Paris, 1978), p. 612.

12. Acquisti e Doni. vol. 293, unfoliated.

13. *Cronica di Jacopo Salviati*, 18: 193.

14. For the sumptuary laws of Bologna, see L. Frati, *La vita privata a Bologna* (Bologna, 1928), pp. 50–53. According to the preamble to the 1377 statutes of Ascoli Piceno, these funerary rubrics were consciously modeled on the 1325 statutes of the Florentine Capitano del Popolo (*Statuti di Ascoli Piceno dell'anno MCCCLXXVII*, ed. L. Zdekauer and P. Sella [Rome, 1910], p. 129).

15. These Roman statutes, along with other sumptuary laws approved by Pope Paul II in 1471, are printed in the preface to Marc Antonio Altieri, *Li nuptiali*, ed. E. Narducci (Rome, 1873), p. 48.

16. B. Cecchetti, "Funerali e sepolture dei Veneziani antichi," *Archivio veneto*, 1st ser., 34 (1887): 265–84, at p. 284n. I discuss the Mantuan ambassador's description of Lucia Terziani da Marsciano's funeral at the Sforza court later in this chapter.

17. Anonymi Ticinensis, *Commentarius de Laudibus Papiae*, ed. L. A. Muratori, in *Rerum Italicarum Scriptores* (Milan, 1727), vol. 11, col. 25.

18. Davidsohn, *Storia*, 7: 710.

19. The classic work on Mediterranean mourning customs is Ernesto de Martino, *Morte e pianto rituale* (repr., Turin, 1975). The sixteenth-century northern Italian humanist Tommaso Porcacchi discussed the tenacity of mourning customs among the ancient Romans and other peoples in his *Funerali antichi di diversi populi et nationi* (Venice, 1574), archived as a rare book (R. a. 59) in Biblioteca Marucelliana, Florence. For graphic depictions of these gestures, see Moshe Barasch, *Gestures of Despair in Medieval and Early Renaissance Art* (New York, 1976).

20. Franco Sacchetti, *I sermoni evangelici, le lettere, ed altri scritti inediti o rari*, ed. Ottavio Gigli (Florence, 1857), p. 154. Sacchetti was constructing an analogy of the Church as the "widow" of Christ as part of a Good Friday sermon. Porcacchi, *Funerali antichi*, p. 65, described similar practices, gestures, and self-inflicted injuries among the ancient Romans when widows mourned their husbands, sisters their dead brothers, and mothers their young children.

21. *Cronica volgare di anonimo fiorentino dall'anno 1385 al 1409, già attribuita a Piero di Giovanni Minerbetti*, ed. E. Bellondi, in *Rerum Italicarum Scriptores*, new ed., (Città di Castello, 1915), vol. 27, pt. 2, p. 183.

22. For the additional, harsh ambivalence toward widows, see Christiane Klapisch-Zuber, "The 'Cruel Mother': Maternity, Widowhood, and Dowry in Florence in the Fourteenth and Fifteenth Centuries," in her *Women, Family, and Ritual in Renaissance Italy*, trans. Lydia G. Cochrane (Chicago, 1985), pp. 117–31; and Nino Tamassia, *La famiglia italiana nei secoli decimoquinto e decimosesto* (Milan, 1910), p. 350.

23. David Herlihy, *Medieval Households* (Cambridge, Mass., 1985), pp. 82–92.

24. For the funerals of Giovanni de' Medici and Matteo Castellani, see BNF. Conv. Sopp. C. 4. 895, fols. 124, 125v. Accounts of Giuliano de' Medici's funeral appear in *Ricordanze di Bartolomeo Masi dal 1478 al 1526* (Florence, 1906), pp. 195–99; and *Istorie di Giovanni Cambi, cittadino fiorentino*, in Ildefonso di San Luigi, ed., *Delizie*, vols. 20–23, at 21: 92–95.

25. Diane Owen Hughes, "From Brideprice to Dowry in Mediterranean Europe," *Journal of Family History* 3 (1978): 262–96; Paolo Cammarosano, "Les structures familiales dans les villes de l'Italie communale XIIe–XIVe siècles," in *Famille et parenté dans l'Occident médiéval*, ed. Georges Duby and Jacques Le Goff (Rome, 1977), pp. 181–94.

26. Carte Strozz. 5. vol. 1747, fols. 82r, 86v, 88r, 154v, 155v.

27. Manoscritti. vol. 88, fols. 141r, 142v, 144r, 160v. Mea's husband Bartolomeo had squandered the dowry for which she and her natal family

had provided no legal guarantees, leaving her penniless. The same household was responsible for burying Bernardo's unmarried, rather profligate brother Tommaso, who had spent most of his life in Rome. Tommaso died in his brother's house in October 1500 and was buried at his own expense in Santissima Annunziata (Manoscritti. vol. 88, fol. 146v).

28. Herlihy, *Medieval Households*, p. 83.

29. Diane Owen Hughes discusses the way this conflict surfaced in artistic representations in "Representing the Family: Portraits and Purposes in Early Modern Italy," *Journal of Interdisciplinary History* 17 (1986): 7–38. I take up this problem in the context of religious commemoration in my article "Remembering the Family: Women, Kin, and Commemorative Masses in Renaissance Florence," *Renaissance Quarterly* 42 (1989): 635–54.

30. On the legal status of women in late medieval and Renaissance Florence, see Thomas Kuehn, " 'Cum Consensu Mundualdi': Legal Guardianship of Women in Quattrocento Florence," *Viator* 13 (1982): 309–33; and idem, "Women, Marriage, and *Patria Potestas* in Late Medieval Florence," *Revue d'histoire du droit* 49 (1981): 127–47. On the legal claims of wives and their natal families, see Julius Kirshner, "Wives' Claims against Insolvent Husbands in Late Medieval Italy," in *Women of the Medieval World*, ed. J. Kirshner and S. Wemple (Oxford, 1985), pp. 256–303.

31. Klapisch-Zuber, *Women, Family, and Ritual*, pp. 185–86.

32. Carte Strozz. 2. vol. 9, fol. 125r.

33. Libri di Commercio. vol. 102, fol. 17v.

34. Mercanzia. vol. 14150, fol. 14r.

35. Carte Strozz. 2. vol. 10, fol. 59r. A similar account of Matteo's funeral appears in a later manuscript compendium (BNF. II. IV. vol. 378, fol. 368r).

36. Richard A. Goldthwaite, *The Building of Renaissance Florence* (Baltimore, 1980), esp. pp. 267–73.

37. Mercanzia. vol. 14150, fol. 14v, dated 1451.

38. Carte Strozz. 2. vol. 17, fol. 24r.

39. For Temperani's will, see NA. S 20. 1462–70. fol. 175r/v. For Petrucci's burial, see Carte Strozz. 2. vol. 15, fol. 62r.

40. Libri di Commercio. vol. 102, fol. 17v.

41. *Vita di Filippo Strozzi il Vecchio scritta da Lorenzo suo figlio*, ed. G. Bini and P. Bigazzi (Florence, 1851), pp. 31–32.

42. For Francesco's funeral, see Gregory P. Lubkin, "The Court of Galeazzo Maria Sforza, Duke of Milan, 1466–1476" (Ph.D. diss., University of California, Berkeley, 1982), pp. 319, 348n. For the funeral of Lucia Terziani da Marsciano, see Archivio di Stato, Mantua. Archivio Gonzaga. 1621. My thanks to Dr. Evelyn Welch, who generously made available to me her transcription of this letter, and the one cited in n. 44.

43. Ralph Giesey, *The Royal Funeral Ceremony in Renaissance France* (Geneva, 1960).

44. Archivio di Stato, Milano. Archivio Ducale Sforzesco. Potenze Sovrane. 1475. Bosio's funeral is described in this letter from Giovanni da Castelnovate and Giovanni Giapanno (Galeazzo's seneschals-general) and Giovanni Si-

monetta to Galeazzo, dated March 17, 1476. Following the initial group of relatives and diplomats came "tutti li altri parenti secondo il grado suo."

45. Archivio di Stato, Mantua. Archivio Gonzaga. 1621.

46. L. Beltrami, "L'annullamento del contratto di matrimonio fra Galeazzo Maria Sforza e Dorotea Gonzaga, 1463," *Archivio storico lombardo*, ser. 2, 6 (1889): 126–32.

47. Archivio di Stato, Mantua. Archivio Gonzaga. 1621. After describing the hand washing, Scalone remarked, "Come se sia facto dal canto delle done nol so ancor ben."

48. The following discussion is indebted to Edward Muir and Ronald F. E. Weissman, "Social and Symbolic Places in Renaissance Venice and Florence," in *The Power of Place: Bringing Together Geographical and Sociological Imaginations*, ed. John A. Agnew and James S. Duncan (Boston, 1989), pp. 81–103.

49. For the role of neighbors in social relations, see Klapisch-Zuber, "Kin, Friends, and Neighbors: The Urban Territory of a Merchant Family in 1400," in idem, *Women, Family, and Ritual*, pp. 68–93; D. V. Kent and F. W. Kent, *Neighbours and Neighbourhood in Renaissance Florence: The District of the Red Lion in the Fifteenth Century* (Locust Valley, N.Y., 1982).

50. Capitoli. vol. 12, fol. 72v. This law of 1377 was redacted in 1415 (*Statuta Populi et Communis Florentiae Anno Salutis 1415*, 3 vols. [Fribourg, 1778–83], 2: 374–75).

51. *Ricordanze di Bartolomeo Masi*, p. 196.

52. Ibid., p. 199.

53. On Giuliano's Roman citizenship, bestowed on him and his nephew Lorenzo in 1513 with great pomp, see Janet Cox-Rearick, *Dynasty and Destiny in Medici Art* (Princeton, N.J., 1984), pp. 98n, 104.

54. For Leo's personal *imprese* and other Medici symbols, see ibid., p. 31.

55. *Istorie di Giovanni Cambi*, 22: 94. Domenico Moreni, *Continuazione delle memorie istoriche dell'ambrosiana imperial basilica di San Lorenzo di Firenze*, 2 vols. (Florence, 1816), 1: 213–15, cites another description of the event by an anonymous diarist.

56. John Shearman, "The *Entrata* of Leo X, 1515," *Journal of the Warburg and Courtauld Institutes* 38 (1975): 136–54. Cox-Rearick, *Dynasty*, p. 34, stresses the dynastic uses of the entry.

57. *Ricordanze di Bartolomeo Masi*, p. 197.

58. Ibid. "Partivonsi, e sopradetti religiosi, della via Larga e venivone giù per la via de' Martegli, e poi si voltavano in sulla mano manca, et andorno drieto a santa Maria del Fiore, cioè dal canto de' Tedaldi e dall'Opera, dal canto de' Bischieri e da santa Maria in Campo e dal canto de' Pazzi e dalla Badia di Firenze e dal palazzo de' Gondi, e volsano dal Capitano [now the Via de' Gondi], e passorno per la piazza de' Signiori, e entrorno in Vacchereccia, e volsano per Por Zanta Maria e per Mercato Nuovo e per Porta rossa, a santa Trinita, e volsano in verso el canto de' Tornaquinci e da' Tornabuoni, e passorno dalla piazza di santo Michele Berteldi e dal canto de' Carnesecchi, e volsano, in verso al canto alla Paglia, e dal canto alla Paglia volsano per borgo santo Lorenzo e su per la piazza di santo Lorenzo,

et entrorno in chiesa per la porta del mezzo di detta chiesa: e questa è la via che fecie el sopradetto morto."

59. *Istorie di Giovanni Cambi*, 22: 95. "Nota la ruota di questo mondo, che tre mesi, e mezzo erano passati, che il Papa venne in Firenze con gran trionfo per portarossa, e per Merchato nuovo, e piazza de' Signori, e da' fondamenti, e dal chanto alla paglia, portato in sur una barella con gran trionfo, e oggi el suo fratello charnale portato morto per la medesima via a riscontro di lui, ed era tutta la Ciptà a vederlo morto detto Giuliano, quanto a vedere il Papa vivo." Cambi also recorded other details of the route. Once the oration was finished, "venono giuso per la via de' Martelli, e andorono da' fondamenti, e passorono per Piazza, e andorono per Vachereccia, e per Merchato nuovo, e per portarossa, e da' Tornaquinci, e dal Canto de' Charnesecchi, e dal chanto alla paglia, e volsano per Borgho S. Lorenzo, e andorono in S. Lorenzo."

60. Shearman, "*Entrata*," p. 143.

61. Cox-Rearick, *Dynasty*, esp. p. 223.

62. BNF. Conv. Sopp. C. 4. 895, fol. 184r.

63. Guido Monaldi, *Diario del Monaldi*, in idem, *Istorie pistolesi* (Milan, 1845), pp. 427–64, at pp. 443–44.

64. Medici's funeral is described by an anonymous diarist in BNF. Panciatichi. vol. 158, fols. 179v–180r.

65. Manoscritti. vol. 77, fol. 20v.

66. Manoscritti. vol. 82, fol. 35v. Ugolino, an active officeholder who had been podestà of Pistoia in 1412, was obligated for the repayment of three dowries: the first, in the amount of 300 florins, to his mother Giemma; the second, in the sum of 1,500 florins (900 of which was tied up in two workshops in Por Santa Maria), to his deceased wife Checcha Panciatichi; and the third, 1,050 florins in Monte credits, to his second wife, Lapa. Negotiations over funeral costs began with a question by Giemma to the other executors: "Siche si domando loro quello volessino fare delle spese delmortoro e dopo molte parole chonvenne che monna Giemma sobrighi asi alle spese del mortoro in sino in quantita di fiorini 25. E creditori altre spese echoreano nellonorare mona lapa vestire e veli e tutto cio che lla promesse e cosi fe rimandare uno de due vestiri neri mando la cioppa e ritenne il mantello e rimando il mantello del vaio siche la seppoltura si fe honestamente chome si richiedea."

67. Catasto. vol. 44, fols. 190r–191v, tax return of Luca di Matteo, a gravedigger, shopkeeper, and neighborhood messenger.

68. Manoscritti. vol. 77, fol. 20v. Valorino spent a total of twenty-five florins to clothe himself, the manservant Meo, and his father's corpse.

69. Carte Strozz. 2. vol. 9, fol. 23r. Normally a woman's mourning outfit required twelve braccia of cloth.

70. For Checcha Masi, see Manoscritti. vol. 89, fol. 18r; Caterina Parenti's mourners are recorded in Carte Strozz. 2. vol. 17 bis, fol. 1r.

71. Carte Strozz. 2. vol.17 bis, fols. 30r, 128v–129v. My thanks to Dr. Elaine Rosenthal for clarifying these Parenti connections.

72. The relevant bibliography is cited in n. 4, above.

73. Pier Nolasco Cianfogni, *Memorie istoriche dell'ambrosiana real basilica di S. Lorenzo di Firenze* (Florence, 1804), p. 234.

74. G. Salvadori and V. Federici,"I sermoni d'occasione, le sequenze e i ritmi di Remigio Girolami fiorentino," in *Scritti vari di filologia* (Rome, 1901), pp. 455–508; some of these sermons are extant in BNF. Conv. Sopp. G. 4. 936. For customary practice in the late Dugento, see Davidsohn, *Storia*, 7: 714–15.

75. The following account is based on *Ricordanze tratte da un libro originale di Tribaldo de' Rossi*, in Ildefonso di San Luigi, ed., *Delizie*, 23: 236–303, at pp. 289–91.

76. Conv. Sopp. 83. vol. 239, p. 37. The Rossi had a long involvement with the convent. According to this same document (pp. 34–35), in 1332 three of the convent's thirteen nuns, including the abbess, Gostanza di Fornacio Rossi, came from Rossi households.

77. Tribaldo listed the five Rossi kinsmen as Nofri di Piero, Gabrielo d'Antonio, Pagolo di Nofri di Piero, Lionetto, and himself.

78. Conv. Sopp. 83. vol. 115, fol. 27v.

79. *Ricordanze di Tribaldo de' Rossi*, 23: 289. Benedetta Machiavelli's election and confirmation as abbess is also recorded in Conv. Sopp. 83. vol. 115, fols. 27v–28r.

Chapter 2: Symbols, Objects, Bodies

Epigraph. Abner Cohen, *Two-Dimensional Man: An Essay on the Anthropology of Power and Symbolism in Complex Society* (Berkeley, Calif., 1974), p. 30.

1. The most elegant discussions of these themes come from Natalie Zemon Davis, especially in her "The Sacred and the Body Social in Sixteenth-Century Lyon," *Past and Present* 90 (1981): 40–70; and her "The Rites of Violence," in idem, *Society and Culture in Early Modern France* (Stanford, Calif., 1975), pp. 152–88.

2. Eve Borsook, "Art and Politics at the Medici Court, I: The Funeral of Cosimo I de' Medici," *Mitteilungen des Kunsthistorischen Institutes in Florenz* 12 (1965–66): 31–54, at p. 40–41.

3. The quote is from Randolph Starn, "Demand for Art in Renaissance Florence: Three Recent Books," *Art Bulletin* 65 (1983): 333.

4. Carte Strozz. 2. vol. 16 bis, fols. 2r, 3r.

5. Camera del Comune. Campioni d'Entrata e Uscita. vol. 13, fol. 330r. "Per onorare beneno di ghucio per suo mortoro e per uno penone e targia donate a Messer pantaleone podesta e spese fatte nel ghonfalone della schala e 3 penoni e spese fate nel mortoro di davanzato e zanobi di semone fei in somma Fl. 82 L. 75.16.8."

6. Writing to Piero di Lorenzo de' Medici on July 29, 1493, Carlo d'Andrea da Prato reminded him that his family had supported the Medici during the attempted coup of 1466, and further noted that "we have your coat-of-arms mounted in our house" (F. W. Kent with Patricia Simons, "Renaissance Patronage: An Introductory Essay," in *Patronage, Art, and Society in Renaissance*

Italy, ed. F. W. Kent and Patricia Simons [Oxford, 1987], pp. 1–21, at p. 9).

7. In 1474 Marco Parenti successfully defended an abandoned family tomb in Santa Croce in part by demonstrating that the Parenti arms were posted there (Carte Strozz. 2. vol. 17 bis, fol. 71v). For the despoiling of arms and pictorial images, see Samuel Y. Edgerton, Jr., *Pictures and Punishment: Art and Criminal Prosecution during the Florentine Renaissance* (Ithaca, N.Y., 1985), pp. 69, 73–74, 109.

8. When Francesco di Tommaso Giovanni ended his term as Captain of Cortona, for example, he was touched that the municipal priors had the Giovanni arms and device painted over the door to the principal room of the communal palace, thereby "demonstrating to me their goodwill most affectionately" (Carte Strozz. 2. vol. 16 bis, fol. 3r). Similarly, the Florentine commune commissioned "a great painting" of the emblem of Emperor Frederick III when he visited the city amid great pomp in 1452 (Camera del Comune. Camera dell'Arme. vol. 52, fol. 3v).

9. Domenico Moreni, *Pompe funebri celebrate nell'imperial e real basilica di San Lorenzo dal secolo XIII a tutto il regno mediceo* (Florence, 1827), p. 9.

10. F. W. Kent, "The Making of a Renaissance Patron of the Arts," in *Giovanni Rucellai ed il suo Zibaldone, II: A Florentine Patrician and His Palace* (London, 1981), pp. 9–95, at p. 94.

11. *Cronica fiorentina di Jacopo Salviati*, in *Delizie degli eruditi toscani*, ed P. Ildefonso di San Luigi, 24 vols. (Florence, 1770–89), 18: 191–95.

12. The deliberations of the Studio officials are quoted in *Ricordi storici di Filippo di Cino Rinuccini dal 1282 al 1460 colla continuazione di Alamanno e Neri suoi figli fino al 1506*, ed. G. Aiazzi (Florence, 1840), p. 146n.

13. Carte Strozz. 2. vol. 9, fol. 23r.

14. For gift giving and exchange in Florentine society, see Christiane Klapisch-Zuber, *Women, Family, and Ritual in Renaissance Italy* (Chicago, 1985), esp. chap. 10.

15. Such items were listed in the inventory of Orsanmichele, dated June 8, 1436 (Capitani di Orsanmichele. vol. 26, fol. 13v).

16. Marcia B. Hall, "The Tramezzo in Santa Croce, Florence, Reconstructed," *Art Bulletin* 56 (1974): 340n.

17. Luigi Passerini, *Genealogia e storia della famiglia Ricasoli* (Florence, 1861), p. 143; Luca della Robbia, "Vita di Bartolomeo Valori," *Archivio storico italiano* ser. 1, 4 (1843): 280n. For other aspects of the renovation, see Marcia B. Hall, *Renovation and Counter-Reformation: Vasari and Duke Cosimo in Santa Maria Novella and Santa Croce, 1565–1577* (Oxford, 1979).

18. "Item dictus testator considerans quod capella Sancte Lucie posita in ecclesia Sancti Spiritus de Florentia super ostium sacristie dicte ecclesie que olim fuit Simonis Giorgii Baronis hodie pertinet et expectat ad ipsum Agustinum et Christonfanum eius fratrem, et cupiens providere ut continuo imperpetuum in dicta cappella celebrentur missa et alia divina officia et ad hoc ut dicta cappella imperpetuum ad memoriam dicti testatoris et suorum conservetur et manteneatur: et si et in quantum sic fiat, et non incontrarium

aliquid fiat vel attentetur, sed semper stet ad memoriam dicti testatoris et cum arma ipsius, et ibidem missa et alia divina officia celebrentur, et si et in quantum fratres capitulum et conventus Sancti Spiritus predicti imperpetuum non ponat nec poni faciat consentiant vel permittant quod ponantur alique bandiere vel targhe vel alia signa iuxta ipsam cappellam vel in anditu seu verone a dicta cappella usque ad locum in quo itur ad organa dicte ecclesie vel in aliquo alio loco in quo vel per quod impeditur aspectionem totius dicte ecclesie et seu alicuius eius particulem in minime vel dicti anditus." Conv. Sopp. 122. vol. 75, fols. 40r–41r, dated June 19, 1417.

19. See Richard C. Trexler, "Florentine Religious Experience: The Sacred Image," *Studies in the Renaissance* 19 (1972): 7–41; idem, "Ritual Behavior in Renaissance Florence: The Setting," *Medievalia et Humanistica*, ser. 2, 4 (1973): 125–44.

20. A. N. Galpern, *The Religions of the People in Sixteenth Century Champagne* (Cambridge, Mass., 1976).

21. Carte Strozz. 2. vol. 17 bis, fol. 86r/v. Piero's flags and funeral expenses are described on fols. 128v–129v.

22. Conv. Sopp. 89. vol. 75, fol. 46r.

23. For Marsili's tomb slab, see Giuseppe Richa, *Notizie storiche delle chiese fiorentine*, 10 vols. (Florence, 1754), 6: 125–26. Medici's costume is described in BNF. Panciatichi. vol. 158, fols. 179v–180r: "Cho' inumerabile numero di gente tutti valenti e gran cittadini poi i chalonici di Duomo con tutto il chericato e giunti a casa sua in Borgo Santo Lorenzo ivi trovarono il corpo suo nuno richo letto chon una cioppa di sciamito di dosso e una beretta di scharlatto foderata di vaio in chapo e una cintura fornita d'ariento erata [*sic*] chon una choltelessa chon ghiere d'ariento orate e cogli sproni dorati i' pie e cosi fatto il misono nella bara."

24. Franco Sacchetti, *Le Sposizioni di Vangeli*, in *I sermoni evangelici, le lettere, ed altri scritti inediti o rari*, ed. Ottavio Gigli (Florence, 1857), p. 154.

25. Edgerton, *Pictures*, pp. 65–66.

26. These examples are taken from Pompeo Molmenti, *La storia di Venezia nella vita privata dalle origini alla caduta della repubblica*, 3 vols. (Bergamo, 1906–8), 2: 573.

27. This point is made by Richard C. Trexler, *Public Life in Renaissance Florence* (New York, 1980).

28. Another moralist who voiced similar opinions was Giovanni Domenici, *Regola del governo di cura familiare* (Florence, 1860).

29. There are numerous descriptions of fine cloths draping the biers of affluent women, as when Marco Parenti purchased "uno drappo bello per la bara" for his mother Tommasa in October 1456 (Carte Strozz. 2. vol. 17 bis, fol. 43r). However, more detailed descriptions are seldom given. Ecclesiastical accounts that record the donation and resale of bier cloths generally note the donors and/or the deceased, and the cloth's value, but not a precise description.

30. Diane Owen Hughes, "Sumptuary Law and Social Relations in Renaissance Italy," in *Disputes and Settlements: Law and Human Relations in the*

West, ed. John Bossy (Cambridge, 1983), pp. 69–99, cites a number of women's gowns, overdresses, and sleeves embroidered with armorial emblems.

31. Ibid. See also Diane Owen Hughes, "Earrings for Circumcision: Distinction and Purification in the Italian Renaissance City," in *Persons in Groups*, ed. Richard C. Trexler (Binghamton, N.Y., 1985), pp. 155–77. On the importance of clothing for a woman's dowry and status, see Christiane Klapisch-Zuber, "Le 'zane' della sposa: La fiorentina e il suo corredo nel Rinascimento," *Memoria* 11–12 (1984): 12–23. More detailed descriptions of women's clothing with illustrations can be found in E. Polidori Calamandrei, *Le vesti delle donne fiorentine nel Quattrocento* (repr., Rome, 1973); and Elizabeth Birbari, *Dress in Italian Painting, 1460–1500* (London, 1975).

32. Mary Douglas argues that the human body "communicates information for and from the social system in which it is a part" (*Implicit Meanings: Essays in Anthropology* [London, 1975], p. 83). For a more general examination of body symbolism, see idem, *Natural Symbols: Explorations in Cosmology* (London, 1970).

33. Edgerton, *Pictures*, p. 65n. Klapisch-Zuber argues that a husband's gifts of clothing allowed him on the one hand to mark the status and identity of his wife, and on the other to divest her of that status by reclaiming his gifts ("The Griselda Complex: Dowry and Marriage Gifts in the Quattrocento," in idem, *Women, Family, and Ritual*, pp. 213–46).

34. Cf. David Herlihy and Christiane Klapisch-Zuber, *Les Toscans et leurs familles* (Paris, 1978), p. 612.

35. San Pier Maggiore. vol. 52, fol. 2r. On Venetian funeral customs, see B. Cecchetti, "Funerali e sepolture dei Veneziani antichi," *Archivio veneto*, ser. 1, 34 (1887): 265–84.

36. For the production and cost of luxury fabrics, see John H. Munro, "The Medieval Scarlet and the Economics of Sartorial Splendour," in *Cloth and Clothing in Medieval Europe*, ed. N. B. Harte and K. G. Ponting (London, 1983), pp. 13–70; and Odile Blanc, "Le luxe, le vêtement et la mode à la fin du Moyen Age," *Bulletin du Centre d'histioire économique et sociale de la région lyonnaise* 4 (1983): 23–44. Polidori Calamandrei, *Le vesti*, p. 38, remarks that in the fifteenth century "il colore rosato era uno de piú preziosi." Edgerton, *Pictures*, p. 65n, also notes the uses and meanings of color symbolism. In punishments by humiliation, Jews had to wear black, gray, or yellow caps, while a red or brown hat distinguished a respected person. The red caps given to slaves on their emancipation during the Roman Republic became a sign of the dignity of their freedom. The imperial associations of the color purple continued to have resonances in the early modern period: the *salle d'honneur* in which French kings lay in state was draped with violet hangings.

37. Guido Monaldi, *Diario del Monaldi*, in idem, *Istorie pistolesi* (Milan, 1845), pp. 427–64, at pp. 443–44, 445, 464. Rinuccini's *prestanza* ranking is given by Gene Brucker, "The Medici in the Fourteenth Century," *Speculum* 32 (1957): 6.

38. Quote cited in Carlo Ginzburg, *The Enigma of Piero* (London, 1985), p. 17.

39. Carte Strozz. 2. vol. 16 bis, fol. 16v.

40. For Giuliano de' Medici's hat, see *Ricordanze di Bartolomeo Masi dal 1478 al 1526* (Florence, 1906), pp. 195–99. The healing miracles ascribed to Antoninus's relics are recorded in *Acta Sanctorum*, ed. Johannes Bollandus et al., 67 vols. (Paris, 1863–1919), entry for May 2. For example, a Florentine official residing in Pisa cured a young Pisan boy who had fallen from a great height by placing the saint's hat on the boy's body. Contact with the hat also cured the sick of fevers, healed a broken arm and a concussion, and helped a woman through a difficult childbirth.

41. Carte Strozz. 2. vol. 16, fol. 7v.

42. BNF. Conv. Sopp. C. 4. 895, fol. 114v.

43. Franklin Toker, "Excavations below the Cathedral of Florence, 1965–1974," *Gesta* 14 (1975): 17–36.

44. San Pier Maggiore. vol. 51, fol. 13v. The source for Federighi is Conv. Sopp. 88. vol. 73, fol. 92r/v, published in Hannelore Glasser, "The Litigation concerning Luca della Robbia's Federighi Tomb," *Mitteilungen des Kunsthistorischen Institutes in Florenz* 14 (1969): 1–32, at p. 31, my translation. Robert Davidsohn, *Storia di Firenze*, 7 vols. (Florence, 1965), 7: 108, confirms the burial of laity and clerics in similar garments and insignia in the late Dugento and the Trecento.

45. Ralph Giesey, "The Royal Funeral Ceremony in Renaissance France: Its Origin and Development" (Ph.D. diss., University of California, Berkeley, 1954), p. 195. For the burials of English knights, see Judith W. Hurtig, *The Armored Gisant before 1400* (Ann Arbor, Mich.: University Microfilms, 1978).

46. Quoted in Richard C. Trexler, *Synodal Law in Florence and Fiesole, 1306–1518* (Città del Vaticano, 1971), p. 128, Trexler's translation.

47. Podestà. Atti Condanne. vol. 127, fols. 115v–116r, dated June 10, 1345. "Et ex jude ipsum corpum extrassit et expoliarut omnibus pannis lane et linos quos idem spinellus habebat in dorso." The grave robbers found the money in a "bracherium quod erat cum serabulis apud spinellum in quo erant centum cinquagintum florenum." Lorenzo and Lotto were sentenced to have their right hands amputated and their tongues removed, and were further obligated to restore the money to Spinello's heirs. See also Trexler, *Public Life*, p. 47n, who argues that the use of graves as depositories was a stimulus to grave robbery.

48. Otto di Guardia. vol. 64, fol. 36r. Michael Rocke kindly brought this document to my attention.

49. Henri Hauvette, *La "Mort Vivante"* (Paris, 1933), pp. 70–75, discusses this legend, which was set in 1396. The earliest written version is probably the short poem of Antonio Velletti, composed near the end of the fifteenth century and redacted in 1522.

50. Mircea Eliade, *The Sacred and the Profane: The Nature of Religion*, trans. Willard R. Trask (New York, 1959), p. 148.

51. Edgerton, *Pictures*, pp. 23–29, notes that Fra Angelico frequently depicted heaven as a cityscape bearing strong resemblances to Florence.

52. The standard work on tomb sculpture remains Erwin Panofsky, *Tomb*

Sculpture (New York, n.d.). For inventories of tomb sculpture and slabs, see Fritz Burger, *Geschichte des florentinischen Grabmals von den ältesten Zeiten bis Michelangelo* (Strasbourg, 1904); F. A. Greenhill, *Incised Effigial Slabs*, 2 vols. (London, 1976); and Margaret Longhurst, *Notes on Italian Monuments of the Twelfth through the Sixteenth Centuries* (London, 1962).

53. J. von Schlosser, "Geschichte der Porträtsbildnerei in Wachs," *Jahrbuch der Kunsthistorischen Sammlungen des alterhoehsten Kaiserhauses* 29 (1911): 171–258; Eric Maclagen, "The Use of Death Masks by Florentine Sculptors," *Burlington Magazine* 43 (1923): 303–4; Gino Masi, "La ceroplastica in Firenze nei secoli XV–XVI e la famiglia Benintendi," *Rivista d'arte* 9 (1916): 124–42; and more generally, Ernst Benkard, *Undying Faces*, trans. Margaret M. Green (London, 1929). For the development of portraiture, see also Jane Schuyler, *Florentine Busts* (New York, 1976); and John Pope-Hennessy, *The Portrait in the Renaissance* (New York, 1966).

54. For Lorenzo de' Medici's bust, see Maud Cruttwell, *Verrocchio* (London, 1904), pp. 98–99. The Capponi bust, now preserved in the Victoria and Albert Museum in London, was originally purchased from a Capponi villa in San Frediano, where it was displayed in the library; for this and the Pitti bust, see Schuyler, *Florentine Busts*, pp. 139–41; and von Schlosser, "Porträtsbildnerei," p. 219n.

55. Maclagen, "Death Masks," p. 304. Several prominent examples of later Quattrocento death masks include one taken by Buggiano of his adoptive father Brunelleschi (d. 1446) for eventual use in a marble bust, and the mask of the saintly bishop Antoninus made eight days after his death, which was later employed in terra-cotta busts. Although death masks had been used rather extensively in Italian tomb effigies dating from the thirteenth and fourteenth centuries, the medieval artist generally used the mask only as the starting point for his depiction. In the fifteenth century, artists used the original mask to achieve a more realistic likeness in their effigies (Schuyler, *Florentine Busts*, pp. 8, 118–19, 134–37, 142–45; Pope-Hennessy, *Portrait*, p. 8; and Joseph Pohl, *Die Verwendung des Naturabgusses in der italienischen Porträtplastik der Renaissance* [Wurzburg, 1938], p. 51).

56. This placement was noted in the inventory of marbles seized by the Signoria in 1495 (Cruttwell, *Verrocchio*, pp. 98–99).

57. The contract between Antonio da Bologna and Archangelo di Giovanni was published by Aby Warburg in his "Bildniskunst und Florentinisches Bürgertum," in idem, *Gesammelte Schriften*, ed. Gertrud Bing, 2 vols. (Leipzig, 1932), 1: 117–18. The Risaliti niche is surrounded by a polychrome glazed terra-cotta frame from the della Robbia workshop. The date probably refers to Jacopo di Geri's death date rather than his daughter's (Schuyler, *Florentine Busts*, pp. 8–9).

58. For the Medici images, see Edgerton, *Pictures*, p. 109. The convent record noting the addition of shelves in Santissima Annunziata appears in Warburg, "Bildniskunst," p. 117. Giorgio Vasari, *Le vite degli artisti più eccellenti* (Florence, 1550), 3: 373, noted that already in his day the production of votive images had declined "either because the devotion is lacking, or

for some other reason." The popularity of votive images continued to decline into the seventeenth century; in 1665 the Annunziata moved all of its images from the church to the small cloister (Ferdinando Leopoldo del Migliore, *Firenze città nobilissima illustrata* [Florence, 1684], p. 287).

59. For Bardi and Antella, see *Diario del Monaldi*, pp. 437, 460. Guccio's ceremonies are reported in *Cronica di Jacopo Salviati*, 18: 192–93.

60. Giesey, "Royal Funeral Ceremony," esp. pp. 147–217. The classic formulation of the relationship between the body natural and the body corporate is Ernest Kantorowicz, *The King's Two Bodies* (Princeton, N.J., 1957). See also Leonard Barkan, *Nature's Work of Art: The Human Body as Image of the World* (New Haven, Conn., 1975); and Marcel Mauss, "Les techniques du corps," *Journal de la psychologie* 31 (1936): 277–93.

61. For Giuliano's funeral, see *Istorie di Giovanni Cambi, cittadino fiorentino*, in Ildefonso di San Luigi, ed., *Delizie*, vols. 20–23, at 22: 92–95; *Ricordanze di Bartolomeo Masi*, pp. 195–99; Domenico Moreni, *Continuazione delle memorie istoriche dell'ambrosiana imperial basilica di San Lorenzo di Firenze*, 2 vols. (Florence, 1816), 1: 213–15.

62. For Pazzi, see *Ricordanze di Bartolomeo Masi*, pp. 124–25; and *Istorie di Giovanni Cambi*, 22: 13–14. For Antoninus, see *Acta Sanctorum*, entry for May 2.

63. *Acta Sanctorum*, entries for May 20 and August 26, respectively. A Latin account of Villana's life, written by Fra Girolamo di Giovanni, and copied by Fra Giovanni Caroli of Santa Maria Novella in 1452, has been published with Italian translation by Stefano Orlandi, *La Beata Villana: Terziaria domenicana fiorentina del secolo XIV* (Florence, 1955).

64. Marin Sanudo, *Cronachetta* (Venice, 1880), pp. 79–82.

65. For a fuller discussion of the funeral ceremonies for Venetian doges, see Edward Muir, *Civic Ritual in Renaissance Venice* (Princeton, N.J., 1981), pp. 263–77.

66. Sanudo, *Cronachetta*, p. 80; Muir, *Civic Ritual*, p. 273n.

67. Johann Huizinga, *The Waning of the Middle Ages* (New York, 1954), esp. pp. 138–51. On *transi* tombs and sepulchral symbolism, see the excellent work by Henriette s'Jacob, *Idealism and Realism: A Study of Sepulchral Symbolism* (Leiden, 1954); and Katherine Cohen, *Metamorphosis of a Death Symbol* (Berkeley, Calif., 1973). Philippe Ariès, *The Hour of Our Death*, trans. Helen Weaver (New York, 1981), does not develop the differences between the attitudes and practices of northern and southern Europe in any detail.

68. Sanudo, *Cronachetta*, p. 81. The notification made to the dogaressa is cited by Molmenti, *Storia di Venezia*, 2: 568–69. She was informed by magistrates "che quando sarete morta vi saranno cavate le cervelle, li occhi et le budelle, et sarete portata in questo loco medesimo dove che per tre giorni haverete a stare avanti che siate sepolta."

69. *Statuti dell'arte dei Medici e Speziali*, ed. Raffaele Ciasca (Florence, 1922), p. 286. The statutes were made "per cagione delle ismisurate storsioni che continuamente si fanno pe' beccamorti." Even with the new guild rulings, fees paid to gravediggers could be quite high in plague years. Paolo Sassetti

recorded that he paid one hundred lire in gravediggers' fees to bury eleven family members during the 1383 epidemic (Carte Strozz. 2. vol. 4, fol. 102r). Katharine Park, *Doctors and Medicine in Early Renaissance Florence* (Princeton, N.J., 1985), pp. 15–24, discusses the evolution of the guild's structure and early regulations, while Herlihy and Klapisch-Zuber, *Les Toscans*, p. 446, take up the social position and regulation of gravediggers. *Beccamorti* continued to be regulated by the Grascia, the main overseers of Florence's food supply, during the Medici principate (*Statuto della Grascia del dì 4 Marzo 1579*, in *Legislazione toscana*, ed. Lorenzo Cantini, 32 vols. [Florence, 1800–1808], 9: 300).

70. *Statuti Medici e Speziali*, pp. 290–93. The statutes allowed a maximum of two lire to wash, shave, and dress the corpse, and ten soldi each for keeping watch over the body, carrying the corpse into the main room of the house, and preparing the bier. Domestic evidence suggests that in non-plague years these ceilings were generally observed. The Parenti family, for example, paid roughly these fees when burying Parente, Tommasa, and Marco in 1452, 1456, and 1497, respectively (Carte Strozz. 2. vol. 17 bis, fols. 29r, 43r, 86r/v). On the books of the dead, see G. Parenti, "Fonti per lo studio della demografia fiorentina: I libri dei morti," *Genus* 6–8 (1943–49): 281–301, esp. pp. 290–91; and Ann G. Carmichael, *Plague and the Poor in Renaissance Florence* (Cambridge, 1986), pp. 28–35.

71. Carte Strozz. 2. vol. 16 bis, fol. 11r.

72. Mary Douglas, *Purity and Danger: An Analysis of Concepts of Pollution and Taboo* (London, 1966); and idem, *Implicit Meanings*, esp. p. 260. For the way in which ritual circumscribes danger, see the classic work of Arnold van Gennep, *The Rites of Passage*, trans. Monika B. Vizedom and Gabrielle L. Caffe (London, 1960).

73. See Sarah B. Pomeroy, *Goddesses, Whores, Wives, and Slaves* (New York, 1975), pp. 43–44. For modern survivals of these caretaking functions and mourning routines, see Margaret Alexiou, *The Ritual Lament in Greek Tradition* (Cambridge, 1974), pp. 39–42. Beth Ann Bassein looks at the cultural connections drawn between women and death in modern literature in *Women and Death: Linkages in Western Thought and Literature* (Westport, Conn., 1984).

Introduction to Part II: The Making of a Ritual Form

1. Michel Foucault sees the control of the body by individuals, state, and society as a hallmark of the modern world, a theme put forth most explicitly in his *Discipline and Punish: The Birth of the Prison*, trans. Alan Sheridan (New York, 1977).

2. Christiane Klapisch-Zuber, "Zacharias, or the Ousted Father: Nuptial Rites in Tuscany between Giotto and the Council of Trent," in idem, *Women, Family, and Ritual in Renaissance Italy*, trans. Lydia G. Cochrane (Chicago, 1985), pp. 178–212.

Chapter 3: The Social World of Late Trecento Funerals

1. The bibliography on plague can be approached through Katherine Park, *Doctors and Medicine in Renaissance Florence* (Princeton, N.J., 1985), esp. pp. 3–6. See also Ann G. Carmichael, *Plague and the Poor in Renaissance Florence* (Cambridge, 1986); and the detailed analysis of mortality patterns by Alan S. Morrison, Julius Kirshner, and Anthony Molho, "Epidemics in Renaissance Florence," *American Journal of Public Health* 75 (1985): 528–35.

2. Among the basic works on late Trecento Florence are Gene Brucker, *Florentine Politics and Society, 1343–1378* (Princeton, N.J., 1962); idem, *The Civic World of Early Renaissance Florence* (Princeton, N.J., 1977); Marvin Becker, *Florence in Transition*, 2 vols. (Baltimore, 1967–68); and John M. Najemy, *Corporatism and Consensus in Florentine Electoral Politics, 1280–1400* (Chapel Hill, N.C., 1982). For Florence's fight with the papacy, see Richard C. Trexler, *The Spiritual Power: Republican Florence under Interdict* (Leiden, 1974).

3. Samuel K. Cohn, Jr., examines the effects of plague on piety in *Death and Property in Siena, 1205–1800: Strategies for the Afterlife* (Baltimore, 1988).

4. Lewis Binford, "Mortuary Practices: Their Study and Their Potential," *Memoirs of the Society for American Archaeology* 25 (1971): 6.

5. Aliberto Benigno Falsini, "Firenze dopo il 1348: Le conseguenze della peste nera," *Archivio storico italiano* 129 (1971): 436, estimates the preplague population at just over ninety thousand, with that figure falling to slightly under fifty thousand after the epidemic.

6. *Cronaca fiorentina di Marchionne di Coppo Stefani*, ed. N. Rodolico, in *Rerum Italicarum Scriptores*, new ed. (Città di Castello, 1955), vol. 30, pt. 1, 231–32.

7. Falsini, "Firenze dopo il 1348," p. 466; Conv. Sopp. 113. vol. 81, fols. 1r–13r.

8. Richard A. Goldthwaite, *The Building of Renaissance Florence* (Baltimore, 1980), pp. 317–50, esp. p. 338.

9. Giovanni Boccaccio, *The Decameron*, trans. Richard Aldington (New York, 1930), pp. 30–36.

10. Falsini, "Firenze dopo il 1348," pp. 460–61.

11. Newberry Library, Chicago. MS. 27, fol. 35v. Pepo listed the family plague victims in terms of their ties of kinship to his father Antonio: June 4, Giovanni d'Antonio; June 11, Paola, daughter of Antonio and Monna Mattea d'Aldobrandino; June 15, Giovanna, Antonio's wife; June 16, Schiata, Antonio and Giovanna's son; June 25, Sandra, daughter of Antonio and Monna Bartola Biliotti, and Giano, son of Jacopo d'Antonio; July 12, Filippo d'Antonio; July 18, Jacopa, daughter of Antonio and Giovanna; July 27, Jacopo d'Antonio; July 31, Antonio di Lando, "in Pisa recosi il corpo suo in firenze venderdi matina dì ij daghosto e sopellissi i sanpero magiore."

12. The following discussion of masses at the Carmine is based on Conv. Sopp. 113. vol. 81.

13. *Croniche di Giovanni, Matteo e Filippo Villani* (Milan, 1857–58), bk. 3, chap. 63.

14. Details of Acciaiuoli's career are discussed by Leopoldo Tanfani, *Niccola*

Acciaiuoli: Studi storici fatti principalmente sui documenti dell'Archivio fiorentino (Florence, 1863), pp. 23–129; Giovanni Battista Ubaldini, *Origine della famiglia de gli Acciaioli, e i fatti de gli huomini famosi d'essa* (Florence, 1588), p. 173; Curzio Ugurgieri della Berardenga, *Gli Acciaioli di Firenze nella luce dei loro tempi, 1160–1834*, 2 vols. (Florence, 1962), vol. 1, esp. chaps. 5 and 6. Lorenzo's own brief career as knight, lieutenant of King Lodovico, and castellan of Naples is reported in Ubaldini, *Origine*, pp. 173–74; and in P. Litta, *Famiglie celebri italiane*, 15 vols. (Turin, 1819–1902), dispensa 104, table 3.

15. Litta, *Famiglie*, dispena 104, table 3, under "Lorenzo," suggests the tensions Acciaiuoli's behavior provoked. See also Ugurgieri della Berardenga, *Acciaioli*, 1: 213–14.

16. Tanfani, *Acciaiuoli*, pp. 46–48, reviews the documents endowing the Certosa. See also Caterina Chiarelli and Giovanni Leoncini, *La Certosa del Galluzzo a Firenze* (Milan, 1982), pp. 17, 274–77. The tombs for Lorenzo and Niccolò are the only two examples of the armored gisant type in central Italy (Judith W. Hurtig, *The Armored Gisant before 1400* [Ann Arbor, Mich.: University Microfilms, 1978], pp. 168–87).

17. Matteo Villani noted the "mirabile pompa d'esequie" staged for Farnese (*Croniche di Giovanni, Matteo e Filippo Villani*, bk. 11, chap. 59), but his more detailed description of the event apparently is no longer extant. Antonio Pucci praised Farnese in verse in *Quinto cantare della guerra pisana*, in *Delizie degli eruditi toscani*, ed. P. Ildefonso di San Luigi, 24 vol. (Florence, 1770–89), 6: 231–35, quote at p. 235. Some of the funerary tributes to Pier Farnese are discussed by A. Medin, "La morte di Giovanni Aguto," *Archivio storico italiano*, ser. 4, 17 (1886): 161–77. See the remarks on Farnese and his monument by John Temple-Leader and Giuseppe Marcotti, *Sir John Hawkwood*, trans. Leader Scott (London, 1889), pp. 292–93.

18. Conv. Sopp. 113. vol. 81, esp. fols. 161r–171r, 224v–231v.

19. Manoscritti. vol. 8, fol. 121r.

20. Guido Monaldi, *Diario del Monaldi*, in idem, *Istorie pistolesi* (Milan, 1845), pp. 427–64, at p. 439.

21. Acquisti e Doni. vol. 293, unfoliated, dated October 19, 1379; Manoscritti. vol. 8, fol. 125r.

22. Cohn, *Death and Property*, esp. pp. 40–46.

23. Diane Owen Hughes, "Sumptuary Law and Social Relations in Renaissance Italy," in *Disputes and Settlements: Law and Human Relations in the West*, ed. John Bossy (Cambridge, 1983), pp. 69–99.

24. Statuti. vol. 34; the preamble at fol. 3r offers a justification for the rulings; the funerary rubrics are at fols. 11v–13v.

25. Provv. e Massai. Campioni. vols. 1–8; for the 1390 permits, see Provv. e Massai. Campioni. vol. 6, fol. 310r/v.

26. The 1374 plague restrictions are reported in *Cronaca di Marchionne Stefani*, vol. 30, pt. 1, p. 289. For the Sassetti burial, see Carte Strozz. 2. vol. 4, fol. 67v, where Paolo noted that he buried Bernardo "in quello onore che a tempo di moria ed ordinamento per lo chomune ordinato."

27. Henri Hauvette, *La "Mort Vivante"* (Paris, 1933), pp. 70–75.

28. Capitoli. Registri. vol. 12, fols. 72v–73v, dated October 21, 1377.

29. Mario Righetti, *Manuale di storia liturgica*, 3d ed., 4 vols. (Milan, 1969), 2: 478; Arlotto Mainardi, *Motti e facezie del Piovano Arlotto* (Milan, 1953), facezia no. 15.

30. On the commune's fiscal problems resulting from war in the late Trecento, see Anthony Molho, "The Florentine Oligarchy and the Balie of the Late Trecento," *Speculum* 43 (1968): 23–51; and idem, "Politics and the Ruling Class in Early Renaissance Florence," *Nuova rivista storica* 52 (1968): 401–20. Roberto Barducci discusses the fiscal restructuring under the short-lived Ciompi regime in "Le riforme finanziarie nel tumulto dei Ciompi," in *Il tumulto dei Ciompi: Un momento di storia fiorentina ed europea* (Florence, 1981), pp. 95–102.

31. Jacques Chiffoleau, *La comptabilité de l'au-delà: Les hommes, la mort et la religion dans la région d'Avignon à la fin du Moyen Age, vers 1320–vers 1480* (Rome, 1980), quote at p. vii; idem, "Pratiques funeraires et images de la mort à Marseilles, en Avignon, et dans le comtat Venaissin, vers 1280–vers 1350," *Cahiers de Fanjeaux* 11 (1976): 271–303.

32. For example, Francesco Rinuccini (d. 1381) was outfitted in vermillion velvet and gold brocade, and Valorino Ciurianni bought a silver brocade bier cloth in 1380 for his father Barna (*Diario del Monaldi*, p. 443; Manoscritti. vol. 77, fol. 20v).

33. *Diario del Monaldi*, p. 444, remarking on the "gran quantità di danaro per dare a Dio."

34. BNF. Panciatichi. vol. 158, fols. 179v–180r. See, for instance, Matteo Villani's description of Biordo degli Ubertini's funeral in 1359, which featured "molti fanti e donzelli vestiti a nero" (*Croniche di Giovanni, Matteo e Filippo Villani*, bk. 9, chap. 43).

35. Chiffoleau, *Comptabilité*, p. ix.

36. Ibid., pp. ix, 153–201.

37. Lapo Niccolini, *Il libro degli affari proprii di casa de Lapo di Giovanni Niccolini de' Sirigatti*, ed. C. Bec (Paris, 1969), p. 69. For the Niccolini tomb in Santa Croce, see Christiane Klapisch-Zuber, *Women, Family, and Ritual in Renaissance Italy*, trans. Lydia G. Cochrane (Chicago, 1985), pp. 70–71.

38. Conv. Sopp. 89. vol. 10, fol. 46r; Carte Strozz. 2. vol. 16 bis, fol. 11r; Conv. Sopp. 83. vol. 113, fol. 8v.

39. This section, except where otherwise stated, is based on Provv. e Massai. Campioni. vols. 1–8.

40. Provv. e Massai. Campioni. vol. 2, fol. 13r. The permit was bought on March 3, 1385, by Lionardo di Neri di Ser Benedetto for his *nipote* Benedetto. Lionardo's heirs, unspecified by name or relation, in turn bought a sumptuary exemption for him on December 14, 1387 (Provv. e Massai. Campioni. vol. 4, fol. 308r).

41. The remarks on fathers and sons, by Leon Battista Alberti, are given by Thomas Kuehn, *Emancipation in Late Medieval Florence* (New Brunswick, N.J., 1982), p. 57, Kuehn's translation. For a different sense of father-son relations, see Richard C. Trexler, "In Search of Father: The Experience of

Abandonment in the Recollections of Giovanni di Pagolo Morelli," *History of Childhood Quarterly* 3 (1975): 225–51. Of the five remaining permits purchased by men without surnames, two were obtained by men identified by four generations of patronymics: Filippo di Ghino di Piero di Ghino, for his brother Tommaso, and Guccio di Rinieri di Gieri di Berto, for his brother Messer Giovanni (Provv. e Massai. Campioni. vol. 6, fol. 310r/v).

42. Richard A. Goldthwaite, "Organizzazione economica e struttura famigliare," in *I ceti dirigenti nella Toscana tardo communale* (Florence, 1980), pp. 1–13; and idem, *Private Wealth in Renaissance Florence* (Princeton, N.J., 1968).

43. For Niccolò's other sons, Angelo, Benedetto, and a second Lorenzo, see Ubaldini, *Origine*, p. 174; for Angelo, who was next in succession after Lorenzo's death, see Litta, *Famiglie*, dispensa 104, table 3. The Florentine Signoria wrote a consolatory letter to Angelo dated December 10, 1365, a month after his father's death, which appears in Tanfani, *Acciaiuoli*, pp. 235–36.

44. For the Nobili licenses, see Provv. e Massai. Campioni. vol. 5, fol. 291v. Francesca's funeral is described in Acquisti e Doni. vol. 293, unfoliated.

45. Nofri di Andrea di Neri bought a permit for his sister Monna Fora in 1390 (Provv. e Massai. Campioni. vol. 6, fol. 310r). The buyers of the remaining sumptuary exemptions for women's funerals were as follows: seven were designated only as the woman's heirs, six bore an unspecified relationship, two buyers shared the woman's surname, and one was the hospital of Santa Maria Nuova, which purchased a permit as the decedent's executor.

46. For masses, see my article, "Remembering the Family: Women, Kin, and Commemorative Masses in Renaissance Florence," *Renaissance Quarterly* 42 (1989): 635–54.

47. Carte Strozz. 2. vol. 135, no. 2, fol. 10v.

48. Carte Strozz. 2. vol. 4, fols. 66v–68v.

49. *Diario del Monaldi*, p. 460; Provv. e Massai. Campioni. vol. 8, fol. 9v.

50. Richard A. Goldthwaite, "The Renaissance Economy: The Preconditions for Luxury Consumption," in *Aspetti della vita economica medievale: Atti del convegno di studi nel X anniversario della morte di Federigo Melis* (Florence, 1985), pp. 659–75; idem, *Building*, esp. p. 338.

51. For Giovanni di Giano's bequests to San Pier Martire, see Conv. Sopp. 102. vol. 326, fols. 13v, 20v; Nepo della Tosa's bequests are at fol. 29r. Della Tosa's testament dated 1363 is partially recorded in Conv. Sopp. 102. vol. 106, pt. 1, unfoliated, under date. Giovanni di Giano's heirs paid 25 florins for his sumptuary permit on May 26, 1387 (Provv. e Massai. Campioni. vol. 4, fol. 307v), while della Tosa's heirs paid 100 florins on December 23, 1392 (Provv. e Massai. Campioni. vol. 8, fol. 9v). The normal fee was 10.5 florins. On patterns of confraternal life and social relations, see Ronald F. E. Weissman, *Ritual Brotherhood in Renaissance Florence* (New York, 1982).

52. Provv. e Massai. Campioni. vols. 1–8. For the mercer Marco di Tommaso, see Provv. e Massai. Campioni. vol. 2, fol. 23v, dated June 3, 1385;

for Francesco d'Agnolo, see Provv. e Massai. Campioni. vol. 5, fol. 291v, April 22, 1388; for Rinieri di Jacopo, see Provv. e Massai. Campioni. vol. 6, fol. 310r, September 15, 1390; for Messer Giovanni Gherardini, see Provv. e Massai. Campioni. vol. 2, fol. 15r, March 27, 1385; for Monna Betta di Bertino, see Provv. e Massai. Campioni. vol. 4, fol. 307v, August 31, 1387; for Bernardo di Lipi, see Provv. e Massai. Campioni. vol. 6, fol. 310r, August 6, 1390; for "Jacopo, called Bianco", see Provv. e Massai. Campioni. vol. 5, fol. 291v, June 10, 1388.

53. In addition to the works cited in n. 2, above, see also Molho, "Oligarchy"; idem, "Politics"; and Ronald G. Witt, "Florentine Politics and the Ruling Class, 1382–1407," *Journal of Medieval and Renaissance Studies* 6 (1976): 243–67.

54. *Croniche di Giovanni, Matteo e Filippo Villani*, bk. 11, chap. 65.

55. *Diario del Monaldi*, pp. 443, 457, 463; Brucker, *Politics*, pp. 199, 230–31, 250–51.

56. For Simone Peruzzi, see Provv. e Massai. Campioni. vol. 3, fol. 35v, dated November 2, 1386; for Vieri de' Medici, see Provv. e Massai. Campioni. vol. 11, fol. 275r, September 11, 1395; for Andrea Salviati, see Provv. e Massai. Campioni. vol. 3, fol. 26v, August 9, 1386; for Benedetto di Nerozzo Alberti, see Provv. e Massai. Campioni. vol. 5, fol. 291v, April 4, 1388; for Salvestro de' Medici, see Provv. e Massai. Campioni. vol. 3, fol. 33v, October 3, 1386.

57. Franco Sacchetti, *Il Trecentonovelle*, ed. Antonio Lanza (Florence, 1984), novella 153, p. 325; Brucker, *Politics*, pp. 50–56.

58. Matteo Villani, in *Croniche di Giovanni, Matteo e Filippo Villani*, bk. 9, chap. 43; *Diario del Monaldi*, pp. 443–45.

59. The five highest fees were one hundred florins for Nepo della Tosa, and sixty florins for Stoldo Altoviti in 1392 (Provv. e Massai. Campioni. vol. 8, fol. 9v); and fifty florins each, for Vieri de' Medici in 1395 (Provv. e Massai. Campioni. vol. 11, fol. 275r), for Rinieri Peruzzi in 1396 (Provv. e Massai. Campioni. vol. 12, fol. 275r), and for Soldo Soldani in 1397 (Provv. e Massai. Campioni. vol. 13, fol. 275r).

60. For the Nobili description, see Acquisti e Doni. vol. 293, unfoliated. The same volume contains an excerpt from the diary of Filippo di Gherardo Nozzi, who noted that he spent sixty florins for the illness and burial of his sister Monna Bancha in May 1372. Similarly, Barna Ciurianni paid about seventy florins to bury his wife Agnesa in 1362 (Manoscritti. vol. 77, fol. 8v).

61. For 1385, see Provv. e Massai. Campioni. vol. 2, fols. 21v, 23v; for 1387, see Provv. e Massai. Campioni. vol. 4, fol. 307v; for 1390, see Provv. e Massai. Campioni. vol. 6, fol. 310r/v; for 1391, see Provv. e Massai. Campioni. vol. 7, fols. 2r–9r; for 1392, see Provv. e Massai. Campioni. vol. 8, fols. 1r–9v.

62. Provv. e Massai. Campioni. vol. 6, fol. 310r/v.

63. Acquisti e Doni. vol. 293, unfoliated.

64. Becker, *Florence in Transition*, 2: 160.

65. Najemy, *Corporatism*; Molho, "Oligarchy"; idem, "Politics"; Trexler, *Spiritual Power*, esp. p. 135; Samuel K. Cohn, Jr., *The Laboring Classes in Renaissance Florence* (New York, 1980), esp. pp. 130–31.

66. *Diario del Monaldi*, pp. 460, 464; Brucker, *Politics*, p. 318.

67. For the tensions surrounding the War of the Eight Saints, see Brucker, *Politics*, esp. pp. 308–15; and Trexler, *Spiritual Power*. In 1377 the commune also dedicated a tournament in front of Santa Croce to "Madonna Libertà."

68. *Diario del Monaldi*, p. 443. For the grant of the "Liberty" motto, see Manoscritti. vol. 8, fol. 130v.

69. Luigi Passerini, *Gli Alberti di Firenze*, 2 vols. (Florence, 1870) summarizes Alberti's career (1: 74–79) and lists his offices (2: 54–57). See also Giovanni di Pagolo Morelli, *Ricordi*, ed. V. Branca (Florence, 1956), pp. 306–7.

70. G. Salvemini, *La dignità cavalleresca nel Comune di Firenze* (repr., Turin, 1960), doc. 48, p. 447. Leon Battista Alberti recalled this event with great pride when reviewing his ancestry (*I libri della famiglia*, ed. R. Romano and A. Tenenti [Turin, 1969], pp. 209–10).

71. *Le "Consulte" e "Pratiche" della Repubblica fiorentina nel Quattrocento, 1401* ed. Elio Conti et al., (Florence, 1981), 1: 22–25, 36–37.

72. *Diario del Monaldi*, pp. 443–44.

73. Alberti's lengthy testament dated August 6, 1376, is printed in Passerini, *Alberti*, 2: 155–85 (the dress stipulations are given on p. 157). *Cronaca di Marchionne Stefani*, vol. 30, pt. 1, p. 309, records the "più di 500 poveri lo piansero alla bara senza quelle e quelli che 'l piansero per Firenze."

74. Cf. the views of Richard C. Trexler, *Public Life in Renaissance Florence* (New York, 1980), who interprets the reliance on feudal forms as indicating the lack of a distinctive communal identity.

75. Salvemini, *Dignità*, pp. 470–71, documents the example of Lorenzo di Antonio Ridolfi, Matteo di Michele Castellani, and Palla di Nofri Strozzi, ambassadors to Naples together with Benedetto Acciaiuoli. These ambassadors had been knighted by King Jacopo of Naples. On February 17, 1416, they petitioned the Signoria to recognize them as Florentine knights. The commune voted its approval, granting the first three men the right to use the emblem of the Popolo on a shield, on a pennant, and on a caparisoned horse and its groom, spending sixty florins for each knight. Because Benedetto Acciaiuoli was already a knight, his nephew Angelo di Jacopo Acciaiuoli received these honors in his place, except for the use of the emblem on the horse, at a cost of fifty florins. Bartolomeo Corazza described the ceremony, which was held on February 27, 1416 ("Diario fiorentino di Bartolomeo di Michele del Corazza, 1405–1438," *Archivio storico italiano*, ser. 5, 13–14 [1894]: 255). See Salvemini, *Dignità*, appendix B, pp. 464–74, for other documents by which the commune recognized the status of those knighted by outside authorities.

76. Benedetto Dei, *La cronica dall'anno 1400 all'anno 1500*, ed. Roberto Barducci (Florence, 1984), p. 179. This action must have substantially increased the number of knights; Dei puts the number of the highest-ranking gold-

spurred knights at sixty-five in 1338, while Salvemini, *Dignità*, p. 402, puts it at seventy-five.

77. Salvemini, *Dignità*, esp. pp. 430–32, 467–70; Najemy, *Corporatism*, p. 267.

78. Salvemini, *Dignità*, pp. 421–28, 431–32, quote at p. 432.

79. The standard biography of Hawkwood is still Temple-Leader and Marcotti, *Sir John Hawkwood*. See E. Ricotti, *Storia delle compagnie di ventura in Italia*, 2 vols. (Turin, 1845), for Hawkwood's military activities (2: 143–56) and his funeral (2: 200–202). Hawkwood's pension contract, dated July 12, 1375, was negotiated with Coluccio Salutati, and is published in *I Capitoli del comune di Firenze: Inventario e regesto* (Florence, 1866), 1: 48. Geoffrey Trease, *The Condottieri: Soldiers of Fortune* (London, 1970), p. 35, gives details of the negotiations.

80. *Capitoli di Firenze* 1: 49.

81. *Cronica volgare di anonimo fiorentino dall'anno 1385 al 1409, già attribuita a Piero di Giovanni Minerbetti*, ed. E. Bellondi, in *Rerum Italicarum Scriptores*, new ed., (Città di Castello, 1915), vol. 27, pt. 2, pp. 183–84.

82. Pucci, *Quinto cantare*, 6: 231–35, quote at 6: 235.

83. *Croniche fiorentine di Ser Naddo da Montecatini*, in Ildefonso di San Luigi, ed., *Delizie*, 18: 141; *Ricordi storici di Filippo di Cino Rinuccini dal 1282 al 1460 colla continuazione di Alamanno e Neri suoi figli fino al 1506*, ed. G. Aiazzi (Florence, 1840), p. xlii; *Cronica attribuita a Piero Minerbetti*, vol. 27, pt. 2, p. 183. For the anonymous poem about Hawkwood's funeral known by Dei, see Medin, "Morte di Aguto," pp. 170, 172–77.

84. In 1394 the commune paid out 410 florins, 1 lira, 11 soldi, "per spese fatte . . . innonorare ilcorpo di Messer Giovanni aghuto" (Provv. e Massai. Campioni. vol. 10, fol. 328r). In addition, the Camera dell'Arme paid a total sum of 38 florins, 27 lire, 2 soldi, the following year, "per spese fatte in Giovanni Bonizi ghonfaloniere e per resto di spese fatte in Messer Giovanni aghuto e onorare Messer Giovanni da Spoleto prossimo passato podesta" (Provv. e Massai. Campioni. vol. 11, fol. 328r).

85. Morelli, *Ricordi*, p. 316. Morelli's assessment was probably accurate, since on April 16, 1394, a month after the ceremony, the commune voted to reimburse Hawkwood's son for his father's funeral expenses (document published in Medin, "Morte di Aguto," pp. 166–67).

86. *Cronica attribuita a Piero Minerbetti*, vol. 27, pt. 2, p. 183. The ceremonies for the deposed pope Baldassare Coscia in 1419, for instance, were partially staged in the Baptistry as well as in the cathedral (BNF. Conv. Sopp. C. 4. 895, fols. 100v–101r). The commune had held a ceremony in the Baptistry for Piero Farnese in 1363, after which he was buried in the cathedral. The Baptistry ceremony, however, was a requiem mass rather than a public lamentation, and there was no subsequent service held in the cathedral. The commune voted to build a marble tomb for Farnese, just as it did thirty years later for Hawkwood (Pucci, *Quinto cantare*, stanzas 13–15; *Croniche di Giovanni, Matteo e Filippo Villani*, bk. 11, chap. 59).

87. Tomb documents published by Medin, "Morte di Aguto," pp. 164–

65, dated August 20, 1393. The marble tomb was to be built in an "eminent, high, and honorable" place within one year of Hawkwood's death, at whatever cost seemed appropriate to the operai of the cathedral. The tomb was to be made "tam pro magnificentia comunis florentie, quam pro honore et fama perpetua dicti domini Iohannis"; no other body was to be placed with Hawkwood in the tomb. For the fresco, see Eve Borsook, "L'Hawkwood' d'Uccello et la *Vie de Fabius Maximus* de Plutarque," *Revue de l'art* 55 (1982): 44–51, which also gives relevant bibliography for the tomb.

88. Catasto. vol. 44, fols. 190r–91v. The remark by Piovano Arlotto (Mainardi) is found in Mainardi, *Motti e facezie*, facezia no. 15.

89. *Statuti delle arti dei Corazzai, dei Chiavaioli, Ferraioli e Calderai, e dei Fabbri di Firenze, 1321–1344*, ed. Giulia Camerani Marri (Florence, 1957), p. 25; *Statuti delle arti dei Fornai e dei Vinattieri di Firenze, 1337–1339*, ed. Francesca Morandini (Florence, 1956), p. 17; *Statuti dell'arte dei Medici e Speziali*, ed. Raffaele Ciasca (Florence, 1922), pp. 143–44.

90. John Henderson, "Religious Confraternities and Death in Early Renaissance Florence," in *Florence and Italy: Renaissance Studies in Honour of Nicolai Rubinstein*, ed. Peter Denley and Caroline Elam (London, 1988), pp. 383–94. The popularity and the functions of various types of confraternities are discussed by Weissman, *Ritual Brotherhood*; and are discussed for Italy generally by G. G. Meersseman, *Ordo Fraternitatis: Confraternite e pietà dei laici nel medioevo*, 3 vols. (Rome, 1977).

91. Of the 156 confraternities active in Florence between 1250 and 1500, 17 were founded before 1300, 51 appeared in the fourteenth century, and another 87 appeared in the fifteenth (John Henderson, "Confraternities and the Church in Late Medieval Florence," *Studies in Church History* 23 [1986]: 69–83).

92. Ibid.

93. *Capitoli della Compagnia dei Disciplinati della città di Firenze*, ed. Pietro Ferrato (Padua, 1871), pp. 13–14 (dated July 1354).

94. These burial items were stipulated in the company's 1333 statutes (*Capitoli della Compagnia della Madonna d'Orsanmichele dei secoli XIII e XIV*, ed. Leone del Prete [Lucca, 1859], p. 50). An inventory of the company's goods dated June 8, 1436, lists similar items on hand for members' use (Capitani di Orsanmichele. vol. 26, fol. 13v).

95. Henderson, "Confraternities and Death."

96. Conv. Sopp. 102. vol. 296, fol. 165r.

97. Statuti del Comune di Firenze. vol. 34, fol. 13r; *Statuta Populi et Communis Florentiae Anno Salutis 1415*, 3 vols. (Fribourg, 1778–83), 2: 377.

98. For Gesù Pellegrino, see Vincenzo Fineschi, *Memorie sopra il cimitero antico della chiesa di Santa Maria Novella di Firenze* (Florence, 1787; repr., Rome, 1977), p. 96. On the development of private family chapels and tombs in the fourteenth century, see Howard Saalman, *The Church of Santa Trinità in Florence* (New York, 1966), esp. p. 37.

99. Catasto. vol. 185, fol. 706r. The company listed among its assets "uno luogho overo chapella overo oratorio chon cimitero dintorno la dove si

raghunavano ichapittani della detta chonpagnia el quale cimitero eluogho e ne insula piazza delachiesa di san lorenzo di firenze."

100. For women's involvement in confraternities, see Meersseman, *Ordo Fraternitatis*, 1: 498–504; and Nicholas Terpstra, "Gender and Class in the Organization of Lay Piety in Bologna, 1260–1600" (Paper given at 22d International Congress on Medieval Studies, Kalamazoo, Mich., May 7–9, 1987).

101. Meersseman, *Ordo Fraternitatis*, 2: 707.

102. Trexler, *Spiritual Power*, p. 131; Terpstra, "Gender and Class."

103. Conv. Sopp. 102. vol. 326, fols. 8r, 8v, 9r, 35v.

104. Conv. Sopp. 102. vol. 296, fol. 141r; Conv. Sopp. 102. vol. 293, fol. 29r.

105. Statuti del Comune di Firenze. vol. 34, fol. 13r, which gave permission for confraternal torches to accompany the body of any "mortui seu mortue."

106. The confraternal tombs of San Pier Martire are mentioned throughout Conv. Sopp. 102. vol. 326. For the separate tomb slabs for men and women at Gesù Pellegrino, see Fineschi, *Memorie*, p. 96. The company of Santa Maria della Neve at Sant'Ambrogio was also ceded "due sepolture in detta chiesa cioe una per Gliomini et una per le donne di detta conpagnia" (Comp. Relig. Sopp. Capitoli. vol. 606, fol. 22v). Private family tombs were similarly segregated by sex; for example, in 1429 Valorino Ciurianni buried his seventeen-year-old granddaughter Tessa in Santo Stefano a Ponte "nel nostro avello delle donne" (Manoscritti. vol. 77, fol. 38r).

107. Comp. Relig. Sopp. Capitoli. vol. 439, fol. 6r. A similarly broad kin group was invoked by the commemorative routines of Santa Maria della Neve at Sant'Ambrogio (Comp. Relig. Sopp. Capitoli. vol. 606, fol. 49v).

108. Strocchia, "Remembering the Family."

109. Terpstra, "Gender and Class."

110. Cohn, *Laboring Classes*, p. 15.

111. For the difficulties of defining parish boundaries, see ibid., pp. 25–32.

112. Cohn, *Laboring Classes*; D. V. Kent and F. W. Kent, *Neighbours and Neighbourhood in Renaissance Florence: The District of the Red Lion in the Fifteenth Century* (Locust Valley, N.Y., 1982); Dennis Romano, *Patricians and Popolani: The Social Foundations of the Venetian Renaissance State* (Baltimore, 1987). By contrast, Trexler, *Public Life*, pp. 13–14, argues that parish life was subordinated to broader civic concerns. Henderson analyzes the problem of parish ties for Florence from the perspective of relations between confraternities, friars, and the Florentine bishop in "Confraternities and the Church." Chiffoleau, *Comptabilité*, p. 284, argues for the declining strength of parish ties in late fourteenth-century Avignon.

113. Gene Brucker, "Urban Parishes and Their Clergy in Quattrocento Florence: A Preliminary Sondage," in *Renaissance Studies in Honor of Craig Hugh Smyth*, ed. Andrew Morrogh et al., 2 vols. (Florence, 1985), 1: 17–

28. Of the sixty-two parishes, thirty-two were located in the city's old center within the first circle of walls.

114. Ibid., p. 17; Catasto. vol. 184, fol. 228r; Cohn, *Laboring Classes*, p. 26.

115. Roberto Bizzocchi, "Chiesa e aristocrazia nella Firenze del Quattrocento," *Archivio storico italiano* 142 (1984): 191–281, at p. 193.

116. Catasto. vol. 184, fols. 267r, 99v.

117. For a general examination of canonical rulings, see Antoine Bernard, *La sépulture en droit canonique du décret de Gratien au Concile de Trente* (Paris, 1933).

118. Richard C. Trexler, *Synodal Law in Florence and Fiesole, 1306–1518* (Città del Vaticano, 1971), pp. 62, 70–73.

119. C. Torricelli et al., eds., *La Misericordia di Firenze attraverso i secoli: Note storiche* (Florence, 1975). In 1425 the Misericordia was united under communal direction with the charitable company of the Bigallo, and the combined organization continued its charitable services to the dead.

120. A complete list of Florentine diocesan constitutions is given in Richard C. Trexler, "Death and Testament in the Episcopal Constitutions of Florence, 1327," in *Renaissance Studies in Honor of Hans Baron*, ed. Anthony Molho and John A. Tedeschi (DeKalb, Ill., 1971), pp. 29–74, at pp. 32–33n.

121. On the political conflicts between bishops, the commune, and the papacy in the fourteenth century, see Antonio Panella, "La politica ecclesiastica del comune fiorentino dopo la cacciata del duca d'Atene," *Archivio storico italiano* 71 (1913): 271–370; and Richard C. Trexler, "Florence, by the Grace of the Lord Pope," *Studies in Medieval and Renaissance History* 9 (1972): 115–215.

122. Giuseppe Richa, *Notizie storiche delle chiese fiorentine*, 10 vols. (Florence, 1754), 5: 15.

123. Bernard, *Sépulture*, pp. 70–75.

124. Carte Riccardi. vol. 521, fol. 25r.

125. Piero Ginori Conti, *La basilica di San Lorenzo di Firenze e la famiglia Ginori* (Florence, 1940), p. 68.

126. Conv. Sopp. 82. vol. 13, fols. 14v–15r.

127. Ginori Conti, *Basilica di San Lorenzo*, pp. 24–26; San Pier Maggiore. vol. 1, fol. 3r.

128. Diplomatico. San Pier Maggiore, dated September 4, 1365; copy with additional documents, dated April 23, 1754, in San Pier Maggiore. vol. 4, tome 1, unfoliated.

129. San Pier Maggiore. vol. 68, fols. 19v–22r.

130. With two exceptions, years were sampled at intervals of three to five years, depending on the available documentation. The sample years were 1374 (22.4 percent of income accruing from burials); 1378 (2.8 percent); 1381 (12.4 percent); 1384 (9.7 percent); 1388 (11.8 percent); 1393 (10.3 percent); 1412 (3.1 percent); and 1413 (6.5 percent). These years give an overall average of 9.9 percent (San Pier Maggiore. vols. 68, 69, 70, 72).

131. Catasto. vol. 184, fols. 213r–214r.

132. Conv. Sopp. 113. vol. 81, fols. 230r, 231v, 232r/v.

133. Cesare Guasti, *Santa Maria del Fiore* (Florence, 1887), pp. xliii, 29–32; Franklin Toker, "Excavations below the Cathedral of Florence, 1965–1974," *Gesta* 14 (1975): 17–36.

134. Fineschi, *Memorie*, p. 4; Guasti, *Santa Maria del Fiore*, p. 93.

135. Guasti, *Santa Maria del Fiore*, p. 277.

136. Lana. vol. 47, dated June 26, 1392. In return for this privilege, Vieri was to subsidize a cathedral chaplain. On June 27, 1393, Vieri petitioned the officials again, asking that he be able to move his tomb if the construction then under way impeded his plans (Lana. vol. 47, fols. 78v–79r).

137. Trexler, *Public Life*, p. 19n.

138. For the Medici tomb, see note 136, above. For the Corsini tomb, see Lana. vol. 85, fol. 70r/v. Within two years, the cardinal or his agent had to buy land worth at least one thousand florins to subsidize a chaplain to officiate at the Corsini altar. The chaplain was to be selected by four priests, two named by the Corsini and two by the operai. Corsini died in Avignon August 16, 1405; his tomb is described in Richa, *Notizie*, 6: 27.

139. Cohn, *Laboring Classes*, pp. 25–26. For the organization of the city into sixths, see F. J. Carmody, "Florence: Project for a Map, 1250–1296," *Speculum* 19 (1944): 39–49.

140. Carmichael, *Plague and the Poor*, pp. 99, 103.

141. *Statuti Medici e Speziali*, pp. 286, 290–93; Carmichael, *Plague and the Poor*, pp. 29–30.

142. Grascia. Libri di Morti. vol. 1, fol. 4r. On the development of Florentine Books of the Dead, see Carmichael, *Plague and the Poor*, pp. 28–35; and Giuseppe Parenti, "Fonti per lo studio della demografia fiorentina: I libri dei morti," *Genus* 5–6 (1943–49): 281–301.

143. Grascia. Libri di Morti. vol. 1, fols. 4r, 11r. Between 1363 and 1370, for instance, gravediggers commonly returned to the friars of Santa Maria del Carmine a payment of 2 soldi, 6 denari per burial (Conv. Sopp. 113. vol. 81, fols. 168v–236r). In the first decade of the fifteenth century, the monks of Santa Trinità made regular use of various services offered by the *beccamorto* Marcialla (Conv. Sopp. 89. vol. 10).

144. Carmichael, *Plague and the Poor*, p. 89.

145. Conv. Sopp. 88. vol. 23, fol. 13v.

146. Catasto. vol. 194, fols. 79v–80r. "Avere ognanno delle istinche L. 54 sono per vicitare glinfermi e per sopellire imorti di quelluogho. Ella ispesa della detta chiesa cioe cho torchi echole chandele e ongni ispesa visiriche-desse e per questo debbono dare i detti danari e sono per Rinformagione e posono quando vogliono levagli e dagli e non sono chose ferme."

147. For the use of criminals for anatomical dissection, see Park, *Doctors and Medicine*, p. 61; and Samuel Y. Edgerton, *Pictures and Punishment: Art and Criminal Prosecution during the Florentine Renaissance* (Ithaca, N.Y., 1985), pp. 159–60. Criminals who had no parish and were not given over for dissection were buried in the special cemetery of the Company of Santa

Maria della Croce al Tempio (Edgerton, *Pictures*, p. 188). Examples of Florentine criminals dispatched to their private tombs are found in Manoscritti. vol. 88, fol. 144v; and Manoscritti. vol. 817, fol. 72r.

148. Catasto. vol. 185, fol. 747v. On the charitable activities of the Tempio confraternity, see Weissman, *Ritual Brotherhood*, esp. pp. 88, 117, 191, 194; and Edgerton, *Pictures*, esp. pp. 55, 138–44, 179–80, 182–83, 231–38.

149. Diplomatico. Santa Maria Novella, dated March 15, 1311, and March 22, 1311. My thanks to Carol Lansing for bringing these documents to my attention.

150. Trexler, *Synodal Law*, p. 71. Acciaiuoli's constitutions are printed in J. D. Mansi, comp. and ed. *Sacrorum Conciliorum Nova et Amplissima Collectio* (Florence, 1759–98), vol. 26, cols. 23–70, funerary rubric at col. 47.

151. Catasto. vol. 184, fol. 228r.

152. Bernard, *Sépulture*; Trexler, *Synodal Law*, p. 72; idem, "Death and Testament," pp. 34–35. The same system of apportionment was later upheld by the Council of Trent.

153. Conv. Sopp. 119. vol. 689, fol. 279v.

154. Conv. Sopp. 88. vol. 2, fol. 270r.

155. San Pier Maggiore, vol. 4, tome 1, no. 28, dated June 6, 1578.

156. In the discussion that follows, specific information about burial patterns in San Pier Maggiore is based—unless otherwise indicated—on the following sources: San Pier Maggiore. vol. 68, fols. 19v–22r; San Pier Maggiore. vol. 69, fols. 25r–29v; San Pier Maggiore. vol. 70, fols. 7v–11r, 25v–32v, 53v–58v; San Pier Maggiore. vol. 52, fols. 2r–6v; San Pier Maggiore. vol. 72, fols. 5v–10v, 13r–17v. The choice of years depended on the availability and condition of documentation. Figures for 1400, a plague year, are available only for the period August through December.

157. Romano, *Patricians and Popolani*, p. 118.

158. Thomas Laqueur, "Bodies, Death, and Pauper Funerals," *Representations* 1 (1983): 109–31.

159. Cohn, *Laboring Classes*, pp. 82, 90.

160. San Pier Maggiore. vol. 52, fol. 2r.

161. San Pier Maggiore. vol. 72, fol. 112r; San Pier Maggiore. vol. 50, fol. 25r.

162. San Pier Maggiore. vol. 72, fols. 7r, 9v, 108r/v. Women regularly used churches as well as confraternities as their funeral brokers and executors; for example, in November 1395 the prior of the Carmine, Fra Niccolò Cecchini, paid off the medical and funeral expenses of a Monna Lorenza out of the proceeds realized from her household goods (Conv. Sopp. 113. vol. 82, fol. 260r).

163. Although neither Lapaccio's occupation nor his surname are given, his heirs donated as much as fifty florins to San Pier Maggiore per his bequest two years after his death in 1380, suggesting that he had some means and a particular connection to the convent (San Pier Maggiore. vol. 69, fols. 25v, 49v, 71r).

164. Manoscritti. vol. 817, fol. 31r.

165. The complaint registered by the rector of San Donato dei Vecchietti in 1427, cited in note 151, above, suggests a similar neighborhood dominance by the Dominicans of Santa Maria Novella.

166. Between 1352 and 1479, the customary minimum donation to friars for participating in funeral processions remained steady at 2 soldi per friar, regardless of the number attending. More generous donors were of course free to offer slightly larger sums. (See Conv. Sopp. 113. vol. 81; Conv. Sopp. 119. vols. 48, 246, 247.) By comparison, gardeners earned 8.2 soldi per day in 1371–75, and 8.8 soldi in 1378–81. Average daily wages for unskilled laborers fluctuated between 8.0 and 11.1 soldi between 1350 and 1380, while daily wages for skilled laborers ranged from 13.3 to 18.3 soldi for the same period (Cohn, *Laboring Classes*, p. 138; Goldthwaite, *Building*, pp. 436–37).

167. Conv. Sopp. 113. vols. 81, 82.

168. In the following discussion, data on the Carmine friars' funeral participation is drawn from Conv. Sopp. 113. vol. 81.

Chapter 4: Civic Ideals and Classicism in the Early Quattrocento

1. Gene Brucker, *The Civic World of Early Renaissance Florence* (Princeton, N.J., 1977).

2. Ann G. Carmichael, *Plague and the Poor in Renaissance Florence* (Cambridge, 1986), pp. 62, 65.

3. Provv. e Massai. Campioni. vol. 15, fol. 330r. The sum given is 452 florins, 2,430 lire, 13 soldi, 6 denari, or 1,083 florins using the equivalents given by Richard Goldthwaite, *The Building of Renaissance Florence* (Baltimore, 1980), appendix 1.

4. Carmichael, *Plague and the Poor*, pp. 98–101.

5. The dates of the epidemics are given by Katherine Park, *Doctors and Medicine in Early Renaissance Florence* (Princeton, N.J., 1985), p. 5.

6. *Cronica volgare di anonimo fiorentino dall'anno 1385 al 1409, già attribuita a Piero di Giovanni Minerbetti*, ed. E. Bellondi, in *Rerum Italicarum Scriptores*, new ed. (Città di Castello, 1915), vol. 27, pt. 2, pp. 250–51.

7. *Cronica fiorentina di Jacopo Salviati*, in *Delizie degli eruditi toscani*, ed. P. Ildefonso di San Luigi, 24 vols. (Florence, 1770–89), 18: 191–95.

8. Manoscritti. vol. 77, fol. 33r.

9. San Pier Maggiore. vol. 52, fol. 8r/v.

10. Hans Baron, *The Crisis of the Early Italian Renaissance*, rev. ed. (Princeton, N.J., 1966).

11. On Salutati's professionalism, see Ronald G. Witt, *Hercules at the Crossroads: The Life, Works, and Thought of Coluccio Salutati* (Durham, N.C., 1983), pp. 113, 120, 123. Demetrio Marzi, *La cancelleria della repubblica fiorentina* (Rocca San Casciano, 1910), p. 148n, briefly quotes Poggio Bracciolini's praise of Salutati's integrity in office. For Ser Niccolò di Ser Venturi Monachi,

who succeeded his father as chancellor (1348–1375), see Witt, *Hercules*, pp. 119–21, and Marzi, *Cancelleria*, pp. 91–105.

12. Witt, *Hercules*. Aspects of Salutati's political thought are also treated by Daniela de Rosa, *Coluccio Salutati: Il cancelliere e il pensatore politico* (Florence, 1980), pp. ix–x; Ronald G. Witt, "The *De Tyranno* and Coluccio Salutati's View of Politics and Roman History," *Nuova rivista storica* 53 (1969): 434–74; and Baron, *Crisis*, esp. pp. 104–20, 146–66.

13. Fortini served as Salutati's colleague in the chancery from June 22, 1376, to June 21, 1377. He also served as chancellor of the Ten of War after 1384, as one of the Twelve Good Men in 1384 and 1403, as one of the sixteen standard-bearers of justice in 1396, and as ambassador on several occasions (Marzi, *Cancelleria*, p. 154; de Rosa, *Salutati*, p. 7; and Witt, "The *De Tyranno*," p. 451n).

14. Witt, *Hercules*, p. 129, and de Rosa, *Salutati*, p. x, discuss the chancellor's limited power and the admission of Salutati to secret meetings of the city's leaders during the war with the papacy.

15. Witt, *Hercules*, pp. 119–21; Marzi, *Cancelleria*, pp. 91–105.

16. Lauro Martines, *The Social World of the Florentine Humanists, 1390–1460* (Princeton, N.J., 1963), pp. 241–45, briefly analyzes the rites staged for Salutati and his successors as an indication of the growing social prestige of humanists.

17. Marzi, *Cancelleria*, p. 149; Witt, *Hercules*, p. 415. In reporting Salutati's burial in the cathedral, the *Cronica attribuita a Piero Minerbetti*, vol. 27, pt. 2, p. 349, also noted the Signoria's approval of "una bellisima sipoltura di marmo gli fosse fatta dal Comune in detta chiesa." For the tomb, which was never built, and other pertinent iconography, see *Epistolario di Coluccio Salutati*, ed. Francesco Novati, 4 vols. (Rome, 1891–1911), 4: 167–70, 559–65.

18. The committee charged with handling Marsuppini's funeral consisted of Giannozzo Manetti, Niccolò Soderini, Matteo Palmieri, Ugolini Martelli, and Piero de' Medici (BNF. Conv. Sopp. C. 4. 895, fol. 163r/v). I have been unable to locate a record of a similar committee for Salutati.

19. "Diario fiorentino di Bartolomeo di Michele del Corazza, 1405–1438," *Archivio storico italiano*, ser. 5, 13–14 (1894): 241.

20. *Epistolario di Coluccio Salutati*, 4: 168n, gives the total sum spent on Salutati's funeral as 973 lire, 10 soldi; for Hawkwood, see Provv. e Massai. Campioni. vol. 10, fol. 328r; for Jacopo Salviati's festivities, see *Cronica di Jacopo Salviati*, 18: 224–26.

21. *Cronica attribuita a Piero Minerbetti*, vol. 27, pt. 2, pp. 348–49.

22. *Epistolario di Coluccio Salutati*, 4: 168n, cites the expenses "pro panno, drappis, vario et zendatis, et pro cera et pro factura cuiusdam cuperte pro equo et palio et stendardo et pro pluribus aliis rebus et expensis factis de mense maii proxime preteriti pro honorando funus domini Colucci Pierii olim cancellarii Fiorentini pro remuneratione servitiorum per eundem factorum comuni Florentino, libr. 973, sold. 10."

23. BNF. Conv. Sopp. C. 4. 895, fol. 86v. "Et fu coronato dalloro come

poeta per mano di ser Viviano di Neri Viviano notaio delle Riformagioni del comune di firenze Et sindacho del comune di firenze per una autorita auta il comune di firenze da Carlo [blank] imperadore in potere coronare e poeti." On the friendship and collegial relations between Salutati and Viviani, see Witt, *Hercules*, pp. 138, 140, 274n, 414.

24. Witt, *Hercules*, esp. pp. 193, 220–23, 291n, 302; idem, "Coluccio Salutati and the Conception of the *Poeta Theologus* in the Fourteenth Century," *Renaissance Quarterly* 30 (1977): 538–63.

25. *Cronica attribuita a Piero Minerbetti*, vol. 27, pt. 2, pp. 348–49; BNF. Conv. Sopp. C. 4. 895, fol. 86v.

26. Various epigrams, epitaphs, and letters praising Salutati are collected in *Epistolario di Coluccio Salutati*, 4: 470–87; the quotation is from *Cronica attribuita a Piero Minerbetti*, vol. 27, pt. 2, p. 348.

27. See *Epistolario di Coluccio Salutati*: for Manetti's life of Salutati (4: 509–13) and for the medallion (4: 167–70, 559–65). The use of coins as a lasting reminder of late antique imperial exegesis is discussed by Sabine G. MacCormick, *Art and Ceremony in Late Antiquity* (Berkeley, Calif. 1981), p. 12.

28. Ernest Hatch Wilkins, *The Making of the "Canzoniere" and Other Petrarchan Studies* (Rome, 1951), pp. 9–21.

29. Ibid., pp. 21–24.

30. Ibid., pp. 61–66. On the circumstances surrounding Cola di Rienzo's coronation as Roman tribune, see Francesco Petrarch, *The Revolution of Cola di Rienzo*, ed. Ronald G. Musto, 2d ed. (New York, 1986), pp. 75–118.

31. References by Poggio and Vergerio to Salutati as father are given in *Two Renaissance Book Hunters: The Letters of Poggius Bracciolini to Nicolaus de Niccolis*, trans. Phyllis Gordon (New York, 1974), pp. 22, 221n.

32. David Quint, "Humanism and Modernity: A Reconsideration of Bruni's *Dialogues*," *Renaissance Quarterly* 38 (1985): 423–45.

33. *Epistolario di Coluccio Salutati*, 4: 471–74; Poggio's letter is printed in Gordan, trans., *Two Renaissance Book Hunters*, pp. 22–24, quote at p. 24, Gordan's translation.

34. For the mixed composition of the regime, see Brucker, *Civic World*, pp. 248–62; and Dale Kent, "The Florentine *Reggimento* in the Fifteenth Century," *Renaissance Quarterly* 28 (1975): 575–638. The priors holding office at the time of Salutati's death were Benino di Francesco Benino, *setaiuolo*; Antonio di Niccolò Alberti; Antonio di Messer Luca da Panzano; Jacopo di Piero di Bonaventura; Ugolino di Jacopo Mazinghi; Lippozzo di Cipriano Mangioni; Benintendi di Nuccio, *tavolacciaio*; Niccolò di Chiaro, *fabbro*; and the gonfaloniere Ruggieri di Messer Giovanni de' Ricci (*Istorie di Giovanni Cambi, cittadino fiorentino*, in Ildefonso di San Luigi, ed., *Delizie*, vols. 20–23, at 20: 131).

35. Eve Borsook, "L' Hawkwood' d'Uccello et la *Vie de Fabius Maximus* de Plutarque," *Revue de l'art* 55 (1982): 44–51; Teresa Hankey, "Salutati's Epigrams for the Palazzo Vecchio at Florence," *Journal of the Warburg and Court-*

auld Institutes 22 (1959): 363–65. Salutati's epigram for Dante is printed in Giuseppe Richa, *Notizie storiche delle chiese fiorentine*, 10 vols. (Florence, 1754), 6: 128.

36. John M. McManamon, *Funeral Oratory and the Cultural Ideals of Italian Humanism* (Chapel Hill, N.C., 1989), p. 17.

37. *Cronica di Jacopo Salviati*, 18: 224–26.

38. *Statuti del Capitano del Popolo, 1322–25*, ed. Romolo Caggese, in *Statuti della repubblica fiorentina*, 2 vols. (Florence, 1910–21), vol. 1, at p. 224.

39. Ronald G. Witt, "A Note on Guelfism in Late Medieval Florence," *Nuova rivista storica* 53 (1969): 134–45.

40. For the Latin text, see Marzi, *Cancelleria*, p. 149; I am using the translation given by Witt, *Hercules*, p. 415.

41. McManamon, *Funeral Oratory*, pp. 6–9. On consolatory letters, see George W. McClure, "The Art of Mourning: Autobiographical Writings on the Loss of a Son in Italian Humanist Thought (1400–1461)," *Renaissance Quarterly* 39 (1986): 440–75.

42. McManamon, *Funeral Oratory*, pp. 10–11; idem, "Innovation in Early Humanist Rhetoric: The Oratory of Pier Paolo Vergerio (The Elder)," *Rinascimento*, n.s., 22 (1982): 3–32.

43. "Diario di Bartolomeo del Corazza," p. 241.

44. For Farnese, see Antonio Pucci, *Quinto cantare della guerra pisana*, in Ildefonso di San Luigi, ed., *Delizie*, 6: 232; for Hawkwood, see *Cronica attribuita a Piero Minerbetti*, vol. 27, pt. 2, p. 183.

45. Quotes are from *Epistolario di Coluccio Salutati*, 3: 140, 142. Witt, *Hercules*, pp. 313–16, situates Salutati's response to Piera's death in the broader development of his thought.

46. *Epistolario di Coluccio Salutati*, 3: 126–128, 133–42; Witt, *Hercules*, pp. 313–14.

47. *Epistolario di Coluccio Salutati*, 4: 347–49.

48. Ibid., 4: 513; Witt, *Hercules*, pp. 313–14, 357.

49. Francesco Petrarch, "How a Ruler Ought to Govern His State," in *The Earthly Republic: Italian Humanists on Government and Society*, ed. Benjamin C. Kohl and Ronald G. Witt (Philadelphia, 1978), pp. 35–78, at p. 78, Kohl's translation.

50. McClure, "Art of Mourning," pp. 444–51; Poggio's remarks are given in Gordan, trans., *Two Renaissance Book Hunters*, p. 22, Gordan's translation.

51. Vespasiano da Bisticci, *The Vespasiano Memoirs: Lives of Illustrious Men of the XVth Century*, trans. William George and Emily Waters (London, 1926), p. 237, their translation. Bruni's remarks are taken from his 1428 funeral oration for Nanni degli Strozzi, excerpted in *The Humanism of Leonardo Bruni: Selected Texts*, ed. Gordon Griffiths, James Hankins, and David Thompson (Binghamton, N.Y., 1987), p. 123, Griffiths's translation.

52. Marzi, *Cancelleria*, pp. 195–96; Carte Strozz. 2. vol. 177, fol. 148: "essendo morto messer Gregorio Marsuppini, padre di messer Carlo cancelliere . . . , et essendo solito nella Città . . . che i cittadini induuntur per totum dorsum de nigro, e, considerato che detto messer Carlo, alla pena di

lire 300, non poteva farlo, pero scrivono a detto messer Carlo che possa venire per una volta tanto in Palazzo vestito di panno di qualsivoglia colore fuorche nero e con quello stare finche tunica et epitorgium suantur."

53. Richard C. Trexler, "La prostitution florentine au XVe siècle: Patronages et clientèles," *Annales* 36 (1981): 983–1015. In 1432 the commune established a sodomy commission (Ufficiali di Notte), which the following year took over the additional function of policing nunneries from the Conservatori dell'Onestà de' Monasteri set up in 1421 (Michael J. Rocke, "Il controllo dell'omosessualità a Firenze nel XV secolo: Gli 'Ufficiali di Notte,' " *Quaderni storici* 66 [1987]: 701–23). Venice also set up a sodomy commission in 1418 (Patricia Labalme, "Sodomy and Venetian Justice in the Renaissance," *Legal History Review* 52 (1984): 217–54). Maria Serena Mazzi explores other aspects of the sexual economy in "Cronache di periferia dello stato fiorentino: Reati contro il morale nel primo Quattrocento," *Studi storici* 27 (1986): 611–35.

54. Michael J. Rocke, "Sodomites in Fifteenth-Century Tuscany: The Views of Bernardino of Siena," in *The Pursuit of Sodomy: Male Homosexuality in Renaissance and Enlightenment Europe*, ed. K. Gerard and G. Hekma (New York, 1989), pp. 7–31. Again Venice offers a useful comparison in its similar expansion of state authority into previously unregulated areas of social life and behavior (Guido Ruggiero, *The Boundaries of Eros: Sex Crime and Sexuality in Renaissance Venice* [Oxford, 1985]).

55. Among the major works dealing with these changes are Brucker, *Civic World*; Marvin Becker, *Florence in Transition*, 2 vols. (Baltimore, 1967–68); John M. Najemy, *Corporatism and Consensus in Florentine Electoral Politics, 1280–1400* (Chapel Hill, N.C., 1982); Anthony Molho, "Politics and the Ruling Class in Early Renaissance Florence," *Nuova rivista storica* 52 (1968): 401–20; idem, "The Florentine Oligarchy and the Balie of the Late Trecento," *Speculum* 43 (1968): 23–51; and Ronald G. Witt, "Florentine Politics and the Ruling Class, 1382–1407," *Journal of Medieval and Renaissance Studies* 6 (1976): 243–67.

56. Between 1385 and 1421 Florence added Arezzo, Pisa, Cortona, and Livorno to its territorial dominion (Giorgio Chittolini, *La formazione dello stato regionale e le istituzioni del contado: Secoli XIV e XV* [Turin, 1979]).

57. Brucker, *Civic World*; Kent, "Florentine 'Reggimento.' "

58. Giovanni Cavalcanti, *Istorie fiorentine*, 2 vols. (Florence, 1838–39), 1: 77–78; Brucker, *Civic World*, pp. 473–74.

59. Brucker, *Civic World*, esp. pp. 292–95, 335.

60. Goldthwaite, who views the fifteenth-century Florentine economy as far healthier than other scholars judge it to have been, states that after the first third of the fifteenth century, money that had been previously absorbed by military ventures and territorial expansion became more available for consumption spending (*Building*, pp. 29–30, 77–83).

61. Ibid., pp. 14–16; Brucker, *Civic World*, p. 38n; Christiane Klapisch-Zuber, *Women, Family, and Ritual in Renaissance Italy*, trans. Lydia Cochrane (Chicago, 1985), pp. 13–14.

62. Julius Kirshner and Anthony Molho, "The Dowry Fund and the Marriage Market in Early Quattrocento Florence," *Journal of Modern History* 50 (1978): 403–38.

63. Ronald E. Rainey, *Sumptuary Legislation in Renaissance Florence*, (Ann Arbor, Mich.: University Microfilms, 1985), pp. 435–37.

64. *Statuta Populi et Communis Florentiae Anno Salutis 1415*, 3 vols. (Fribourg, 1778–83), 2: 374–81, at p. 375.

65. Brucker, *Civic World*, pp. 482–83. See, for example, the joust held in Piazza Santa Croce in January 1429 described in *Istorie di Giovanni Cambi*, 20: 172–73. Among the eleven participants were the sons of several important political figures: Giovanni di Francesco Giovanni, who won the tournament; Lorenzo di Palla Strozzi, bringing five horses covered in richly embroidered silks; Domenico di Benedetto Benini; Filippo di Filippo di Messer Simone Tornabuoni, who placed second; and Lamberto di Bernardo Lamberteschi. Judging the contest was a group of older, socially established knights: Messers Giovanni Guicciardini, Agnolo Acciaiuoli, Matteo Castellani, and Rinaldo degli Albizzi.

66. Richard A. Goldthwaite, "The Empire of Things: Consumer Demand in Renaissance Italy," in *Patronage, Art, and Society in Renaissance Italy*, ed. F. W. Kent and Patricia Simons (Oxford, 1987), pp. 153–75.

67. Manoscritti. vol. 84, fol. 36r; Capitani di Orsanmichele. vol. 62, fols. 11v, 12v, 13r; Provvisioni. vol. 123, fols. 264r–265r.

68. BNF. Conv. Sopp. C. 4. 895, fol. 124r.

69. Niccolò Alberti's funeral (1377) cost 3,000 florins and Matteo Soldi's (1379) 1,000 florins (Guido Monaldi, *Diario del Monaldi*, in idem, *Istorie pistolese* [Milan, 1845], pp. 427–64, at pp. 443–44, 460).

70. Rainey, *Sumptuary Legislation*, pp. 431–33. For the relative values of dowry and trousseau, see Klapisch-Zuber, *Women, Family, and Ritual*, pp. 220–21.

71. For Nofri's funeral and requiem, see Conv. Sopp. 89. vol. 10, fol. 31v; and Conv. Sopp. vol. 46, fol. 14r. For Strozzi's tomb, chapel, and artistic ensemble, see Marcel Reymond, "La tomba di Onofrio Strozzi nella chiesa di Santa Trinità in Firenze," *L'Arte* 1 (1903): 7–14; Darrell D. Davisson, "The Iconology of the S. Trinità Sacristy, 1418–1435: A Study of the Private and Public Functions of Religious Art in the Early Quattrocento," *Art Bulletin* 57 (1975): 315–34. The last-named work contains several factual errors noted and corrected by Roger Jones, "Palla Strozzi e la sagrestia di Santa Trinità," *Rivista d'arte*, ser. 4, 37 (1984): 9–106.

72. Carte Strozz. 3. vol. 132, no. 60, letter of Palla to Simone di Filippo Strozzi, Venice, March 28, 1422. My thanks to Heather Gregory for bringing this document to my attention. On Strozzi's wealth, see Martines, *Social World*, pp. 316–18. Vespasiano, *Memoirs*, pp. 237–38, notes the heavy burden of taxation and other debts borne by Strozzi.

73. Manoscritti. vol. 84, fols. 26r–33r, 36r.

74. For Guicciardini, see Richa, *Notizie*, 9: 303–4. For the Scali and Ardingelli projects, see Conv. Sopp. 89. vol. 1, fols. 10r, 11v, 16v, 18r; Conv.

Sopp. vol. 31, fols. 1–40, devoted entirely to the Ardinghelli chapel; and Conv. Sopp. vol. 128, fols. 10v, 25r, 26v, relating to roof payments for the Ardinghelli chapel.

75. Carte Strozz. 2. vol. 9, fol. 23r. Contemporaries identified the "customary" consumption of cloth for mourning garb as ten braccia for men and twelve braccia for women, with an additional two veils and one kerchief for women.

76. BNF. Conv. Sopp. C. 4. 895, fol. 124r.

77. Excerpts of Bruni's translation of Aristotle's *Economics* are printed in Griffiths, Hankins, and Thompson, eds., *Humanism of Bruni*, pp. 305–17.

78. Alberti's remarks, taken from his *Della famiglia*, are quoted and translated by Thomas Kuehn, *Emancipation in Late Medieval Florence* (New Brunswick, N.J., 1982), p. 57.

79. Catasto. vol. 57, fols. 139r–142v, at fol. 142r.

80. Each brother agreed to pay thirty-nine florins as his share, after a fifty-florin down payment had been made. Catasto. vol. 42, fols. 11r/v, 443v; Catasto. vol. 43, fol. 843v; Catasto. vol. 45, fols. 704v, 773v. Of the five brothers—Ser Antonio, Giovanni, Ser Tommaso, Carlo, and Ser Francesco—Ser Tommaso was the only one with a solid financial base (D. V. Kent and F. W. Kent, *Neighbours and Neighbourhood in Renaissance Florence: The District of the Red Lion in the Fifteenth Century* [Locust Valley, N.Y., 1982], pp. 84, 90).

81. Manoscritti. vol. 89, fol. 14r. The entry, dated 1456, recounts the funeral debts first incurred in 1405 and still owed fifty years later.

82. E. Polidori Calamandrei, *Le vesti delle donne fiorentine nel Quattrocento* (repr. Rome, 1973), p. 63.

83. Carte Strozz. 2. vol. 9, fol. 23r.

84. Carte Strozz. 2. vol. 11, fols. 12v, 13v.

85. Provv. e Massai. Campioni. vols. 15, 18, 21, 24–27, 29, 30, 32, covering the period 1400–1429. For Agnolo da Uzzano's permit for his first wife, Lena, purchased in June 1390, see Provv. e Massai. Campioni. vol. 6, fol. 310r.

86. The tomb inscription is printed in Domenico Moreni, *Pompe funebri celebrate nell'imperiale e real basilica di San Lorenzo dal secolo XIII a tutto il regno mediceo* (Florence, 1827), p. 6. Medici's deathbed speech is reported in Manoscritti. vol. 817, fols. 37v–38v.

87. Carte Strozz. 2. vol. 16, fol. 7v; Carte Strozz. 2. vol. 9, fols. 104v, 122r.

88. Manoscritti. vol. 77, fols. 8v, 21v, 24v, 27r, 37v.

89. Manoscritti. vol. 82, fol. 35r/v.

90. Brucker, *Civic World*, pp. 348–52, 396, 400–406, quote at p. 396. On the creation of the Catasto commission, see David Herlihy and Christiane Klapisch-Zuber, *Tuscans and Their Families* (New Haven, Conn.; 1985), pp. 4–6.

91. Brucker, *Civic World*, pp. 403–6.

92. Provv. e Massai. Campioni. vol. 6, fol. 310r/v; Provv. e Massai. Campioni. vol. 26, fols. 9v, 15v.

93. Provv. e Massai. Campioni. vol. 27, fol. 3r; Provv. e Massai. Campioni. vol. 29, fol. 3v.

94. Conv. Sopp. 89. vol. 10, fols. 5r, 7r, 12v, 17r, 21v, 31v.

95. *Cronica di Buonaccorso Pitti*, ed. A. Bacchi della Lega (Bologna, 1905), p. 247n.

96. Brucker, *Civic World*, pp. 481–83.

97. For the procedure of communal allocations for funerals, see Martines, *Social World*, pp. 240–41; and Brucker, *Civic World*, p. 37n. These subsidies ranged from thirty to about fifty florins for leading figures, and from fifteen to twenty florins for lesser ones. Messer Cristofano Spini, identified by Brucker as one of five men at the apex of the regime between 1403 and 1414, was voted seventy-three florins. Maso degli Albizzi was allocated forty florins in 1417, Filippo Corsini up to thirty florins in 1421, Messer Giovanni Guicciardini sixty florins in 1427, and Giovanni de' Medici thirty florins in 1429.

98. *Statuta Communis Florentiae 1415*, 2: 380.

99. BNF. Conv. Sopp. C. 4. 895 describes Gianfigliazzi's funeral (fol. 114v), and Guadagni's (fol. 117r/v; quote at fol. 117v); *Istorie di Giovanni Cambi*, 20: 164–65, 167, offers similar descriptions of these events. For Gianfigliazzi's career, see Brucker, *Civic World*, pp. 249, 276–78, who cites Gianfigliazzi's renown as a knight (p. 278). Vieri Guadagni's political contributions are discussed by Luigi Passerini, *Genealogia e storia della famiglia Guadagni* (Florence, 1873), pp. 54–65.

100. For Petriboni's remarks, see BNF. Conv. Sopp. C. 4. 895, fol. 124r. Another description of Medici's funeral is given in *Istorie di Giovanni Cambi*, 20: 174. Despite the reported sum of 3,000 florins spent on the ceremonies, I have been unable to locate a record of a sumptuary license purchased for the event. However, the volume of communal accounts for 1429, where the licenses normally appear, does record the 30 florins, 4 soldi, for "spese fatte per honorare Ilgregio homo Giovanni di Bicci de Medici" (Provv. e Massai. Campioni. vol. 32, fol. 287v, dated July 4, 1429). It is also worth noting that, according to the descriptions cited earlier in this note, Medici's body was displayed uncovered on the bier, as was Matteo Castellani's, in violation of the 1415 sumptuary code.

101. Machiavelli's assessment of Giovanni is excerpted in Moreni, *Pompe funebri*, p. 7; see also Scipione Ammirato, *Istorie fiorentine*, 3 vols. (Florence, 1641–47), 3: 1047.

102. Carte Strozz. 2. vol. 10, fol. 59r. Matteo had served as consul of the silk guild on twenty-two occasions. His funeral cortege reportedly involved about 280 priests.

103. Brucker, *Civic World*, pp. 313–16.

104. Robert Wuthnow, *Meaning and Moral Order* (Berkeley, Calif., 1987).

105. Brucker, *Civic World*, p. 270. Vespasiano, *Memoirs*, p. 316, said of

Ridolfi that "though he had great influence in state affairs and might have done whatever he willed, he was like an ancient Roman in integrity—a poor man who lived on his own income." Guadagni's five sons and heirs listed combined net capital of 5,352 florins in 1427, which ranked them sixty-fourth in their quarter, San Giovanni (Martines, *Social World*, p. 370). Four of the five sons shared the household, which owed a debt of 300 florins for mourning clothes purchased for their father's funeral the previous year (Catasto. vol. 57, fols. 139r–142v, at fol. 142r).

106. Carte Strozz. 2. vol. 9, fol. 23r; G. Canestrini, "Vita di Bartolomeo Valori (il Vecchio)," *Archivio storico italiano* 4 (1843): 280n.

107. Vespasiano, *Memoirs*, pp. 247–50, who also remarks that Pandolfini "was always in favor of peace." The claim is borne out by Pandolfini's opposition to the war with Genoa (Brucker, *Civic World*, p. 352). A brief sketch of his life is given by Martines, *Social World*, pp. 313–14. For the tomb, see the preface to Agnolo Pandolfini, *Trattato del governo della famiglia* (Florence, 1734), pp. 10–11.

108. Najemy, *Corporatism*, pp. 13, 312–13; Richard C. Trexler, "A Widow's Asylum of the Renaissance: The Orbatello of Florence," in *Old Age in Preindustrial Society*, ed. Peter N. Stearns (New York, 1982), pp. 119–49.

109. F. W. Kent with Patricia Simons, "Renaissance Patronage: An Introductory Essay," in Kent and Simons, eds., *Patronage, Art, and Society*, pp. 15–16.

110. Carte Strozz. 2. vol. 9, fols. 6r, 23r; Petriboni's remarks are found in BNF. Conv. Sopp. C. 4. 895, fol. 114v.

111. Quoted in Dale Kent, *The Rise of the Medici: Faction in Florence, 1426–1434* (Oxford, 1978), p. 303, Kent's translation.

112. Klapisch-Zuber, *Women, Family, and Ritual*, pp. 283–309. Naming patterns differed from this practice, of course, in that names generally skipped one generation.

113. For the Medici, see Manoscritti. vol. 817, no. 3, fols. 37v–38v; for Capponi's remarks, see Brucker, *Civic World*, p. 316.

114. Vespasiano, *Memoirs*, p. 257.

115. BNF. Conv. Sopp. C. 4. 895, fols. 125v–126r; *Istorie di Giovanni Cambi*, 20: 176–77. A shorter account of the ceremony is given by Lorenzo Strozzi, who called it a "ceremonia rara e degna d'esser vista" (*Le vite degli uomini illustri della casa Strozzi*, ed. P. Stromboli [Florence, 1890], p. 27). Castellani listed net Catasto assets of 13,234 florins, ranking him eleventh in his quarter, Santa Croce (Martines, *Social World*, p. 365). Castellani generally maintained a conservative stance, with strong political connections to former magnate houses. After Matteo's death, the family's political fortunes began to wane. There was no representative of the house in the inner regime between 1429 and 1434, and contemporaries frequently named the Castellani as leaders of the Medici opposition in 1434. However, Leonardo Bruni married his son into the Castellani family (Kent, *Rise of the Medici*, pp. 137–38, 158, 161–63).

116. Letter of Giovanni de' Medici to Coscia's nephew Michele, dated

December 31, 1419, quoted and translated in R. W. Lightbown, *Donatello and Michelozzo: An Artistic Partnership and Its Patrons in the Early Renassiance*, 2 vols. (London, 1980), 1: 12, with full text of the letter in 2: 290–91.

117. For the tomb, see Lightbown, *Donatello and Michelozzo*, 1: 24–51; and Harriet Caplow, *Michelozzo*, 2 vols. (New York, 1977), 1: 98–140, which focuses on Michelozzo's involvement in executing the tomb. Sarah Blake McHam examines the political circumstances surrounding the tomb's creation and design in "Donatello's Tomb of Pope John XXIII," in *Life and Death in Fifteenth-Century Florence*, ed. Marcel Tetel, Ronald G. Witt, and Rona Goffen (Durham, N.C., 1989), pp. 146–73. My thanks to Professor McHam for allowing me to consult the typescript before publication.

118. Peter Burke, *The Historical Anthropology of Early Modern Italy* (Cambridge, 1987), p. 168.

119. For biographical material in addition to that contained in the works cited above, see Eustace J. Kitts, *In the Days of the Councils: A Sketch of the Life and Times of Baldassare Cossa* (London, 1908).

120. Lightbown, *Donatello and Michelozzo*, 1: 7; McHam, "Donatello's Tomb," p. 153n, quoting Bruni's *De temporibus suis*.

121. George Holmes, "How the Medici Became the Pope's Bankers," in *Florentine Studies: Politics and Society in Renaissance Florence*, ed. Nicolai Rubinstein (Evanston, Ill., 1968), pp. 357–80, esp. 362–63, 375–76. Coscia asked Giovanni de' Medici to provide the ransom, equivalent to 3,500 cameral florins. Medici quickly responded, probably by drawing on funds Coscia had left on deposit, then transacted the exchange with Niccolò da Uzzano's assistance and dispatched the money through his agent Bartolomeo de' Bardi via the Venetian branch of the Medici bank.

122. On the intellectual ties between Florence and Coscia's papacy, see George Holmes, *The Florentine Enlightenment, 1400–50* (New York, 1969), pp. 59–61. Bruni's relations with Coscia are discussed in Holmes, "How the Medici," pp. 373–74; and in Griffiths, Hankins, and Thompson, eds., *Humanism of Bruni*, pp. 33–36. Poggio referred to Coscia's generosity in his funeral oration for Bruni ("Oratio in funere Leonardi Aretini," in *Leonardi Bruni Arretini Epistolarum Libri VIII*, ed. L. Mehus, 2 vols. (Florence, 1741), 1: cxx–cxxi).

123. The Signoria appointed four men to prepare the celebration for Martin's entry. Martin was met at Porta San Gallo by all the communal magistrates and important citizens dressed in their best garments with olive garlands on their heads. Heading the procession were one hundred youths dressed in communal livery, each carrying a large torch (BNF. Conv. Sopp. C. 4. 895, fols. 98v–100v; *Istorie di Giovanni Cambi*, 20: 140–43). See Conv. Sopp. 89. vol. 46, fol. 20r, for Santa Trinità's payment for the banquet celebrating Martin's entry.

124. Giuseppi Conti, *Fatti e aneddoti di storia fiorentina, secoli XIII–XVIII* (Florence, 1902), pp. 143–50.

125. Brucker, *Civic World*, pp. 422–23; and Peter Partner, "Florence and the Papacy in the Earlier Fifteenth Century," in Rubinstein, ed., *Florentine*

Studies, pp. 381–402, esp. 389–90. Partner also points out (p. 388) that the Florentines were not always entirely faithful to John XXIII but equivocated in their attitude toward him on occasion: when he arrived at the city while fleeing from Ladislaus in June 1413, the city refused to admit him.

126. Canestrini, "Vita di Bartolomeo Valori," pp. 429–38; Lightbown, *Donatello and Michelozzo*, 1: 7.

127. For Coscia's death, see BNF. Conv. Sopp. C. 4. 895, fol. 100v; "Diario di Bartolomeo del Corazza," pp. 264–65, which mistakenly gives the death date as November 23; and *Istorie di Giovanni Cambi*, 20: 147–48. Coscia's appreciation of the meaning of his death for Martin's security is related in *Le croniche di Giovanni Sercambi, Lucchese*, ed. Salvatore Bongi, 3 vols. (Rome, 1892), 3: 248–49.

128. Coscia's will is printed in Canestrini, "Vita di Bartolomeo Valori," pp. 292–96. The will is described in part by Petriboni in BNF. Conv. Sopp. 4. 895, fols. 100v–101r; and discussed by Lightbown, *Donatello and Michelozzo*, 1: 8–10.

129. BNF. Conv. Sopp. C. 4. 895, fol. 100v. Lightbown, *Donatello and Michelozzo*, 1:14–16, 76, 79–80, 83–84, discusses the correspondence between Giovanni de' Medici and Coscia's nephews regarding the estate, and compares Coscia's obsequies with the funeral plans projected by other cardinals in their testaments. McHam, "Donatello's Tomb," pp. 156–57, argues that Giovanni de' Medici was the central figure in securing the tomb's favorable location in the Baptistry, and that the tomb represents a disguised strategem for Medici self-promotion.

130. Provvisioni. vol. 109, fol. 209r/v, dated December 27, 1419. Lightbown, *Donatello and Michelozzo*, prints both the original communal provision (2: 289–90) and a translation (1: 12–13).

131. On Coscia's insufficient estate, see Lightbown, *Donatello and Michelozzo*, 1: 14–16. For the relative simplicity of fourteenth-century papal funerals compared to those of the fifteenth and sixteenth centuries, see M.-E. Déprez, "Les funérailles de Clement VI et d'Innocent VI d'après les comptes de la cour pontificale," *Mélanges d'archéologie et d'histoire de l'Ecole française de Rome* 20 (1900): 235–50, esp. p. 236.

132. Déprez, "Funérailles"; John W. O'Malley, *Praise and Blame in Renaissance Rome* (Durham, N.C., 1979), p. 11. The concern with following ceremonial formulas is apparent in the funeral of Sixtus IV (d. 1484), overseen by Johannes Burchard, papal master of ceremonies. The ceremony is described in *Il diario di Gaspare Pontani*, in *Rerum Italicarum Scriptores*, ed. S. Lapi, n.s., 34 vols. (Città di Castello, 1900–17), vol. 3, pt. 2, pp. 37–41.

133. "Diario di Bartolomeo del Corazza," pp. 264–65. Details of Coscia's ceremonial dress, which are portrayed on his tomb effigy, are discussed by Lightbown, *Donatello and Michelozzo*, 1: 44–46.

134. The Ordo Romanus compiled in the late fourteenth century by Pierre Ameilh stipulated that cardinals lie in state for nine days. (Lightbown, *Donatello and Michelozzo*, 1: 81). In practice, public exposure of the body showed considerable variation, especially in papal funerals. The body of Innocent

VI (d. 1362) was exposed for only two days before his obsequies began, and that of Sixtus IV (d. 1484) only five days, from August 12 to August 17 (Déprez, "Funérailles," p. 241; *Diario di Gaspare Pontani*, pp. 37–39).

135. Lightbown, *Donatello and Michelozzo*, 1: 44, argues that a death mask was probably made in preparation for the tomb. The body of Clement VI was not embalmed after his death in 1352 but was simply placed in the cold to avoid putrefaction, while the corpse of Sixtus IV was washed and the orifices stopped up (Déprez, "Funérailles," p. 236; Lightbown, *Donatello and Michelozzo*, 1: 44). "Diario di Bartolomeo del Corazza," p. 282, reports that when news of Martin's death reached the city, "cominciorono a sonare i doppi nelle chiese per l'anima sua e sonorono nove sere, ogni sera nove doppi per chiesa; non compierono sonare detti novi di." Similarly, Francesco Giovanni noted that when news of the death of Nicholas V reached Florence in 1455, "secondo il consueto sonorono la sera tutte le campane" (Carte Strozz. 2. vol. 16 bis, fol. 20r). For the importance of bell ringing in early modern funeral rites, see Clare Gittings, *Death, Burial, and the Individual in Early Modern England* (London, 1984), pp. 133–35.

136. "Diario di Bartolomeo del Corazza," pp. 266–67; BNF. Conv. Sopp. C. 4. 895, fols. 100v–101r; Lightbown, *Donatello and Michelozzo*, 1: 13.

137. The description of the ceremony above, and in the next three paragraphs, is based on BNF. Conv. Sopp. C. 4. 895, fol. 100v.

138. "Diario di Bartolomeo del Corazza," p. 251.

139. The enabling legislation, passed on December 27 by 157 votes to 34 and ratified the following day, is printed in Lightbown, *Donatello and Michelozzo*, 1: 12–13, Lightbown's translation. For the Parte Guelfa's contribution see BNF. Conv. Sopp. C. 4. 895, fol. 100v.

140. Quoted and translated in Lightbown, *Donatello and Michelozzo*, 1: 14.

141. McHam, "Donatello's Tomb," p. 155n.

142. Ammirato, *Istorie*, 2: 985, Lightbown, *Donatello and Michelozzo*, 1: 19–20; McHam, "Donatello's Tomb," p. 159; Holmes, "How the Medici," p. 376.

143. Déprez, "Funérailles," pp. 238–39.

144. McManamon, *Funeral Oratory*, p. 24.

145. *Istorie di Giovanni Cambi*, 20: 172, gives the date of Bruni's election to the office of chancellor as November 27, 1427. However, according to Marzi, *Cancelleria*, p. 190, this was only a provisional election and was followed by another definitive election in December.

146. The political dimensions of the oration are discussed by Baron, *Crisis*, pp. 412–18; Griffiths, Hankins, and Thompson, eds., *Humanism of Bruni*, pp. 37–38; and McManamon, *Funeral Oratory*, pp. 95–97.

147. Quoted in Baron, *Crisis*, p. 414, Baron's translation.

148. I am citing the translation given by Griffiths, Hankins, and Thompson, eds., *Humanism of Bruni*, pp. 121–27, at p. 122. The full Latin text is printed in E. Baluze, comp., *Miscellaneorum . . . Hoc Est, Collectio Veterum Monumentorum*, 7 vols. (Paris, 1690), 3: 226–48.

149. McManamon, *Funeral Oratory*, p. 24. Paul O. Kristeller states that

the diffusion of humanist orations was dependent "on the public success of the oration, which was indeed regarded by the audience as a public entertainment like a theater performance or a concert, as well as on the fame of the speaker" ("The Scholar and His Public in the Late Middle Ages and the Renaissance," in *Medieval Aspects of Renaissance Learning*, ed. Edward Mahoney [Durham, N.C., 1974], pp. 1–25, quote at p. 11).

150. McManamon, *Funeral Oratory*, pp. 107–8.

151. Griffiths, Hankins, and Thompson, eds., *Humanism of Bruni*, pp. 121–22, Griffiths's translation. MacCormack, *Art and Ceremony*, examines similar connections between oratory and ceremony in the late antique world.

152. The texts of Poggio's orations for both Niccoli and Lorenzo de' Medici are printed in Poggius Bracciolini, *Opera Omnia*, ed. Riccardo Fubini, 4 vols. (Turin, 1964), 1: 270–77, 278–86. See also McManamon, *Funeral Oratory*, pp. 118, for Pacini's oration for Lorenzo, which was not recited at the funeral; and Alison M. Brown, "The Humanist Portrait of Cosimo de' Medici, Pater Patriae," *Journal of the Warburg and Courtauld Institutes* 24 (1961): 186–221, esp. p. 190.

153. McManamon, *Funeral Oratory*, p. 5.

154. Bruni claimed in his *Laudatio*, for example, that "so excellent and caring is the government of this city under these magistracies that one may say that there was never a household with better discipline under a watchful *paterfamilias*"; he echoed similar sentiments about the city as a "multitude of households" in his notes to Aristotle's *Economics* (Griffiths, Hankins, and Thompson, eds., *Humanism of Bruni*, pp. 120, 307, Griffiths's translation).

155. See McManamon, *Funeral Oratory*, for a finding list of orations (pp. 249–92), and an analysis of several of these orations (pp. 113–14).

156. This passage is taken from a consolatory letter of 1433 from Bruni to Nicola di Vieri de' Medici, printed in Griffiths, Hankins, and Thompson, eds., *Humanism of Bruni*, pp. 337–39, quote at p. 337, Hankins's translation.

157. Ibid., p. 338, Hankins's translation.

158. Susannah K. Foster, *The Ties That Bind: Kinship Association and Marriage in the Alberti Family, 1378–1428* (Ann Arbor, Mich.: University Microfilms, 1985).

159. Griffiths, Hankins, and Thompson, eds., *Humanism of Bruni*, p. 338, Hankins's translation.

160. Pier Giorgio Ricci, "Una consolatoria inedita del Marsuppini," *Rinascità* 3 (1940): 363–433; Brown, "Humanist Portrait," pp. 189–90.

Chapter 5: Spectacle at Mid-Century

1. For the procedures by which the Medici achieved and retained political control, see Dale Kent, *The Rise of the Medici: Faction in Florence, 1426–1434* (Oxford, 1978); Nicolai Rubinstein, *The Government of Florence under the Medici, 1434 to 1494* (Oxford, 1966); Anthony Molho, "Cosimo de' Medici: Pater Patriae or Padrino?" *Stanford Italian Review* 1 (1979): 5–33. Cosimo's character

is ably explored by Alison Brown, "The Humanist Portrait of Cosimo de' Medici, Pater Patriae," *Journal of the Warburg and Courtauld Institutes* 24 (1961): 186–221; and by Curt Gutkind, *Cosimo de' Medici il Vecchio* (Florence, 1940).

2. For the Magi ceremonies, see Rab Hatfield, "The Compagnia de' Magi," *Journal of the Warburg and Courtauld Institutes* 33 (1970): 107–61. F. W. Kent discusses the Medici-Rucellai wedding in "The Making of a Renaissance Patron of the Arts," in *Giovanni Rucellai ed il suo Zibaldone, II: A Florentine Patrician and his Palace* (London, 1981), pp. 9–95, at pp. 67–68, quote at p. 68 (my translation). Communal outlays for ceremonies grew commensurately. For example, in June 1442 the commune paid 364 florins for the *palio* used in the civic feast of San Giovanni, in comparison to 247 florins spent in 1394 (Camera del Comune. Uscite di Paghe, vol. 72, fol. 2r; Provv. e Massai. Campioni. vol. 44, fol. 105v).

3. A. D. Fraser Jenkins, "Cosimo de' Medici's Patronage of Architecture and the Theory of Magnificence," *Journal of the Warburg and Courtauld Institutes* 33 (1970): 162–70, at p. 162.

4. For the fifteenth-century building boom, see Richard A. Goldthwaite, "The Florentine Palace as Domestic Architecture," *American Historical Review* 77 (1972): 977–1012; and idem, *The Building of Renaissance Florence* (Baltimore, 1980).

5. Both Molho, "Cosimo de' Medici"; and Samuel K. Cohn, Jr., *The Laboring Classes in Renaissance Florence* (New York, 1980), highlight class tensions under Medici rule.

6. When Eugenius IV consecrated the cathedral in March 1436, for example, the commune constructed for the occasion an elegant arcade of fine tapestries, armorial hangings, and leaf-covered colonnades stretching from Santa Maria Novella to the cathedral; under this arcade walked thirty-seven bishops and archbishops, seven cardinals, Eugenius himself, assorted ambassadors, and the Florentine priors (Carte Strozz. 2. vol. 16, fol. 12r; Giuseppe Conti, *Fatti e aneddoti di storia fiorentina, secoli XIII–XVIII* [Florence, 1902], pp. 173–77).

7. For the funeral of the cardinal of San Marcello, the Sienese jurist and canonist Antonio Casini, see "Diario fiorentino di Bartolomeo di Michele del Corazza, 1405–1438," *Archivio storico italiano*, ser. 5, 13–14 (1894): 295. A brief biography of Casini is given by Vespasiano da Bisticci, *The Vespasiano Memoirs: Lives of Illustrious Men of the XVth Century*, trans. William George and Emily Waters (London, 1926), p. 154. The ceremonies surrounding the 1438 proclamation of unity between the Greek and Latin churches are described in Conti, *Fatti e aneddoti*, pp. 179–89. Among the many ecclesiastical ceremonies in the late 1430s were a number of obsequies for foreign or visiting clerics, some of which were quite impressive. Most of the obsequies took place in Santa Maria Novella, which traditionally housed papal entourages. From 1435 to 1439, the church provided the funeral locale and burial sites for the papal secretaries Bernardo Labrua and Dionisio Dohene (both d. 1435); the Dominican Giovanni Casanova, cardinal of San Sisto, and one of his chaplains (both d. 1436); and the patriarch of Constantinople (d. 1439)

(Stefano Orlandi, *Necrologia di S. Maria Novella*, 2 vols. [Florence, 1955], 2: 213, 571–73, 575).

8. Francesco di Giovanni's description of the processions are in Carte Strozz. 2. vol. 16 bis, fols. 17r, 21r. The obsequies for James, cardinal of Portugal, cost his estate 368 cameral florins, not including the chapel in San Miniato designed by Antonio Rossellino (BNF. Conv. Sopp. C. 4. 895, fol. 184r; Mercanzia. vol. 14150, fol. 16r; and F. Hartt, G. Corti, and C. Kennedy, *The Chapel of the Cardinal of Portugal* [Philadelphia, 1964], p. 42).

9. Carte Strozz. 3. vol. 91, fol. 90v; BNF. Conv. Sopp. C. 4. 895, fol. 183r; *Istorie di Giovanni Cambi, cittadino fiorentino*, in *Delizie degli eruditi toscani*, ed. P. Ildefonso di San Luigi, 24 vols. (Florence, 1770–89), vols. 20–23, at 20: 374. According to canonization proceedings in 1522, Antoninus's corpse showed no spots or signs of decay, or evidence of stiffening, after being displayed for eight days. During this time there was a tremendous outpouring of public affection, and contact with his body worked several miracles among the crowds flocking to see him (*Acta Sanctorum*, ed. Johannes Bollandus et al., 67 vols. [Paris, 1863–1919], entry for May 2). A death mask was taken only after the public display of the body, which may account for the distorted features on the terra-cotta busts employing the mask (Jane Schuyler, *Florentine Busts* [New York, 1976], pp. 142–45).

10. Mercanzia. vol. 14150, fols. 11v, 12v, 14r/v; Miscellanea Repubblicana. Busta 4, no. 130, dated October 29, 1460; Deliberazioni Signori e Collegi. Speciale Autorità. vol. 34, fols. 131v–132v. For communal protocol, see Richard C. Trexler, *The Libro Cerimoniale of the Florentine Republic* (Geneva, 1978).

11. Randolph Starn and Loren Partridge, "Representing War in the Renaissance: The Shield of Paolo Uccello," *Representations* 5 (1984): 33–65, at p. 57.

12. Francesco di Tommaso Giovanni made lengthy preliminary notes about major public events, from which he later reconstructed detailed and deceptively neat descriptions. See, for example, the paired descriptions of the entry of Frederick III in 1452 (Carte Strozz. 2. vol. 16 bis, fol. 14r and carte sciolte no. 15) and of the Marsuppini funeral in 1453 (Carte Strozz. 2. vol. 16 bis, fol. 16v and carte sciolte no. 16). I borrow the notion of "thinking with things" from Robert Darnton, *The Great Cat Massacre* (New York, 1984), who argues that ordinary people do not develop logical propositions about the world around them; rather, "they think with things, or with anything else that their culture makes available to them, such as stories or ceremonies" (p. 4).

13. Cf. Richard C. Trexler, *Public Life in Renaissance Florence* (New York, 1980), esp. p. 40.

14. Gordon Griffiths, "The Political Significance of Uccello's *Battle of San Romano*," *Journal of the Warburg and Courtauld Institutes* 41 (1978): 313–16; C. C. Bayley, *War and Society in Renaissance Florence* (Toronto, 1961), p. 120. Cosimo's cousin Averardo died six weeks after their return and was given

a respectable state funeral (Kent, *Rise of the Medici*, p. 315; *Istorie di Giovanni Cambi*, 20: 202).

15. Unless otherwise noted, the following discussion of the funeral is based on BNF. Conv. Sopp. C. 4. 895, fol. 135r/v; *Croniche di Giovanni di Jacopo Morelli*, in Ildefonso di San Luigi, ed., *Delizie*, 19: 1–164, at 129–32; *Istorie di Giovanni Cambi*, 20: 203. Griffiths, "Political Significance," mistakenly reports the date of the ceremony as March 20.

16. For Averardo's remarks, see Starn and Partridge, "Representing War," p. 57, their translation. Tolentino's funeral expenses, plus huge payments for military expenses to Tolentino's sons Cristofano, Giovanni, and Baldovini, are found in Provv. e Massai. Campioni. vol. 38, fols. 90v, 91r, 92r.

17. Uccello's depiction of the battle of San Romano marked a similar disintegration of chivalric symbolism (Starn and Partridge, "Representing War," p. 55). For the knighting of Davanzati, see Carte Strozz. 2. vol. 16, fol. 12r.

18. Bruni's speech is quoted and translated in Griffiths, "Political Significance," p. 314; Griffiths also discusses Palmieri's evaluation of Tolentino's abilities.

19. Aspects of these arguments are discussed by Bayley, *War and Society*, pp. 196–218; Starn and Partridge, "Representing War"; Griffiths, "Political Significance"; and Eve Borsook, "L' 'Hawkwood' d'Uccello et la *Vie de Fabius Maximus* de Plutarque," *Revue de l'art* 55 (1982): 44–51.

20. Starn and Partridge, "Representing War."

21. Borsook, "L' 'Hawkwood,' " p. 49.

22. Sarah Blake McHam, "Donatello's Tomb of Pope John XXIII," in *Life and Death in Fifteenth-Century Florence*, ed. Marcel Tetel, Ronald G. Witt, and Rona Goffen (Durham, N.C., 1989), p. 172. Bruni had specified, in his will made five years before his death, that if he died in the city he wanted to be buried in Santa Croce. The tomb site was to be appropriate to his rank, but the tomb itself should be simple and of plain marble (Vito R. Giustiniani, "Il testamento di Leonardo Bruni," *Rinascimento*, n.s., 4 (1964): 259–64, at pp. 260–61. For the Marsuppini tomb, see John Pope-Hennessy, *Italian Renaissance Sculpture*, 2 vols. (London, 1971), 2: 37–38.

23. On Bruni's career and character, see Ronald G. Witt, *Hercules at the Crossroads: The Life, Works, and Thought of Coluccio Salutati* (Durham, N.C., 1983), p. 116; Demetrio Marzi, *La cancelleria della repubblica fiorentina* (Rocca San Casciano, 1910), p. 192; Gordon Griffiths, James Hankins, and David Thompson, eds., *The Humanism of Leonardo Bruni: Selected Texts* (Binghamton, N.Y., 1987), pp. 37–43; Lauro Martines, *The Social World of the Florentine Humanists, 1390–1460* (Princeton, N.J., 1963), pp. 117–23, 254–56. Vespasiano's remark is quoted and translated in Griffiths, Hankins, and Thompson, eds., *Humanism of Bruni*, p. 42.

24. Martines, *Social World*, p. 256.

25. Naldus Naldius, quoted and translated in Griffiths, Hankins, and Thompson, eds., *Humanism of Bruni*, p. 44.

26. The quotes are taken from ibid. For other accounts of the ceremony,

see *Ricordi storici di Filippo di Cino Rinuccini dal 1282 al 1460 colla continuazione di Alamanno e Neri suoi figli fino al 1506*, ed. G. Aiazzi (Florence, 1840), p. lxxiii; *Istorie di Giovanni Cambi*, 20: 245; BNF. Conv. Sopp. C. 4. 895, fol. 146r; Martines, *Social World*, pp. 241–42.

27. Giannozzo Manetti, "Oratio Funebris in Solemni Leonardi Arretini Historici, Oratoris, ac Poetae Laureatione," in *Leonardi Bruni Arretini Epistolarum Libri VIII*, ed. L. Mehus, 2 vols., (Florence, 1741), 1: lxxxix–cxiv, at pp. civ–cxiv; John J. McManamon, *Funeral Oratory and the Cultural Ideals of Italian Humanism* (Chapel Hill, N.C., 1989), pp. 57–58, 130.

28. Griffiths, Hankins, and Thompson, eds., *Humanism of Bruni*, p. 44, quoting Naldius, Griffiths's translation.

29. McManamon, *Funeral Oratory*, p. 29.

30. This conviction that there was harmony between learning and government service was common among humanist orators of the earlier Renaissance (ibid., p. 120).

31. Vespasiano's remarks are quoted in Marzi, *Cancelleria*, pp. 197–98n.

32. McManamon, *Funeral Oratory*, pp. 121–22; Griffiths, Hankins, and Thompson, eds., *Humanism of Bruni*, p. 43.

33. *Croniche di Giovanni di Jacopo Morelli*, 19: 131–32; on soldiers' laments, see Ernesto de Martino, *Morte e pianto rituale* (repr., Turin 1977), pp. 44–45.

34. The inscription is as follows: "Historia luget, eloquentia muta est, ferturque Musas tum Graecas tum Latinas lacrimas tenere non potuisse" ("History is in mourning and eloquence is dumb, and it is said that the Muses, Greek and Latin alike, cannot restrain their tears"); it is quoted and translated in Pope-Hennessy, *Italian Renaissance Sculpture*, 2: 36–37.

35. Poggio gave Salutati a greater role in the revival of letters in his oration for Niccolò Niccoli. Even here, however, he assigned much credit to Niccoli for bringing Greek letters back to Italy because Niccoli footed the bills (McManamon, *Funeral Oratory*, pp. 128–31). Poggio praised Bruni in his "Oratio Funebris in Obitu Leonardi Arretini," in *Leonardi Bruni Epistolarum*, 1: cxv–cxxvi. According to McManamon, *Funeral Oratory*, p. 258, this oration was written in Rome in 1444, and the final redaction was apparently completed at Florence, not before 1453.

36. Griffiths, Hankins, and Thompson, eds., *Humanism of Bruni*, p. 46.

37. Palmieri praised Marsuppini for using his learning to help knit society together, and for influencing others toward moral living and good citizenship (McManamon, *Funeral Oratory*, p. 58).

38. BNF. Conv. Sopp. C. 4. 895, fol. 163r/v.

39. Camera del Comune. Camera dell'Arme. no. 51. The supervising officials, listed by quarter inside the front cover, were Francesco di Niccolò Benino, Lorenzo di Gino Capponi, Bernardo di Messer Lorenzo Ridolfi, and Tommaso di Lorenzo Soderini (from Santo Spirito); Alamanno di Messer Jacopo Salviati, Bernardo di Bartolomeo Gherardi, Lorenzo di Antonio Spinelli, the stationer (*cartolaio*) Pero di Dino, and Giovanni del Zacherro di Jacopo (from Santa Croce); Piero di Cardinale Rucellai, Francesco di Jacopo

Ventura, Domenico di Tano Petrucci, and Giovanni Bartoli, who replaced Roberto di Antonio de' Nobili (from Santa Maria Novella); and Niccolò d'Ugo Alessandri, Francesco di Nerone di Nigi, Piero di Cosimo de' Medici, and Niccolò di Marco Cerretani (from San Giovanni).

40. For contemporary descriptions of Marsuppini's funeral, see Carte Strozz. 2. vol. 16 bis, fol. 16v; BNF. Conv. Sopp. C. 4. 895, fol. 163r/v; *Ricordi storici di Filippo Rinuccini*, p. lxxix; *Istorie di Giovanni Cambi*, 20: 310–11. See also Martines, *Social World*, p. 242.

41. Camera del Comune. Camera dell'Arme. no. 51, fol. 101v. That the sum spent on Frederick's entry was larger than that spent on Marsuppini's funeral should not be surprising, given the far greater number of participants in the former case, their lengthy stay, and the conventions governing the respective occasions. The ceremonial entry is described by Francesco di Tommaso Giovanni, in Carte Strozz. 2. vol. 16 bis, fol. 14r/v. Trexler's claim that the Florentine master of ceremonies Francesco Filarete saw this event as the beginning of the commune's history appears to be unfounded (Trexler, *Libro Cerimoniale*, pp. 57–58, 71–74).

42. Libri del Giglio. vol. 54, fol. 67r; Libri del Giglio. vol. 56, fol. 70r; Libri del Giglio. vol. 58, fol. 80r. The low number of sumptuary permits for the mid-Quattrocento is no doubt also due to poor record keeping, to gaps in the records, and almost certainly to violations.

43. NA. S 20 (1462–70), fol. 175r/v. For Sacchetti's remark, see Gene Brucker, *Renaissance Florence* (Berkeley, Calif., 1969), p. 259.

44. For descriptions of the funeral, see BNF. Conv. Sopp. C. 4. 895, fol. 143r; Pier Nolasco Cianfogni, *Memorie istoriche dell'ambrosiana real basilica di San Lorenzo di Firenze* (Florence, 1804), p. 195; and Domenico Moreni, *Continuazione delle memorie istoriche dell'ambrosiana imperial basilica di San Lorenzo di Firenze*, 2 vols. (Florence, 1816), 1: 41–42. Martines, *Social World*, p. 241, notes that the commune allocated thirty florins for the funeral. Poggio's eulogy for Lorenzo is printed in Poggius Bracciolini, *Opera Omnia*, ed. Riccardo Fubini, 4 vols. (Turin, 1964–69), 1: 278–86.

45. Mercanzia. vol. 14150, fol. 14v.

46. Federighi's obsequies are recorded in Conv. Sopp. 88. vol. 23, fol. 15v. For the tomb by Luca della Robbia for San Pancrazio, see Hannelore Glasser, "The Litigation concerning Luca della Robbia's Federighi Tomb," *Mitteilungen des Kunsthistorischen Institutes in Florenz* 14 (1969): 1–32. Receipts for Orlando de' Medici's funeral are in Conv. Sopp. 119. vol. 689, fols. 76v, 77r, 78v. For Rucellai's architectural involvement with San Pancrazio, see Marco Dezzi Bardeschi, "Il complesso monumentale di S. Pancrazio a Firenze ed il suo restauro," *Quaderni dell'Istituto di storia dell'architettura*, ser. 13, fasc. 73–78 (1966): 1–66, at pp. 15–26. Rucellai died on October 28, 1481; his 1465 testamentary instructions regarding his funeral are printed in Kent, "Making of a Patron," p. 94.

47. Goldthwaite, *Building of Renaissance Florence*; Samuel K. Cohn, Jr., *Death and Property in Siena, 1205–1800: Strategies for the Afterlife* (Baltimore, 1988), esp. p. 97; Gene Brucker, *The Civic World of Early Renaissance Florence* (Prince-

ton, N.J., 1977); Martines, *Social World*; Eugenio Garin, *L'Umanesimo italiano: Filosofia e vita civile nel Rinascimento* (Bari, 1964). On the rise of the Ginori and their building activities, see F. W. Kent, *Household and Lineage in Renaissance Florence: The Family Life of the Capponi, Ginori, and Rucellai* (Princeton, N.J., 1977), esp. pp. 102–4, 178–79, 255–56; and Piero Ginori Conti, *La basilica di San Lorenzo di Firenze e la famiglia Ginori* (Florence, 1940), esp. pp. 47–52, 199–200. The Bonvanni record is in Catasto. vol. 924, pt. 2, fol. 552r.

48. Kent, "Making of a Patron," esp. pp. 12–13, 22–31.

49. Conv. Sopp. 89. vol. 75, fol. 28v.

50. Conv. Sopp. 88. vol. 23, fols. 54v, 131v. Giuliano di Particino's activities in his parish and ward of the Red Lion are discussed by D. V. Kent and F. W. Kent, *Neighbours and Neighbourhood in Renaissance Florence: The District of the Red Lion in the Fifteenth Century* (Locust Valley, N.Y., 1982), pp. 79–80, 120, 132.

51. Conv. Sopp. 119. vol. 689, fol. 35r.

52. This survey is drawn from Biblioteca Laurenziana, Florence. Archivio della Parrocchia di San Lorenzo. vol. 2214, quotation on fol. 1r, dated 1463. There is an insert (fols. 20r–23r), probably dating from the eighteenth century, that lists tomb-owning families who had died out or who were buried elsewhere.

53. Conv. Sopp. 88. vol. 23, fols. 56v, 58r. Although the cemetery opened in 1456, burials began to become more frequent there only in the early 1460s (Dezzi Bardeschi, "Complesso di S. Pancrazio," p. 15).

54. Carte Strozz. 2. vol. 16 bis, fols. 5r, 13r, 23r.

55. The next three paragraphs are based on Carte Strozz. 2. vol. 16 bis, fol. 11r. Francesco's use of language is quite idiomatic, and his system of abbreviations borders on the unique. I have taken some liberties in translating the passage to make it more readable in English. The original reads: "Ricordo come a dio piaque che martedì a dì 14 di luglo 1450 cioè la notte dinanzi tralle 6 et 7 hore La Nanna mia figluola et donna fu di Giovanni di Filippo Arrigucci. Passassi di questa vita, et pocho prima cioè a hore 6 di notte passò Filippo suo figluolo ch'era il magiore di 3 che aveva. Et lei et lui ebbono il segno, lei nella coscia et lui sotto il braccio. Erano tutti alloro luogo da montughi allato a Santa Maria. Et cominciò loro la febre el venerdì dinanzi a dì X di detto; poi la domenica s'avidono del segno. Di poi detto Giovanni Arigucci lunedì mattina a dì 13 venna a noi in Pian di Ripoli col segno suo et prima l'aveva mostro a maestro Girolamo medico et lui disse essere morbato. Et allora avengha ch'io fussi malato di scesa, la Mea mia donna andò con lui a Montughi dove era solo una loro schiava et balia di Bernardo loro figluolo in fasce et con assai disordine di casa d'ogni provedimento. Et trovolla che certe lavoratori la confortavano perchè ebbe la mattina grande isfinimento per non aversi confortata del cibo. Ancora mandai Tomaso mio figluolo et Pippo mio fattore a procurare per la cura di lei et Tomaso vi mandò da Firenze 2 donne, cioè Mona Simona balia di Giovanbatista et mona Katerina, che torna in casa con lei, la quale parve che Idio

mandassi per subventione di quelli 2 infermi et per aiuto della mona. Inperò che il dì medesimo Giovanni levò glaltri 2 fanciulli et lui et la schiava et vennono a Firenze et solo la mona con queste 2 donne rimasono con glinfermi. Et allei convenne non andandovi per vigitarle, racomandare l'anima alla figluola et da una camera all'altra tutta quella notte non finire a procurare detti infermi et quando segnarono l'uno poi l'altro per non esservi candele benedette davanzo. dipoi avestire e governare e corpi morti. E così il martedì mattina procurare per fare lesequia loro. Avengha che Giovanni vi mandò Francesco dello Scrinato e 4 doppieri e candele e una cassa dove misono lei et il fanciullo e sono nella chiesa di santo [ ] di montughi. A dio piacci avere avuto lanime. Adomandò assai volte il prete e i sacramenti e non si pote avere per non esservi chi andassi per lui di notte. Fatto lesequia alla isconsolata madre convenne ragovernare la masseritia di casa et serare la casa et vennero a Firenze." In the right margin: "La detta Nanna era confessata adì [ ] di gugno in Santo Spirito et al suo fine si confessò a Dio non avendo il prete così divotamente et con perfetto conoscimento sanza travaglo alchuno passò." The passage then continues: "Intesi di poi che a dì [ ] 1450 Giovanni fece arecare e loro corpi a Santa Maria Novella dove sono le loro sepolture. Non so se mai fe' farne uficio alchuno ma io feci piatanza di dire messe 5." These masses and the Gregorian series performed for Nanna at the Carmine are recorded in Carte Strozz. 2. vol. 16 bis, fol. 5r.

56. Kent, *Rise of the Medici*, pp. 181, 187; Rubinstein, *Government*, p. 45; P. Litta, *Famiglie celebri italiane*, 15 vols. (Turin, 1819–1902), dispensa 72, table 18.

57. Letter of Filippo Strozzi to Lorenzo Strozzi, dated August 26, 1459, three days after Matteo's death, in Alessandra Macinghi Strozzi, *Lettere di una gentildonna fiorentina del secolo XV ai figliuoli esuli*, ed. C. Guasti (Florence, 1877), pp. 190–91; for legal strictures on exiles' funerals, see pp. 140–41, 181.

58. Quoted in Mark Phillips, *The Memoir of Marco Parenti* (Princeton, N.J., 1987), p. 91, Phillips's translation.

59. *Motti e facezie del Piovano Arlotto*, ed. G. Folena (Milan, 1953), facezia no. 15.

60. Strozzi, *Lettere*, pp. 184–85.

61. Matteo's testament, dated August 22, 1459, is printed in ibid., pp. 191–93; for other pertinent correspondence, see pp. 181–82. Writing to Lorenzo on October 18, 1459, Filippo noted, "La spesa che ho fatta ne l'asequio di Matteo monta presso a 100 fiorini, con quello panno hanno auto a Firenze le nostre sirocchie, non vi mettendo niente de' mia vestimenti" (ibid., p. 215).

62. Manoscritti. vol. 85 (Dietisalvi Neroni, 1429–39), fols. 23v, 48r, 63v, 68r; Manoscritti. vol. 86. (Giovanni Venturi, 1439–41), fols. 4r–6v; Manoscritti. vol. 91. (Dietisalvi Neroni, 1457–64), fol. 140r; Libri di Commercio. vol. 13 (Antonio Segni, 1463–69), fol. 125r.

63. The statutes of April 28, 1449, are transcribed in Ronald E. Rainey, *Sumptuary Legislation in Renaissance Florence* (Ann Arbor, Mich.: University

Microfilms, 1985), pp. 766–72; for the statute of July 3, 1459, see E. Polidori Calamandrei, *Le vesti delle donne fiorentine nel Quattrocento* (repr. Rome, 1973), pp. 22–23.

64. "Giunto in Milano e volendo andare a visitare quel Signore, vestito di pagonazzo come era in commissione, perchè non pareva conveniente avere a vestire di nero per la morte di una donna, e intendeno come il Duca ne faceva pazzie, gli parve minore male vestire di nero" (Francesco Guicciardini, *Ricordi autobiografici e di famiglia*, in *Opere inedite*, ed. Giuseppe Canestrini, 10 vols. [Florence, 1857–67], 10: 40). For condolences paid to Francesco Sforza, see *Ricordi storici di Filippo Rinuccini*, p. xcviii.

65. Carte Strozz. 5. vol. 1749, fol. 31v; Carte Strozz. 2. vol. 17 bis, fols. 29r, 30r; Carte Strozz. 2. vol. 9, fol. 125r.

66. Carte Strozz. 2. vol. 16, fol. 25v.

67. Manoscritti. vol. 89, fol. 18r; Carte Strozz. 2. vol. 17 bis, fol. 43r.

68. See my article, "Remembering the Family: Women, Kin, and Commemorative Masses in Renaissance Florence," *Renaissance Quarterly* 42 (1989): 635–54.

69. Carte Strozz. 2. vol. 16 bis, fol. 15v. I am grateful to Dr. Elaine Rosenthal for helping to clarify these family relationships.

70. Manoscritti. vol. 89, fol. 18r.

71. Conv. Sopp. 78, vol. 313, no. 292.

72. Vespasiano, *Memoirs*, pp. 445–62; quotes at pp. 460–61, Waters's and George's translation; Strozzi, *Lettere*, p. xiv. For widows' customary mourning clothes, see Polidori Calamandrei, *Le vesti*, pp. 49–52.

73. Miscellanea Repubblicana. vol. 66, fols. 111v–112r, at fol. 111v, dated November 29, 1459.

74. Miscellanea Repubblicana. vol. 66, fols. 111v–112r, at fol. 111v, dated November 29, 1459. For the 1456 law, see Polidori Calamandrei, *Le vesti*, p. 64.

75. Diane Owen Hughes, "Sumptuary Law and Social Relations in Renaissance Italy," in *Disputes and Settlements: Law and Human Relations in the West*, ed. John Bossy (Cambridge, 1983), pp. 69–99, at pp. 89–90; Rainey, *Sumptuary Legislation*, pp. 545–46.

76. Hughes, "Sumptuary Law," pp. 86–87. Sanuti's oration is printed in L. Frati, *La vita privata a Bologna* (Bologna, 1928), pp. 251–62.

77. Comp. Relig. Sopp. Capitoli. vol. 606, fols. 14v, 18r, 22v, quote at fol. 30v.

78. Acquisti e Doni. vol. 293, unfoliated.

79. Conv. Sopp. 79. vol. 144. I plan to study this group as part of a larger study of Florentine nuns and nunneries currently under way.

80. Carte Strozz. 2. vol. 16 bis, fol. 16r; Acquisti e Doni. vol. 293, unfoliated.

Chapter 6: The Return of an Aristrocratic Ethos

1. See chapter 5, n. 42 and the corresponding text, for sumptuary permits

issued between 1457 and 1466. Vols. 60–63 of the Libri del Giglio, covering the period 1467–73, record no licenses sold during these years. Vol. 64 (1474) is missing; vols. 65–68 (1475–82) record no licenses but were kept very sketchily. Vol. 69 (1489–91, with some additions dated 1493) is also devoid of licenses, but more importantly reveals that changing communal accounting procedures make the systematic use of these permits unfeasible for the 1480s and 1490s. The series ends with vol. 73 (1503–11). However, I have located the record of the sumptuary permit bought in April 1475 for Matteo Palmieri by his heirs for twenty-five florins, in Deliberazioni Signori e Collegi. Speciale Autorità. vol. 34, fol. 153r.

2. Some of these developments are discussed by Maurizio Fagiolo dell'Arco and Silvia Carrandini, *L'Effimero barocco: Strutture della festa nella Roma del '600*, 2 vols. (Rome, 1977–78).

3. Nicolai Rubinstein, *The Government of Florence under the Medici, 1434 to 1494* (Oxford, 1966); Dale Kent, *The Rise of the Medici: Faction in Florence, 1426–1434* (Oxford, 1978); Alison Brown, "The Humanist Portrait of Cosimo dé Medici, Pater Patriae," *Journal of the Warburg and Courtauld Institutes* 24 (1961): 186–221. The remark about Cosimo is quoted and translated in Isabelle Hyman, "Fifteenth Century Florentine Studies" (Ph.D. diss., New York University, 1968), p. 92.

4. Niccolò Machiavelli, *Istoria fiorentina*, ed. M. Bonfantini (Florence, 1954), p. 880.

5. Quoted and translated in Hyman, "Florentine Studies," p. 92; Janet Ross, *Lives of the Early Medici* (London, 1910), pp. 67–68.

6. On Cosimo's last days, see Ivan Cloulas, *Lorenzo il Magnifico*, trans. Cesare Scarton (Rome, 1986), pp. 80–82. Alison Brown, *Bartolomeo Scala, 1430–1497, Chancellor of Florence* (Princeton, N.J., 1969), p. 40, states that Scala heard Cosimo's dying speech to Piero.

7. Mediceo Avanti il Principato (hereafter abbreviated as MAP). vol. 163, fols. 2r–12v. Extracts of Piero's *ricordi* concerning Cosimo's death and burial are published by Angelo Fabroni, *Magni Cosmi Medicei Vita*, 2 vols. (Pisa, 1789), 2: 253–57, quote at p. 254.

8. Bonsi's letter to Filippo Strozzi, dated September 15, 1464, is printed in Alessandra Macinghi Strozzi, *Lettere di una gentildonna fiorentina del secolo XV ai figliuoli esuli*, ed. C. Guasti (Florence, 1877), p. 327. Alamanno Rinuccini commented that Cosimo "volle esser seppellito, e cosi fu, sanza pompa o onoranza alcuna" (*Ricordi storici di Filippo di Cino Rinuccini dal 1282 al 1460 colla continuazione di Alamanno e Neri suoi figli fino al 1506*, ed. G. Aiazzi [Florence, 1840], p. xciv). These remarks have formed the basis of scholarly lore regarding the funeral: see, for example, Curt S. Gutkind, *Cosimo de' Medici, Pater Patriae* (Oxford, 1938), pp. 245–46. For Machiavelli's remarks, see Mark Phillips, *The Memoir of Marco Parenti* (Princeton, N.J., 1987), p. 8, Phillip's translation.

9. MAP. vol. 163, fols. 3r–4r.

10. MAP. vol. 163, fols. 3r–4r; Manoscritti. vol. 817, fols. 41v–42r.

11. MAP. vol. 163, fols. 3r–4r.

12. MAP. vol. 163, fols. 3r–4r. Each of Cosimo's male and female kin, and professional associates, received fourteen braccia of cloth, while the factors, stewards, serving women, and slaves received ten braccia each. On Scala's career and relationship with Cosimo, see Brown, *Bartolomeo Scala*, esp. pp. 22–41; Brown (p. 36) quotes and translates Scala's description of himself as a Medici servant. It was highly unusual to allocate money for servants' mourning clothes, except for the "honor guard" surrounding the bier in the later Trecento. Those outfitted were typically "tutti parenti," as were the ten persons clothed by the lawyer Virgilio Adriani for the funeral of his father Andrea in February 1464 (Carte Strozz. 2. vol. 21, fol. 3r).

13. On Cosimo's patronage, see Kent, *Rise of the Medici*; Anthony Molho, "Cosimo de' Medici: Pater Patriae or Padrino?" *Stanford Italian Review* 1 (1979): 5–33; F. W. Kent with Patricia Simons, "Renaissance Patronage: An Introductory Essay," in *Patronage, Art, and Society in Renaissance Italy*, ed. F. W. Kent and Patricia Simons (Oxford, 1987), pp. 1–21. *Cronaca di Lionardo di Lorenzo Morelli dal 1347 al 1520*, in *Delizie degli eruditi toscani*, ed. P. Ildefonso di San Luigi, 24 vols. (Florence, 1770–89), 19: 179, notes Cosimo's donations to poor girls and prisoners. For Piero's donations, see MAP. vol. 163, fols. 10v–12v.

14. MAP. vol. 163, fols. 4v–10r. In most cases, Piero did not specify the number of masses per commemorative office, which could range anywhere from twelve to thirty. However, since Piero wanted the office at San Lorenzo to have thirty masses, a very common request for the elite, I have used this figure to estimate the total for the 401 offices stipulated. In addition, Piero gave money to thirteen houses of religious women, presumably in exchange for their prayers for his father's soul.

15. The circle of Giovanni and his wife Ginevra deserves closer attention. A number of nuns and abbesses in various houses wrote to Giovanni requesting particular favors; for examples, see MAP. filza 6, nos. 532, 628, 720, 739, 745. For letters to Ginevra, see MAP. filza 6, nos. 236, 375, 421, 436, 456, 585, 736. I am currently preparing a study of women's patronage networks at five Benedictine convents, including Ginevra's involvement with the Murate and San Pier Maggiore.

16. Cosimo and his brother Lorenzo had placed 800 florins in the Monte to subsidize "un solennissimo anniversario" for their father. In addition to this yearly office, the chapter of San Lorenzo was required to celebrate an office for Giovanni every Monday, at which the priests sang the seven penitential psalms, and the deacon and the subdeacon helped celebrate the mass (a practice generally reserved for feast days). Following the office, the chapter assumed the processional cross and marched through the candlelit cloister (Domenico Moreni, *Continuazione delle memorie istoriche dell'ambrosiana imperial basilica di San Lorenzo di Firenze*, 2 vols. [Florence, 1816], 1: 27–28).

17. Giuseppe Richa, *Notizie storiche delle chiese fiorentine*, 10 vols. (Florence, 1754), 5: 30.

18. The phrase is from Marco Parenti (Phillips, *Memoir of Marco Parenti*, p. 8, Phillip's translation).

19. For Santa Verdiana, see Conv. Sopp. 260. vol. 217, fol. 80r; for examples of the correspondence between the Murate abbess and the Medici in the 1460s, see MAP. filza 10, no. 291; MAP. filza 17, no. 532; MAP. filza 20, no. 452.

20. MAP. vol. 163, fols. 14r–41v. Lorenzo and Giuliano's letter is printed in Lorenzo's de' Medici, *Lettere*, ed. Riccardo Fubini (Florence, 1977), 1: 11–12.

21. Pier Giorgio Ricci, "Una consolatoria inedita del Marsuppini," *Rinascità* 3 (1940): 363–433.

22. For Piera Berti's letter, see MAP. filza 6, no. 436, dated December 22, 1459, Siena. Ginevra's young son Cosimino died on November 18, 1458, not in 1461 as erroneously reported by Lorenzo in his *ricordi*. It is unclear why the letter was written after a year's delay. Dei's letter is excerpted in Acquisti e Doni. vol. 293, unfoliated.

23. Brown, "Humanist Portrait," p. 202n.

24. Ibid., pp. 202n, 211n; Castiglione's letter to Lorenzo and Giuliano is printed in *Reden und Briefe italienischer Humanisten*, ed. K. Müllner (Vienna, 1890), pp. 214–19.

25. Cosimo's body was moved to the new tomb in front of the main altar on October 22, 1467. On that occasion, the monks of the abbey of Fiesole and the friars of San Marco were on hand to help perform an elaborate office. Beneath the inscription referring to the public decree of Cosimo's title ("Cosmus Medices hic situs est Decreto publico Pater Patriae. Vixit annos LXXV. menses III. dies XX") was another inscription, ("Petrus Med. Patri faciundum curavit") referring to Piero's commission of the tomb (Domenico Moreni, *Pompe funebri celebrate nell'imperiale e real basilica di San Lorenzo dal secolo XIII a tutto il regno mediceo* [Florence, 1827], p. 13). For medals commemorating Cosimo, see Janet Cox-Rearick, *Dynasty and Destiny in Medici Art* (Princeton, N.J., 1984), p. 57.

26. The enabling legislation and decree appear in Fabroni, *Magni Cosmi Medicei*, 2: 257–62. The ten members of the citizens' committee entrusted with devising a fitting tribute were Luca Pitti, Bernardo Ridolfi, Bernardo Neri, Bernardo Giugni, Franco Sacchetti, Angelo Acciaiuoli, Giovanni Bartoli, Carlo Pandolfini, Dietisalvi Neroni, and Bartolomeo Puccini. Contemporaries discussed other projects for permanent memorials or monuments to Cosimo before deciding on the public decree of a title (Moreni, *Pompe funebri*, p. 13). For later eulogies of Cosimo, see John M. McManamon, *Funeral Oratory and the Cultural Ideals of Italian Humanism* (Chapel Hill, N.C., 1989), pp. 49–50.

27. Brown, "Humanist Portrait."

28. Kent with Simons, "Renaissance Patronage," esp. pp. 4, 6–8, 14–16. Much work remains to be done on women's patronage and on the use of maternal imagery and metaphors in political discourse. For an invocation to Ginevra Alessandri Medici as "magnifica et generosa madonna et come madre honoranda" by Caterina di Ugo Berti, see MAP. filza 6, no. 421, dated November 30, 1459, Siena.

29. Simon Price explores the kinship implications of the title in ancient

Rome in "From Noble Funerals to Divine Cult: The Consecration of Roman Emperors," in *Rituals of Royalty*, ed. David Cannadine and Simon Price (Cambridge, 1987), p. 64. For other useful discussions of the title, see McManamon, *Funeral Oratory*, pp. 106, 118-19; and Molho, "Cosimo de' Medici."

30. This passage is taken from Acciaiuoli's preface to several of Plutarch's *Lives*, quoted and translated in Margery Ganz, "Donato Acciaiuoli and the Medici: A Strategy for Survival in '400 Florence," *Rinasciemento* 22 (1982): 49-50.

31. On the financial crisis of 1465, see Raymond de Roover, *The Rise and Decline of the Medici Bank, 1397-1494* (Cambridge, Mass., 1963), pp. 359-60. For contemporary assessments of Piero's regime, see Rab Hatfield, "A Source for Machiavelli's Account of the Regime of Piero de' Medici," *Studies on Machiavelli*, ed. Myron Gilmore (Florence, 1972), pp. 319-33.

32. Rubinstein, *Government*, pp. 174-75; Manoscritti. vol. 817, fol. 43r, printed in Angelo Fabroni, *Laurentii Medicis Magnifici Vita*, 2 vols. (Pisa, 1784), 2: 42.

33. Giovanni Soranzo, "Lorenzo il Magnifico alla morte del padre e il suo primo balzo verso la Signoria," *Archivio storico italiano* 111 (1953): 42-77, at p. 45. Scipione Ammirato argued that another motive behind the simplicity of Piero's funeral was the desire to avoid envy (Moreni, *Continuazione delle memorie istoriche*, 1: 123).

34. Manoscritti. vol. 817, fol. 43r; Acciaiuoli's letter is printed in Fabroni, *Laurentii Medicis*, 2: 42-44.

35. Samuel Y. Edgerton, *Pictures and Punishment: Art and Criminal Prosecution in the Florentine Renaissance* (Ithaca, N.Y., 1985), pp. 104-8; Moreni, *Pompe funebri*, pp. 14-15. For the votive images, see Gino Masi, "La ceroplastica in Firenze nei secoli XV-XVI e la famiglia Benintendi," *Rivista d'arte* 9 (1916): 124-42, at p. 133; Giorgio Vasari, *Le vite degli artisti* (Florence, 1550), 3: 373; and Karla Langedijk, *The Portraits of the Medici*, 2 vols. (Florence, 1981), 1: 27-28.

36. Edgerton, *Pictures*, p. 69, notes the desecration of the Pazzi conspirators' ancestral tombs. The printing history of the lament honoring Giuliano is given by Emilia Nesi, *Il diario della stamperia di Ripoli* (Florence, 1903), pp. 20, 40-41.

37. Richard C. Trexler, *The Libro Ceremoniale of the Florentine Republic* (Geneva, 1978). Various financial accounts and descriptions of important ceremonies honoring foreign visitors from 1475 to 1484 are found in Camera del Comune. Camera dell'Arme. nos. 53-58. For the episode of the giraffe, see Giuseppe Conti, *Fatti e aneddoti di storia fiorentina* (Florence, 1902), pp. 224-25.

38. Cited and translated in Guido Biagi, *The Private Life of the Renaissance Florentines* (London, 1896), pp. 82-83.

39. Richard C. Trexler, *Public Life in Renaissance Florence* (New York, 1980), pp. 409-10; Rab Hatfield, "The Compagnia de' Magi," *Journal of the Warburg and Courtauld Institutes* 33 (1970): 107-61.

40. After Lorenzo's death, Rinuccini claimed that he had coopted "all dignity, power and public authority" in attempting to establish himself as *signore* of Florence (Moreni, *Continuazione delle memorie istoriche*, 1: 128). On the legality of the regime, see Brown, *Bartolomeo Scala*, p. 334. Cf. the viewpoint of J. N. Stephens, *The Fall of the Florentine Republic, 1512–1530* (Oxford, 1983), pp. 21–23, who emphasizes the constitutional "subterfuge" of Lorenzo's regime.

41. Palmieri's heirs paid twenty-five florins for a sumptuary exemption in April 1475 (Deliberazioni Signori e Collegi. Speciale Autorità. vol. 34, fol. 153r). In 1476 Matteo's nephew Antonio was granted a chapel site in San Pier Maggiore, for which he paid 150 florins and Matteo's widow Cosa paid 100 florins (San Pier Maggiore. vol. 6, doc. 556). The Palmieri chapel contained an altarpiece supposedly painted according to Palmieri's design, which reportedly remained covered for a long time because it was thought to express Palmieri's unconventional opinions about the soul (San Pier Maggiore. vol. 4. tome 1, no. 107). Rinuccini's eulogy of Palmieri, which was subsequently reworked and polished, is printed in Alamanno Rinuccini, *Lettere ed orazioni*, ed. V. Giustiniani (Florence, 1953), pp. 78–85.

42. Cristoforo Landino, *Reden Cristoforo Landinos*, ed. M. Lentzen (Munich, 1974), pp. 65–76. For a discussion of the oration in its philosophical context, see Arthur Field, *The Origins of the Platonic Academy of Florence* (Princeton, N.J., 1988), pp. 202–4; I am using Field's translations here, quotes at pp. 202, 203.

43. For Ficino's funeral and epitaph, see Richa, *Notizie*, 6: 128. Rinuccini's bronze medal bore his likeness on one side, and a chimera with the motto "Humana cuncta sic vana" on the other; the chancellor Marcello Adriani delivered the funeral oration (*Ricordi storici di Filippo Rinuccini*, p. 146).

44. Field, *Platonic Academy*, esp. pp. 8–9, 10–17, 272–73.

45. Stephens, *Fall of Florentine Republic*, pp. 17–18, 21–22.

46. Some of the pertinent correspondence is printed in A. Luzio and R. Renier, "Delle relazioni di Isabella d'Este Gonzaga con Ludovico e Beatrice Sforza," *Archivio storico lombardo*, ser. 2, 17 (1890): 74–119, 346–99, 619–74. For detailed descriptions of articles from Beatrice's wardrobe, see Julia Cartwright, *Beatrice d'Este* (London, 1912), pp. 161–75, 181–82.

47. Patricia Simons, "Patronage in the Tornaquinci Chapel, Santa Maria Novella, Florence," in Kent and Simons, eds., *Patronage, Art, and Society*, pp. 221–50; Conv. Sopp. 102. vol. 106, pt. 1, no. 31; Carte Strozz. 2. vol. 17 bis, fol. 71v; Conv. Sopp. 89. vol. 75, fol. 52v.

48. Carte Strozz. 2. vol. 17 bis, fol. 71v.

49. For unknown reasons, controversy erupted in December 1473 between Barone and Agnolo Spini over the burial of Batista di Salvestro Spini in the family tomb. The dispute was decided in the archbishop's court to permit burial on this occasion only, with the agreement that it did not confer "alcuna giuridictione sopra detta sepultura" (Conv. Sopp. 89. vol. 75, fol. 52v). As a lineage the Spini had other collective obligations toward Santa Trinità; for example, "la casa degli Spini tutti insieme" owed three pounds of wax

annually in perpetuity as homage to the church (Conv. Sopp. 89. vol. 75, fol. 68v).

50. Conv. Sopp. 88. vol. 23, fol. 34r bis. See also D. V. Kent and F. W. Kent, *Neighbours and Neighbourhood in Renaissance Florence: The District of the Red Lion in the Fifteenth Century* (Locust Valley, N.Y., 1982), p. 132.

51. Conv. Sopp. 119. vol. 49, fol. 176v.

52. Strozzi's biography and building activities can be approached through Richard A. Goldthwaite, *Private Wealth in Renaissance Florence* (Princeton, N.J., 1968), esp. pp. 52–73; idem, "The Building of the Strozzi Palace: The Construction Industry in Renaissance Florence," *Studies in Medieval and Renaissance History* 10 (1973): 99–194; and more recently idem, *The Building of Renaissance Florence* (Baltimore, 1980). Strozzi is called a "symbol of successful repatriation" by F. W. Kent, "'Più superba de quella de Lorenzo': Courtly and Family Interest in the Building of Filippo Strozzi's Palace," *Renaissance Quarterly* 30 (1977): 311–23, at p. 313. David Friedman, "The Burial Chapel of Filippo Strozzi in Santa Maria Novella in Florence," *L'Arte* 9 (1970): 108–31, offers another useful study of Strozzi's activities. For Piero Masi's remarks, see Manoscritti. vol. 88, fol. 141v.

53. Lorenzo Strozzi, *Vita di Filippo Strozzi il Vecchio scritta da Lorenzo suo figlio*, ed. G. Bini and P. Bigazzi (Florence, 1851), p. 49.

54. This excerpt from Strozzi's will appears in Eve Borsook, "Documents for Filippo Strozzi's Chapel in Santa Maria Novella and Other Related Papers, Part II: The Documents," *Burlington Magazine* 112 (1970): 801, my translation. Strozzi's testament is partially printed in Strozzi, *Vita di Filippo Strozzi*, pp. 65–66.

55. Borsook, "Documents," p. 742, states that the relevant entries in Strozzi's account book show a total sum of 1,222 florins spent on the obsequies in Florence and Naples. Of this figure, 380 florins subsidized the ceremony in Naples.

56. Descriptions of the funeral can be found in Strozzi, *Vita di Filippo Strozzi*, pp. 31–32; and Manoscritti. vol. 88, fol. 141v. The quotes are taken from *Ricordanze tratte da un libro originale di Tribaldo de' Rossi*, in Ildefonso di San Luigi, ed., *Delizie*, 23: 236–303, at p. 257. P. Litta, *Famiglie celebri italiane*, 15 vols. (Turin, 1819–1902), fasc. 68, table 1, gives the number of Strozzi eligible for office.

57. Strozzi, *Vita di Filippo Strozzi*, pp. 31–32.

58. Goldthwaite, "Construction Industry," pp. 172–73, states that during peak employment in the summers of 1491, 1492, and 1493, workers numbered in the forties and fifties, and that Strozzi's stipulation in his testament to keep at least fifty men employed on the project was respected. The quotes are taken from Strozzi, *Vita di Filippo Strozzi*, pp. 31–32.

59. Molho, "Cosimo de' Medici," pp. 13–17.

60. Goldthwaite, "Construction Industry," pp. 170–71.

61. Ronald Weissman, "Taking Patronage Seriously: Mediterranean Values and Renaissance Society," in Kent and Simons, eds., *Patronage, Art, and Society*, pp. 25–45.

62. Conv. Sopp. 119. vol. 49, fol. 145r.

63. For Lena Mancini's donations, see Conv. Sopp. 89. vol. 47, fol. 44r; and Conv. Sopp. 89. vol. 75, fol. 31r. The other examples are cited in Conv. Sopp. 89. vol. 75, fols. 52r, 53r, 62r.

64. Conv. Sopp. 89. vol. 75, fol. 90v; Conv. Sopp. 119. vol. 59, quote at fol. 21v.

65. Conv. Sopp. 119. vol. 49, fol. 170v. Conv. Sopp. 89. vol. 75, fol. 61v, records the 1481 burial of a Spaniard who died in the house of Leonardo Spini and was buried in the confraternal tomb of San Giovanni Gualberto.

66. Conv. Sopp. 102. vol. 106, pt. 2, unfoliated, dated respectively May 18, 1495, and July 5, 1499; Conv. Sopp. 88. vol. 65, fol. 99v.

67. Conv. Sopp. 102. vol. 106, pt. 2, unfoliated, dated May 21, 1482.

68. Conv. Sopp. 102. vol. 106, pt. 1, unfoliated, dated April 17, 1482. This *fede* apparently was not notarized until April 27, 1521.

69. Conv. Sopp. 88. vol. 1, fols. 118v, 120v, 121v; Conv. Sopp. 89. vol. 75, Gianfigliazzi commission and quote at fol. 46r.

70. The following examples are drawn from Manoscritti. vol. 88, esp. fols. 9r, 140r, 141r, 142v, 144r, 146v, and 160v.

71. Hatfield, "Magi," p. 119; Richa, *Notizie*, 3: 267–68.

72. *Ricordanze de Tribaldo de' Rossi*, 23: 287.

73. Carte Strozz. 2. vol. 17 bis, fols. 29r–30r, 43r, 86r/v, 128v–129v.

74. See Kent and Kent, *Neighbours and Neighbourhood*. F. W. Kent's recent remarks on the problem of neighborhood are devoted to conceptualizing the importance of local ties for social experience rather than examining change over time ("Ties of Neighbourhood and Patronage in Quattrocento Florence," in Kent and Simons, eds., *Patronage, Art, and Society*, pp. 79–98.)

75. Conv. Sopp. 88. vol. 65, fol. 36r.

76. Gene A. Brucker, "Monasteries, Friaries, and Nunneries in Quattrocento Florence," in *Christianity and the Renaissance*, ed. Timothy Verdon and John Henderson (Syracuse, N.Y., 1990), pp. 41–62, esp. pp. 52–53.

77. Biblioteca Laurenziana, Florence. Archivio San Lorenzo. vol. 2219. Ricordi di funerali, 1483–1724, p. 1, portions of which are printed in Moreni, *Pompe funebri*, pp. 15–16.

78. BLF. Archivio San Lorenzo. vol. 2219, pp. 1–2, 4–6, quote at p. 2. This account is partially printed in Moreni, *Pompe funebri*, pp. 24–27.

79. Catasto. vols. 184, 185, 194, 989.

80. Catasto. vol. 185, fols. 763r–796v; Catasto. vol. 989, fols. 670r–679v.

81. NA. P 357. no. 180. For the tomb, see Manoscritti. vol. 623, fols. 4r, 5r; and Conv. Sopp. 89. vol. 75, fol. 91v.

82. Conv. Sopp. 102. vol. 106, pt. 2, unfoliated, under the dates March 20, 1494 and June 29, 1489, respectively.

83. Federighi's testament is in NA. P 357. no. 2, dated November 26, 1463. For the dispute, see Conv. Sopp. 88. vol. 68, fol. 111r/v; Conv. Sopp. 88. vol. 70, fols. 13v–14r; and Catasto. vol. 1012, fol. 402r. The Rustichi program is recorded in Carte Strozz. 2. vol. 11, fol. 10r.

84. *Constitutiones Capituli Ecclesie Florentine Secunde de Anno 1483* (Florence, 1505), unpaginated.

85. Conv. Sopp. 102. vol. 106, pt. 2, unfoliated, dated May 18, 1496.

86. Conv. Sopp. 102. vol. 106, pt. 2, unfoliated, dated May 19, 1480, June 7, 1498, and May 21, 1482, respectively.

87. Conv. Sopp. 88. vol. 1, fols. 122v, 124r; Conv. Sopp. 102. vol. 106, pt. 2, unfoliated, dated August 22, 1498.

88. Samuel K. Cohn, Jr., *Death and Property in Siena, 1205–1800: Strategies for the Afterlife* (Baltimore, 1988), esp. pp. 113–114. Jacques Chiffoleau, *La comptabilité de l'au-delà: Les hommes, la mort et la religion dans la région d'Avignon à la fin du Moyen Age, vers 1320–vers 1480* (Rome, 1980), argues that this obsession with the performance of large numbers of masses signaled uncertainty about their effectiveness.

89. For the epidemic, see Ann G. Carmichael, *Plague and the Poor in Renaissance Florence* (Cambridge, 1986). p. 103. According to Stefano Orlandi, *Necrologio di Santa Maria Novella*, 2 vols. (Florence, 1955), 2: 301–2, eighteen friars of Santa Maria Novella perished of plague in the summer of 1479. Richa, *Notizie*, 3: 339–40, cites the following inscription in church of San Martino: "In questo cimitero sono seppelliti XX mila corpi i quali morirono in questo luogo di peste l'anno MCCCCLXXIX."

90. As noted, for example, by A. N. Galpern, *The Religions of the People in Sixteenth-Century Champagne* (Cambridge, Mass., 1976); Jacques Toussaert, *Le sentiment religieux en Flandre à la fin du Moyen Age* (Paris, 1963); and for England by J. T. Rosenthal, *The Purchase of Paradise* (London, 1972).

91. Galpern, *Religions of the People*, pp. 16–20; Cohn, *Death and Property*, p. 155.

92. Marvin Becker, "Aspects of Lay Piety in Early Renaissance Florence," in *The Pursuit of Holiness in Late Medieval and Renaissance Religion*, ed. Charles Trinkaus with Heiko Oberman (Leiden, 1974), pp. 177–200; and additional comments in Cohn, *Death and Property*, pp. 16–17.

93. John Henderson, "The Hospitals of Late Medieval and Renaissance Florence: A Preliminary Survey," in *The Hospital in History*, ed. Lindsay Granshaw and Roy Porter (London, 1989), pp. 63–92; idem, "Charity in Late Medieval Florence: The Role of Religious Confraternities," in *Florence and Milan: Comparisons and Relations*, 2 vols. (Florence, 1989), 2: 67–84; Richard C. Trexler, "A Widow's Asylum of the Renaissance: The Orbatello of Florence," in *Old Age in Preindustrial Society*, ed. Peter N. Stearns (New York, 1982), pp. 119–49; idem, "Charity and the Defense of Urban Elites in the Italian Communes," in *The Rich, the Well-Born, and the Powerful*, ed. F. C. Jaher (Urbana, Ill., 1973), pp. 64–109.

94. Patterns of sponsorship of masses are discussed in my article "Remembering the Family: Women, Kin, and Commemorative Masses in Renaissance Florence," *Renaissance Quarterly* 42 (1989): 635–54. The phrase "great age of selfishness" is from Cohn, *Death and Property*, p. 97.

95. Werner Gundesheimer, "Patronage in the Renaissance: An Exploratory Approach," in *Patronage in the Renaissance*, ed. G. F. Lytle and S. Orgel (Princeton, N.J., 1981), pp. 3–26, makes the point that concentration on the patron-client relationship should not obscure the "networks of mental attitudes and social connections that provide its supportive structures."

96. John Henderson, "Religious Confraternities and Death in Early Renaissance Florence," in *Florence and Italy: Renaissance Studies in Honour of Nicolai Rubinstein*, ed. P. Denley and C. Elam (London, 1988), p. 384, puts the number of (mainly flagellant) confraternities founded between 1400 and 1499 at eighty-seven. For San Pancrazio, see Conv. Sopp. 88. vol. 1, fol. 116r.

97. Conv. Sopp. 88. vol. 1, fols. 118v, 120v, 121v, 132v; Conv. Sopp. 88. vol. 2, fols. 3r, 29v, 44r.

98. On the 1480s as the "golden age" of judicial tolerance for sodomites, see Michael J. Rocke, "Male Homosexuality in Late Medieval Florence: The Forms, Meanings, and Regulation of Non-Normative Sexual Behavior" (Ph.D. diss., State University of New York–Binghamton, 1989).

99. For Francesco Buonaparte's will, see NA. P 357, no. 94, fols. 197r–199v, dated November 25, 1489; for Gino Capponi, see NA. L 130. no. 115, dated March 24, 1480; for Angelo Strozzi, see NA. P 357. no. 53, fols. 123r–124r, dated January 29, 1480; for Girolamo Martini, see NA. P 357. no. 115. fols. 240r–245v, dated January 17, 1490; for Alberto Serruchi, see NA. P 339. fol. 184r, dated March 29, 1475. The terms of Antonio Albizzi's will are given in San Pier Maggiore. vol. 7, unfoliated, dated October 13, 1476. My thanks to Rab Hatfield for bringing several of these documents to my attention.

100. Piero Masi implies that Filippo Strozzi was buried in the white robes of this confraternity (Manoscritti. vol. 88, fol. 141v. For Spinelli's testament (1468), see NA. P 357. fols. 69r–74r. Spinelli also wanted to be carried by "dignified persons" rather than by Franciscan friars. Money that would otherwise be spent on flags was instead directed toward the purchase of silver chalices and a missal for Santa Croce. By Spinelli's own calculations he spent about 6,820 florins in patronizing the church (F. Moise, *Santa Croce di Firenze* [Florence, 1845], p. 482).

101. Ronald E. Rainey, *Sumptuary Legislation in Renaissance Florence* (Ann Arbor, Mich.: University Microfilms, 1985), pp. 524–38, quote at p. 524, Rainey's translation. The legislation is found in Deliberazioni Signori e Collegi. Speciale Autorità. vol. 34; funerary rubrics at fols. 125v–129r, dated April 27, 1473, with additional measures governing the use of flags and draperies, dated June 4, 1473, at fol. 131r/v.

102. The pertinent rubric for the first quote reads: "Et perchè gli e consueto farsi le messe con pompa di ragunate duomini e di lumi assai con spesa sanza fructo dellanima del morto" (Deliberazioni Signori e Collegi. Speciale Autorità. vol. 34, fol. 128r). The second quote is cited and translated by Rainey, *Sumptuary Legislation*, p. 524.

103. For Machiavelli's remarks, see Rainey, *Sumptuary Legislation*, pp. 536–38. Francesco Guicciardini reported that "sendo di poi pacificate per qualche tempo le cose d'Italia . . . e perchè la città era in quieta e il Magistrato con poche faccende, attese la fare leggi nuove e rinnovare le antiche appartenenti a' costumi, come circa alle pompe di nozze e mortori, circa agli ornamenti delle donne e uomini, circa a' giuochi e cose simili" (*Ricordi autobiografici e*

di famiglia, in *Opere inedite*, ed. Giuseppe Canestrini, 10 vols. [Florence, 1857–67], 10: 28). For Trexler's argument, see *Public Life*, esp. p. 409.

104. Deliberazioni Signori e Collegi. Speciale Autorità. vol. 34, fols. 126v–127v; Samuel K. Cohn, Jr., *The Laboring Classes in Renaissance Florence* (New York, 1980), pp. 197–203. Edgerton, *Pictures*, esp. appendix B, argues that beginning in the late 1460s there was a shift in capital punishment from beheading to hanging, which degraded the victim more.

105. The statutes are printed in Marc Antonio Altieri, *Li nuptiali*, ed. E. Narducci (Rome, 1873), appendix, p. xlviii.

106. For Bruni's mourning restrictions, see Demetrio Marzi, *La cancelleria della repubblica fiorentina* (Rocca San Casciano, 1910), pp. 195–96. For the 1473 regulations, see Deliberazioni Signori e Collegi. Speciale Autorità. vol. 34, fol. 127r.

107. The duration of public mourning by men, specified as the wearing of a long mantle with hood, was limited to one year for the death of one's father or grandfather, and to six months for a brother. Women other than widows could wear mantles only for their fathers or mothers, with a limitation of six months; however, widows were exempt from time restrictions in mourning their husbands (Deliberazioni Signori e Collegi. Speciale Autorità. vol. 34, fol. 128v). Marco Parenti commented that he buried his beloved wife Caterina in May 1481 "honoratamente quanto si pote secondo la legge," although the four formal mourners—her two daughters Gostanza and Marietta, sister Alessandra, and sister-in-law Selvaggia—actually exceeded the provisions (Carte Strozz. 2. vol. 17 bis, fol. 1r).

108. One indication of the growing expense of men's mourning mantles is the greater frequency with which they were rented rather than purchased. Piero Parenti rented three such garments for his father Marco's funeral in 1497, and Piero's seven sons rented mourning mantles when he died in 1519 (Carte Strozz. 2. vol. 17 bis, fols. 86v, 129v).

109. Filippo Strozzi noted that his mother Alessandra Macinghi Strozzi was buried "honoratissimamente" in Santa Maria Novella in 1471 but gave no details (Strozzi, *Lettere*, p. xl). Bartolomeo Masi recorded the burial of his maternal grandmother Agnola and mother Caterina in 1484 and 1495 in similar fashion (*Ricordanze di Bartolomeo Masi dal 1478 al 1526* [Florence, 1906], pp. 8, 29).

110. Dei's remarks on the funeral are printed in Biagi, *Private Life*, pp. 88–89, Biagi's translation.

111. The quote is from ibid., p. 88, Biagi's translation. Other contemporary accounts of Lorenzo's death, funeral, and burial are found in Acquisti e Doni. vol. 301, fol. 104r, recorded by Giovanfrancesco Mazinghi; and *Diario fiorentino di Agostino Lapini dal 252 al 1596* (Florence, 1900), p. 28. *Ricordanze di Tribaldo de' Rossi*, 23: 275, states that there were four orders of friars involved but does not specify their affiliations. Piero Parenti's description, included in his *Storia fiorentina*, is printed in Moreni, *Pompe funebre*, pp. 17–23.

112. Biagi, *Private Life*, pp. 88–89, Biagi's translation.

113. Moreni, *Pompe funebri*, pp. 21–22.

114. The quote is from *Ricordanze di Tribaldo de' Rossi*, 23: 287; Poliziano's poem, "In morte del magnifico Lorenzo de' Medici," is printed in his *Le Stanze, l'Orfeo, e le Rime* (Florence, 1863), pp. 382–92. For the orations, see Moreni, *Pompe funebri*, p. 19; and McManamon, *Funeral Oratory*, pp. 50–51.

115. Quoted in E. L. S. Horsburgh, *Lorenzo the Magnificent* (London, 1909), p. 357, Horsburgh's translation.

116. Donald Weinstein, *Savonarola and Florence* (Princeton, N.J., 1970), p. 62. The epitaphs for Ficino and Pico are printed in Richa, *Notizie*, 6: 128, and 7: 141. Ghirlandaio died in 1493 and was buried in the old cemetery in Santa Maria Novella. In the seventeenth century his bones were transferred to a more prestigious location in one of the *avelli* (Orlandi, *Necrologio*, 2: 588).

117. Melissa M. Bullard, "Lorenzo de' Medici, Anxiety, Image Making, and Political Reality in the Renaissance," typescript, pp. 28–34. A version of this paper is scheduled to appear in a forthcoming volume edited by Giancarlo Garfagnini.

118. For accounts of the entry, see Luca Landucci, *A Florentine Diary from 1450 to 1516*, ed. I. del Badia (London, 1927), pp. 60–67; Bonner Mitchell, *The Majesty of the State: Triumphal Progresses of Foreign Sovereigns in Renaissance Italy, 1494–1600* (Florence, 1986), pp. 63–69. Communal expenditures for Charles's lavish reception are recorded in Camera del Commune. Camera dell'Arme. vols. 62–64.

119. Stephens, *Fall of Florentine Republic*, pp. 30–35; Gene Brucker, *Renaissance Florence* (repr., Berkeley, Calif., 1983), pp. 268–69.

120. Francesco Guicciardini, *Ricordi*, ed. Raffaele Spongano (Florence, 1951), pp. 137–38.

121. Soderini also asked friars and friends to pray for his soul (NA. G 432 [1484–1516], fols. 44r–48v). Caponni in 1499 left long instructions defining the religious who were to take part in the funeral, while providing for Gregorian masses and prohibiting "gloria mundana"; he wanted his funeral expenses to be met by the sale of his clothes and, if necessary, his rings and silverware (NA. P 339, no. 160, fols. 421r–421 bis verso). For Rinuccini's will, dated 1497, see NA. P 357 (1454–1505), no. 166, fols. 349r–351v. Francesco di Filippo Pugliese was similarly adamant in 1503 that he "prohibit[ed] and [did] not wish that there be made for him observances or other pomp that are done very often for funerals" (NA. V 356 [1500–1503], fols. 94–99v).

122. For debates over women's clothing, see E. Polidori Calamandrei, *Le vesti delle donne fiorentine nel Quattrocento* (repr., Rome, 1973), pp. 65–66. The Savonarola quotation is in Cohn, *Death and Property*, p. 97, Cohn's translation.

123. Landucci, *Diary*, pp. 214, 229; for a description of Orsini's requiem, with a wax apparatus prefiguring the great "cappelle ardenti" of the later sixteenth century, see *Ricordanze di Bartolomeo Masi*, p. 82. The political ma-

neuvers behind Pazzi's accession to office are discussed by Humphrey C. Butters, *Governors and Government in Early Sixteenth-Century Florence, 1502–1519* (Oxford, 1985), pp. 127–29.

124. Between 1494 and 1515 the number of communal accounts of entries—including descriptions by Filarete and Manfidi in the *Libro ceremoniale*—decreases noticeably. Expenses for various ambassadorial receptions circa 1501 are given in Camera del Comune. Camera dell'Arme. vol. 65.

125. Landucci, *Diary*, p. 120; Molho, "Cosimo de' Medici," p. 32. For the inventory of marbles seized by the Signoria in 1495, see Maud Cruttwell, *Verrocchio* (London, 1904), pp. 98–99.

126. J. R. Hale, *Florence and the Medici: The Pattern of Control* (London, 1977), p. 89.

127. For Capponi's funeral, see *Istorie di Giovanni Cambi, cittadino fiorentino*, in Ildefonso di San Luigi, ed., *Delizie*, vols. 20–23, at 21: 97. Ginori's republican credentials were impeccable. Serving as *gonfaloniere* in 1494, Ginori wrote to Charles VIII to dissuade him from reinstating the Medici; in 1497, he was a member of the prestigious Ten on Liberty for the third time, which office he held at the time of his death (Piero Ginori Conti, *La basilica di San Lorenzo di Firenze e la famiglia Ginori* [Florence, 1940], pp. 199–200). Savonarola mobilized thousands of Florentine youth for greater moral purity (Richard C. Trexler, "Ritual in Florence: Adolescence and Salvation in the Renaissance," in Trinkaus and Oberman, eds., *Pursuit of Holiness*, pp. 200–264).

128. Weinstein, *Savonarola and Florence*, esp. pp. 295–303.

129. *Ricordi storici di Filippo Rinuccini*, p. 146.

130. Rainey, *Sumptuary Legislation*, pp. 560–61.

131. Physically buffering the two groups of canons was a clerical retinue of grand proportions: the city's Dominican and Franciscan friars, both Conventuals and Observants, one hundred priests, and the bishop of Volterra (Biblioteca Laurenziana, Florence. Archivio San Lorenzo. vol. 2219, pp. 1–2; Moreni, *Pompe funebri*, pp. 24–25).

132. Landucci, *Diary*, p. 211.

133. Attending Lorenzo's funeral were the friars of Santa Maria Novella, San Marco, and Santa Croce, the canons of the cathedral and San Lorenzo, 158 additional priests, and five bishops (Moreni, *Pompe funebri*, pp. 27–29).

134. Conti, *Fatti e aneddoti*, pp. 277–88.

135. Carmichael, *Plague and the Poor*, pp. 103–6.

136. In 1490 the Misericordia set its core number at seventy-two members (thirty priests and forty-two laypersons), although others could participate in the spiritual benefits of the company. The principal obligation assumed by the company was burial of the dead poor, especially plague victims. This duty was similarly stressed in the company's revised statutes of 1501 (C. Torricelli et al., eds., *La Misericordia di Firenze attraverso i secoli: Note storiche* [Florence, 1975], pp. 53–68; *Documenti inediti o poco noti per la storia della Misericordia di Firenze, 1240–1525* (Florence, 1940), pp. 64–66, 73–76, 104–15).

137. Cohn, *Laboring Classes*, pp. 120–21.

138. Except where otherwise noted, this discussion of burial sites of parishioners of Sant'Ambrogio is based on Conv. Sopp. 79. vol. 458, "Libri di morti, 1478–1511." There are some slight gaps in the evidence: no burials were recorded for January 1505, or for March and August 1510.

139. See Table 3.1, above.

140. Pierre Chaunu, *La mort à Paris: 16, 17, et 18e siècles* (Paris, 1978), pp. 324–25. The remaining 24 percent chose burial in one of the city's many convent churches.

141. The displacement of the laboring classes is discussed in Cohn, *Laboring Classes*, pp. 104, 127–28.

142. *Concilium Florentinum Provinciale Anno 1517*, in J. D. Mansi, ed., *Sacrorum Conciliorum Nova et Amplissima Collectio*, 53 vols. (reissued, Paris, 1900–1927), 35: cols. 215–318, at col. 268. For a similar process of privatization of ecclesiastical space in Siena, see Cohn, *Death and Property*, pp. 106–9.

143. Conv. Sopp. 88. vol. 2, fol. 267v.

144. Conv. Sopp. 81. vol. 3, fol. 30v. Butters, *Governors and Government*, p. 96, notes the criticisms leveled against Soderini because of his wife's epistolary activities.

145. Ronald F. E. Weissman, *Ritual Brotherhood in Renaissance Florence* (New York, 1982), pp. 173–74, 205–6.

146. Comp. Relig. Sopp. Capitoli. vol. 606.

147. San Pier Maggiore. vol. 4. tome 1, doc. 147, dated August 4, 1493, July 1516.

148. Conv. Sopp. 79. vol. 144; Weissman, *Ritual Brotherhood*, pp. 207–8.

149. *Constitutiones Synodales Cleri Florentini: Cosmi de Pacciis Archiepiscopi Florentini Anno Domini Incarnationis 1508* (Florence, 1509), bk 3 (*De Sepulturis*), unpaginated; *Concilium Provinciale 1517*, col. 240.

150. Conv. Sopp. 102. vol. 106, pt. 2, unfoliated.

151. Butters, *Governors and Government*, p. 150; Richard C. Trexler, *The Spiritual Power: Republican Florence under Interdict* (Leiden, 1974), pp. 178–86. Those churches instructed to continue celebrating mass were Santo Spirito, Santa Croce, Santa Maria Novella, the Carmine, Ognissanti, and Santissima Annunziata.

152. *Ricordanze di Bartolomeo Masi*, pp. 76–77n. Other contemporaries remarked on the severity of the terms as well: see *Istorie di Giovanni Cambi*, 21: 278; and Manoscritti. vol. 88, fol. 150v.

153. Conv. Sopp. 79. vol. 27, fol. 285v; Conv. Sopp. 79. vol. 458, fol. 39v.

154. *Istorie di Giovanni Cambi*, 21: 278–79.

155. Weinstein, *Savonarola and Florence*, pp. 345–46.

156. Manoscritti. vol. 88, fol. 162r; *Ricordanze di Bartolomeo Masi*, p. 118; Hale, *Florence and the Medici*, pp. 96–97; Cox-Rearick, *Dynasty and Destiny*, p. 98n.

157. *Ricordanze di Bartolomeo Masi*, pp. 124–25; *Istorie di Giovanni Cambi*, 22: 13–14; for the funeral oration attributed to the chancellor Marcello Adriani, see McManamon, *Funeral Oratory*, p. 250.

158. *Istorie di Giovanni Cambi*, 22: 92–95; see also *Ricordanze di Bartolomeo Masi*, pp. 195–99.

159. For the tomb commission, see *Istorie de Giovanni Cambi*, 22: 161–62.

160. Roy Strong, *Art and Power: Renaissance Festivals, 1450–1650* (Berkeley, Calif., 1984), p. 52.

161. Giovanni delle Bande Nere of a collateral branch carried the first flag displaying the papal insignia; Piero di Jacopo Salviati, Giuliano's nephew, carried the second; the lord of Piombino, married to Giuliano's niece Emilia Ridolfi, carried the command baton (*bastone*).

162. Moreni, *Pompe funebri*, pp. 29–36, at p. 31.

163. McManamon, *Funeral Oratory*, pp. 49–51, 264–65, 289; Moreni, *Pompe funebri*, p. 41. The humanist Stefano Sterponi also composed an oration for Lorenzo which did not form part of the obsequies.

164. Cox-Rearick, *Dynasty and Destiny*.

165. Rosemary Devonshire Jones, "Lorenzo de' Medici, Duca d'Urbino: 'Signore' of Florence?" in Gilmore, ed., *Studies on Machiavelli*, pp. 299–315.

166. *Ricordanze di Bartolomeo Masi*, pp. 241–42; see also *Istorie di Giovanni Cambi*, 22: 149–52; Moreni, *Pompe funebri*, pp. 40–46; Hale, *Florence and the Medici*, pp. 106–7.

167. For the liturgical offices honoring Leo held on December 6, 1521, in San Lorenzo and the following day in the cathedral, see *Ricordanze di Bartolomeo Masi*, pp. 253–54.

168. Ibid., pp. 240, 242–43, 244–45; *Istorie di Giovanni Cambi*, 22: 158–59. Madeleine predeceased her husband by a few days and was initially buried without pomp, since it was feared that news of her death would further debilitate the sick Lorenzo. Her requiem was celebrated only three days after Lorenzo's burial, on May 10, 1519. Alfonsina died in her native Rome; her requiem, held on February 11, 1520, in San Lorenzo, featured a huge catafalque filled with torches and a richly draped nave "come si fece al figliuolo." According to Masi, both events drew large crowds, "come si costuma fare et ire quando si fanno le Messe per qualche gran maestro" (*Ricordanze di Bartolomeo Masi*, p. 245).

169. Acquisti e Doni. vol. 293, unfoliated.

170. Devonshire Jones, "Lorenzo de' Medici," p. 305; Stephens, *Fall of Florentine Republic*, pp. 86–89, 91; Kent with Simons, "Renaissance Patronage," pp. 7–8.

171. Eleonora's obsequies are described in *Diario di Agostino Lapini*, pp. 135–38. For the development of a "liturgy of state" in sixteenth-century ceremonies, see Strong, *Art and Power*, p. 19.

172. Ginori Conti, *Basilica di San Lorenzo*, p. 214.

173. Carte Strozz. 2. vol. 17 bis, fols. 128v–129v.

174. Libri di Commercio. vol. 102, fols. 17v, 29v.

175. Acquisti e Doni. vol. 274, I, ii.

176. Carte Strozz. 2. vol. 17 bis, fols. 128v–129r.

177. The first polyphonic mass setting, now lost, was written by Dufay circa 1470–74; the first preserved polyphonic setting, by Ockeghem, dates from 1485–90. Ockeghem's pupil Brumel, who worked at the courts of Leo X and the duke of Ferrara, also composed polyphonic requiems. See Alec Robertson, *Requiem: Music of Mourning and Consolation* (London, 1967).

178. Conv. Sopp. 102. vol. 106, pt. 2, unfoliated, dated September 1525.

179. Conv. Sopp. 102. vol. 106, pt. 1, unfoliated, dated October 31, 1513.

180. C. Lis and H. Soly, *Poverty and Capitalism in Pre-Industrial Europe* (Atlantic Highlands, N.J., 1979), p. 95; *Diario di Agostino Lapini*, p. 95. The population estimate of eighty thousand is given by John Henderson, "Epidemie nella Firenze del rinascimento: Teoria sanitaria e provvedimenti governativi," in *Sanità e società: Emilia-Romagna, Toscana, Marche, Umbria, Lazio, secoli XVI–XX*, ed. A. Pastore and P. Sorcinelli (Udine, 1987), p. 40. For other accounts of the 1527–28 plague, see Cecil Roth, *The Last Florentine Republic* (London, 1925), pp. 74–77.

181. *Istorie di Giovanni Cambi*, 22: 238–39; Henderson, "Epidemie," p. 53; Lis and Soly, *Poverty and Capitalism*, p. 95.

182. *Istorie di Giovanni Cambi*, 22: 239–40.

183. Henderson, "Epidemie," p. 50; for plague policy in the seventeenth century, see Giulia Calvi, *Storie di un anno di peste* (Milan, 1984).

184. Henderson, "Epidemie," pp. 44–45.

185. Torricelli et al., eds., *Misericordia attraverso i secoli*, p. 70; Henderson, "Epidemie," p. 40; Carmichael, *Plague and the Poor*, p. 106.

186. Hale, *Florence and the Medici*, pp. 109–18; Roth, *Last Florentine Republic*, esp. pp. 37–54.

Conclusion

1. Thomas Coryat, *Coryat's Crudities: hastily gobbled up in five months trauells* (London, 1611), p. 255.

INDEX

Acciaiuoli: Bishop Angelo, 89, 94; Donato, 187, 188, 191; Lorenzo di Niccolò, funeral of, 59–60, 67, 68, 257n43
Adimari family, 27, 69
Adriani: Marcello, 191, 219, 229; Virgilio, 288n12
Agostino di Francesco di Ser Giovanni, 36
Albanese, Cardinal, 141
Alberti: family, 61; Leon Battista, 5, 125, 146, 259n70; Niccolò, 24, 40, 64, 73, 76–77
Albizzi: family, 58, 69, 99, 254n11; political faction, 55, 72; Maso, 273n97; Rinaldo, 120, 152
Alessandri: Alessandro, 133; Ginevra, 184, 186, 187, 215, 288n15, 289n22, 289n28
Almieri, Ginevra degli, 44, 62, 250n49
Altoviti family, 61, 73
Antoninus, Saint, 41, 48, 151, 250n40, 280n9
Ariès, Philippe, xiv, 252n67
Arrigucci, Giovanni, 66, 167, 168
Avignon: funeral pomp in, 63–67

Badia of Fiesole, 21, 185
Baldovinetti, Niccolò, 78
Baldovino da Empoli, 61
Baptistry, 91, 134, 139
Baracci family, 61
Barbadori, Gherardo, 122
Bardi, Alessandra, 173–74
Bardi family, 47, 61
Baron, Hans, 108, 144
Baroncelli, Piero, 128
Battle of San Romano, 153–54, 155
Bernardino of Siena, Saint, 10, 49, 119–20, 122
Bertoldi family, 61
Bilateral kinship, 13–14, 68, 214. See also Funerals; Mourners; Requiem
Biliotti, Bishop Antonio, 43, 89, 94
Boccaccio, Giovanni, 42, 57, 113
Bonichi, Piero, 164, 165, 166
Bonvanni family, 163
Books of the Dead, 50, 93
Botti, Beata Villani de', 49, 252n63
Bourdieu, Pierre, 5

Brogliole, Messer, 107
Brown, Alison, 187
Brucker, Gene, 128, 163
Bruni, Leonardo, 112, 118, 120, 125, 136, 146, 154, 277n145, 278n154; consolatory letter for Bicie Medici, 147; funeral of, 114, 155–59; oration for Nanni Strozzi, 143–45; tomb of, 156, 158, 162, 281n22, 282n34
Bryant, Lawrence, xv
Bueri: Domenico, 61; Piccarda, 147
Burke, Peter, 135

Cambi, Giovanni, 22, 226
Capponi: family, 46, 61, 68, 133, 251n54; Piero, 217, 218, 219, 297n121
Cardinal of Portugal, 23, 151
Castagno, Andrea del, 155
Castellani: family, 69; Messer Matteo, 13, 133–34, 273n100, 274n115
Castiglione, Francesco da, 186
Catafalques, 7, 21, 22, 31, 37
Cathedral. See Santa Maria del Fiore
Cavalcanti family, 60–61, 68, 72, 164
Certosa of Galluzzo, 59, 60, 68
Chapels: family, 124, 192
Charity: shift in public, 208–9
Charles VIII (king), 43, 217
Chaunu, Pierre, xiv, 221
Chiffoleau, Jacques, xiv, 63–66, 262n112
Chrysoloras, Manuel, 136, 159
Ciompi revolt, 33, 55, 75, 78, 83
Ciurianni: burial of family members, 24, 25, 107, 127, 245n68, 258n60, 262n106
Civic chivalry, 78–79, 259n75
Clement VI (pope), 138, 143, 277n135
Clerics: obsequies for foreign, 279n7
Coffins, 39–40
Cohen, Abner, 30, 31
Cohn, Samuel, xiv, 61, 88, 163, 208, 209
Commemorative images, 46–47
Commemorative medals, 111–12, 190
Commemorative practices, 3, 133, 196, 225
Confraternities, 261n91, 295n96; provision of funeral goods, 8, 34, 38,

Confraternities (*cont'd*)
85, 261n94, 265n162; role of, in
burials, 84–86; tomb sites of, 86, 87,
198, 261n99, 262n106, 293n65;
women's involvement with, 86–88,
176–77
Consolatory letters, 115, 146–47,
185–86
Corazza, Bartolomeo, 116
Corbizzi family, 68
Corpse: care of, 45, 50–51, 253n70;
dress of, 38–45, 64, 74, 249n32,
249n36, 256n32
Corsini: family, 92, 264n138; Filippo,
273n97
Coryat, Thomas, 236, 237
Coscia, Baldassare (deposed pope):
276n125; funeral of, 134–43, 260n86,
277n139; tomb of, 134, 142, 156,
276n129, 276n133, 277n135

Da Casale, Guccio, Lord of Cortona:
funeral of, 9, 10, 33, 47, 107
Da Diacceto, Francesco Cattani, 229
Da Filicaia family, 99, 101
Dante Alighieri, 112, 113
Da Panzano: Antonio, funeral of, 25,
34, 124, 132; Gostanza, 2, 15; Luca,
1–3, 15, 126, 171; Lucrezia, 1–3;
Messer Luca, 2
Da Uzzano: Agnolo, funeral of, 122,
124, 128; Niccolò, 136, 137
Davanzati, Messer Giuliano, 153
Davidsohn, Robert, 11
Death: historiography of, xiv–xv
Death masks, 46, 47, 251n55
Death rites: nature and function of,
xiii–xviii, 1–3, 5, 6–7, 29, 30–31,
51; representation in narrative, 5–6,
27, 28, 152; style of, 53–54, 106,
121–22, 152, 178–80, 231, 236–38
Dei, Benedetto, 80, 215, 259n76
Dell'Antella, Alessandro, 47
Della Rena family, 99, 101
Della Robbia, Luca, 162
Della Tosa family, 27, 70, 71, 73
Del Tovaglia, Piero, 196
Desiderio da Settignano, 156
Doge, Venetian, 41; funeral of, 49–50
Dominicans, Observant, 8, 184, 202
Dominici, Fra Giovanni, 110
Donatello, 134, 219
Donati family, 100
Dowries, 121, 127

Ecclesiastical constitutions, 43, 89, 94,
206, 223, 225
Effigies, 45–46, 47–50
Eugenius IV (pope), 33, 150, 151

Farnese, Pier, 56, 60, 76, 80, 260n86
Federighi: Bishop Benozzo, 42, 162;
Federigo, 206
Ficino, Marsilio, 191, 216
Field, Arthur, 191
Florence: territorial expansion of,
270n56
Fortini, Benedetto, 109, 267n13
Fra Angelico: *Last Judgment*, 44–45,
250n51
Franceschi, Ser Luca: funeral of, 125,
272n80
Franciscans, Observant, 8, 185, 202
Frederick III (emperor), 150, 159, 160,
247n8, 282n39, 283n41
Funeral banners, 35, 36, 37
Funeral goods, 34–35, 95, 96, 248n29
Funeral orations, Latin, 111, 115–16,
143, 146, 278n149, 282n30; for
women, 146
Funerals: function of, 7, 23;
proliferation of clergy in, 201–3, 210,
224, 232; representation of kinship
in, 12–15; route of, 20, 28; structure
of procession, 7–17; symbolic
trappings of, 9, 31–38
Funeral sermons, 27, 28, 115

Galpern, A. N., 36
Garin, Eugenio, 163
Geertz, Clifford, xvi
Ghirlandaio, Domenico, 216, 297n116
Gianfigliazzi: burial of family members,
37; Rinaldo, 42, 130, 133
Giesey, Ralph, xv
Ginori: family, 163, 232; Gino, 219,
298n127
Giovanni: Francesco di Tommaso, 9, 32,
41, 126, 167–68, 172, 247n8,
280n12; Mea, 50–51, 172–73, 177
Girolami, Fra Remigio, 27
Giuliano di Particino, 164
Goldthwaite, Richard, 68, 163, 270n60
Gonzaga, Barbara (marchioness of
Mantua), 18
Grain Office (Grascia), 50, 93
Gravediggers, 50–51, 56, 57, 93,
252n69, 264n143
Graverobbery, 43–44

Gregory XI (pope), 55, 75, 76
Grief: control of, 12, 116–20, 158, 169, 173; experience of, 1, 3; expressions of, 11–12, 115, 119. *See also* Humanism; Mourning practices
Guadagni, Vieri, 125, 129–30, 131, 137, 274n105
Guicciardini: family, 134, 211, 217; Giovanni, 273n97
Guilds: Calimala, 91; doctors' and spicers', 50; Lana, 91; role of, in funerals, 83–84

Hanley, Sarah, xv
Hawkwood, John: funeral of, 12, 32, 48, 56, 79–82, 110, 134, 153, 155, 260n79, 260n84, 260n85, 261n87
Herlihy, David, 14
Huizinga, Johann, 50
Humanism: effect of, on death rites, 105–6, 116–20, 158, 169

Innocent VI (pope), 138, 277n134
Interdict of 1511, 225–26, 299n151

John VIII of Paleologus (emperor), 40
Jousts, 271n65
Julius II (pope), 225

Kent, F. W., 163
Klapisch-Zuber, Christiane, xvi

Landini, Lisabetta: funeral of, 8–9, 10, 15, 17, 232, 241n7, 241n10
Landino, Cristoforo, 191
Landucci, Luca, 218
Lapini, Agostino, 234
Last Judgment (Fra Angelico), 44–45
Laurel crown: symbolism of, 112–15
Lebrun, François, xiv
Leo X (pope), 21, 22–23, 41, 218, 226
Libro ceremoniale, 151, 189, 298n124
Lippi, Filippino, 194
Luca di Matteo (gravedigger), 82–83

Machiavelli, Niccolò, 28, 130, 181, 211
Magalotti, Giovanni, 72, 76
Magli, Vaggia (widow of Piero), 66
Malespina, Argentina, 223
Manetti, Giannozzo, 111, 114, 117, 159; oration for Leonardo Bruni, 157–59
Manutius, Aldus, 37
Marsili, Fra Luigi, 37

Marsuppini, Carlo, 118, 147; funeral of, 9, 40, 48, 110, 155–56, 159–61, 267n18, 282n37; tomb of, 156
Martelli, Ugo, 159
Martin V (pope), 137, 139, 142, 275n123
Martines, Lauro, 163
Marzocco, 21, 228
Masi: Bartolomeo, 21; burial of family members, 14, 199–201, 242n27, 296n109; Checcha, funeral of, 25, 172, 173; Ser Tommaso, funeral of, 125
Masses; commemorative, 58–59, 87–88, 91, 233; Gregorian, 3, 58, 205; multiplication of, 204–9; requiem, 2, 63, 232–33, 301n177
Matteo di Lorenzo (goldsmith): funeral of, 16, 130, 273n102
Medici (de'): family, 21, 23, 47, 73, 162, 186, 246n6; ousting of, 33, 217, 219, 235; palace, 21, 22, 23, 46, 189; restoration of, 226–28
—Cosimo I, 35, 132, 229
—Cosimo il Vecchio, 147, 149–50, 152, 155; commemorative program for, 183–85, 288n14; funeral of, 180–83, 287n8, 288n12; title *pater patriae*, 186–87, 289n26; tomb of, 184–85, 187, 219, 289n25
—Giovanni di Bicci: death and funeral of, 13, 122, 123, 124–25, 126, 130, 133, 273n97, 273n100, 288n16; relations with Baldassare Coscia, 134, 136, 137, 138, 142, 275n121
—Giovanni di Pierfrancesco, 8, 203, 220, 298n131
—Giuliano di Piero, 188–89
—Giuliano di Piero (duke of Nemours): funeral of, 21–23, 41, 48, 228–29, 300n161
—Lorenzo di Giovanni, 27, 33, 145, 161–62, 278n152, 283n44
—Lorenzo di Pierfrancesco, 220, 298n133
—Lorenzo di Piero (duke of Urbino): funeral of, 13, 228–29, 300n163
—Lorenzo il Magnifico, 46, 188–89, 291n40; funeral of, 201, 215–16, 296n111
—Piero di Cosimo, 159, 182, 188, 290n33
—Piero di Lorenzo, 216, 217, 220
—Vieri di Cambio, 24, 32, 37, 65, 92,

Medici (de') (cont'd)
    248n23, 264n136
Merchants' Court (Sei dei Mercanzia),
    16, 151, 162
Michelangelo, 219, 228
Michelozzo, 134
Michi, Ugolino: funeral of, 24–25, 127,
    245n66
Misericordia, 57, 89, 221, 234,
    263n119, 298n136
Mitchell, Bonner, xv
Monachi, Ser Niccolò, 109, 266n11
Monaco, Lorenzo, 123
Monaldi, Guido, 24, 61, 64
Morelli, Giovanni, 63, 80
Mourners: arrangement of, in cortege,
    9–10, 17–19; identity of, 15–17,
    64–65; sexual segregation of, 10–11,
    19, 241n11
Mourning clothes, 10, 24–26, 125–26,
    171, 192, 213, 245n69, 272n75,
    296n108; women and, mid-fifteenth
    century, 170–76
Mourning practices, 2, 6, 19, 116–20,
    173, 242n20; 1473 regulation of,
    212–14. See also Grief
Muir, Edward, xvi
Mussato, Alberto, 112

Naddo da Montecatini, Ser, 80
Neighborhood: characteristics of,
    19–20; ties to, 88, 202, 224, 293n74
Niccoli, Niccolò, 112, 145
Niccolini, Lapo, 66
Nicholas V (pope), 277n135
Nobili, Francesca de': funeral of, 10, 69,
    74

Ognissanti, 89
Orlandini family, 68
Orsanmichele, 47, 88
Orsini: Alfonsina, 230–31, 300n168;
    Giordano, 203; Archbishop Rinaldo,
    218, 227, 297n123
Otto di Guardia, 44

Pacini, Antonio, 145, 216
Palmieri, Matteo, 132, 154, 190–91,
    287n1, 291n41; oration for Carlo
    Marsuppini, 159, 160
Pandolfini, Agnolo, 132, 133, 274n107
Parenti: Caterina, funeral of, 25, 214,
    296n107; family burials compared,
    201; Marco, 36, 169, 192–93, 247n7;

Parente, funeral of, 26, 171; Piero,
    funeral of, 26, 36–37, 232–33;
    Tommasa, 172
Parish: 263n113; burial revenues, 91,
    94–95, 263n130, 266n166; loyalties
    to, 88, 95–104, 202, 221–23, 224,
    262n112; role of, in burials, 88–91;
    role of, in civic administration, 92–94
Parte Guelfa: emblems of, 33–34, 131
Patriarch of Venice, 48
Patriliny, 13–14, 15, 46, 68, 125, 171,
    214. See also Funerals; Mourners;
    Requiem
Patronage, 191–92, 294n95
Pazzi: family, 99; conspiracy, 33,
    188–89; Archbishop Cosimo, 48,
    218, 227
Peruzzi family, 73
Petrarch, Francesco, 112, 113, 117
Petriboni, Pagolo, 13, 124, 125, 130,
    133
Petrucci: burial of family members,
    16–17
Pico della Mirandola, Giovanni, 216,
    297n116
Piero della Francesca, 40
Piovano Arlotto, 63, 82
Pisan War, 75, 76, 77
Pitti family, 46, 61, 69
Pius II (pope), 48, 181, 185
Plague: of 1348–49, 55–59, 64, 254n5;
    of 1363, 60–61; of 1374, 62; of 1400,
    106–7; of 1479, 208, 294n89; of
    1490s, 221; of 1520s, 234–35
Platonic Academy, 191
Poggio Bracciolini, 112, 118, 136, 145,
    159, 161, 282n35
Poliziano, Angelo, 216
Pontormo, 232
Pucci, Antonio, 60, 112
Pugliese, Francesco, 297n121

Quarta, 94–95, 265n152

Rangone, Tommaso, 38
Requiem: function of, 3, 7, 23–24;
    liturgy, 7, 26–27; participants in, 10,
    16, 23–24, 25–26; style of, sixteenth
    century, 179, 230. See also Masses
Ricasoli, Albertaccio, 35
Ricci (political faction), 55, 72
Ridolfi: family, 68; Lorenzo, 132, 134,
    274n105
Rienzo, Cola di, 112

Rinuccini: family, 68; Alamanno, 34, 190, 191, 218, 219, 291n43; Francesco, 40, 75
Risaliti family, 46–47, 251n57
Ritual: historiography of, xv–xvi
Rossellino, Bernardo, 156, 162
Rossi (de'): family, 246n76; Piera di Antonio, funeral of, 27–29, 246n77; Tribaldo, 27–29
Rucellai, Giovanni, 33, 149, 150, 162, 163, 283n46

Sacchetti, Franco (commentator), 161
Sacchetti, Franco (novelist), 11–12, 27, 37, 38, 46, 51, 73
Salutati, Coluccio, 48, 108–17, 134, 159, 160, 267n17, 267n20, 267n22, 268n34
Salviati: family, 100, 101; Jacopo, 9, 10, 33, 110, 114
San Donato dei Vecchietti, 88, 94
San Felice in Piazza, 102
San Frediano, 89, 101, 102
San Giovanni: feast of, 279n2
San Jacopo sopr'Arno, 8
San Lorenzo: canons of, 8, 90, 203, 220; parish of, 89, 102; tombs in, 164–66
San Marco, 21
San Niccolò, 91
San Niccolò da Bari: confraternity of, 87
San Pancrazio, 42, 93, 95, 166, 202, 209, 284n53
San Pier Gattolino, 89
San Pier Maggiore, 42, 90–91, 95, 224; parish burial patterns, 96–101, 221, 265n163
San Pier Martire: confraternity of, 71, 87, 204
San Sebastiano: confraternity of, 234
San Simone, 47, 93
Santa Croce, 35, 95, 96, 100, 102, 222
Santa Felicità, 27, 28, 102
Santa Maria del Carmine, 57, 58–59, 91, 101–2, 177
Santa Maria del Fiore: canons of, 8, 94, 203, 220; tombs and burial in, 42, 91–92
Santa Maria della Croce al Tempio: confraternity of, 94, 264n147
Santa Maria Novella, 35, 44, 94, 95, 102, 266n165
Santa Maria Ughi, 89
Sant'Ambrogio, 89, 95, 96, 99, 176, 177, 224; parish burial patterns, 221–23

Sant'Appollonia, 90
Santa Trinità, 42, 101, 197–98
Santissima Annunziata, 46, 47, 95, 100, 102, 164, 198
Santo Spirito, 36, 101, 102
Sanudo, Marin, 49–50
Sassetti: burial of family members, 14, 62, 69–70
Savonarola, Fra Girolamo, 38, 189, 217, 218, 219
Scala, Bartolomeo, 181, 182–83, 190
Scalone, Vincenzo, 18–19
Scipione Ammirato, 130, 142
Secondary burial, 58, 66, 67, 107–8, 168
Sexuality: regulation of, 119–20, 209, 270n53, 270n54
Sforza: court funerals, 17–19, 171
Sixtus IV (pope), 276n132, 277n134, 277n135
Soderini: Niccolò, 159; Piero, 217, 218, 220, 223, 297n121
Soldani family, 73
Soldi, Matteo, 70, 72, 75
Spinelli, Tommaso, 210, 295n100
Spini: family, 193, 291n49; Cristofano, 128, 129, 273n97
Spiritual anxiety, 209–10
Stecchuti, Giovanni, 233
Stefani, Marchionne di Coppo, 56
Strong, Roy, xv
Strozzi: family, 61, 66; Alessandra Macinghi, 169–70, 296n109; Filippo, 17, 169, 194–96, 210, 214, 292n55, 292n58; Lorenzo, 17, 194, 195; Matteo, 169–70, 285n61; Nanni, oration for, 143–45; Nofri, 89, 123, 129; Palla di Francesco, 40, 73; Palla di Nofri, 118, 123, 134
Studio, Florentine, 34, 40, 191, 219
Subsidies: civic funeral, 273n97
Sumptuary exemptions, 62, 67–69, 71–74, 126, 128, 161, 256n40, 256n41, 257n45, 257n51, 258n59, 283n42, 287n1
Sumptuary laws, 11, 43, 61–63, 85–86, 87, 241n14; changing strategies of, fifteenth century, 121, 123, 129, 170–71, 174–75, 219; of 1473, 204, 211–14, 295n102, 295n103, 296n107

Tanaglia family, 68
Tedaldi, Messer Maffeo, 69
Temperani, Messer Manno, 17, 161
Theory of magnificence, 105, 149–50
Tolentino, Niccolò da: funeral of,

Tolentino, Niccolò da (cont'd)
152–55, 281n16
Tombs: availability of, 164–66,
197–201, 223; claims to, 192–94;
types of, 50, 60, 255n16; women's,
198–201
Tornabuoni family, 122, 232, 233
Tour de l'Auvergne, Madeleine, 230,
300n168
Trexler, Richard, xvi, 86, 212, 259n74,
262n112, 283n41
Triumph of Death, 31

Ubertini, Biordo degli, 73
Uccello, Paolo, 81, 155, 281n17

Valori, Bartolomeo, 35, 100, 132, 136,
137
Vasari, Giorgio, 46, 189, 232
Vergerio, Pier Paolo, 112, 115
Verrocchio, 46
Vespasiano da Bisticci, 118, 156, 158,
173, 174
Vettori: Francesco, 189; Messer Pagolo,
90
Vigil, 2, 6
Villani: Filippo, 71–72; Matteo, 59, 60
Visconti, Bianca Maria (duchess of
Milan), 19
Visconti wars, 75, 108
Viviani, Ser Viviano, 108, 111, 115
Votive images, 46–47, 251n58
Vovelle, Michel, xiv

War of the Eight Saints, 55, 62, 75, 76,
259n67
Wax consumption, 128–29
Weissman, Ronald, xvi, 196
Witt, Ronald, 108
Women: role of, in exiles' funerals,
169–70

Zabarella, Francesco, 117